Acclaim for Jann S. Wenner's

LIKE A ROLLING STONE

"The planet got much hipper right around the time Jann Wenner arrived on it. It feels like every significant wave that's broken over the surface of the world I have lived in, Jann has been there to bear witness and often to catalyze. In memoir as in life, Wenner lets his serious and his silly get the better of him. And we, his readers — for nearly half the century — get the best of him in these pages. I had a lot of fun getting lost in him and no interest in being found." — Bono

"Rock may be dead, but Jann Wenner is still rolling...A memoir brimming with juicy anecdotes about friendships and feuds with the gods of the golden age of rock." — Maureen Dowd, *New York Times*

"If you were young, alone, and in the far lands of New Jersey, *Rolling Stone* was a dispatch from the front, carrying news of a bigger world and another life waiting. *Like a Rolling Stone* is a touchingly honest memoir from a man who recorded and shaped our times and of a grand life well lived. It is wonderfully deep and rewarding reading. I loved it." — Bruce Springsteen

"It's not possible to overstate the impact Jann Wenner has had on the world's pop culture...Wenner seems to have retained every letter he ever received, and even somehow has copies of letters he sent. It's a treat to hear John Lennon in his own words, as he regrets having eviscerated Paul McCartney, or Mick Jagger feeling betrayed after *Rolling Stone* covered the violence at Altamont. These are priceless historical documents and add reportorial credibility to Wenner's recollection of long-ago events." — Ken Kurson, *Book & Film Globe*

"Thrilling...fascinating...Wenner demonstrated great vision when he created, at age twenty-one, a publication that treated rock and politics as subjects equally deserving of serious examination."

— Chris Klimek, *Washington Post*

"Incredibly candid, open, and honest."

— Walter Isaacson

"A mind-blowing and insightful trip through the life of one of the principal sculptors of rock 'n' roll culture...Thoughtful, opinionated, and open-hearted."

— Tom Morello

"A high-octane story...A sweeping portrait of a generation...Wenner is in a league of his own. This memoir is utterly intoxicating."

— Douglas Brinkley, author of *Silent Spring Revolution*

"*Like a Rolling Stone* takes readers through Jann Wenner's heady years as editor and publisher of *Rolling Stone*, the most influential music and pop culture publication of its era."

— *AARP*

"A frank, sharp memoir by a zeitgeist-savvy entrepreneur who ranks among the earliest of modern influencers."

— *Kirkus Reviews*

ALSO BY JANN S. WENNER

Lennon Remembers
Garcia: A Signpost to New Space
Gonzo: The Life of Hunter S. Thompson
(with Corey Seymour)

LIKE A ROLLING STONE

STONE

A Memoir

JANN S. WENNER

Back Bay Books
Little, Brown and Company   New York · Boston · London

Back Bay Books / Little, Brown and Company
Hachette Book Group
1290 Avenue of the Americas, New York, NY 10104
littlebrown.com

Originally published in hardcover by Little, Brown and Company, September 2022
First Back Bay paperback edition, June 2023

Back Bay Books is an imprint of Little, Brown and Company, a division of Hachette Book Group, Inc. The Back Bay Books name and logo are trademarks of Hachette Book Group, Inc.

The publisher is not responsible for websites (or their content) that are not owned by the publisher.

The Hachette Speakers Bureau provides a wide range of authors for speaking events. To find out more, go to hachettespeakersbureau.com or email HachetteSpeakers@hbgusa.com.

Little, Brown and Company books may be purchased in bulk for business, educational, or promotional use. For information, please contact your local bookseller or the Hachette Book Group Special Markets Department at special.markets@hbgusa.com.

Permissions and credits are listed on page 557.

ISBN 9780316415194 (hardcover) / 9780316415293 (paperback)
Library of Congress Control Number: 2021950062

Printing 1, 2023

LSC-C

Printed in the United States of America

For Jane and Matt and our progeny, Alex, Theo, Gus, Noah, India, and Jude.
Love forever.
In memory of my parents, Ed and Sim. Forever young.

Hail, hail rock and roll
Deliver me from the days of old

— Chuck Berry

Later, I found myself taking the song ["Pirate Jenny"] apart, trying to find out what made it tick, why it was so effective. I could see that everything in it was apparent and visible but you didn't notice it too much. Everything was fastened to the wall with a heavy bracket, but you couldn't see what the sum total of all the parts were, not unless you stood way back and waited 'til the end.

— Bob Dylan, *Chronicles*

CONTENTS

THE LAST DAYS

I WENT TO THE *Rolling Stone* offices on a Monday morning in mid-May 2019. My assistant met me downstairs to take my attaché case, as I was still walking with two canes. It was a gray day in New York, one of rain, with a forecast for more all week. When I got to our second-floor lobby, workmen were putting up plywood to protect the walls from the movers.

The spacious cubicles, which the great furniture designer Ward Bennett had chosen twenty-eight years earlier, and the glass-walled private offices with views of Sixth Avenue and Radio City Music Hall, were empty. The staff from the Rock and Roll Hall of Fame were still there, as was Paul Scanlon, who came every day to help me start this book.

I never felt so completely that *Rolling Stone* was over for me as on that day.

The week before, the last fifty people on the editorial staff had packed their desks into boxes. Thursday of that week was their final day at 1290 Sixth Avenue before moving to small "content farm" tables at a new office, with a new owner. We took a group photo and I gave an off-the-cuff farewell speech. It was a sweet moment.

Gus, my twenty-eight-year-old son and heir apparent, my formally announced successor, came into my office, late again, for our weekly meeting. It would be our last one at the offices where I had worked for decades. The subject was paper stock for the cover. I advocated going to glossy, but Gus refused. A barely polite argument followed about who knew best what he was doing. We were each learning that it was not necessary to win every fight, but sometimes to just let it go. When I wrapped up my daily writing and packed up to go home, one or two people were still at their desks; the rest were gone.

The departure of the staff was what finally affected me. The reason I hadn't previously sold *Rolling Stone* was that once someone else owned it, they could do what they wanted, including fire me. I also knew that if the owner told me what to do and I strongly disagreed, I would have to quit. And I would never again find a job as great. Now all that was coming to pass. This was the end of the road.

When I returned the next week after the move, I walked onto a floor of empty offices, the desks and chairs randomly out of place, walls stripped of art, paper and trash scattered on the carpet, the detritus of a once revered and mighty magazine. It conjured up death. When you see the end coming to someone you know, whether from illness, injury, or just age, you handle it however it falls to you and do whatever you need to make sense of it. Even as you watch the person fade and fail, they are still with you, and death is not fully real. Even when the breath is gone, the body is there and you are not alone. Not until the flesh itself has been buried or burned, has gone to dirt or ash, do you grasp the finality of it. That person is gone, gone, gone, and you are alone, on your own. So I felt.

One message that came that day was from Jac Holzman, who had just been cut off the list of people who received a free lifetime subscription to the magazine. In the early years, Jac had loaned me money to keep *Rolling Stone* alive. There must be some karmic juju at work here, I thought, and I didn't intend to be on the slap-back end of that. Jac had once told me the biggest mistake he ever made was to sell Elektra

Records, the idiosyncratic company that he had started. He had accepted millions but became one of many subalterns in a much larger company. I had always kept that in mind as big-name buyers flirted with me. Thanks, but no thanks. I was my own boss; I was having fun and making a difference in my world. I would have regretted losing that for the rest of my life. I almost bit once. It was the big one, right at the peak. But fuck it.

I got on the phone and had Jac's subscription restored.

The movers were ready to bubble-wrap my things. We packed up a bust of Bill Clinton with a Pinocchio nose that Bob Grossman had sculpted for us to use as a cover during Bill's impeachment. I was too partisan to use the funny, truthful, but negative image. It would have been one of our great covers. I kept it to remind me not to forget the higher duty of the magazine.

I took down Annie Leibovitz's portrait of a young Pete Townshend, his hands bloody from playing his guitar. Leaning next to the picture of Pete were skis decorated with Rolling Stones iconography and graffiti. The band had made a few dozen pairs to mark its fiftieth anniversary. Mick sent them. They were serious skis, and I had put a hundred days on them. I packed up the small wood and metal sculpture of a skier that Patti Scialfa sent for my birthday. I had a poster of a Fillmore Auditorium show on one of my best acid-fueled nights before *Rolling Stone*. I took down the four-by-four-foot photograph of me that Hunter Thompson had shot a hole through with his .44 Magnum, spray-painted, framed, that he had presented to me on the twenty-fifth anniversary of *Rolling Stone*.

By the end of the week, workers had finished dismantling the last vestiges of *Rolling Stone*, ripped out the editorial department offices, turned off the telephones and data lines, and shut down the air-conditioning. The desks, chairs, computer screens, and telephones were thrown into dumpsters. The last wall would be breached, and within a few days workers would be tearing apart the private office where for nearly thirty years I had lived and ruled, achieved fame and fortune. When I walked out that last time, I left numb.

As Hunter would say, I see buzzards circling overhead.

FROM THE FIRST issue I thought the readers of *Rolling Stone* shared an understanding, an unspoken feeling about a suddenly new world. We were in this together, the tribe, the gathering of the tribes, strangers in a strange land, and what seemed to be the universal connection, the common tongue, was rock and roll, the music, the song, the dance. It was glue holding a generation together. I felt as spiritually connected to the Beatles and the Rolling Stones five thousand miles away as I did to my friends going to concerts across the Golden Gate Bridge.

I hadn't formed a theory of the historical moment — that came later — I just knew that the Beatles and Bob Dylan spoke to me about the most profound concerns in my life in a form of communication and a language that went through my entire body. I had to learn more, hear more, be a part of it, become it, find "the magic that can set you free."

Somewhere along the line, as a magazine editor and a finder of stories, it was clear that my own story, the saga of *Rolling Stone*, and the breadth and depth of its horizon, could be a great read, and a historically authentic way of telling the story of my generation, our times, and my own mission. The battle about the legacy of the sixties continues, known today as culture wars. From my first days at college, it seemed we were on trial for generational crimes, and that trial has never ceased.

In part it was youthful rebellion, but this time the rebel army was the biggest population cohort in American history. Vast suburbs and a system of the finest free education, kindergartens to universities, were built. The great prosperity and peace, the benefits of having won a world war (in which 100 million people died), gave us the opportunity to study our history, in particular its racism, consider its meaning and its future for us, a process that was intensified and accelerated by the rise of technology.

The "mainstream media" missed this story, treated our early demands as folly, not qualified for serious consideration, not only by just the fact of youth but also due to its own national sclerosis, even a national cirrhosis. The truly subversive language we spoke was rock and roll. It wasn't a secret tongue; anybody of any age could hear it and give it an open listen. It wasn't just words, but also music that resonated with the physical world of adolescence, the truth of that world, not the denial and repression of the glorious spirit of nature.

The battle of the generations was for the soul of America. Rock and roll was soft power. This was the underlying theme of *Rolling Stone:* a charter to examine all aspects of America, to get "the latest spin on the shit we're in," in Jackson Browne's phrase, so this book is in part a report on today's world and how we got here. It was one of the most admirable periods in our nation's history. Young people saw that their leaders could be dreadfully wrong in their judgments, that they could no longer assume that those in high places knew what they were doing. What emerged was a commitment to international peace, to human rights and racial and environmental justice, to shared responsibility and action, the potential for enlightened domestic and foreign policy.

We were in a moral crisis in America. We needed to find out how this happened before we could figure out how to revive the ideals of our American Dream, our belief in and crusade for life, liberty, and the pursuit of happiness.

This book is about the rock and roll era in the age of reckoning. This book is also about my own nine lives and about my failure to observe the posted speed limits. Our readers often referred to *Rolling Stone* as a letter from home. This is my last letter to you.

PART ONE

BEGINNINGS

CHAPTER 1

RAINBOW ROAD

I GREW UP ON Rainbow Road, the name my parents gave the dirt lane that led to the home they had built in a valley filled with oak trees. Lemon bushes surrounded the house and red bougainvillea covered the arbors that shaded the patios. It was where I learned my first lessons about life and what lay ahead.

We lived in the rural suburbs of San Rafael, California, the county seat of Marin, which would become a mecca of the hippies in the sixties and of the hip in the seventies. It lay just north of the Golden Gate Bridge; the highway from San Francisco was a two-lane road. That was before freeways and the new towns that were built to house the baby boom.

My parents, Ruth Naomi "Sim" Simmons and Edward Wenner, were from New York City, where they had met looking to share a ride to ski in Vermont. Both had joined the armed forces during the war. She was stationed in New Orleans as a quartermaster in the Navy; he was a lieutenant based in Monroe, Alabama, with the Army Air Corps, where he taught pilots and navigators how to drop bombs. After they married in 1943 and had me, they decided to leave New York, packed up a car, and set out to find their new life in California. The population of the United States in 1946 was 140 million. Today, it is 350 million.

I was born on January 7, 1946, which put me at the leading edge of the generation that would be the largest, best educated, and wealthiest in American history. My pediatrician in New York City was Dr. Benjamin

Spock, the man who wrote the modern rules for raising children with love, not punishment, which was mocked as "Spare the rod, spoil the child."

My parents started a business when they moved to San Francisco. It was called Baby Formulas, a service that provided custom-made bottles of formula for hospitals in the Bay Area. Work kept them away from home in the early years, and my sisters — Kate, born in 1947, and Martha (Marti), in 1949 — and I were raised most days by our housekeeper, Bea, who lived thirty minutes away in a segregated housing project for blacks — then called "colored people."

The problem with Rainbow Road from a child's point of view was that we didn't have nearby neighbors, so it was hard to make friends. We were never like the neighbors anyway. For one thing, both of my parents worked, and mothers who did were considered strange, almost aliens. And, we were Jews. Being "nonobservant" Jews was not a meaningful difference in the neighborhood.

My sisters and I would walk the two miles to town, over a hill, along the train tracks, leaving pennies on the rails to see them flattened by passing trains. We'd go to movies on Saturday afternoons, buy ten-cent ice cream cones, and get a free See's chocolate candy from the nice lady there, who watched my sisters and me, apparently penniless, stare at her display case.

I was a pudgy kid with freckles, a cowlick, a toothy smile, big ears, and blue eyes. If I was concentrating, say on reading a book, my tongue would hang out. I was also what in those days was called a "problem child." I had been kicked out of two private schools in San Francisco. The first, a nursery school, explained that I was "just too much trouble." In early grade school, I deliberately hid in the bushes on a field trip to the San Francisco Zoo. This caused a panic for my parents, the police, and the school. I showed up at a police station later that day, as I wandered across the city helplessly looking for my parents at the Baby Formulas offices. That school also gave me the heave-ho.

My parents, together with a few other families who lived on the right side of the tracks, founded a private school, Marin Country Day, where my sisters went. As a fifth grader I was too old then and was sent to the local public school. Most of the kids there lived in Rafael Meadows, on the other side of the tracks, about two hundred tract homes built for blue-collar families. My two best friends lived there; one's father was a fireman, the other's dad was an inmate in San Quentin. We would hang out at Danny's, a grocery store where we did most of our shoplifting. It had a pay phone outside where we could make free calls by sticking a bobby pin into the coin box.

In the summers, my sisters and I would cut open cardboard boxes and race them down the dry grass on the hills around the house or splash around in our creek. It had a footbridge that led to a small island where we built a fortress. Every summer we were sent to Camp Lagunitas in the backwoods of rural Marin, a funky place that the Grateful Dead would rent years later. The camp's owner was a full-tilt alcoholic, who could be found asleep in the middle of the day on top of a picnic table. Some of us ten-year-olds would use that time for risky hijinks. I commandeered a boat with a 75-horsepower Evinrude outboard engine and came within an inch of smashing full speed into the dock. My friends and I dove off an old pier until we were warned about the underwater cables that could slice our heads open.

While we were there, our folks took driving trips to Canada, Mexico, and throughout the West. We got picture postcards of giant redwoods, Paul Bunyan statues, and tourist monuments of all kinds, a photo gallery of the fifties. They wrote us lots of letters, all of which I saved, the beginning of my obsession with filing and keeping everything. My mother sent updates on the Sunday comics and on family life: "I am enclosing three news clippings which I thought would interest you. One is about a phone company man who was killed by wild bees. It frightened me when I read it to remember how you and Ricky and Jeff used to stone down the wild bees in our woods. We had a scientist over from Berkeley last night and he told us some interesting things about radioactivity and the fallout from atom bomb tests."

She stopped working in their business full-time and spent her days sitting in the sun at a typewriter. Before she married, she had been a freelancer for magazines in New York, particularly ones about child-rearing. As a "qualified professional," she told me I was the most difficult child she ever encountered. Now she was working on a witty retelling of starting Baby Formulas with my dad, titled *Back Away from the Stove*. It was mildly successful. A glamorous publicity photo of her holding the book appeared in the local papers. She mentioned all our names and said, "One good thing about getting the actual book in hand is this justifies their having an unconventional mother." Everyone in our family was so proud.

When I walked home from school each day, my mother would bring out fresh fruit and make me a peanut-butter-and-jelly sandwich. We would listen to the Army-McCarthy hearings being broadcast on the radio from the U.S. Senate. It was a showdown between Senator Joseph McCarthy, a right-wing thug, a mudslinger from Wisconsin, and the United States Army, which he claimed was infiltrated by communists. All this was above my eight-year-old head, but I was absorbing bits and pieces, learning about democracy, the Red Scare, and politics. I listened as the lawyer for the Army, Joseph Welch, famously challenged McCarthy: "At long last, have you left no sense of decency?"

My parents were active in Democratic politics. They brought the liberal traditions of New York City to Republican California, a hotbed of conservatives and other ultras that gave us Richard Nixon and Ronald Reagan. My sisters and I stuffed envelopes and walked neighborhoods on Saturday afternoons to distribute buttons, bumper stickers, and yard signs. When Adlai Stevenson ran for the Democratic presidential nomination in 1956, my father was his Northern California campaign chairman. I met Stevenson at cocktail parties with my dad and took a bus into San Francisco on my own to hear him speak at a rally. Ten years old. I started reading anything I could find about FDR. Why?

My mother was one of the founders of the California Democratic Council, along with future senator Alan Cranston. It was a citizens' movement organized to win back California from the Republicans, and ultimately helped elect Pat Brown, Jerry's father, as governor. Mom also ran a congressional campaign, defeating a long-term Republican. Politics was mother's milk. It seemed we were never not involved.

Around sixth grade, I decided to become an editor and publisher. I have no clue where or how this odd notion struck me. I was already a fanatic about our daily newspaper, the *San Francisco Chronicle*. My mother and I read the columnists together, discussed the news, and relished Herb Caen's classic three-dot gossip column, "Baghdad by the Bay."

The Weekly Trumpet, as my very first effort was modestly called — actually the initial name was *The Up to the Minute News* — was printed by typing onto a stencil, in opposite directions on each quarter page, so it could be folded into a four-page mini-magazine. The stencil was then copied on a ditto machine. Larry and Doug Ashby and I put together school news, neighborhood comings and goings, some gossip gleaned through our playmates — once about someone's parents discussing divorce — jokes for kids, and even political editorials. A copy cost a dime and we had sixty subscribers. There was a story about us cute junior entrepreneurs on page one of the Marin County newspaper, but after six months, the three of us gave it a rest and divided up our forty-dollar profits. We announced a not-to-be-consummated return in the fall with a monthly magazine, *The Trumpeter*. Instead, there was the seventh-grade school newspaper, the *Santa Venetia Informer*, with announcements for the usual school activities, lists of kids looking to babysit, and a gossip column: "Janice Rhodes likes Larry Ashby an awful lot and maybe it's vice versa . . . Ronnie Reaves and Chris Dauphine are girlfriend and boyfriend. Did you hear about when they went to Chris's house together? Ronnie rode the bike and Chris walked and carried the books . . . Mary Nichol is making it obvious it's a certain boy."

THE FIRST RECORD player I saw was my parents' 78 rpm Garrard turntable, with a component tube amp and a speaker my dad had mounted in the wall of the living room. That was just before rock and roll, which my parents would dislike, but their taste was eclectic enough to encompass

Billie Holiday and Eartha Kitt, the Weavers, Broadway musicals — especially *South Pacific* — and lots of classical music, all of which I still love. My mother had strong training in piano, and most nights she would play "Moonlight Sonata" before sending us to bed. Mom and Dad also took us to see Gilbert and Sullivan comic operettas — I can still sing tunes from *The Mikado*. I think of those two Victorian composers as precursors to the Beatles.

I thought my mother, who was called "Sim," a contraction of her maiden name, was a special and different kind of mom. When I read *Auntie Mame*, it all made sense. My mother was our version of the outspoken, open-minded, and wacky lady who sent her nephew to a nursery school where the kids went naked and pretended they were fish. I fantasized that she really was Auntie Mame.

My mother's father, Maurice Simmons, was a Democrat, an anti–Tammany Hall reformer. He trained to become a Rough Rider in the Spanish-American War, but was too late to serve. He became a municipal judge. I ended up with two of his gavels. He founded the Jewish War Veterans of America. Maurice had married his first cousin Zillah, one of seven sisters from Australia, and had two children, my mom and her older brother, Robert.

My father, Ed, was building a business and we saw him mostly on weekends, when he would spend the days on various household projects. He had a woodshop with table saws. He built beds for us with built-in drawers, made modern coffee tables, and put retaining walls against the hillsides around our house to hold back the mud during the rainy season. He was short, but a powerfully built man. His passion was to make a success of Baby Formulas. His mother had run a lingerie store in New York, where he was the after-school assistant and errand boy. She had gotten him tangentially involved in an insurance-fire scheme, and it soured him on her. I remember meeting her once, exchanging letters with an old lady, but otherwise she was not in our lives. We knew nothing of his father, never met a brother or sister of his, and only knew that he was the youngest child, "baby Eddie." His mother had emigrated from the Ukraine but he had lost touch with all of his siblings except his brother Sam, whom he visited once in Boston. Dad made his business work by honesty and his sweat. Baby Formulas ended up feeding 90 percent of the babies born within 125 miles of San Francisco. He never stopped working, and that was the basis of my family's comfortable life.

Dad only spanked me once. I don't think he liked it. The second time my mom told him he had to spank me, I ran into the woods and didn't come home for an hour. That was the end of that.

My father loved science fiction. He subscribed to monthly pulp magazines with names like *Galaxy* and *Amazing Stories*. He saved every copy and had bookshelves packed with fantasy. When I discovered *Stranger in a Strange Land*, by Robert Heinlein, he had already been there and done that. He smoked pipes and carried around tins or pouches of Edgeworth tobacco, which gave off the scent of cherries. It was the early *Mad Men* era, so we saw a lot of Benson & Hedges cigarettes in boxes, Scotch and sodas, and a steady flow of their friends, couples who also smoked and drank.

As a kid, my father's recreation was hiking in the mountains, and he loved the outdoors until his last days. Our family's winter vacations were to ski areas around Lake Tahoe. The Squaw Valley lodge became a vacation home for us kids. There were rec rooms and snack bars and enough safety to allow us our freedom. On weekends, I would wake up with Dad at 4:30 a.m. and the two of us would pack into his MGB and drive to Squaw Valley for two days of skiing. Our ritual was to have a predawn breakfast at the Black Swan Diner on the way. Once at the mountain he would meet up with his friends and cut me loose to learn how to ski on the rope tows. I quickly discovered that the chairlift was easier and took me all the way to the top. I loved skiing with Dad and having "grown-up" time together. Being the oldest child, the young man of the family, made me feel special. Skiing became my sport: going solo, the need for speed. My dad was a wit, and we used to laugh all the time. Those are my best memories of him from those days.

When I was ten, "Heartbreak Hotel" came out and there was no turning back. What was it about that rhythm, that beat, those loud voices, those romantic harmonies for someone so young? I would pull the bedcovers over my head to listen to a rocket-shaped crystal radio. When I got my first 45 rpm record player, for the free single that came with it I chose Bill Haley's "Rock Around the Clock."

In 1959, as the Eisenhower era was coming to an end, I was in seventh grade. We had a Pat Boone club and an Elvis club. I joined the white-suede shoes side but then admitted I was wrong and switched to the blue-suede kind. The record I could not get enough of was "Party Doll," by Buddy Knox on Roulette Records. Knox was from Happy, Texas. I would wait for that line: "To come along with me when I'm feeling wild, / To be everlovin', true and fair, / To run her fingers through my hair." He would drag out "wild" like "wiiile" and round it all up with "I'll make love to you, to you, / I'll make love to you." This was exciting and dangerous stuff.

I went to Little League tryouts at the school playground, was the last kid chosen, and never returned. There were kids in my class who paid no attention, and it didn't seem to matter to anybody, even the teachers. I thought it was unfair that we were treated the same, even though I was smarter. I learned not to be the kid raising his hand with the answer. On Fridays, half the class attended catechism at the Catholic church across the street. My parents explained why I couldn't go — we didn't believe in God — and I knew not to say a word about that dangerous secret. I walked home at the end of every day alone. It all seems glowing in retrospect, but at the time I was lonely. I had few friends outside of my sisters.

ONE LATE SPRING afternoon, Miss La Chappelle, our homeroom teacher, who had developed an affection for me, her little prodigy, said she had a special announcement for the class: "Jan [as I then spelled it] Wenner won't be with us next year because he is going off to a private boarding school." I had never said a word about it to my classmates and I cringed at Miss La Chappelle's revelation. My folks thought I should get a better education, I presumed. But it also must have been time to get me out of the house; I had become too hard to handle. When my father took me to Los Angeles for the admissions interview at the Chadwick School, I fought for a white jacket with silver threads in it, but of course ended up with a charcoal-gray suit.

It was time to leave. My sisters stood under the giant oak in front of our house and waved goodbye as my dad and I drove off. I was twelve years old. It was the end of Rainbow Road.

CHAPTER 2

THE SCHOOL
ON THE HILL

I ARRIVED AT THE Chadwick School with a sturdy suitcase, an army surplus trunk, and an empty shipping box to mail laundry home. The place where I was to spend the next five years of my life was called the Hill. At the end of a two-mile gated road was the campus with its buildings: Little Boys' Cottage, Little Girls' Cottage, student dormitories, an amphitheater, playing fields, even a chicken farm. I was the first kid to arrive on the Sunday before the fall term began. My father dropped me off, settled me in my dorm, and waved goodbye. I imagine now that he cried. I didn't. I sat in my room quite alone. It was time to man up.

Chadwick was tucked between two wealthy neighborhoods south of Los Angeles: Palos Verdes Estates, with large Spanish-style homes, and Rolling Hills, behind private gates with miles and miles of white fence. Each home had its own stables, corrals, and barns. About half of Chadwick kids were day students from those two communities. They were not only wealthy, but also right wing, of course, and many of them raised to be anti-Semitic.

My homeroom teacher was Virginia Chadwick, a cousin of the headmaster. She was funny but a scold. She reminded me of my mother, and I tried to be her smartest pupil. She lived with Virginia Daniels, the ninth-grade homeroom teacher; they were known as Gin and

Danny. Both wore pants and had short haircuts. No one thought twice about it.

In ninth grade I had a kissing, hand-holding relationship with a day student, a cute blonde who wore madras skirts. One weekend she invited me to supper with her family, in the course of which they asked about my religion. I knew right away this would be a deal breaker, but I answered in full voice. "Jewish" was met with a quick but unmistakable silence before conversation resumed. The next week she broke up with me, no explanation given or necessary. I had gone to Sunday school at a Unitarian church and knew I could fall back on that, but I would have been so ashamed of myself. It was take it or leave it.

We had a chaplain, and mandatory services every Sunday. The Reverend Tourigney would sermonize — I never listened — and when he was done, the hair from the right side of his balding head, which he had carefully combed across the top, would be sticking out at all angles, as if God had driven him mad. The school put on an annual Christmas pageant, "The Drama of the Ages," which consisted of Bible passages selected and arranged by our headmistress, Margaret Lee Chadwick. The students were costumed as shepherds, the Three Wise Men, and, in my case, the prophet Isaiah: "Make straight in the desert a highway for your God!" It all climaxed with the "Hallelujah Chorus," which led to my lifetime love of *Messiah*.

I joined the print shop, a one-man and one-student operation located in a leaky shed near the chicken farm. It had a hand-fed press with a circular inking plate. The faster you fed the paper into the press, the more you risked crushing your fingers or even losing one. I picked up the left-behind knowledge of setting type by hand. It was ink-stained work. I loved the sense of responsibility and having a skill that set me apart from the other kids. But what an odd thing to do for two years, and how pre-ordained it now seems.

My mother wrote me weekly letters about politics, books I must read, our runaway cats and dogs, her new novel in progress, our need to save money, the nice or nasty neighbors, and always a plea for me to write back: "Think of your poor old ma weeping and moping without you, sustaining herself on the thought that there might be one li'l ole letter from her son in the mailbox. SO, WRITE. Right? Much love, Mother. By the way, your letters are such good reading, I wonder if you are not harboring some writing talent...why don't you try writing a short story and sending it up to me?"

In my first year, she sent me an airline ticket and asked me to come home for a visit before Thanksgiving break. My dad met me at San Francisco International Airport, which was then one terminal building with a half-dozen gates, and suggested lunch before heading home to Rainbow Road. After the burger and fries arrived, he got down to business: "Your mom and I have decided that we are not going to live together... get a divorce...nothing to do with you...not your fault...still love each other...will always be best friends..." When we got back to Rainbow Road, it no longer felt like home. Once back at school, I discovered that "broken homes" were common, and I felt a little less tragic.

By tenth grade I had settled into school. I had real, if not many, friends. I had to watch my tongue, especially with the teachers. I was estranged from the school mainstream, but there were two activities I had my heart set on: the school newspaper, *The Main Sheet*, and the yearbook, *The Dolphin*. Frank Quinlan, a retired reporter, a kindly white-haired man with reading glasses hung around his neck, oversaw the publications and taught journalism, all from a room called "Shaft Alley" because of how narrow it was. It became my semi-secret private office on campus for the next three years. To work on the newspaper, you just signed up; to be the editor of the yearbook, your classmates had to elect you in tenth grade, so that the following year, you became the junior-class editor in order to learn the ropes. I was the only candidate, and I was elected. There were serious misgivings among the faculty about this.

I made my first appearance in front of the disciplinary committee, the dozen faculty members who met every two weeks and sat like a tribunal behind a U-shaped arrangement of folding Formica-top tables. I had once again been caught off campus without written permission. A few teachers wanted to seize the opportunity to kick me out, but some of the older faculty thought I was a precious stone in the rough. Mr. Quinlan's journalistic force in waiting was not about to get the boot.

The angel watching over me was Margaret Lee Chadwick. She wore her salt-and-pepper hair in two long braids curled up on the top of her head. She had founded the school in the thirties with her husband, an Annapolis graduate, Commander Joseph Chadwick, who ran the business side but deferred to her in all things, including the question of what to do with the difficult and not terribly necessary Wenner boy. She stopped the disciplinary committee from kicking me out. I was a star in her advanced-placement English class. We stayed in touch until she died at ninety-one.

I had wild times at Chadwick, sneaking off campus in the middle of the night, stealing cars for joyrides, getting drunk, waking up in vomit, and barely making it back to school for my 8:00 a.m. class. In one of those late-night escapades, my friends and I stole a station wagon from a house in Rolling Hills that had a hallway lined with photos of the parents with Richard Nixon and engraved invitations to the White House.

AT CHADWICK, WHEN I was fifteen, I began a handwritten journal in spiral notebooks at my mother's urging, and despite the discipline involved, I took to it. I still have them. It was the record of a pretty happy kid who had become deeply involved in the life of the school. Chadwick was home and family now, and it also engaged my ambition and rebelliousness. My two closest friends were Jamie Moran and Andy Harmon. We were writers and natural allies. Jamie was the class's creative star, fearless and stubborn in his ideas. On his own he studied mysticism and philosophy, way over my head. He was also a varsity football player.

Andy Harmon was my sophomore roommate and best friend. His mom was a madcap heiress to a brewing fortune and his father was a film director. Both my mother and his father thought we might be having an affair — Andy wasn't gay and I didn't have an ounce of sexual interest — but his dad succeeded in getting him a different roommate for reasons that were never explained to us. Andy, Jamie, and I were considered a little "beatnik," but tolerably so, and we managed to get money from the school to publish an anthology of the best student poetry and a literary magazine, *Journey*.

My journal was not deeply introspective. It was reportorial. I was testing out my writing skills, my fancy vocabulary, humor, my knowledge, anything I could try on. I wrote profiles of various teachers and students. I was reading college-level psychology texts then, so I was attempting to analyze everyone. I would work myself up into a lather about the school's dress code. I would rail at hypocrisy and mediocrity. I was writing editorials.

I had also become a semi-BMOC. I was the editor designate of the yearbook, and was making the honor roll. I wrote two theses my senior year, one about the decision to drop the atomic bomb on Hiroshima, a lesson in war, morality, and the power of bureaucracy; the other about Nixon, McCarthyism, and the rise of the radical right in California politics. But what I loved most was playing the Duke of Plaza Toro, a principal role in the annual Gilbert and Sullivan operetta, their Italian opera parody, *The Gondoliers*. "That celebrated, cultivated, underrated nobleman, the Duke of Plaza Toro." We also did *The Pirates of Penzance* and *H.M.S. Pinafore*. I understudied for the Major General and fell in love with the sophomore who played Buttercup, and we had an offstage fling for a weekend, singing and making out. Performing onstage put me in another world. To sing loudly and freely could just take me over; the applause sent waves of warmth through me.

THERE WAS NO openly homosexual culture among the students or faculty; Chadwick wasn't like British boarding schools. One older teacher who taught Spanish couldn't help himself and would leave his classroom every time this one boy would go to the bathroom. He retired that year without notice. There was also the senior English teacher, a sharp-witted man beloved by all, who was having an affair with one of the senior boys, but not a word was said.

Jack Ashton lived just down the hall from me in the boys' dorm. Not a regular friend of mine but a loner — black leather motorcycle jacket, pouty lips, and seriously good-looking. One afternoon as our gym class lined up for towels and showers, I was standing behind Jack and without even thinking twice rubbed up against him. He didn't move, so I did it again a little longer. I had an erection, and he turned around and smiled. Later that day he took me into his dorm room, locked the door, and showed me how to masturbate. I got hooked on masturbation and also got hooked on Jack.

No one had any suspicion of what was going on between Jack Ashton and me. I don't think anyone really knew much about homosexuality. I didn't. It was a secret life of intense sexual desire, but there was nothing about it in popular culture that we came across, nobody knew an openly homosexual person at home or school; all we knew was that somewhere, even among us, there were queers.

There was a day student from Rolling Hills whose dad worked for Secretary of Defense Robert McNamara. He was a football star. He added a second d to his first name and went from Ted to Tedd. I thought that was so cool, a quiet but unmistakable statement of nonconformity. I never liked "Jan" — the name on my birth certificate — and already had asked to be called Eric when I was eight. After I added an extra n to Jan, my mom couldn't resist writing a letter that began "Dear Jannnnnn." Tedd committed suicide in college. I didn't know him at all, but I think he was gay and couldn't belong in the world as it was then.

I was also at war with the master of the boys' dorm. He liked to hold white-glove surprise inspections, a bully who would ride the weakest kids. Once he and a few of his toadies pinned down an unpopular kid and shaved his head, a nakedly cruel move. He was a doppelgänger for Humphrey Bogart's Captain Queeg in *The Caine Mutiny*, given to crazed, spittle-laced speeches. I distributed paperback copies of the book throughout the dorm. I made sure to let him know I had figured him out. Mrs. Chadwick alerted my parents that "Jann has a severe problem with the head of the boys' dorm." It was going to be a fight one of us had to lose.

I got a roll of butcher paper and made a Jackson Pollock–style splatter painting. I papered my entire room with it and hung a mobile made out of wire hangers, a mockery of what a regimented dorm should look like. It was an eyesore, but I was protected by the school tradition of art and self-expression. It was war, not a great way to live unless you are serving the cause of righteousness. I would do anything, and in the end, it came down to shouting matches in front of the whole dorm. He resigned. I was a dorm hero but now was seen as a threat to other teachers; I went to the top of the disciplinary committee's watch list.

When I got back to campus for my senior year, the culmination of a great teenage run, I checked into the senior dorm and discovered that my room was just across the hall from Jack Ashton's. It was a convenient stroke of fate.

AND THEN I fell in love. Her name was Susie Weigel. She was from San Francisco, and we were on the same flight home for Thanksgiving. She knew about serious things, including politics, not to mention her good looks and a flirtatious personality. I was enchanted. We would see each other every day, at every meal, especially in the free hour after dinner when we would find a private alcove, and smoke and kiss until we were worn out. Nightly we fought the Battle of the Bra, and by spring I had gotten into a winning field position. In my journals that winter, I was wrestling with my conflicted sexuality, trying to understand what it was — what I was. Sometimes I would find myself intensely wanting sex with Jack, but then the feeling would recede and I could reassure myself that I liked it less and less, that I could handle an occasional encounter here and there. Susie was the person I loved.

I decided to be on the student council. The only obstacle was that I might not be popular enough to win the vote. My friend Bill Belding, a day student, was captain of the swim team, president of the Lettermen's Club, and dating the homecoming queen. We could run together, on the "Progressive Ticket." Nothing like a "ticket" had ever been done before at Chadwick. It was vaguely conspiratorial, subversive, a little voice whispering "change" and "loss of faculty control." But worse, it was "progressive," an undeniable slap at the local community's right-wing politics.

I was skating right to the very edge this time. To the powers that be it seemed that a student revolt might be brewing. But my strategy left them no way out, unless they openly betrayed the values they had pledged to inculcate in us. We put up banners around campus, a few with our last names, but most read "Vote Progressive." I became the consummate ward heeler: I said hello to students I had ignored all year and also paid off a few small debts. The Progressive platform: seniors would have an expansion of their coffee privileges; the dress code would be relaxed to allow certain styles of jeans; and we would start a student-only newspaper. The Progressive Party won in a landslide, 37–15.

We delivered on all our promises, and I even got the student paper off the ground for three issues. In keeping with Chadwick's nautical theme, I called it *The Sardine*. "Random Notes" was the title of the gossip column; "We employ some of the biggest gossips in the school," I wrote. The motto of *The Sardine* was "All the News That Fits." It had a hand-drawn logo and was published biweekly.

The third issue of *The Sardine* had a parody of a secret faculty meeting about students wearing jeans and a report from an off-campus basketball game where Chadwick students had ditched the game for the local amusement park. The dean of men, a double straight arrow and a faculty member who disliked me and all my works, in a rage that scared me, told me that *The Sardine* would never be printed again.

The final attempt to shut me up or expel me was to call me in front of the disciplinary committee for a little talk, no specific offense. The committee was concerned over the "decline of school spirit." They had been seeing a lack of enthusiasm for sports and organized school activities. Their conclusion was that it resulted from the influence of our class on the whole school, and that was due to the influence of the senior boys' dorm over the class, and that I was the bad influence over the dorm. They wanted a good end to the school year and needed my cooperation. It was the last airing of our grievances. I was strong-willed, but they were the authorities, and it was time to stop. A truce was reached that allowed us all a happy ending.

BY LATE SPRING of 1963 the Hill was settling into the business of sending another class off to college. I got the thin envelope from Harvard and the thick one from UC Berkeley. Bill Belding got into Yale on a scholarship, sponsored by the Navy for his swimming talent and, I think, general strength of character. He joined the Navy SEALs. In Vietnam he was sent ashore from submarines to hunt down and assassinate people. When we caught up with each other as adults, Bill had become president of the Vietnam Vets Against the War and, in recalling the old days, told me about his deeply liberal family. I told him I had no idea they weren't conservatives. "You would have," he said, "if you had ever stopped talking."

My final report card came in. I was a hit in journalism: "To his characteristic enterprise and ambition, Jann, through his work on *The Dolphin*, seems to be adding discretion and diplomacy." And in civics: "It has been a pleasure to have this intelligent, aggressive, and rambunctious young man in my class. Those who complain about the apathy of the younger generation haven't met Mr. Wenner."

The leave-taking was too quick for me to fully appreciate the five years that had passed. The class, in suits and dresses, sat with their parents on the grass steps of the amphitheater. I was one of the student speakers, made the honor roll, and was given the annual journalism prize. My dad and mom didn't sit together. (Mom looked stunning.) My sister Kate flew in from Vermont to surprise me. They were happy: their troubled, unhappy boy was going to be okay.

I didn't go to the senior prom. My crew headed to the Troubadour in West Hollywood to hear Mose Allison. We were on the cusp of the sixties.

MY MOTHER SOLD Rainbow Road and bought a house in one of the new, very modern Eichler homes in Marin. My dad moved to Los Angeles to run the branch of Baby Formulas there, which was based in Anaheim, two exits from Disneyland. I didn't fully understand it, but I had ended up in my dad's custody and my sisters stayed with my mom. By then, my father had married his assistant and sales manager, Dorothy Arnold. She was my only friend on the outskirts of no-man's-land.

Before the year was out, both my mom and dad had cashed out their ownership in Baby Formulas. Dad and Dorothy moved to Newport Beach, on the coast south of Los Angeles, and bought a sailboat. Mom sold the family home in Marin and bought a house in San Francisco and one on the big island of Hawaii. Kate was sent to boarding school in Putney, Vermont, and Marti to one in Colorado, a short drive from Aspen. It was my mom's turn for freedom. The family had been scattered to the winds.

CHAPTER 3

BERKELEY

WHEN I RETURNED to the Bay Area, I had no friends. I had been gone for five years. Susie Weigel connected me to new people and a new crowd. My family had been dismantled, but hers was at home, closely involved with each other and from the same liberal Jewish gestalt as mine. Her world was upper-class San Francisco. The kids I got to know through Susie lived in Pacific Heights mansions or in posh suburbs like Hillsborough and Woodside. Quiet money in big houses.

It was the season for debutantes in my age group, a very serious thing in almost provincial San Francisco. The summer of parties was covered in detail in the newspapers and concluded with the Cotillion Ball, which glittered underneath the chandeliers in the grand ballroom of the Palace Hotel. I was in so deep that I purchased a dinner jacket and pants with the shiny stripe. It was more than just rich families; it was the interconnected world of the San Francisco elite, going back to the turn of the century. I was happy to be a part of that world. I needed pals and ended up making friends who would last for life.

At the same time, my mom, whom I was staying with, was getting a little boho, no more the businesswoman in skirts and heels. She wore leather sandals from North Beach and wraps and muumuus from Hawaii. She had a good friend, Charles Morgan, a man in his fifties who had a deep whiskey voice and was a nonstop smoker — the first working journalist I ever met. He had a mustache and wore a bow tie.

Charles was based at the local NBC radio station, the San Francisco bureau of NBC News. They had a commute-time job for me: five days a week, 6:00 to 9:00 a.m., then back for the 4:00 to 6:00 p.m. shift. It was a classic newsroom: desks pushed together, clutter everywhere, six-line rotary phones, wire-service bells ringing in the background. My job was to listen to police-radio broadcasts about car accidents and traffic tie-ups. I memorized all the police codes. Every fifteen minutes I put the information into listener-friendly scripts for the jocks to read on air, the drive-time commute update. For my own amusement I made up Eddie the Traffic Eagle, in whose voice I started writing the reports. I was also in charge of coffee and donuts for the morning shift.

THE IMPORTANT PART of the summer was Susie. I spent nearly every day and weekend with her and her family. I bought my first car, a 1954 Jaguar, a beast that must have had two tons of iron and steel in it. And no power steering. It cost $200. The beast was a wild card on the highway or the Golden Gate Bridge on the way to her family's summer home. Her father barred Susie from being a passenger in it. He was right, no question. That car was just waiting to get weird. I knew nothing about it when I bought it, just the exotic model name, the XK120. I bought the mechanic's handbook for the car, but had no intuitive mechanical skills, and barely got the fan belt back on.

I remember the summer of 1963 as a sunny time, happy, in love, a job that resonated and was fun, a new family whom I could idealize and who welcomed me as one of their own, a stern father — he was a federal judge — a welcoming mother, and two sisters. Their summer home in Marin near the redwoods was not far from where I grew up. The prep-school Battle of the Bra became the Siege of the Underpants. One morning, after I'd spent another night without permission in the guest cottage, Judge Weigel made loud noises outside as a warning, marched in, had a conversation with his daughter, and ambled around for fifteen minutes while I hid under the bed. He knew I was there, trembling.

The Chadwick world had been a small one, and I had mastered it all while navigating a divorce, sexual confusion, adolescent anger, and an allergy to authority. Life now was full and satisfying. I felt grown-up. My summer job at NBC was over and they asked me to be their paid campus stringer at Berkeley. I gathered up my clothes and off to school I went, again.

THREE MONTHS AFTER settling into life as a newly minted freshman, I was between classes and saw students swelling into Sproul Plaza. Something felt odd; there was no focus, the crowd wasn't doing anything together or engaged in anything I could see. I walked through them into the student union to find everyone quiet, watching television: "President Kennedy was shot today riding in a motorcade in Dallas, Texas." I didn't stick around for the details. I walked back to my apartment and got in bed. I stayed there for the next four days, watching television, a waking narcotic dream.

I planned on a major in English and a minor in political science. I was taught by Pulitzer Prize writers, on a campus with the most Nobel Prize winners in the United States. The university radiated purpose and pride. The reading and homework were heavy going but I loved learning stuff that was new, knowledge that I was finding and putting together on my own. The school year ended uneventfully, which is why I did well in my classes. I was proud to be there and felt both comfortable and at peace with this new vision of myself. Each day I walked through Sather Gate, a three-story arch, a mythologically powerful entrance, a gateway to knowledge. I got my job back at NBC, with new responsibilities. There were parties and friends, but without Susie, who was still at Chadwick in her senior year, the social life was boring. Still, it was what I had and not too bad at all.

I went to demonstrations at the Palace Hotel to protest racial bias in hiring. The hotel was an early-twentieth-century masterpiece of high gilded ceilings. I knew it well from Sunday brunches there with my wealthy friends and from the annual debutante cotillion. Now, the lobby was packed with demonstrators carrying signs and sleeping bags, ready for a confrontation or a night on the lobby floor. I had picketed real estate offices for CORE, but there were too many tedious afternoons. It was the year that colleges were beginning to organize for civil rights.

My bonus assignment from NBC was the Republican National Convention in San Francisco, the year they picked a quirky libertarian conservative from Arizona, Senator Barry Goldwater. I was assigned full-time to the convention staff, starting as soon as the first cable was laid until the day it was taken out. I was the assistant to the executive in charge of NBC's convention operations. Gavel-to-gavel coverage and floor reporters were new; a lot was being done on the fly. I became the gofer in the broadcast booth, fetching Salem cigarettes and ripping wire copy for the anchormen, Chet Huntley and David Brinkley, for four straight days and nights. I watched from the booth with them as the Goldwater delegates booed and shook their fists at the newsmen, urged on by a speech by former President Eisenhower. I was in the heart of the machine, watching it toss and spin, thousands of people screaming and cheering, and millions watching it on television. I was a part of making it all happen.

THAT SAME SUMMER of 1964 I found the Beatles. Two of my classmates from Chadwick had just married — the homecoming queen and the movie star's son — and I was staying with them at their bungalow in Pasadena. I hadn't seen the Beatles on *Ed Sullivan* and was clueless on the subject. My hosts insisted that taking me to see *A Hard Day's Night* was a condition of staying with them. The revelation! The Beatles were young and in love with life. They rang out joyful harmonies on top of a rocking band. It was all of that, and telling some kind of truth, too. They were in rebellion against adult hypocrisy, lit up by the impudence and irreverence we were feeling toward a meaningless society. At the same time, they were a declaration in favor of love and the joy of living. And, they were having fun.

Weren't they just who I wanted to be? Adorable wiseasses making music and being chased by girls. The Beatles were utterly irresistible. That was what we were looking for: life, liberty, and the pursuit of happiness. We didn't realize it then, but they alleviated the heaviness and cynicism of a society that had killed its beautiful young president and had peeled back the mask on its racism. The Beatles were a last flourish of innocence and joy before the war in Vietnam came home.

The music in that movie, my first Beatles music, was exhilarating, jump-out-of-your-seat stuff like "Can't Buy Me Love," something that went to the central nerve that made you want to twitch and shout. The love ballads, the yearning, sad melodies, "And I Love Her," expressed emotions that you couldn't describe on your own. And always that something slightly mysterious, like "I'll Be Back." They were in that ineffable world of fun and happiness. They were a band of brothers.

IN MY SOPHOMORE year I joined a radical student group called SLATE; there were about twenty of us who met weekly. They had led the mass demonstrations against the House Un-American Activities Committee when it held hearings in San Francisco in 1960 and more or less ran them out of town. SLATE wanted to start an independent guide to classes at Berkeley that would give student appraisals of the teachers and everything else worth knowing to help you decide whether you wanted to take a course. We distributed anonymous questionnaires on campus. On the basis of three or five of them — or even one if it seemed smart enough — we would compile our critique. Less than three weeks back at school I found myself the deputy editor, all of eighteen years old, writing the evaluations of the English and drama departments, heavy-duty commentary on some professor's lifework.

I was the odd duck at SLATE; the membership was a lot of beards, thrift-shop wardrobes, work boots, and bad breath. At one meeting each member was asked to tell their true feelings about the wealthy patrician JFK. It was a political purity test — not exactly a purge, but a bridge that had to be crossed. I wasn't concerned because I knew what I wanted to say and said it: I was sad about his death, he was probably a great man, and now we'd never really know. In the spring I came to a meeting in an ankle cast after a skiing accident. A few of my fellow revolutionaries, already doubtful about me, laughed: "You are so bourgeois."

WHEN SCHOOL STARTED SLATE distributed an open letter on campus that called for a small civil rights protest, and by the time winter came, the university and all its souls had been transformed. It was one of those "nothing will ever be the same again" turning points.

A small rally had been held on a twenty-six-foot strip of university property at the Telegraph Avenue entrance to the campus where, by informal tradition, card tables were set up with literature about social clubs, events academic and sporting, political activities, and the many oddities of Berkeley life. A harmless anything goes zone. The next day, the university announced that tables and activities calling for political advocacy were to be banned from that bit of campus property. It was a torch thrown into a gas station.

That was September 16, and on October 2, thousands of students gathered in the main plaza in front of the giant granite columns of the administration building and surrounded a police car in which one of the demonstrators was being held. He was the man who came up with the slogan "Never trust anyone over 30." Five hundred cops were brought in to deal with the trouble.

On the second day of the sit-in, which had trapped the police car, Joan Baez suddenly appeared at the top of the plaza above this sea of students and then sang in that flawless, heavenly voice of hers:

> Oh my name it is nothin'
> My age it means less
> The country I come from
> Is called the Midwest

I's taught and brought up there
The laws to abide
And that the land that I live in
Has God on its side

Bob Dylan's song was a litany of war and death, from the Civil War to Hiroshima, and even the crucifixion of Christ. Each verse ended with the perpetrators saying they had God on their side. Even Judas, the betrayer of Christ, had God on his side.

That day was my epiphany. I was still unsure of where I fit in at Berkeley and which of my contradictory choices I would commit to. I see myself wearing my preppy camo on that day — in the same spot where a year earlier I heard that President Kennedy had been shot — but with my brain in hyperawareness, suffused by the energy of the protesters. And I was hearing the voice of an angel with the message that the hypocrisy must stop, the killing must stop, and the truth shall rule. I knew that I had to commit to what was honest and real. No more dancing between the society world and the left-wing student groups. I had to do something that was deeply felt. Bob Dylan and Joan Baez were guiding stars, for me and my generation.

The confrontation was defused in the early hours of the morning, after an intense show of police force. But it was the opening round in a series of dumb, bungling, obstinate moves by a liberal but calcified university leadership. They were trying to defend "the rules" for no good reason other than to preserve their authority. That was the moment it began, the student protests of the sixties, in front of my eyes.

Within days, a self-selected leadership named itself the Free Speech Movement; many were my comrades from SLATE. The entire campus was caught up in the fight: every student, every faculty member, every committee, every ad hoc committee, everyone. Thousands of students facing off against hundreds of cops was a national news story. I began to transform my part-time job for NBC as campus stringer to Special Correspondent Wenner. I was expected to hire film crews and get broadcast-quality interviews for network television until the situation got so hairy that they sent in a national correspondent, whom I then dropped into the story.

As the battle escalated and a showdown loomed, I tried to understand what my role in this drama should be: Would I watch things go down but not play a part, not fight for the righteous, afraid to take the risk, too fearful to make the commitment? I had read enough to know that this was a well-worn, tortured self-examination common both to journalists and the fainthearted, one that I was not going to solve quickly.

Finally, on a late afternoon in the first week of December, one thousand students and faculty marched into Sproul Hall, the administration building, and occupied all four floors. Mario Savio, a frumpy, charismatic philosophy student who had fallen into the role of the FSM's leader, spoke these words at the rally that turned into an occupation: "There is a time when the operation of the machine becomes so odious, makes you so sick at heart that you can't take part, you can't even tacitly take part, and you've got to put your bodies upon the gears and upon the wheels, upon the levers, upon all the apparatus, and you have got to make it stop." Joan Baez was there and told the demonstrators, "When you go in, go with love in your heart." And they filed in to the clarion of her singing "We Shall Overcome."

At 7:00 p.m., the police locked the doors of the building. One could leave, but no one could go in. The lights were turned off at 1:00 a.m. and people began to sleep. An hour later, six hundred helmeted, baton-equipped police officers assembled behind the building. Then they went inside. I watched as the cops dragged out students, their heads bouncing down the marble stairs. Over seven hundred people were taken to jail.

The university's regents and the protesters finally worked out a convoluted truce. As the peace agreement was presented to a packed amphitheater, Mario Savio appeared onstage to announce a rally later in the day. The campus police seized him and dragged him off. In that moment the university lost any high ground of moral authority. I was on the stage in my trench coat, a few feet behind Savio, with my ten-pound broadcast-quality tape deck. A photograph of that moment was printed in a local anti-communist rag. It identified me as a communist.

At the beginning of the next year, the chancellor (his name was Strong) was hospitalized for stress, and a widely liked liberal was named to succeed him. Agreements with the protesters were quickly made, and it was over. Free Speech had won. But something was dead, and something unknown was stirring. The vision of college as a sanctuary was replaced by the frightening possibility of a more challenging and potentially dangerous arena for the education of children born after World War II, the baby boom.

CHAPTER 4

TURN ON, TUNE IN, DROP OUT

I MOVED OUT OF my digs near campus into the three-bedroom penthouse of a new building about ten minutes away. I took the room with the terrace, which was handy thanks to Berkeley's sunny weather and all the pot everyone was smoking. The apartment was a pit stop for the people I knew from my worlds of student politics, journalism, San Francisco society, and my new drug friends. I no longer struggled to find my place. Things were coming together with a sense of purpose and fun. The girls were pretty and the pot was plentiful, a key to my deep studies of the harmonic intricacies of the Beatles.

THE COOL EATING spot on campus was the Terrace, an outdoor cafeteria. I wandered in one day during the spring and sat down at a table with friends and some people I didn't know, among them Denise Kaufman, a girl with wild curly hair and twinkling eyes. She knew just who I was, and began a conversation. I didn't realize that I was already an ongoing topic of discussion among her friends. I was on my way home with a few caps of acid to try for the first time, because I had chosen the "psychedelic experience" as the topic for my psychology term paper. LSD was just beginning to appear in Berkeley. It wasn't illegal then, but nonetheless it was used discreetly and with caution. "You can't do that by yourself," she said. Denise had tried it a few months earlier. "You need someone with you. I'll be your guide." The handbook for dropping acid then was *The Psychedelic Experience: A Manual Based on the Tibetan Book of the Dead*, by Harvard professors Timothy Leary and Ralph Metzner. The two, along with Richard Alpert (later Ram Dass), believed that psychedelics could, as Aldous Huxley had written, raise one's consciousness by opening the "doors of perception."

We went back to the penthouse, dropped the capsules (no tabs or blotter acid then), and sat listening to records by the Beatles and Sandy Bull, the guitar and oud player. The acid came on gently but unmistakably. I went into a closet and closed the door. Denise stationed herself outside to keep an ear on the proceedings. What I recall most from the trip were the transcendental insights about the oneness of life. It made me see how interconnected everything was, from the butterfly to the bullwhip, from Jesus to John Lennon, from the mud to the Milky Way, and me to everything. All of it was living, interwoven, interdependent and One. All of it deserved awe, worship, and love. According to Denise, tears were streaming down my face and I was "radiant." She said I had "the face of love."

Denise and LSD changed my life. The acid provided so much depth to any experience. It let me understand something in its many dimensions and meanings that would ordinarily be disguised and unknowable to the strictly rational, unspiritual mind. Of all those experiences, music had the most powerful effect on me. Music could express the inexpressible. My listening to rock and roll at that time was infused with the use and impact of LSD. I became an evangelist for music and psychedelics.

Denise was all of this incarnate. It was springtime in Berkeley, with so many places to go, to play, to hear music, to smoke pot and take acid. The Berkeley, Stanford, and San Francisco State campuses were each catalyzing their own psychedelic communities, and the State students were beginning to colonize Haight-Ashbury. Denise and I were always hanging out. She took me further into wonderland. I was falling in love.

We took my mother to see the Jefferson Airplane at the Matrix, a small nightclub at the center of the San Francisco rock scene. Denise asked her how someone as square as I was could have come from a mom so hip. Visiting her parents, I told them I was going to marry Denise. This did not go down terribly well with her, as the very idea defined what she wanted to get away from.

That spring was spent chasing Denise, trying to capture that wild spirit for myself. She played harmonica, something unusual for a "chick," and was doing gigs with a local high school band that had a lot of chops and acid. In June, Ken Kesey saw them play in Big Sur and took Denise out for the evening. A week later he showed up at her apartment in Berkeley and talked her into joining the Merry Pranksters and him. She was now Mary Microgram, and suddenly took off into another world.

I SPENT THAT SUMMER on the big island of Hawaii, in Kailua Kona, a lazy fishing community that had two small hotels. My mother loaned me her house, one of just five on Keauhou Bay. It had shoji screens that opened onto a tropical rain forest. My sister Kate had given me her acoustic guitar and a Peter, Paul and Mary songbook; I traded my tickets for the Beatles — their last-ever show — to Denise and the Merry Pranksters for two dozen hits of acid. I was well equipped for my summer vacation.

Each morning I opened the screens into a tangle of vines and trees set against the blue sky, practiced the guitar, hitchhiked into town for a burger, and picked up the mail. I wrote a nightly journal. Every few days I dropped acid, listened to music, and went to the beach and snorkeled. After two months the acid ran out and I went home.

Back at Berkeley, a drummer I knew wanted to start a band. I had shoulder-length hair and a Gretsch Country Gentleman guitar. We found some other players, including the only one with some spark, a high school dropout nicknamed Scratch, who was the lead guitarist. The songs I ended up with were "In the Midnight Hour" by Wilson Pickett and "Just Like Me" by Paul Revere and the Raiders. The drummer found a cocktail lounge a mile from campus, and we met there every afternoon for rehearsals. I really had to concentrate. It was hard work, and I mixed the exuberance of making loud music with lots of reverb and tremolo. I wrote to my dad asking for money for a van and more amps so we could go on the road.

After a few weeks of rehearsals, we did our first engagement at a North Beach topless club. It was one of the cheaper ones, and the ladies walked naked in front of us on the stage. I was okay but wasn't about to find a special talent in me that would burn anything down. Scratch's parents pulled the plug on his allowance, and he was gone after that gig. I didn't show up for the next rehearsal either. The name of the band: The Helping Handout.

I wasn't meant for a career as a musician, despite how deeply I felt the music and how central it was to my life. I had a good ear, and a decent voice, but I would need disciplined study, and at the end of the day didn't think I would get that good or be particularly special. It would require an obsession and discipline I didn't have and a commitment to a lifestyle much more uncertain than I could handle. I was not ready to float. I liked structure, organization, and leadership.

Around that time, Denise got pregnant by a careless night with a badass musician she was hanging around with. The abortion was cash in advance, over the Mexican border. The next morning she was admitted to a San Diego hospital, bleeding, barely conscious. Despite once again swallowing her rejection, I was at her bedside when she woke up. She smiled with such gratitude and love that a lifelong and unbreakable bond was formed. There was nothing more I could say to her; I had laid myself at her feet.

MUSIC AND LSD took over my life. I liked getting stoned, listening to the Rolling Stones' *Out of Our Heads*, the Byrds' *Mr. Tambourine Man*, and the Mamas and the Papas' *If You Can Believe Your Eyes and Ears*. Dylan had out *Highway 61*. It was a glorious time in rock and roll. I went to the dance concerts in San Francisco produced by the Family Dog or

Bill Graham nearly every weekend and shows in small clubs and ballrooms with Janis Joplin or the Jefferson Airplane.

Early one morning about 3:00 a.m., while living in a house off campus, I was startled awake by flashlights. The cops. They found a shoebox
of grass in the closet but missed the LSD in the ice cube tray and the
DMT in the vegetable crisper. The house we lived in had been a dead
giveaway that we were drug people. The shrubbery had been sprayed
Day-Glo orange, and touches of Day-Glo green highlighted windows,
eaves, doors, and the porch of the otherwise drab cottage. However, as it
turned out, it was a tip from an angry former roommate, whose girlfriend had cheated on him with me, that had brought the cops to the
door. I was booked by the Berkeley police at four in the morning. My
two phone calls were to my boss at NBC, to whom I offered my resigna-
tion, which he graciously and loyally declined, and to an ex-girlfriend
who with her new boyfriend arranged for a lawyer and bail by noon.

The charges later were dropped because there had been no search war-
rant. But the bust spooked me, so I packed up and got out of the house,
jumped on my Honda 50, the one with the "psychedelic transmission," and
moved into a proper redbrick apartment building on the dull side of campus. I thought that might make me take school more seriously.

I BOUGHT A TICKET to see the Rolling Stones on December 4, 1965,
at the 2,500-seat San Jose Civic Auditorium. It was the year of "Satisfaction." I had spent a lot of afternoons lying on the floor with stereo
speakers on each side of my head and knew every word on *Out of Our
Heads.* "Cry to Me" was about the saddest thing I had ever heard: "Loneliness, it's just a waste of your time." The concert was screaming hysteria,
up close and crazy. Mick ran back and forth across the stage, twirling his
blazer in one hand, about to send it, again and again, into the frenzy,
casting his spell.

On the way out of the show I was handed a hand-drawn flyer promoting an event called "The Acid Test" at a private house a few blocks

away. It was a jam-packed party in a Victorian near San Jose State. Kool-Aid laced with acid was being passed around. The band was loud. They looked like rough characters. When they stopped, I asked the bass player who they were. He whispered in my ear, from one head full of acid to another, "We are the Grateful Dead." That is a mind-blowing phrase to hear when you are deep in the psychedelic. They had been the War-locks, and that night was their first performance as the Dead. It was the second Acid Test.

I soon went to a much bigger Acid Test that Ken Kesey put on at the old Fillmore Auditorium, where there was enough room for seven hundred people to dance, get expressive, and freak out to the Dead and other noisemakers. I was wearing a double-breasted naval officer's coat with brass buttons and epaulets. My buddy and new partner in crime, John Warnecke, was with me; he had gone to high school with the Dead's drummer, Bill Kreutzmann, who provided us access to the sugar cubes with acid. John was from the world of society parties and pink shirts, but he was also raucous, rebellious, and discovering drugs. We were naturals, brothers. It was a long, long night, and we left as the sun came up.

I went to the Trips Festival with the Merry Pranksters, the Mime Troupe, and a variety of other like-minded communes and space cases. Thrift-store creative, Salvation Army chic, Day-Glo Warrior, Victorian evening wear, Riverboat Pirate Gambler, and Cowboy Desperado were the looks of the evening. Every lady had long hair and open arms. It was a gathering of the hippie tribes throughout Northern California.

It was the night Denise introduced me to Ralph J. Gleason, who was wearing a trench coat and a Sherlock Holmes hat. Ralph was the jazz critic for the *San Francisco Chronicle* who was also writing about Dylan and the Beatles, and had championed the Free Speech Movement. His home in Berkeley was a gathering place for the FSM leaders and his column was the only thing you could find in print that understood our hippie, rock world. Everyone read him. He was devoted to music, the freedom it represented, and the talent that created it. He saw that same passion in Denise and many others and ultimately in me.

He had actually written about Denise in the *Chronicle*, "a wild-haired girl harmonica player" wailing away at a folk music festival on the Berkeley campus. He ran into her on the street a few weeks later and introduced himself. They became dear friends. Ralph and I fell into this rare and reassuring place where you know an adult—he was forty-nine—who thinks the same way you do and likes the same things, especially the music and the passionate nature of being young.

I WAS WITH DENISE again, which meant a seesaw between sanity and madness. She brought me along on a "Let's go to L.A. for a lark" trip. The driver was Neal Cassady, who was the basis for Dean Moriarty, the hero of Jack Kerouac's *On the Road*. We all ended up crashing at my dad's house. A few months earlier, Neal had given me a 4:00 a.m. ride from Kesey's place in La Honda back to San Francisco. He had a hammer in one hand and the steering wheel in the other, and I listened to him talk, on speed, without pause while he raced through the dark curves of the mountain roads. Kesey had an open-door policy: if you could find his place, set back in the woods, you could just wander in, knowing nobody, and crash. My feeling was that I didn't belong there.

I FREELANCED A LONG article, reporting and essay combined, in *San Francisco Magazine* about the student protest movement and another one about marijuana use in San Francisco's finest families. The pot piece hit the nail on the head a little too hard. There was a small controversy, which generated a story on the *Chronicle's* society page and a panel at a local narcotics conference, with cops, psychiatrists—and me. The pros.

The military draft loomed, and every male on campus reported for the physical, which was hard to fail. You waited in long lines of guys in their underpants. One of them had painted an abstract sun with solar flares that centered on his nipple. I was automatically entitled to a student deferment. The next time I was called, I presented a psychiatrist's letter stating that I was totally unsuited for the military and showed "homosexual ideation." With the filing of my second notice I used my father's address; he had just moved to a suburb of St. Louis, where he had taken a job at Monsanto putting together a deal to sell soybean milk to the Chinese. I never heard from the draft board again.

I HAD A WEEKLY column for the student newspaper, the *Daily Californian*, titled "Something's Happening." I wrote under a pseudonym, Mr. Jones, and a photograph showed me in long hair and a makeup mustache, hippie dark glasses, and a loaded harmonica holder. This was all Dylan imagery, taken from "Ballad of a Thin Man." I became an essayist, thinker, and minor voice of the rock and roll scene. I was an acolyte of Ralph Gleason, channeling his columns about music and our fringe of society.

Two of my early readers were Greil Marcus and another Berkeley student, Jonathan Cott. Both became lifelong friends and *Rolling Stone* editors. Jonathan was on the masthead of the first issue. Bill Graham, who was just starting to produce dance concerts at the Fillmore, also read my column. He tracked me down on campus and confronted me about something I had written about him. We ended on pleasant terms, enough to get me free entrance to the Fillmore.

I would write up my adventures of the previous weekend, taking acid and going to rock and roll shows. I was an amateurish and very bad imitator of Dylan and his flow of strange narrative imagery. The adventures were with my two best friends, John Warnecke and Ned Topham, another fortunate son of San Francisco. Ned and I looked somewhat alike. I started copying his stylish red-striped shirts from Brooks Brothers, and people assumed we were brothers.

Freak Out headquarters was John's street-level apartment in his father's Victorian on Russian Hill. We had a record player and privacy. It was a short ride to the Avalon Ballroom to see the Grateful Dead or Quicksilver Messenger Service, or over to the Fillmore Auditorium in the heart of the inner city to catch the Jefferson Airplane and the Charlatans.

On nights when that wasn't happening, we might wander around North Beach, checking out topless clubs or burger joints — we loved the one called Clown Alley — and coffeehouses. There was an improv comedy club, the Committee, which we would drop into while totally whacked.

My *Daily Cal* column continued throughout the spring and concluded with a 3,000-word essay, "The Future of Psychedelics." I was attempting to defend LSD, all the wonderful things that flowed from using it, and warn about the storm of hysteria on the horizon. Acid was still legal to take, but the Anti-Fun League was on the march.

RALPH J. GLEASON LIVED in an old-style Julia Morgan house with his wife, Jean, and their three young kids, at 2835 Ashby Street, on the border of Berkeley and Oakland. I became a steady visitor, dropping by in the afternoons, looking to just sit around and talk. His living room had floor-to-ceiling shelves stuffed with books and records, as did the foyer, the dining room, and the bedrooms. Ralph liked that I was an enthusiastic student and acolyte, eagerly soaking up everything he had to offer. He was a sage. I nearly always stayed for dinner.

Ralph was born in the Bronx in 1917, the only son of Irish immigrants. His father worked as chief clerk at Bell Telephone. Ralph went to Horace Greeley High School and was editor of the student newspaper. At Columbia University he wrote a jazz column for the *Daily Spectator* and fell into a tight circle of fellow fans, including John Hammond, the A&R man who discovered Billie Holiday and Bob Dylan, and Thomas Merton, who became a religious scholar and monk.

Ralph went back to the early days of Duke Ellington and Dizzy Gillespie. He was a passionate, fearless advocate of Lenny Bruce. He was the guru to the players who made up the "San Francisco Scene," all the local musicians, promoters, and managers sought him out for advice and his wisdom. Every important musician who came to town visited Ralph. I heard this dig about him: "Gleason is a forty-eight-year-old man who can't decide if he is three sixteen-year-olds or four twelve-year-olds."

MEANWHILE, I WAS going nuts because Denise was back with the Merry Pranksters, living at Kesey's place in La Honda. She was on the Bus, which meant her trips to San Francisco were fewer. Seeing Denise less made each time worse. One night we went to a Family Dog show at the Avalon Ballroom. First up was a group that wore cowboy hats, vests, and sideburns, whom I barely heard, and then a band wearing broad-striped T-shirts and wire-frame glasses:

> Do you...believe in the magic of the young girl's soul
> Believe in the magic of rock 'n' roll
> Believe in the magic that can set you free?
> Ah, talking 'bout the magic

When the show was over, Denise and I went into the early morning world of streetlights, empty intersections, and hissing steam. We sat in my car and said nothing, still feeling the acid. I was toggling between painfully sad and angry. I wanted her to say or do something. Without her I had the feeling that I would be helpless.

"Last night," Denise said, "I had a dream about you. We were alone together on a beach in Hawaii and we were living there in a house on that beach. We were married.

"Remember the fun we used to have together? I still dig doing those things and I'd dig doing them with you. But you get uptight about it and put me uptight. You think it's something I'm doing to you, but it's not. It's something you are doing to yourself. People don't do things to other people, other people let them. I love you in a very special way but I am afraid."

But for what other reason, I thought, had we met on the Terrace than to be together always? The fun, the love, the family we shared. She satisfied my image of myself and my emotional needs. We were a natural match. But there was more than that. She was the daughter of magic, music, and love. And she was flying away.

CHAPTER 5

LONDON CALLING

IT WAS TIME to leave town. School was an easy life but not the real world, let alone the one I wanted to live in. Politics on campus after the Free Speech Movement was dreary and small. Politics in the real world without JFK and with droopy-faced Lyndon was for old people, not for the idealists, students, and the young who wanted change to come. Pot and LSD had left politics colorless; the only thing people were making better than drugs was music. Drugs and finals certainly didn't mix. And my "romance" with Denise was over, my hopes and dreams for us dashed. Nothing was holding me in the Bay Area.

I had become rock and roll crazy.

Off I went to the Holy Land. I booked a June ticket out of New York to London on one of the early transatlantic discount airlines. "Swinging London" was on the cover of *Time* magazine two weeks before I left. I took finals for the two out of five classes I was interested in and flunked the rest, thus finishing my junior year as a sophomore. I was turned on, tuned in, and about to drop out.

On the way to London I stopped to visit my sister Marti for her boarding school graduation. I flew standby to Denver and then hitchhiked to Carbondale, just outside Aspen. I stayed at the school infirmary, sleeping twelve hours a day. Drug use had taken its toll on me: poor health and hygiene, dirty teeth and gums, fatigue, and a cold I couldn't shake. I joined the school bad boys, stole a Mobil gas station sign in town, took it back to school, and hung it up where the graduation ceremonies were to take place. Then we stole some dynamite, set it off at 3:00 a.m., and I went back for more sleep at the infirmary.

My mother came to the graduation with her new boyfriend. He made her happy and had money, which meant hotels, rental cars, and, a first for me, a chartered jet back to Denver. I went to visit my father and stepmother in St. Louis. I had a difficult time concealing my disappointment with the dullness of their lives. All I talked to Dad about was money and my travel details; Dorothy was an enjoyable, pretty woman, but not what I wanted for my dad. I was uncomfortable, embarrassed, and I hurt their feelings in my hurry to get on to New York.

I hadn't been in the city where I was born since I was a kid. I stayed on the Upper East Side in an apartment just off Fifth Avenue that belonged to the family of a girl I occasionally dated in San Francisco. John Warnecke's pretty blond girlfriend was also staying there. I caught up with my grandmother, who gave me some travel money, and saw my first and closest cousin, Steve Simmons, with whom I was raised but hadn't seen since we were in single digits. He was writing articles for a teen magazine and volunteering for Hubert Humphrey. We were the designated "most likely to succeed"s of the family. I had my 35mm Pentax, my portable Olivetti Lettera 22 typewriter, and my Gretsch Country Gentleman guitar, and off I went.

FROM HEATHROW I got a ride into town with two people I had met on the plane. The three of us got a cheap hotel room to share; they went to sleep, but I took a shower, a Dexedrine, and went out to see London. I started in Soho, found Regent Street, then Carnaby Street. Within minutes, a Rolls-Royce pulled up to the curb and out came Brian Jones with a walking stick. It was Brian without a doubt, and the wisdom of my trip was confirmed. There were shops and stores crammed into every street. *Melody Maker*, the weekly music newspaper, was on sale everywhere. I bought a pair of Beatle boots (which used to be called Chelsea boots), a pair of tight bell-bottoms, and a flowered belt.

I found a "bedsit," a one-room mini-flat in South Kensington, half-way between Chelsea and Earl's Court. There I read *Seven Pillars of Wisdom*, by T. E. Lawrence, and *Lady Chatterley's Lover*. I started sleeping with a pretty, very British girl who lived next to me, and I wandered around London with my camera, getting lost as a way to learn the city. I had an introduction from Ralph to a friend of his who worked at *Melody Maker* and met him at their Fleet Street offices, hoping for a job. I did a freelance assignment about the Beach Boys' newest record, which earned me ten pounds. I earned twenty-five quid one Sunday taking pictures at a wedding, and another twenty-five for playing the guitar for a few hours at a party in the corner of a cocktail lounge.

I saw the Yardbirds at the Marquee Club, a side-street joint with low ceilings that was packed. I thought I had heard loud in San Francisco, but these guys were at 9½ in a small place where I was jammed against the low stage. On another night I saw John Mayall's Bluesbreakers with a young Eric Clapton. He was loud. The knockout for me was Stevie Winwood, seventeen years old, with the Spencer Davis Group. I saw Simon and Garfunkel one night and hooked up with their manager, who was an old friend of Ralph's. I got a car ride from him, but no invite to hang out or meet the guys. I had a girl in North London who provided me with hash. I wanted to join a rock band, but was firmly told that "guitarists are two a penny." I wasn't looking to be an expat, or set up a life in London, though if *Melody Maker* had given me a job, I would have stayed. I was going to need money not too far down the path. I had no real reason to be in London and no way of entering the rock and roll world.

ONE DAY, A powder-blue airmail letter fluttered through the slot and fell into my room. Denise had written: "I took a trip yesterday with

Robbie and Sue, and got very scared that something might happen to you. I don't know if I want to hurt you — sometimes I do — or what, but please take care of yourself. I'd like to be with you away from old images — rock and roll and all — maybe to places neither of us have known separately but could know together. I'm still scared. I love you."

I was stunned. Her sudden appearance was a miracle. She had confessed her guilt over our splitting up, wanted to go away with me, and she said, "I love you." I loved her and knew that I always would. I wrote back and proposed marriage as soon as we could. We were twenty. Her response came as soon as planes could cross the ocean.

It was a long and qualified "yes," or maybe a "probably." She didn't want to be married by an English judge, but back home in a forest or in gardens with all our friends and family. I should please not sell my guitar, how important it was to keep it — and finally how unhappy she was there, and what did I think she should do. We wrote back and forth discussing where to get married, work permits, beaches in Spain, whether to live together first, but most particularly we talked about the nature of our relationship, knowing that it would change, and what we wanted from each other. In late July, I got a telegram: "OK. Let's. Arriving Aug. 22, Rotterdam. I love you."

Three weeks later I got a letter that started with a line like "I have been doing a lot of thinking lately." Her parents were now in the picture, so were mine, and friends who knew us well were thrilled but sending unmistakable warnings about the fickleness of her enthusiasms and her taking too much LSD. We did love each other, which was what was so painful. I was looking for commitment and stability, and she was a free spirit and was not about to be tied down — to anybody or anything.

I packed my copy of *Revolver*, which had been released in the U.K. but was not due out in the U.S. for another two months, and soon enough was in a New York City taxicab on a muggy August afternoon, a discouraging contrast to London. My grandmother lived on Park Avenue, and when I arrived at her apartment I called Denise. No marriage, not ready to see you. No amount of sobbing or "You told me" was going to make any difference, knowing full well it was no basis for a good relationship or marriage. I went to the bathroom feeling sick and watched the water swiftly circle the toilet bowl until it disappeared with a final swallow. This, I thought, is how it ends.

Andy Harmon, my best friend from Chadwick, was on the East Coast. He invited me to move in with his family at Overly Farms, their estate in Westchester County. At night we would drive into the city. The car radio would be loud: the Beatles, the Troggs, Tommy James, Paul Revere, Sam the Sham, the Rolling Stones, and, every two hours, without fail, the Lovin' Spoonful's "Summer in the City." The asphalt was still sticky in the early evening, and it was T-shirt temperature all night.

Every day we listened to *Revolver*. It was so unlike anything else in pop music, the expansive harmonies, the imaginative, complex arrangements, the lyrical wit and depth. Digging into *Revolver* required pot, many consecutive listens, and usually ended up with a long fan letter, illustrated by Andy, which we would send to the Beatles. I began to write an awkward novel about Berkeley and Denise, titled *Now Those Days Are Gone*, a lyric from John Lennon's song "Help."

DENISE'S PARENTS, AN older couple, devoted to and worried about their talented, spirited, and headstrong little girl, had her "voluntarily" committed to the psych ward of a local hospital. They liked me well enough — I was that nice Jewish boy — but they felt a marriage was wildly premature. They thought Denise had taken too much LSD and had to break the spell of Kesey and the Pranksters. It was time for Mary Microgram to retire. She spent three months as an in-and-out patient and resumed her career playing music, forming the first all-girl rock group, the Ace of Cups. She's the one with the wild hair, wailing on harmonica.

DENISE KEPT RALPH Gleason up to date on my comings and goings, and her worries about my health, mind, safety, and future. Ralph tracked me down at Overly Farms and sent a chatty letter that, near the end, said this: "The reason I write is that *Ramparts* is taking over the *Sun Reporter*, which is the weekly Negro newspaper here, and turning it into a weekly thing roughly in the *Village Voice, New Republic* bag. We will cover local stories the metros don't cover, full coverage to the movement, literary, social, etc. etc. etc. I am going to be on the board of editors of this project. I would like to propose that you might be available for a part or full-time job as a reporter when we get going in October. You would fit into this whole thing very well. We are going to need coverage of flicks, art, books, plays etc., etc., etc. Wide Open."

CHAPTER 6

JANE

WHEN I RETURNED to San Francisco I began battling with my mother. She didn't want Marti to take drugs and threatened to disinherit me if I turned her on. Marti became best friends with Denise and changed her name to Merlyn. Within the year Mom had tried pot herself and became a daily brownie lady from then until she turned ninety. I got a late night–early morning gig at NBC to come to the newsroom for just fifteen minutes at 2:00 a.m. to log in live dispatches from Vietnam, which brought in $120 a week. I still occasionally took acid but it had become too big a commitment of time and energy — two days to trip and recover. Finally, I cut my hair and decided to look for a nine-to-five job, but after one interview at Sears, Roebuck and another with the phone company, I knew that idea was not going to fly. Ever.

I did an interview with Eric Clapton, when Cream came to San Francisco, my first interview with a musician and a rock and roll star. He was staying in Sausalito, and I spent the afternoon with him in the hotel bar. I was a fan of little distinction, but he took it seriously, a very polite and thoughtful man. I sold the story to *Melody Maker* for $50. The full interview showed up as the cover story in *Rolling Stone* number 10.

THE CALL FROM Ralph came in October. It was time to report for work. I was going to become a journalist. I didn't see it as a career path; I just knew I had a knack for it, and had fun. The idea of journalism school had never occurred to me. I did think of myself as a writer — my portable typewriter was my companion and confidante. I could find a groove in softly clicking keystrokes. I should have known.

Ramparts was headquartered on Broadway, the street that ran through the heart of North Beach, the Barbary Coast–era quarter that was now the beatnik district, the nighttime playground of the city. It had City Lights Bookstore run by Lawrence Ferlinghetti, coffee shops, and folk music and jazz clubs. You could buy handmade sandals, purses, and belts, and very carefully score weed. *Ramparts* was in the hands of an editor in his early thirties, Warren Hinckle III, who saw himself as a swashbuckling journalist, a man with a love for spending other people's money, playing pranks, and irresponsible behavior. He had a pet monkey in a cage in his office named Henry Luce; his sister, his right hand, was nicknamed Vampira. There were a few genuine journalists, including the New Left writer Robert Scheer, and a handful of businesspeople, including a three-hundred-pound accountant. When I got there, the magazine was on a hot streak with an exposé of the CIA's infiltration of the National Student Association. Warren had decided to publish a fortnightly newspaper, *Sunday Ramparts*. I was to be employee number one. I showed up on an early Monday morning.

THE FIRST PERSON I met was a beautiful woman sitting behind the reception desk. Her name was Jane Schindelheim. She had just moved from New York, where she had been studying painting. She had dark hair to her shoulders, a seductive smile that she would hold back, high cheekbones, and almond-shaped eyes, distantly Asian, which made her beauty her own. I told her my business and didn't move from the front of her desk. My questions weren't very sparkling and her replies not encouraging, but I had made up my mind. At coffee break that afternoon she told me she had moved to San Francisco to live with her older sister, Linda, who also worked at *Ramparts*. Like me, Jane was just getting over a big breakup. The guy turned out to be a Chadwick classmate and the only fellow student who skied better than I did. I said the coincidence was a sign that we would get married, and she thought, she told me later, there was "no possible chance."

We would be married for twenty-five years and have three children.

JANE AND I set up housekeeping in a tiny Victorian on Potrero Hill. I loved the companionship, the conversation, the cooking. It was family, freedom, and fun. Jane was very smart, she had a great eye and taste, and was just plain beautiful. Both of us were still in recovery from too much love — or too little — too soon. I had found someone who would put up with my eccentricities, including the drugs, my musical passion, and writing; a woman who could deflect my manic energy and share in my inchoate ambitions. Jane charmed and bewitched my friends and forged friendships with other couples I knew. She liked to go to concerts. She was sophisticated. Herb Caen once referred to her as "Bloomingdale's by the Bay." We were twenty. And then we got a dog. Sooner or later, that has to add up to love.

I had my first full-time job and a reliable paycheck. I was doing something I liked. My duties included coming up with odd news items, like the mating practices of the California condor or any kind of unsigned rewrite that could take a witty headline or the ironic touch of *The New Yorker's* Talk of the Town. I wrote short reviews of movies, plays, museum exhibits, and music to fill calendar listings. In exchange for those duties, I was allowed to write rock and roll stories. My debut was about the first anniversary of the very first San Francisco rock-and-dance concert produced by the Family Dog, "A Tribute to Dr. Strange." That column ended thusly: "Mainly though, it's just been a gas. Freaking on the weekends hasn't been so much fun since grandma first turned on — and as grandma once said to me: Happy Birthday." My second article was an interview with Joan Baez, about her difficulties trying to make a rock record, despite how much she loved it. The headline was "Looking for Heaven in Rock and Roll." I read the review copy of *Hell's Angels* by Hunter S. Thompson that was sent to us.

I covered pot laws, books about hippies, Buddhism, and Tim Leary, who was on his "Turn on, tune in, drop out" lecture tour. The two of us ended up on an all-day road trip to a college where he was speaking. Tim was a magician with words and had the spirit of a leprechaun. He was Irish to the core, talkative and charming. I fancied myself his wingman, an accomplice on his mission to convert the next audience. Along the way, we stopped for a hamburger and a bottle of champagne. I was a newbie and thought LSD and alcohol weren't compatible. We also stopped at his ex-wife's house. I sat in the car, listening to them arguing and screaming. Tim had feet of clay, and I had to accept that. He was some kind of visionary or saint, a holy man or a fool, or all of them together. I liked him.

My favorite phrase those days, which I saw on a Family Dog poster, was "May the Baby Jesus Shut Your Mouth and Open Your Mind," which came from a Captain Beefheart record.

The *Ramparts* gang was a voice of the New Left. At best they ignored rock and roll, and several of them openly hated it — and me. Their lack of interest allowed me a chance to do whatever I wanted. I gave the Steve Miller Band its first write-up, a glowing one. I was not even a way distant second to Ralph Gleason in impact with the artists and the business, but it felt real. The sea would part when Ralph showed up at a nightclub or concert; I was just earning my "drop in" wings. We would go out together, he in his Sherlock Holmes hat, pipe, and trench coat and me with long hair, jeans, and a baby face. We looked like a beatnik Batman and a hippie Robin, the Boy Wonder. I went down to Los Angeles to cover the "Sunset Strip riots," the LAPD crackdown on the nightclubs and rock joints flooded by hippies and music-crazed kids. Stephen Stills' famous song with Buffalo Springfield, "For What It's Worth," was written about that moment: "It's time we stop, children, what's that sound? Everybody look, what's goin' down."

Ramparts was always running out of money, in large part because of

Hinckle's profligacy, which included his inspiration to start *Sunday Ramparts* with no apparent business plan. The Sunday edition was sacrificed in April 1967. I was out of a job, but I had hopes and some prospects in a very small world.

IN JUNE I went to the Monterey Pop Festival. I called Jane after the first night, insisting she join me, that it was mind-blowing. Ralph and I had been guiding the organizers to bring San Francisco music and culture in a righteous way into the weekend mix. It was the coming together of the rock and hippie scenes in London and New York and the West Coast, for the first time ever. Few people had a vision of how quickly and how far our local renaissance had traveled, how rock and roll had spread the word. It was also the summer of *Sgt. Pepper's Lonely Hearts Club Band*, an announcement to the entire world to join in the fun. In that same year, FM underground radio and *Rolling Stone* were born in San Francisco. The word was going out.

THAT SUMMER I had to face up to my homosexuality. Jane and I were regular weekend guests of John Warnecke at the ranch his father owned on the Russian River. His dad had restored a large Victorian where he used to bring Jackie Kennedy, whom he was dating at the time. Visitors got a modern bunkhouse that could sleep eight people. One Saturday afternoon, Jane and I were at the swimming hole in the river where I first saw a boy from Wales, a year younger than me with a beautiful, impish smile and a soft laugh. I watched him splashing around in the sun at the edge of the wooded riverbanks.

When I thought I wouldn't be too obvious, I swam over. Robin Gracey was a student at Cambridge, spending the summer traveling through the States on a ninety-nine-dollar unlimited bus pass. On one of those buses he had met a girl who had just finished working for Jackie Kennedy as an au pair for her children and was on her way to stay at the ranch. And so, along came Robin. Splashing each other was harmless but it got a little physical, so I swam away and tried to let the rest of the weekend pass quietly. I gave him my phone number.

My desire to see him again was frightening and unmistakably sexual. While I waited, hoping he would call, everything seemed to take on some extra level of nervous energy and anxiety. It was excitement, for sure, but it was also unpleasant to need something so badly; and, thinking back on it, I was experiencing not only an overwhelming need, but the fear that comes with doing something you think is wrong, the fear of doing it or the fear of getting caught. I knew this was going to hurt Jane.

Robin and I arranged to meet for a walk through the Haight, where he was staying a few days. We ended up in Golden Gate Park, trying to get to know each other as quickly as we could. I was amazed how insightful and educated he was as we each told our stories and discovered how alike they were. We kissed tentatively, a quick test of the waters, and agreed to meet the next day at my apartment and take LSD together. We both knew what would happen.

I convinced Jane to visit her sister for the day and leave me alone to take drugs with Robin. There were no specific grounds for suspicion. On the other hand, she was intuitive and knew something might be waiting in the wings. The apartment was filled with the light and dust of the afternoon sun. Robin and I kissed and undressed. Moments of doubt were followed by delight and discovery. The sex was nice. It was innocent. When Jane came back that night, she knew. She could smell it and could see it and she said so. We didn't have a fight; neither of us tried to discuss what this was about. I gave her a warning: I have the devil in me; it's not a good idea for you to be around me, but I love you and want to be with you.

I didn't love Jane in that swept-away sense. I didn't put her needs first or think about trying to surprise or delight her. I didn't take time out of my daily life to find that "special something" for her. Date night? It was always about me and what I wanted to do.

Jane was womanly but easily breakable. Being so beautiful made her less secure, not more. Maybe she felt she didn't deserve her beauty and felt guilty about it? Maybe I was her punishment? Jane wrote a lot of notes to me, really not to me, but more like journal entries. They were never sent, and I found some in one of the many drawers she never cleaned out.

"I have lived with Jann now for almost six months. I am in love with him, so much in love, and for just once I am unaware of the part I am playing in this love. I hope he can see over the fence of his glory."

"My darling, I am not trying to erupt the bit of calm we have at times, just trying to see love through the transparent film that holds things together and permits us to exist. Wrap yourself in mine and let me fall deep into the you I barely know. I have opened my legs for you many times, but now my soul, too. I love you. I don't want to want more of you than I can find until you show me that more is there."

We never talked directly in those terms. I concealed too much to be fully honest. Jane was willing to live with my selfishness, whether because of better qualities she saw in me or because she feared rejection. But my behavior silently tore at her. Like it or not, I wasn't "losing" my homosexuality. I had lusted after Robin. The feeling was powerful and just took over.

The next day Jane decided to go to New York. She told me she would think about staying together and let me know. She left me with the dog.

PART TWO

ROLLING STONE

CHAPTER 7

THE FIRST ISSUE

I DIDN'T HAVE A job, and waited for the results of the civil service exam so I could work at the United States Postal Service as a happy hippie and smoke dope all day. I bemoaned my fate with Ralph; we looked at each other and said it was time for plan B, a rock and roll magazine.

England had *Melody Maker* and *New Musical Express*, newspapers that were reported, written, and designed like any other Fleet Street product. In the U.S. there were trade magazines or fan magazines like *Sixteen* and *Tiger Beat* for teenage girls. There was nothing that gave Bob Dylan his due gravitas nor spoke to what amazing musicians and writers the Beatles and the Stones were. Nothing showed any awareness of the cultural revolution under way.

Ralph had written an essay for the academic journal *American Scholar* titled "Like a Rolling Stone," in which he argued that Dylan and the Beatles, as well as Simon and Garfunkel and the Stones, were poets, the truth tellers about the current state of the world. He quoted Plato, who wrote that "the walls of the city will shake and fall. Forms and rhythms in music are never changed without producing changes in the most important political forms and ways." What Ralph wrote was everything I believed about rock and roll, how serious it was, about its deeper meanings and how it had become an act of freedom and liberation. His essay was the philosophical underpinning of *Rolling Stone*, our thesis, and ultimately our name. It was the title of Bob Dylan's greatest hit and also a salute to the Rolling Stones, whom I worshipped. The Stones took their name from Muddy Waters' first hit record, "Rollin' Stone."

And, lo, it came to pass.

WE CREATED ROLLING STONE in Ralph's living room, sitting in his green, cracked-leather armchairs. We would need volunteers, rent-free offices, investors, a design, articles and photos, and a logo. I wanted to have the logo done in the style of the posters that the Family Dog jobbed out to local artists to promote their weekly dance concerts. My favorite artist among the group was Rick Griffin, an ex-surfer who did antique, circus-like lettering, rendered with just the right psychedelic flourish. He also specialized in drawing bloodshot eyeballs with legs and wings. I went to Rick's apartment to pick up the logo as if it were a newborn child. The place reeked of pot, which he insisted I sample. He had lost an eye in a motorcycle accident, and that side of his face was a mass of scar tissue. He hadn't had a haircut or a shave in weeks. He hadn't finished the logo, so I left with a copy of the working draft. We used it until he sent me the finished drawing a year later.

I had to find money. I sent long letters to my mother, my mother-in-law-to-be, my stepmother, and my Berkeley adopted mother, Joan Roos, whom I had met at SLATE and who turned out to be Robert De Niro's first cousin. I estimated how much income we expected to make on ad sales and subscriptions. Of course, I knew nothing about that, but the projections looked rosy and made me appear more confident and thus reassuring to my potential backers. Ralph put in $2,000 and I put up $1,500. All in all, I raised $7,500 to start *Rolling Stone*. I had two turndowns, my best pal, John Warnecke, who was backing a play at the time called *High Mass*, about marijuana, and Bill Graham, the emerging rock impresario. God had spared me. I would have never survived Bill looking over my shoulder.

I met Michael Lydon and his wife, Susan, at the Monterey Pop Festival. Michael was a correspondent for *Newsweek*, doing their hippie and culture reporting. He was a lean, tweedy Bostonian who had been a history major at Yale. I asked him to help out at my new magazine. Ralph would be the wise man, but Michael and I would do the work. He would also add a little journalistic prestige and Ivy League pedigree. Michael agreed, though he couldn't quit *Newsweek*, as I offered no money.

I wanted good photography. I felt that rock and roll was also about imagery — looks, sex, and attitude — good or bad. I didn't want public-relations portraits or performance shots with microphones in everyone's face. I needed a photographer, not a rock fan with a hobby. There was a guy in San Francisco, Jim Marshall, who was a devout fan and an outstanding photographer. He was the obvious choice, except that he was a full-time hothead who usually packed heat. I wasn't up for dealing with that.

I met Baron Wolman at a rock symposium at a local college and told him of my plans and that I needed someone to do great photography. Baron was thirty. He came from Columbus, Ohio, and had gone to Northwestern, where he majored in philosophy. In 1958 he found himself in West Berlin, a counterintelligence agent in the U.S. Army. When the Berlin Wall went up three years later, he wrote and shot the story for his hometown newspaper. After that, he was hooked on photojournalism.

JANE RETURNED FROM New York to find me in a fever, assembling all the bits and pieces of the magazine. She jumped right in, bringing her sister, Linda, and her sister's roommate with her. Since Jane had worked at *Ramparts* taking orders for subscriptions, she became the subscriptions director. Michael Lydon later wrote, "Jann's pretty girlfriend, Janie Schindelheim, did a little of everything; she and Jann made a good couple, but I sensed that Jane had fallen in love with a whirlwind and was now holding on for dear life."

OUR PRINTER WAS located in the San Francisco warehouse district, two blocks from the Hall of Justice, among the dive bars and bail bondsmen storefronts. Across the alley was a slaughterhouse. The printer primarily did shopping inserts for newspapers, a left-wing publication, *People's World,* and had printed the defunct *Sunday Ramparts.* They let us set up a rent-free office on their second floor, where they stored racks of one-ton rolls of newsprint and had a four-machine Linotype shop, with a furnace that melted lead type and filled the air in the mornings with the smell of burned ink. The Linotype machine, now extinct, was a forklift-like contraption that had a seat attached to it for a person who could operate a keyboard that controlled the flow of molten lead into letter forms, punched out in cascading three-inch metal strips, while wheels and levers clanked and shuttled. This was how *Rolling Stone* was produced for three years, by union men who were furious about having to typeset words like "fuck" and "bullshit," the first of many mini-crises to come.

We put up drywall to make an office space for ourselves, bought five folding cafeteria tables for desks, rented typewriters, bought a used file cabinet, and had two phone lines installed. Jane started to find odds and ends at thrift shops to make it a little homelike and put up a poster of the Marx Brothers smoking a hookah over my table. I had stationery printed, over Ralph's objections. I didn't think it would look very promising if we sent out letters written on the back of press releases, as he had suggested.

Michael and I wrote, rewrote, edited, and proofread everything in the issue — the headlines, the pieces with no bylines, our own stories. Ralph had a column; Michael did the news; I handled the record reviews. Michael and I worked like that until the end of the year, when we were joined by three groupies who had been working for Bill Graham. They had volunteered to type up the red-and-yellow mailing labels for our first issues. One of them, Henri Napier, a tough young lady who sported a hard-to-miss Afro, was my first assistant.

Three days before we were scheduled to go to press, Baron got a call that the Grateful Dead had been arrested for drugs, their house in San Francisco raided, and the group taken to jail. The city had a narcotics division that was at war with the rock bands. The police had tried to shut down the Fillmore the year before. In fact, Ralph had kept the venue alive by mobilizing the *Chronicle's* front-page editorial support. Baron and I went to the Dead's house, at 710 Ashbury, at the corner of Haight Street, the heart of the hood, where they would be holding a press conference. I went from bedroom to bedroom interviewing everyone, scoping out the darkly lit commune. The group gathered on the front steps for a photo, Pigpen, their singer, a Hell's Angels look-alike, clenching a rifle, defiance on his face.

THE NIGHT FINALLY came — Tuesday, October 17, 1967. A red button was pushed, a bell rang out three times, and we watched our first issue roll off the small web offset press. The ink was cheap and came off on everyone's fingers. Baron brought a bottle of champagne and plastic glasses. It was anticlimactic for me, and I remember thinking that the issue was so good we would never be able to do better.

We printed 40,000 copies of a twenty-four-page tabloid, then boxed and shipped them throughout the country to tiny magazine wholesalers who had not ordered the magazine and had never even heard of us. This was done through the one small-magazine distributor located in San Francisco. The date on the cover was November 9, at the request of the distributor, so no one would think we were the previous week's edition. Some 33,000 copies were returned in unopened boxes. Those that sold did the trick, though; we began to get letters from people in the oddest places. My favorite was from Cookie Sills, in Paducah, Kentucky, because of the name and place. In San Francisco, Los Angeles, Boston, and New York City, *Rolling Stone* triggered a small but excited response, enough to make me feel that we had something and that we should keep going.

John Lennon was on the first cover. It was the best of the free photos I could find and was an auspicious choice that combined our specialties to come: music, movies, and politics. And one of the greatest, if not the greatest, rock and roll stars in history.

The masthead of the first issue listed the future Mrs. Wenner and a few volunteers, including my Berkeley friend Jonathan Cott, who also had been recruited by Ralph for *Ramparts* along with me. Jonathan had a full head of curly hair, talked fast, and looked every bit the graduate student. He wrote poetry and always had a beautiful girlfriend. Jon Landau was also on the masthead, an East Coast writer I had corresponded with but not yet met. I also listed the names of three people — in key roles such as ad sales and our New York City bureau chief — who didn't exist.

We cobbled together the news that David Crosby had been tossed out of the Byrds; Al Kooper was starting a new group called Blood, Sweat & Tears. Mike Bloomfield and his new group, Electric Flag, had been arrested at 4:00 a.m. in Orange County, California, on drug charges. Procol Harum's tour would launch in the U.S., not the U.K. The first *Rolling Stone* interview was with Donovan.

In addition to an investigation of Monterey Pop Festival profits, Michael Lydon did a quick story about Bill Haley, still touring forty-five weeks a year, and a report about Haight-Ashbury hipsters burning a coffin to expunge the commercialization of hippies. I led the record review section with Arlo Guthrie's *Alice's Restaurant* ("excellent"), and it all ended with a newsy letter from London. We clipped stuff from *Melody Maker*, added some additional reporting by phone, and rewrote. Our staff and friends ran with the local groups, and we had a lot of their news, such as what it looked like inside the opulent house in Los Angeles that the Airplane had leased. Jonathan Cott reviewed a James Brown show in Paris. I wrote the headline: "Sock It *à Moi*."

Ralph began "Perspectives," his series of columns that would appear in nearly every issue. The first was about racial discrimination in the music business, how ugly it was but that it would inevitably disappear.

Jon Landau wrote a mixed review of the newly formed Cream, founded by Eric Clapton, saying they needed more rhythmic foundation, and the new *Jimi Hendrix Experience* album, which was a rave with a few quibbles. Jon had been writing lengthy, almost academic pieces for the first rock and roll fanzine, *Crawdaddy*, which had published a half-dozen issues before *Rolling Stone* began. I didn't care for the *Crawdaddy* approach. But Jon, as a reasonably accomplished guitar player himself, could clearly describe the music and communicate his enthusiasm for it.

I wrote to Jon two months before the first issue, as he was starting his sophomore year at Brandeis. He wrote back to explain his situation: he was not a reporter, but an essayist; "To be altogether candid, Jann, I have never been happy with *Crawdaddy*, and would be delighted to be exclusive to *Rolling Stone*. In the future, unless you ask me to work on something else, you'll be getting a lot of copy on Motown, Atlantic, and Stax/Volt performers. I am not a tremendous fan of the major West Coast groups, although I have spent hours listening to their music. I am much more into English rock and colored things, like the Big O [Otis Redding], the Four Tops, and Stevie Wonder..."

I wrote back: "I don't care if you are wordy or obscene, just as long as it says something. There are no minimums or maximum, although I would prefer you to stay between 750–1,000 words on most things. I like to edit. This does not mean rewrite...I have noticed, in both your pieces and my own, that the introductory paragraph can usually be eliminated to the betterment of the whole piece. We don't do any wholesale slaughtering, but sometimes a piece, anybody's, including my own, can be improved by judicious cuts."

A year passed before Jon and I met in person. In the meantime, there was a constant correspondence, soon supplemented by long and pricey collect phone calls. I liked the San Francisco groups; he didn't. Most of all, Jon loved R&B, which in those years had some of the greatest artists, producers, and songwriters of all time. Jon gave me an education; he introduced me to and gave me my love for soul and rhythm and blues, which is still my favorite music. Because of Jon's passion for R&B and Ralph's love of jazz and blues, *Rolling Stone* introduced black music to an expanding white audience — not as music for white people created by black people, but as black music in and of itself.

THIS IS WHAT I wrote in my first Letter from the Editor: "We have begun a new publication reflecting what we see are the changes in rock and roll and the changes related to rock and roll … We hope that we have something here for the artists and the industry and every person who believes in 'the magic that can set you free.' *Rolling Stone* is not just about the music, but also about the attitudes that the music embraces. We have been working quite hard on it and hope you can dig it. To describe it any further would be difficult without sounding like bullshit, and bullshit is like gathering moss."

CHAPTER 8

A FAMILY AFFAIR

I**T TOOK THREE** months to do the first issue. For the next one, two weeks later, there wasn't enough time to plan anything. The cupboard was empty; we were down to seeds and stems. Ralph and I saw Ike and Tina Turner tear it up the week before deadline at the Hungry i — the North Beach nightclub that regularly featured Lenny Bruce — so my photo of Tina belting it out and a short review became the cover. Ralph lucked into page one news: "Dylan Is Alive and Well in Nashville," the first story about his reemergence from Woodstock after a motorcycle accident and his return to the studio for what became *John Wesley Harding*. Baron went to a Janis Joplin concert with Big Brother at a Marin beach where "large crowds, near to 2,000," had come one weekend. We published two pages of his photos.

Ralph's second "Perspectives" column came from the opposite side of the cultural divide. Zal Yanovsky, the lead guitarist of the Lovin' Spoonful, had been arrested by the San Francisco police for possession of pot and was offered a chance to avoid deportation — he was Canadian — if he would set up a local dealer. Once that got out, various underground papers started a boycott of the Spoonful. Ralph wrote a plea for compassion and civility, and against a rush to judgment. He stood against fashionable hypocrisy, even if it was dressed like a hippie. His last line was "Do we *really* want to be selling postcards of the hanging?" It was Dylan's great line from "Desolation Row."

Jon Landau's second column was about Aretha Franklin's new

Atlantic album, produced by Jerry Wexler, one of the greatest R&B producers of all time. Jerry was a pal of Ralph's from the fifties in New York and would become a mentor and friend to both Jon and me, particularly Jon. I sent the first two issues to Jerry, and he returned the note, having scrawled in the margin: "First issue strong, second one weak. Giant, Ralph Gleason, ever. *Rolling Stone* needs professionalism, detachment, needs identity. Are you a trade publication? Or a critical journal? Or a combo of the two?" We ran an ad selling subscriptions on the last page, where you could choose one of two coupons to mail in. The first one got you a year's subscription for $10 and the other simply said, "*Rolling Stone* sucks."

BARON AND I went to the Cow Palace, south of San Francisco, to see the Who perform as part of a tour package. This one was headlined by the Association. I had already seen the Who at Monterey Pop and had a few of their records, but the group was not established in the States. I found Pete Townshend backstage between the afternoon and evening performances. He was sitting alone in his dressing room and we talked on and on. Pete couldn't have been more open and intelligent. I liked him a lot. I profiled him in the next issue. And Baron shot a great portrait of Pete staring at him from the stage, arms spread, guitar hanging down, ready to kill.

JANE AND I were driving to dinner in Berkeley when we heard the news on the radio that Otis Redding had died in a plane crash. He was twenty-six. He had recorded "Dock of the Bay" a week earlier. We pulled over; this was a tough one to take, and we were crying. We reacted like everyone at Monterey Pop the night Otis strolled out onstage in his lime-green suit and, just before singing "I've Been Loving You Too Long," said, "So, this is the love crowd?" He had more energy than any other performer, songs that killed, and a voice with intense emotional character. He was the same age as most of his audience, and most, like me, had never seen him before. It was my first exposure to soul music in all its power and glory. *Otis Redding Live in Europe* was the soundtrack of our first office. We were just about to close issue 3. I asked Michael Lydon to write the obit, but he put his arm around me and said, "You gotta do it yourself. You can do it. You love the guy, you love his music, come on, man, get to it."

MY SOON-TO-BE SISTER-IN-LAW was dating my soon-to-be art director, Bob Kingsbury, a committed pothead and wood sculptor. Bob was a stoic old-school Swede, salt-of-the-earth good guy. In his woodshop, for a hobby, he made roach clips, lathing high-quality wood dowels and attaching an alligator clip you could use to smoke that last bit of a joint and spare yourself a singed lip or finger. I asked him to make a few hundred so we could offer them as a premium with subscriptions. The ad read, "This Handy Little Device can be yours free." We described its many uses around the house, the recording studio, your bedroom, and concluded, "Act now, before this offer is made illegal." We gave away thousands of them.

Jon Landau wanted his freedom, his autonomy, and not to be edited. The first two needs were fine with me, the same as Ralph had. But Jon was an academic writer and needed help. We went mano a mano. In January 1968, three months after we launched, I received this: "If you touch the stuff about the Byrds, Grape, Airplane, or Doors I will be really burned. And don't give me this crap about how it's not that you disagree with me. I know that every time I get cut it's because what's being cut is going to offend the West Coast audience. I thought *Rolling Stone* was supposed to have balls. I warn you now: never again. I am a critic and I intend to criticize. I am not some irrelevant expert on soul music who is nice to have around to balance the content and throw a few crumbs to advertisers. I do not intend to be part of it in the future. That is, I intend to have *my* say and that means that, within reason, I expect you are going to publish what *I write*."

The West Coast groups were nearly all white and hippies. I loved them. I had seen them live, up close, and high during my "formative years." Jon was right about my not-very-well-disguised effort to not print what I thought was his biased opinion. I didn't want to admit it. He was right to call bullshit on it in strong terms. Jon was a formidable individual even at that age. He loved to talk, and did so carefully and slowly, and he oozed gravitas. He was a North Star to me from then on.

Finally, we met in person. I flew up to Boston on one of my business trips to New York, and he picked me up at the airport. It was like a reunion of long-lost brothers. You don't quite know what to say other than "I can't believe it's you." Jon was a gangly college kid, long hair, wire-frame glasses, altogether a very studious look. The conversation didn't stop for two days. We went to see the Four Tops, the first Motown act I'd ever seen. I watched Jon pounding the drum patterns on his knees, like he was in a trance.

We had reached our understanding about his freedom to say whatever he wanted. However, I couldn't totally restrain myself. I wrote a letter to the editor, under the pseudonym Kevin Altman from Chicago, objecting to what Jon had written an issue earlier: "The group, both on record or in person, is nowhere near what Landau claims they are capable of. I have yet to see one head 'taken apart and reassembled' except perhaps Landau's." Jon figured it out immediately and busted me. Although I tried to deny it, he started writing me notes addressed "Dear Kevin."

When rock artists came to San Francisco, they had little to do except shop, sleep, and spend time hanging out with *Rolling Stone*. Stevie Winwood, on Traffic's first tour, was our first office visitor from the world of music. It was a small world then; the money wasn't big and we were outside the orbit of the record biz in New York and Los Angeles. We had direct access to the artists, not through a PR machine. They left us alone. Baron and I spent an afternoon with Jimi Hendrix, smoked a lot of dope, turned on the tape and took a lot of pictures. I edited it into a less disjointed conversation than had taken place. This happened too frequently.

WITH JANE, HER sister, Linda, and Linda's boyfriend, Bob Kingsbury, working at *Rolling Stone*, the magazine's seven "employees" felt more like family than our original half-hippie volunteer crew. Bob was now my art director and closest partner in putting together the magazine; we would all hang out in the evenings and talk, talk, talk *Rolling Stone*. Bob also started playing around with photographs, cutting out the backgrounds if he didn't like them. He found a book of antique engravings with typefaces and odd lettering styles that started to give us a look — one that was playful and funky. It had a message about who we were, smart but homespun. I decided to pay for heavier, whiter paper for our cover, and Bob had the idea to solarize a photo of Eric Clapton for that cover. It conveyed a sense of our own style.

Three pieces became legend to *Rolling Stone* insiders. Jon Landau wrote an analysis of a live Cream show, and while giving the group their full due for virtuosity and musicianship, he made the point that the music was clichéd and uninteresting. This faced a full-page advertisement for two Cream records, in addition to being in the issue with Eric on the cover. Eric told everyone that this piece caused him to break up Cream.

Ralph wrote in his "Perspectives" column a broadside titled "Stop This Shuck, Mike Bloomfield." I had done an interview with Bloomfield, a Jewish kid from a wealthy Chicago family, just two years older than me. After being kicked out of a bunch of schools, he ended up on the South Side at the feet of Muddy Waters, B. B. King, and Buddy Guy, who all got him, this oddball, dorky whiz kid. Mike had talked about how he had been schooled by all the great bluesmen, spoke their language, and belittled his fellow San Francisco musicians who didn't. "There is one thing I can guarantee you, come hell or high water," wrote Ralph. "No matter how long he lives and how well he plays, Mike Bloomfield will never be black. You can count on that...He will always be a Jewish boy from Chicago, not a black man from the Delta. It won't rub off. You can't become what you are not and it's not for sale. Play your own soul, man, and stop this shuck." That didn't land well with the many white blues guitarists, then in fashion.

The main story of that issue was an editorial I wrote: "A self-appointed coterie of political 'radicals' with no legitimate constituency has formed the Youth International Party, the Yippies, and have started a blitzkrieg to organize a hip protest at the 1968 Democratic National Convention. What makes this otherwise transparent event worthy of notice is that these leftover radical politicos will rise and fall on their ability to exploit the image and popularity of rock and roll."

I had disliked Jerry Rubin when he organized two bloody antiwar protests in Berkeley. Nothing about him struck me as genuine. I thought he was a hustler who saw protest primarily as a way to become famous. And then he hooked up with Abbie Hoffman, who had wit and madness in him but was also a prodigious hustler. These two were the so-called Youth International Party.

They had decided to have a "Festival of Life" at the Democratic convention that would attract hundreds of thousands of kids because of all the big rock groups they said would be coming. To do anything in Chicago without Mayor Daley's okay, to get all those long-haired rock fans to show up in the face of Daley's police, was a reckless risk of lives.

Nobody would call bullshit on it, whether out of fear or left-wing political correctness. I called around and found that every group they attempted to recruit had said no. We printed this banner headline over my piece: "Musicians Reject New Political Exploiters." Hundreds were injured and gassed, but I think our warning had been heard.

I WAS GIVEN A copy of a demo that Bob Dylan had just made in Woodstock. I reviewed the songs in a page one story headlined "Dylan's Basement Tapes Should Be Released." We had Jerry Hopkins write "A Special Report on the Los Angeles Scene," a take on how deeply the business was connected to the city and a quick gossipy look at the canyons, Laurel and Topanga: who was living there and with whom. It was also an introduction to the new talent coming up: Jackson Browne, Buffalo Springfield, and Linda Ronstadt. Don Henley and Glenn Frey were in Linda's band.

Jerry Hopkins had taken up my offer to be our unpaid L.A. bureau chief. He had an enthusiastic chipmunk-like smile that belied his reportorial cynicism. After graduating with a master's from Columbia Journalism School, he ended up in the TV business before starting the first head shop in Los Angeles. He was on the *Rolling Stone* masthead for the next twenty years.

While staying at Jerry's cottage in leafy Laurel Canyon on a trip to Los Angeles, I was moved by the warmth and ease that he and his wife, Jane, shared. Look how wonderful this is, I thought. I have this with my Jane, too, and I should hold on to her. (Later I learned that Jerry's Jane was number two of his four wives.) When I got back to San Francisco, I asked Jane how she felt about marriage. It was a discussion, not a surprise diamond ring, though I did get on my knee to make the proposal. I think Jane, like I, knew that we were a natural fit. We were family. She was the girl for me. We were more special together than apart, and our life side by side was important and fun.

We chose July first as our wedding date and a traditional Jewish ceremony in a synagogue. We didn't invite our parents or extended family. Jane's sister, my sister Merlyn, and Bob Kingsbury came. Baron and his wife were there, and he took the photos. John Warnecke, who looked innocent and boyish in a yarmulke, as if it were a baseball hat turned sideways, was my best man.

I wore a suit; Jane wore a white lace dress. We read the vows, those ancient words of wisdom, looking into each other's eyes. I will do this, I thought to myself, and be happy doing it. I crushed the glass on the second try. Everyone at the office had the day off and joined us at a party in the afternoon — wedding cake and champagne at our loft.

The next day Jane and I drove north over the Golden Gate Bridge to honeymoon in Bodega Bay, but it was foggy. We only spent the night and decided to wait a week and take up an invitation from Steve Miller to go to Los Angeles with his band while they were making a record.

CHAPTER 9

MICK JAGGER, PETE TOWNSHEND, AND THE NAKED BEATLE

I MET MICK JAGGER when I was twenty-two and he was twenty-five. It was in July 1968. Jane and I were on our honeymoon, poolside with the Steve Miller Band, at a hotel in Hollywood. Mick was in town remixing *Beggars Banquet* with Glyn Johns, who was also producing Steve's record. Mick had a soft handshake and a soft voice; he was wearing a dress shirt with pressed trousers, definitely not a rock star outfit. But a rock star he surely was. He made me feel comfortable right away.

I sat at the mixing board between Glyn and Mick, and suddenly out of this supersonic sound system came "Street Fighting Man." They played it again and again as they mixed it, stunning on first listen, absolutely incredible as the song became more familiar. They also worked on "No Expectations." Then Mick stopped the mixing and told me he had finished one more, and would I like to hear it? It was "Sympathy for the Devil." The final take had been done the day after Bobby Kennedy had been gunned down, and Mick added the lines, "I shouted out, 'Who killed the Kennedys?' After all, it was you and me."

Mick took me in his red Cadillac convertible to the house he had rented in Beverly Hills. A couple of cars with groupies tailed us for a while. He had the test pressing of a new record to play for me that had knocked him out. It was the first time I heard *Music from Big Pink*. We spent a long time talking about music and so many other things. It was a great start to a friendship.

BOOKER T. & THE MG's played the Fillmore. I found them packed into their dressing room, keeping their distance from the druggie and rock-and-roll chaos backstage. They were four properly dressed Southern boys with polite manners: Steve Cropper, a consummate and widely respected guitar player; bassist "Duck" Dunn, the kid in the group; bandleader and organist Booker T. Jones; and Al Jackson, "the human drum machine." I invited them to my loft the next day to do a "turntable talk" about some of their landmark records: "Soul Man," "Knock on Wood," "Hold On, I'm Coming," "Respect," and "Dock of the Bay." For two hours they told the stories of how the songs were conceived and written, what the creative process was like, and how much fun and accidental it all was. "Hold On, I'm Coming," for example, was what Sam Moore had yelled while sitting on the can when Steve Cropper was trying to get him back into the studio. It was one of my favorite interviews about making music.

Pete Townshend was my next big interview. This time the Who was in town headlining for hippies at the Fillmore, and Pete performed in a T-shirt and white pants instead of setting off smoke bombs for teenagers in a glitter outfit. He suggested we meet at my house, after his last show. He arrived at 2:00 a.m. He was not ready to wind down.

Pete loves to talk, he loves to think, and he loves to ramble about his many strong opinions, which often contradict one another. We talked about his guitar smashing: when he started it and why, how he felt while doing it and after it was over. We mostly talked about the history of the Who and their future. Pete said: "We have been talking about doing an opera called *Deaf, Dumb, and Blind Boy*, and the hero is played by the Who. We really want to create the feeling that when you listen to the music you can actually become aware of the boy. He sees things basically as vibrations, which we translate as music. The boy elevates and finds something incredible and overwhelming."

Pete told me later that this was the first time he had articulated the concept for *Tommy*. I took him to the airport the next day. He asked if I had spiked his orange juice with acid the night before. I hadn't. It was pure Pete. The interview was so long we ran it in two parts. The first cover was an artsy photo I took of Pete windmilling onstage.

The cover of the issue with part two was a pistol-packing Mickey Mouse in boots, lighting a cigar, perhaps a large joint, and getting ready to shoot. It was a cartoon by Rick Griffin, who had drawn the *Rolling Stone* logo. We were covering the arts that were growing in the same cultural soil as the rock scene: the poster artists, the underground comics crew, and the world of people who put on the light shows at dance concerts. We also had a review of John Lennon's first-ever solo art exhibition by Jonathan Cott, who had gotten a fellowship to study in London just as *Rolling Stone* was getting started. I asked him to be our correspondent, $25 for articles, $50 for interviews.

That issue debuted "Random Notes," our gossip column, modeled on the column of the same name that had run in the student newspaper I had started in high school. We had been running a silly gossip column by the pseudonymous John J. Rock (ahem), but I was up to my neck and had to retire that dude. In the same issue Janis Joplin announced she was leaving Big Brother. Jon Landau had written earlier that she was at a whole other level than her band, and Ralph had predicted that show biz was going to swoop in and take Janis. It did.

We put Mick on the cover again, with an interview Jonathan Cott had conducted at Mick's office in London. Mick never took interviews seriously; they were a trivial genre of music journalism then, and the idea bored him. But he had never been interviewed by Jonathan, who had developed a way of getting what he wanted from a subject by profusely apologizing in advance for interrupting, asking too much, and even doing the interview to begin with. By which point the subject was desperate to help Jonathan and answer any question he asked. Once that dynamic was established, no matter who the subject, Jonathan would pull out some arcane reference, quote, or bit of knowledge that clearly indicated that he knew the interviewee's area of expertise stone-cold and had his own provocative insights on the subject at hand. This was Jonathan's *modus operandi* for all the years to come. One had no choice but to surrender, and that included Mick. Ours was probably the first serious interview he had ever done. He gave us the artwork for *Beggars Banquet*, which had been banned, and we ran it as a center spread. It was a photo of a bathroom stall, with the album credits written in graffiti on the walls.

RALPH DECIDED TO resign. He sent me a letter saying he didn't like the way I handled "business, personnel relations, and editorial policy." Maybe it was growing pains for all of us. In any case, his hot temper cooled and he stayed. Ralph declared in writing that he would no longer be responsible for *Rolling Stone* content other than his own column. But he continued to offer sharp and shrewd advice to me and the editors. He had just given me two great story ideas. One was to report on what we were hearing about drugs in Vietnam. We couldn't afford to send a reporter, but why not send a questionnaire to every subscriber who had an Army or Air Force mailing address and ask them about drugs and music? Questionnaires came back from Air Force bases, ships at sea, up-country Vietnam, stateside, and from all the branches, especially from personnel in the Medical Corps. As it turned out, even Green Berets and Marines were getting high. Questionnaires from Vietnam came back with red dirt in the folds. Charlie Perry edited all of this into a detailed, in-their-own-words survey of how the tendrils of the counterculture were sinking into the wartime military. It was what we would see a few years later in *Apocalypse Now*.

Charlie, a balding, mustachioed grad student who always wore a yellow shirt, tie, and a yellow fedora, was the first full-time employee of *Rolling Stone*. He came in as a volunteer copy editor and the must-have jack of all trades. He worked three issues for free and then had an offer from the San Francisco Zoo. He wanted $40 a week to stay, which was all we could afford. At Princeton he had wanted to be a writer but ended up in Middle Eastern studies, took a year in Lebanon at a school started by T. E. Lawrence, and became fluent in Arabic. He enrolled at Berkeley and ended up sharing a flat with Owsley Stanley, who started quietly manufacturing his own LSD. Charlie took care of beagles for the UC psych department, which qualified him for the job as zookeeper.

Ralph's other idea put *Rolling Stone* on the map. John Lennon and Yoko Ono had released their first record together, *Two Virgins*, and John's record company banned the cover photo of the two of them standing naked, a photo John had taken with a timer on his Nikon. Ralph said I should get in touch with John and Yoko and offer to print it in *Rolling Stone*.

THE BEATLES LIVED in a highly protected bubble. I had one line to them, through Derek Taylor, an ascot-wearing Englishman who had been Brian Epstein's assistant and the Beatles' publicist. He also helped put on Monterey Pop, where we first met. I wrote him, offering to print the banned photographs in our first-anniversary issue in November 1968. We quickly got a yes from John and Yoko, without conditions, and a week later a mailing tube covered with shipping labels and customs stamps arrived at our printer's loft. Inside were the family jewels.

Jonathan Cott met with John in his and Yoko's basement flat in London and taped a conversation about Beatles songs, meeting Bob Dylan, and the naked pictures. It was our first interview with a Beatle. For the cover we used the photo of them looking back over their shoulders, butt naked. To caption the picture, I added this from the Bible: "And they were both naked, the man and his wife, and were not ashamed."

The straight-on, fully naked self-portrait of John and Yoko with their arms around each other ran inside as the center spread. It was a picture of an ordinary couple with ordinary bodies, who were comfortable in their own skin. There was nothing erotic or shocking. It was a message of humility that renounced both shame and fame. To leave behind all that stardom and power, to risk career and respectability, required courage. However, I think it was easy for John. He was being his true self, and in being that person found enormous freedom and happiness. That was the message he sent through his work, and now through *Rolling Stone*.

"Nude Beatle Perils S.F." was the headline in the *San Francisco Chronicle*. It was our first notice in the press. The issue was banned in a few places, including Boston. But it sold out everywhere else. We went back to press and doubled our normal run. In the following issue I wrote a Letter from the Editor sharing with our readers the brouhaha we had caused, how the post office delayed mailing our East Coast copies and the San Francisco police arrested a street vendor in an attempt to bring us to court. We were now on the national radar. All the fuss, I said, came down to an ancient principle of public relations: "Print a famous foreskin and the world will beat a path to your door."

At the one-year mark we had established who we were, where we were going, and what we would cover. Between the record ads and our readers, we were probably grossing $25,000 a month. We could afford to pay a few small salaries, and freelancers could get $10 to $15 for a record review and $100 for a longer story. I tried to give the magazine an essential attitude about the times we were in: hopeful, humorous, and committed. I wanted *Rolling Stone* to be both as knowledgeable and passionate as an insider and simultaneously clear and convincing to an outsider. I had strict notions of what was hip and what we should and shouldn't be writing about. I wanted to establish that we were having a good time but were very serious about our mission. And furthermore, we were in this together with our readers.

We were in the music business, the hippie business, and the magazine business. Each had its own priorities, values, and ideas. They often conflicted. I had to manage all that push and shove while trying to establish that our highest loyalty was as truth tellers to our readers.

There was nothing substantive about rock and roll in the newspapers or on television beyond superficial reports from guys with crew cuts. Little glimmers appeared in a movie or two and occasionally a magazine, usually in the *Saturday Evening Post*, of all places. For *Time* and the other titans of the mainstream, rock and roll was at best a curiosity—look what the kids are up to now—and at worst something ominous and subversive. They didn't like what was happening to young people, their rebelliousness, their very youth. Rock and roll was connecting kids throughout the country, in big cities and on campuses, where they had the strength of community behind them, and in small towns and strict families, where they were isolated and stigmatized because of the music they loved and that spoke to them. By the end of our first year, we had given a national voice to our beliefs. The tribal telegraph for young people had been the radio—now it included *Rolling Stone*.

In addition to sales to subscribers and on newsstands, thousands of copies of *Rolling Stone* were being sold by CBS Records and A&M through record stores. We sold more issues at Tower Records in San Francisco than anyplace else in the world. We gave free albums to new subscribers. We started selling several thousand copies an issue in London. We kept growing.

Jane found a round oak table for me to use as a desk, behind which she put an old postal sorting shelf, which I used for my papers and paraphernalia, like the Beatle bobblehead dolls. She replaced the poster of the Marx Brothers with a framed print of Daniel in the lion's den. I used that round table and postal desk for many years and never worked at a proper desk again.

WE MADE NEWS again in the February 15, 1969, issue. Baron told me he was taking studio pictures of girls who followed around rock stars. In the forties they were called "band girls"; now they were called "groupies," and we decided they would make a noteworthy special issue. Many were legends in the rock and roll world, my first assistant included. The biggest sensations were two plain-Jane Chicago girls who called themselves the Plaster Casters. They were getting their hands on various well-known musicians and making plaster casts of their erect penises. We had a sincere and serious debate about how to handle that, deciding in the end — naturally — to run pictures of the girls with their collections. Jimi Hendrix was the star.

I was blown back by the attention this got. The text and photos were published as a paperback, our first *Rolling Stone* book. I put together a full-page ad in the *New York Times* that promoted our groupie issue as an example of how *Rolling Stone* was "the gateway to understanding American youth." That advertisement was a big-ticket price, but I wanted to promote *Rolling Stone* in the very heart of the establishment.

GREIL MARCUS HAD been sending in record reviews, which we were happily running. One day someone told me he was bitching about the quality of some of the other reviews in the section. I called him up with an "If you're so fucking smart, why don't you try editing it?" And he did, running a serious section, bringing in Lenny Kaye, Lester Bangs, J. R. Young, Peter Guralnick — idiosyncratic and important. That was in the short-lived era of the "super group," when star musicians would perform with other star musicians. Greil wrote a review of *The Masked Marauders*, a record with Bob Dylan, Mick Jagger, George Harrison, John Lennon, and Paul McCartney — the all-time super group who had recorded secretly at the Hudson Bay Colony in Canada. Record stores began calling, asking how to get copies; record labels were calling to find out how to get the tapes and which manager to call. No one realized it was a joke. Warner Bros. signed Greil's coconspirators and rushed out a low-cost album with songs like "I Can't Get No Nookie." It reached 114 on the *Billboard* chart. There was even a reissue. It was another (slightly notorious) feather in our cap.

WE HAD BEEN publishing freelance music pieces by Ben Fong-Torres. He had a part-time job writing the English-language page for the *Daily Chinese World*. His full-time gig was editing the telephone company's in-house employees' magazine. I scrawled "Call me" on one of his check stubs and offered him a $135-a-week salary to work for us. I also suggested he either pick Fong or Torres as his professional name, or no one would believe he was real. He did not take the advice. Joni Mitchell was Ben's first cover and the last time she talked to *Rolling Stone* for a decade. Jerry Hopkins had created a diagrammatic sidebar on the interlocking love lives of the Laurel Canyon musicians. Joni was pretty much the most interlocked, and that was it for us and her for many years.

A SCHISM OPENED IN the heady new world of rock criticism. We were the eight-hundred-pound gorilla in the room. Partially it was geographic, as *Rolling Stone* in San Francisco had become the center of gravity, not the clubby New York critics' circle, which I thought was somewhat more a circle jerk. Robert Christgau, who is now deservedly called the Dean of Rock Critics, sent in a review of a minor record by John Fred and the Playboys. I cut it by a third, stripping it of all the intellectual candy, printed it, and sent him a scathing letter condemning him and every other critic on the East Coast, except Landau, as a species. He wrote back: "I think you are bright and earnest and have the worst case of San Francisco pompousness I've ever observed. I think you should teach in college, it would be a good life for you, and you could disseminate your ideas about art from there without hurting anyone seriously. Your aesthetic assumptions are hopelessly outdated. I agree Landau is the best. Do you always write letters when you are high or have you merely developed the faculty of sounding that way when you are straight? Bob Christgau, Secular Music, Esquire."

CHAPTER 10

A BRIEF VISIT
TO PLANET NEW YORK

O N MY FIRST business trip for *Rolling Stone* to New York, I wanted to see the people who bought ads in the trade publications. They were not interested in seeing me. The publicity people, on the other hand, welcomed me; they saw the magazine as a new outlet for stories on their artists. Ralph's friend at Atlantic didn't have much of a clue about us, but promised an ad for a jazz artist and took me in to shake hands with Ahmet Ertegun. Atlantic's offices, just off Columbus Circle, were a mess, jammed with desks and endless boxes of records.

Columbia was a world away from Atlantic, in the CBS building nicknamed Black Rock on Fifty-Second Street and Sixth Avenue. The skyscraper was severe, clad in black granite, stripped of detail. Everything inside was black-and-white; the lettering and numbers in the elevators were thin and without flourishes. You knew it was expensive. Ralph's longtime buddy from the forties, Bob Altschuler, was a hearty-voiced, arm-around-your-shoulder-style PR guy, a collector of rare jazz and blues records. He got me; I was a fellow fan on the way up. Bob persuaded Clive Davis to have Columbia Records create an advertising campaign custom-designed for us.

We depended on those ads. We spent the money we had as needed. I had no idea how long it would last. There were no business plans, no projections. It was just a blind jump off a cliff. The priority was to get the next issue out. I was still doing most of it by myself. Magazine distribution, advertising, and marketing were all unknown to me. Let alone financial management. Our bookkeeping was done by the printer's wife. One day I received a letter from a law firm representing Allen Klein, manager of the Rolling Stones, telling me to stop using their name. I couldn't imagine that the band would give a shit, and certainly hoped so. I wrote the lawyer back asking him to prove that this was what the band wanted. I said something like "This is not where their heads are at." My toughest legalese. I never heard back.

THE OTHER LABEL diving big into the new music was Elektra, founded by Jac Holzman in his dorm room at St. John's College. When I met him, he had signed the Butterfield Blues Band, the Doors, Love, and very shortly the Stooges. Jac was originally a folkie — Judy Collins was the alluring face of Elektra — and he had fallen into rock with an avant-garde, cerebral twist. Jac took me under his wing and began advertising immediately.

Jac had hired Danny Fields specifically to push the Doors and the rock acts. Soon every label had to have its emissary to "the underground," a so-called house hippie. Danny had graduated Phi Beta Kappa at Penn and quit Harvard Law School after a year to follow his muse. He affected a mannered weariness. He introduced me to Andy Warhol's demimonde and the New York rock-critic clique.

Danny arranged a dinner for me with an up-and-coming rock photographer, Linda Eastman, a comely blonde from Scarsdale, New York. Everyone assumed she was an heiress to the Eastman Kodak fortune, though she was Jewish and the daughter of an entertainment lawyer. We had a little flirt that didn't go far. At her Upper East Side apartment she had binders and file drawers full of her photographs. I picked out about a hundred to take back to San Francisco; they were the foundation of the *Rolling Stone* photo library. She was a good photographer, and we became good friends. Soon enough she asked if I would assign her to shoot the Beatles in London; she would pay her own way. Sure, why? To meet Paul. She would send me postcards from London, detailing her pursuit of him. Soon enough a card arrived saying she'd been on a date with him. Then another: "All is well. Thanks to you. x Linda."

Danny also introduced me to Gloria Stavers, editor in chief of *Sixteen* magazine, which sold hundreds of thousands of copies during the reigns of Herman's Hermits and the Monkees. I felt like I was secretly in the enemy camp of teen magazines, since that was the kind of journalism we were supposed to wipe off the face of the earth. I visited her offices at 745 Fifth Avenue, the building with the FAO Schwarz toy store on the ground floor, the same building *Rolling Stone* settled in when we moved to Manhattan a decade later. It was just Gloria, a onetime model in tight black leather, a half-dozen assistants, and black file cabinets lined up against every wall. I had never seen a magazine office before, other than the Alice in Wonderland world of *Ramparts*. Gloria told me that when she shot a teen idol, she would not only take his shirt off, but also undo the top button of his pants. Those would prove to be wise and useful words.

ONE DAY I got a call from the office that a friend of Robin Gracey's was in New York and wanted to see me. I hadn't heard Robin's name in more than a year but had often thought about him after our few days together. I never got his address; he just disappeared, much as Jane and I had hoped he would. We didn't discuss him or "it." But for me the longing had never gone away. The fantasy about a future meeting was faded but remained real enough.

His friend filled in bits of the fairy tale: Robin's seven-day hitchhiking odyssey back to Canada, his return to Oxford, his harsh family life, his girlfriend. He gave me an address. When I got back to San Francisco, I wrote him a single-spaced, ten-page typewritten letter in which I tried to figure out what this all meant, the complications, the sexual attraction, and to see what he thought and where this was going.

I wanted to go to London and find him.

CHAPTER 11

TRANS-OCEANIC
COMICS COMPANY

WHEN I HAD gone to London as a college dropout, the headlines on the tabloids at Heathrow were about Donovan's hashish bust. Now, in 1969, they were beating the drums about George Harrison and his wife, Pattie Boyd, busted for pot, apparently a setup by the police to rain on the parade for Paul McCartney, who was marrying Linda Eastman that day. I was there now to do business with Mick Jagger.

I traveled on Pan Am, in the glory days of first class, catering by Maxim's, champagne and tins of caviar. A car was waiting to take me to a hotel looking over Hyde Park, where Mick's office had booked me a room. Brian Jones and Bill Wyman were staying down the hall. The British Invasion was still under way; the Beatles hadn't broken up; the Stones were getting ready to come to America again. The Who, the Kinks, the Animals, Clapton, Traffic... it seemed endless. London felt like magic.

My counterpart in London in the "counterculture press" was Richard Neville, who founded OZ magazine in 1967. Richard treated me as a very distinguished person, a brother in arms, the real deal from world hippie headquarters in San Francisco. Tony Elliott, who founded *Time Out*, and Felix Dennis, who worked at OZ, had a magazine distribution business, and I gave them the rights to handle *Rolling Stone*. Tony was my age, a straightforward guy with a great magazine idea, *Time Out*. Felix was a good-hearted, loudmouthed buccaneer who became a major magazine publisher, philanthropist, and poet, none of which would have seemed likely at the time. *Rolling Stone* was selling almost as many copies in London as in Los Angeles and had a big reputation.

John and Yoko invited me to visit their new home, Tittenhurst Park, in Ascot, a small town twenty-five miles west of London. I knew they had felt enormously buoyed by our support on *Two Virgins*. Yoko was petite, no small talk, all business. She told me John was sleeping, not feeling well, and wasn't coming down to meet me. She told me much later that he had been "too nervous." She poured tea and let me propose a long interview with John, a serious one about what it was like to be in the Beatles and where all the songs came from. I didn't know that the group was in the early stages of breaking up. She said no for the time being. But it was a start.

Pete Townshend asked me to dinner with his wife at his house in Twickenham, on the Thames. Pete was as talkative as ever and loved to play music, so I didn't leave until long after midnight. He was a Stones fan and obsessed with Mick. I took him to one of the *Let It Bleed* over-dubbing sessions at Olympic Studios. Pete became a pen pal. "Roger," he wrote about Roger Daltrey, "is buying mansions after being told he is a dollar millionaire. I bought my seventh Revox to celebrate credit where it's due. The big drag about the Who is that they always lean so heavily on their history. Anything slightly daring throws everyone into panics. For the first time in six years, I feel I can put a time limit on how much longer we'll be together. I give it eighteen months…It's very sunny on the Thames. Lots of Love, Pete."

I HAD STAYED in touch with Mick ever since Los Angeles. Everyone knew he had gone to the London School of Economics and was well educated. He was more polished and sophisticated than anyone I was meeting in the land of rock and roll. We talked about doing a British version of

Rolling Stone. We shared the same passions in music and culture. Magazines were important voices then, and there was romance and magic about them. I sent Mick a to-do list: office space, staff, legal issues. I wrote, "We didn't really discuss what exactly we each had in mind. I would like to see basically similar editions for each country...but local reviews, news, calendars and advertising would be different."

Mick wrote back with his thoughts: "As far as control is concerned, I would like it to be simply between yourself and myself. For my part, I assumed that I would more or less have control from week to week on this side of the Atlantic. I was prepared to find the finance myself. What I really want it to be is not a carbon copy of American *Rolling Stone.* I don't want a circulation of 10,000 every two weeks. I think we should aim for at least 60,000 within a year. I don't think these issues are insurmountable."

Would their ruthless former business manager, Allen Klein, be in the mix, I asked. Mick wrote, "There is no possibility of Allen Klein being involved, so we can get that particular gremlin out of your head." And the name, *Rolling Stone.* Who owned that? I had let it slide, but if we established a business, lawyers would insist that we formalize control. I had never worried about it because I trusted Mick's judgment and honesty. He must have felt the same about me. Thirty-five years passed before we signed an agreement over the name we shared.

Mick was indirect about the business issues. I worked out the legal agreements with his advisor, Prince Rupert Loewenstein. Rupert owned Leopold Josephs and Sons, a private bank, and did Mick's banking, advised him on deals, and set up tax havens. He was fleshy and effeminate and spoke with a generic aristocratic accent. He nearly gagged when I told him we had decided to call our company Trans-Oceanic Comics, Ltd.

I met Marianne Faithfull briefly. Mick and I were having drinks at a pub near his house on Cheyne Walk, a pretty side street just off the Thames in Chelsea. We headed back to his house and were having a smoke upstairs in his upholstered living room when in burst Maria crying and running to the bedroom. Strange, I thought, and went back to my hotel.

MICK WANTED BRITISH *Rolling Stone* to have its own voice and writers. London was then in a renaissance, not just in rock, but also the arts: experimental theater, happenings, photography, fashion, and galleries. Everything was touched with a rebellious but well-behaved spirit. *The International Times, OZ,* and *Time Out* were thriving as the chroniclers and arbiters of it all. The scene was underground, but quite trendy as well. Mick was interested in the full cultural mix rather than just the music. I was enthralled to be in partnership with Mick Jagger. He would find the editor, hire the staff, and take charge personally. As a practical matter, I couldn't do it from five thousand miles away, and Mick was paying for it. We had a press conference to announce the plan. Mick and I sat at a table with a flower arrangement, answering Fleet Street's questions. Mick's hair was down to his shoulders; mine was below my ears. Mick had on an embroidered vest; I wore a cream-colored silk shirt with ruffles from neck to navel.

Mick was polite and generous with me. I was in his bubble of fortune and fame. There was no use pretending not to be a fan. Everybody else was, too. Best to just be straightforward and not stare. I watched how people got bent by the force field around his fame, how they maneuvered and competed to get closer to him, and how often they tripped up anticipating his wishes and how they liked to assert their closeness.

MICK WAS WELL past his teen idol days. The Stones were writing material that defined a harder-edged view of life. "Sympathy for the Devil" was beginning to deal with his knowledge of the largest political and moral issues of the day, and the presence of evil in the world. Things changed with that song; the Stones were transmuted not only by the crossfire hurricane of the sixties, but soon enough by a song about Satan and death, one that soon had its own true-life murder attached. It was inescapable that Mick would become the personification of the song in a time of war and bloodshed. This was weight Mick was not yet carrying, at least not for a few months. When I was around then, Mick was setting up their first modern tour of the USA. It ended up plagued with logistical mishaps one after the other, mishaps that culminated in Altamont.

ROBIN HAD WRITTEN back. We had been briefly brought together in San Francisco by desire and curiosity. We were two people who didn't know each other, trying to fill in a history that we didn't have. I wasn't clear about his sexuality, but he had been open-minded.

When I arrived in London, I called him. I took him to the Stones sessions, and he watched Mick at the microphone, recording the vocals for "You Can't Always Get What You Want." Mick gave us a ride back to my hotel. It didn't occur to me to worry about what he might think. Once back in my room, Robin and I began to kiss. He said he wasn't gay, and then we made love. I had no idea then of how to find sex with another man, and I had to fly thousands of miles for that opportunity.

When I got back to London from a weekend with Robin in Oxford, a letter from Jane was waiting: "I feel that I am losing you. Your face slips away. Nonetheless my husband there are great times when I need you. I know you must be away, but when I need you, give that to me sometimes. Last week I was weak from loneliness because I was worried. I am sitting in your chair typing this; I always do things in your chair when you are gone because it's like the forbidden candy. I want to be special for you Jann because I love you so."

MICK FOUND OFFICES, put together a staff, and it was under way. He was now in the magazine business, and I was in the Mick Jagger business, and I would stay in that business for life. The new offices were on Hanover Square, one of the nicest spots in London, a full floor of parlors and windows with views, very much smarter than my offices or Mick's.

The small staff was nice but more interested in being quasi-hippies than journalists. I had no real power to fire anyone nor countermand orders Mick had given. Not being in control was a disassociated state for me. I had become used to being in charge; it was my comfort zone. The staff struggled with not only editorial but also the difficulties of distribution, printing, and advertising sales. The police were confiscating issues of other magazines for being obscene; printers were demanding indemnities, and advertisers were demanding editorial coverage for advertising. *OZ* was put on trial on charges of publishing obscenities. By the time I returned to London a few months later, they had printed an issue with a black-and-white cover by Jim Dine, a "neo-Dadaist" American living in London. He was a highly regarded artist, but the cover was of four crudely drawn hearts growing hair. I flipped. They told me that Mick — now filming *Ned Kelly* in Australia — had commissioned it.

Robin came back to London. We had been writing letters back and forth, imagining a relationship as if we were two young poets in the nineteenth century, British university students, which in fact Robin was. We talked literature, music, dreams of going away. We fell in love with a fantasy. I knew it was a delusion. I was married, and he wasn't gay. We never found the basis for romance. My life was with Jane and *Rolling Stone*.

On the flight back on a Pan Am Clipper, using its onboard stationery, I wrote Mick a long report on my visit: "The situation at the office was uninspiring, loosely run, haphazard and the resultant product a reflection of all this, mediocre. The staff is characterized by a kind of pleasant happy-go-luckiness, which by itself is harmless enough, but seen in the context of what *RS* has already achieved and what we are trying to do in the U.K., must come to an end." I wrote out my recommendations for the future and my hope that this would work out. I was expecting the managing editor to spend two weeks with me in San Francisco; she didn't come. I decided to get rid of the whole crew at Hanover Square, sink the whole leaking ship, and start over on my own. I shut it down.

Mick cabled from Australia that he would be in Los Angeles

mid-October and hoped we could meet. "Love to you and Straight Arrow. Mick." He was unreachable in Australia, but I took the responsibility for doing it. I knew I was right and that Mick would agree. Hopefully. I sent my New York bureau chief, Jan Hodenfield, to take over *Rolling Stone* in London and run a small business and editorial operation. Mick was a gentleman. He paid off the bills, the employee salaries, and their severance.

It never came up again.

CHAPTER 12

ME AND BOZ, SITTIN' ON OTIS' PORCH

B OZ SCAGGS AND his soon-to-be wife, Carmella Storniola, lived across the street from us in our old house on Potrero Hill. Jane had become best friends with Carmella, a flamboyant Sicilian who loved a good time. Boz and I became inseparable; I sent him a press card so he could get into shows free, and he sent me back a note saying, "I'm going out to look for a scoop now." By that time he had quit as the rhythm guitarist for Steve Miller. Boz was deeply polite, always well dressed. He had gone on a scholarship to a private school in Dallas where he'd met Steve, the son of a wealthy doctor. His real name was William Royce Scaggs.

We would talk, play guitars, listen to Van Morrison, Dylan, and Bobby Blue Bland. Boz wanted to make a solo record and asked if I would help him think it through. Wilson Pickett, Clarence Carter, and Otis Redding had the feel and style he wanted. They had noticeable things in common: musicians from Memphis and Muscle Shoals, guitarist Duane Allman, and the same label, Atlantic Records.

We took Boz's songs into a local studio, made some demos, and flew to New York in May 1969 to see Jerry Wexler. He wanted to put Boz on their new rock label, Atco, but we insisted on being considered part of the historic tradition of Atlantic. We walked out with a first timer's contract: a $5,000 advance, another $2,000 on delivering a record, and a

7 percent royalty, reducible to 5 percent if a producer had to be paid. We were thrilled. We were going to make a record. We packed Jane and Carmella off to Acapulco and went south for two weeks to make what we called the "joyful noise."

First stop was Macon, Georgia, the home turf of Phil Walden, an artists' manager about my age, whom I had called to book Duane Allman for the sessions. Phil worked out of a small stucco building in Macon where he ran Capricorn Records with his brother and a guy named Speedo, a guy named Blue, and two ladies with beehives. There were gold records by Otis Redding on the wall. Phil had been his manager and best friend from the beginning to the end. Otis was a Macon boy, too. As were Little Richard and James Brown. Phil was now managing the Allman Brothers, who had just formed and were finishing a month of rehearsals. We went to see their very first gig in a local nightclub and ended up sleeping on mattresses at a former fraternity house they used as a crash pad.

We rented a Thunderbird convertible and headed for Muscle Shoals through Georgia and across northern Alabama, almost to the Tennessee border. It was deep South and we had long hair. We made the run nonstop except for gas stations, got a room at the Downtowner Hotel in Florence, Alabama, and drove out to the studio. Muscle Shoals Sound Recorders was just off a two-lane highway in an unmarked, windowless cement building that looked like it might be an appliance-repair business.

I was expecting to find a group of black musicians waiting for us inside. Instead, it was young white guys in their twenties and thirties, local boys who liked fishing the Tennessee River. Nothing hippie about them, except for Duane, whom they already knew and loved. They called him Skydog. His guitar jumped and swooped — gutsy, lyrical, swampy. I had been in studios before and was comfortable with musicians, even though my knowledge of production and its technical language was quite basic at best. But I could run the sessions by feel and read Boz well. I was confident about what I liked and what I thought worked, when to stop and start again, or move something around. We had brought ten songs with us and a couple of notions. Boz had remembered a fragment from a slow blues, "Loan Me a Dime." We ran it down with the musicians, and I indicated places for Duane to take extended solos. When we began, Duane caught fire, found a lick he could keep working and come back to, and the musicians fell in. As they jammed, it got bigger, louder, longer. After about eight minutes I could feel the fade coming, so I ran out of the control booth into the middle of the studio waving my arms in a circle for them to keep going. You can hear it drop for a few bars and then Duane pushing it into overdrive.

After seven days we were about done, never more than three takes on any song. I played a bit of "Loan Me a Dime" over the phone to Jerry Wexler, who called the next day screaming that we were spending too much money and he was pulling the plug. We never got the chance to do the overdubbing that would have polished, filled out, and finished the album.

The record was released in August 1969. I invited the Bay Area FM jockeys to a listening party at a local studio, got them all high, and played them "Loan Me a Dime" at a brain-imprinting volume. It became a big FM radio favorite. *Rolling Stone* couldn't give the record the coverage it deserved and help kick it off because of my involvement. We buried it in the review section.

Many consider it a classic. It was an intense shared experience. We were partners in it and stayed great friends for years. We still call each other Luke and Elrod. That's Boz and me in the photo in the center spread of the album, sitting on the porch of Otis Redding's cabin in Georgia's piney woods.

CHAPTER 13

TALKING BOB DYLAN

I WANTED TO INTERVIEW Bob Dylan more than anything. His language had reached me and my own uncertain sense of self like no one else had. It still did. He was an incandescent moral and literary figure as well as a lyrical and musical genius. The idea that he spoke for a generation was true, no matter what he said. If *Rolling Stone* was going to fulfill its mission, we had to have Bob in our pages, honor him, and give our readers a deeper understanding of the man and his work.

Bringing It All Back Home was the first Dylan record I bought, just as I started dropping acid. Acoustic and electric guitars, pianos, harmonicas, and tambourines danced in the brain, along with lyrics like "If my thought dreams could be seen, they'd probably put my head in a guillotine. But it's alright, Ma, it's life, and life only."

Six months later I had *Highway 61 Revisited* in hand. It was rougher and tougher, fully rocked out and cascading and exploding with psychedelic energy and imagery. My personal mindblower was "Desolation Row," but the song that cut the deepest was "Like a Rolling Stone." The song was about discovering what was actually going on around you, realizing that life isn't all that you've been told it is. You're liberated from your false knowledge and hang-ups, but that's frightening, and you have to face that. Suddenly you're scrounging for your next meal, but "say, do you want to make a deal?" There's fear in that line, in that melody, in that voice. The key line is "You're invisible now, you've got no secrets to conceal." Everything has been stripped away and you're on your own, there is nothing to hide, you're alone, with no direction home. But you're free. That was the message. It was a song of innocence and experience.

I always thought it was my story. I used to go to the finest schools. Nobody had ever taught me how to live out on the street. Now all of a sudden, I was on the streets of Berkeley, in a world of radicals, Hell's Angels, harmonica queens, drug dealers, and dope kings. One of them is called the Mystery Tramp. And then I'm at an acid test, and some stranger with a top hat on comes up to me, and I stare into the vacuum of his eyes and he asks, "Do you want to make a deal?" That happened to me, many times.

BOB HAD BEEN in seclusion, living a quiet family life near Woodstock, New York, since his motorcycle accident in 1966. He had recorded *John Wesley Harding* and *Nashville Skyline*, but other than that, he was out of sight, a mystery. An interview with Bob would be a big scoop for us, and hopefully something meaningful in his own history.

Ralph — who had met Bob a few times when he played San Francisco and Berkeley — suggested I write Bob through his manager, Albert Grossman, and ask to meet the next time I was in New York. I sent a few issues of the magazine with a letter in which I tried to be hip and persuasive, using jargon of the times, like "groovy" and "dig it." In retrospect, cringeworthy.

One early summer afternoon I got back to my hotel in New York to find a message that "Mr. Dillon called." I had to leave the next day. "Mr. Dillon" had left no call-back number. On my next trip, nothing. When I was back in town with Boz to make our record deal with Jerry Wexler, Bob called. He said we could meet, and I could tell him what I had in mind.

Boz and I were sharing a room at the Drake Hotel. The next morning I was awakened by a knock on the door. I got up, answered the door, and in Bob walked, dressed in jeans, sheepskin jacket, and cowboy boots.

I scrambled into my clothes, and Bob and I sat and talked. By that time Boz was awake and having a "holy shit" moment. Bob peppered me with questions. What was *Rolling Stone* about? Why? Why did "they" want to interview him? What do you want to know? Do you know the Grateful Dead? Nice to meet you; I'll be in touch.

A month later Bob agreed to an interview.

I MET WITH Bob at the Stanhope Hotel on East Eighty-First Street and Fifth Avenue. Usually the neighborhood was tranquil, but on that day the streets were packed with people who had come to show their love for Judy Garland, who had died five days earlier. Her service was under way at Frank Campbell's funeral home around the corner.

Bob was clean-cut, neatly dressed, and carried a book bag. He came alone; this was in those less fraught early days without PR people. His answers were simple and direct. If Bob didn't want to answer, he wasn't evasive but he would just stay silent until I felt completely awkward and moved on.

"Well, Jann," he said. "I'll tell ya, I was on the road for almost five years. It wore me down. I was on drugs, a lot of things. A lot of things just to keep going. And I don't want to live that way anymore. I'm just waiting for a better time."

"Do you think you've played any role in the change of popular music in the last four years?"

"I hope not."

"Well, a lot of people say you have."

"Well, you know, I'm not one to argue. I don't want to make anyone worry about it, but boy, if I could ease someone's mind, I'd be the first one to do it. I want to lighten every load. Straighten out every burden. I don't want anybody to be hung up ... especially over me or anything I do."

"A lot of people, your audience, seem to regard you as a great 'youth leader' ... What do you feel about unwillingly occupying that position?"

"I can see that position filled by someone else. I play music, man, I write songs. I have a certain balance about things, and I believe there should be an order to everything. Underneath it all, I believe there are people trained for this job that you're talking about, the 'youth leader' type of thing, you know? I mean there must be people trained to do this type of work. And I'm just one person, doing what I do. Trying to get along…"

It was the Bob of the *Nashville Skyline* era. I asked about his new singing voice on that record, and he said it was because he had stopped smoking and told me I should do the same. I spent a lot of time on how he made records, touring, being a musician. I asked technical questions about songs, not about their origins and intent, which I knew he wouldn't answer, but I wished later I had tried. If he didn't answer a question literally, he would do so figuratively or metaphorically. He was very funny.

It wasn't a tell-all conversation; that was never going to happen. But he was straightforward with me; you got a sense of him, lighthearted, careful, likable, a man in an extraordinary circumstance. I liked Bob. I thought that, even with the awkwardness of my awe, we would be able to work together and find a level of friendship that would last.

I WAS GIVING a lot of thought at the time to an ongoing question in the hippie community over the profit motive: whether making money, or more than you needed, was wrong and created bad karma and bad vibes, as we liked to say at the time. A nasty sandbox debate was under way over "hip capitalism." I was trying to find a paradigm for "rock and roll values." I asked Jerry Garcia for advice on how big an organization should get. He said I should stop hiring people once I started not remembering everyone's name.

The high-water mark of "free" — the hippie ideal — was Woodstock in August. It wasn't meant to be free, quite the opposite. Tickets were oversold and the movie rights auctioned off. But the promoters were amateurs who skimped on security guards and fences, which were overrun by thousands of fans coming from New York and New Jersey at the height of summer. I had no desire to travel so far, but we had it covered around the clock out of our New York bureau. Then came the rain and the mud. It turned out to be a triumphant moment for rock and roll culture, and for young people more broadly. It was a moment when the stars and the heavens were aligned. But all the best-laid plans couldn't make it happen again.

The Dylan interview was the cover of our second-anniversary issue in November 1969. By then every issue was selling nearly 100,000 copies. We had hired a research firm to do a survey. The average *Rolling Stone* reader was twenty-two years old, and four out of five were between sixteen and twenty-five, roughly late high school through college and beyond. Ninety percent were men. The pass-along readership — the number of other people who read one reader's copy — meant that close to half a million people saw each issue.

I wrote a Letter from the Editor that was a report to our readers about what had happened during the past year. I concluded with these words: "Rock and roll is an idea with great power. In this last year, this energy has flashed with great power at Woodstock, but in so many other areas has diffused and scattered. *Rolling Stone* is wailing along at a nice little clip. This country is also wailing along at a nice little clip on the road to destruction. If there is any hope left, I think before the next two years are out, the culture we represent will make a serious effort at and succeed in taking for itself the political power it represents."

CHAPTER 14

ALTAMONT AND THE END OF THE INNOCENCE

THE ROLLING STONES were planning their first tour of the States since 1966 when I first saw them, twenty-four shows between November 7 and December 6, 1969. They had released *Beggars Banquet* and their audience was now wrapped up in the imagery and message of "Street Fighting Man" — "Everywhere I hear the sound of marching, charging feet, boy / 'Cause summer's here and the time is right for fighting in the street, boy." What could you interpret in that but insurrection, a challenge to authority more directly spoken than anything we had heard before in rock and roll.

The most potent song on the record was the masterpiece "Sympathy for the Devil." It was a historical essay on the power of Satan. I'm everywhere, but won't you guess my name? "I've been around a long, long year, stole many a man's soul and faith..." *Sgt. Pepper's* had caught the mood of 1967 and the Summer of Love but this was something else altogether, written for and about an America inflamed by riots, assassinations, and war. The Stones were also about to release *Let It Bleed*, with "Midnight Rambler" and "Gimme Shelter." I think by this point the magazine had anointed them "the world's greatest rock and roll band." They certainly were, and they unhesitatingly embraced our phrase. We planned start-to-finish coverage of the tour.

The Stones were based out of Los Angeles, a city on edge from the Tate-LaBianca murders. Their arrival was a welcome distraction from the unsolved crimes. Local radio and TV ran daily updates on the band's whereabouts and followed their nighttime club-hopping. KRLA, the local Top 40 station, was running a ticket contest, whipping up Stones mania the way they once had done for the Beatles. If you listened to AM radio while driving in your car, which everybody in Los Angeles did, you could easily think an invasion by the British was under way.

I watched them rehearse in the living room of a rented mansion jammed with microphones, cables, guitars, drums, and amplifiers. Mick never brought up anything about my pulling the plug on our partnership in British *Rolling Stone*. It was late at night and they were already set up and playing. Mick nodded and gave a little wave of his hand. I didn't know the rest of them. Mick Taylor was with them, and he played beautifully. I sat in a chair in a corner as they worked up old stuff, like "I'm Free" or "Carol," and new material, like "Midnight Rambler." It was loud, the way I liked it. After an hour or so I noticed Mick call over his road manager and say something in his ear. Two minutes later the road manager came over and said that in his opinion, it might be a good time for me to go. He never mentioned that it was Mick's call. This, I was to learn, was classic Mick. There were always someone else's fingerprints.

Crazy energy was swirling around the band. There was public protest over the price of tickets because they cost from $5.00 to $7.50, with those in the front section going for $12.50. The promoters blamed the Stones, and there was grumbling, led in part by Ralph Gleason in the pages of *Rolling Stone*. He asked if the Stones "really need all that money" and "Can't they share the loot?" Los Angeles was the first sellout— 36,000 tickets in eight hours.

I saw the show in Oakland. B. B. King and Ike and Tina Turner opened. Mick's outfit was a black shirt with an omega sign on it, a rhinestone-studded belt, tight black pants, an Uncle Sam hat, and a long, dangling red scarf. The whole thing—the look, the dancing, the music— was charged with sex and violence. Greil wrote a rave review of the concert; he had been transported by "this devastating band and their devouring leader." The show ended with "Street Fighting Man" at 3:30 a.m. It was the first of the modern rock tours, and one of the greatest of all time. I couldn't imagine what else you could want for your $7.50, or even your $12.50.

THE PRESSURE ON the Stones to do a free concert had been building since they announced their American tour. It was an idea in the air at the time, something our generation believed was the right thing; in fact, the Stones had done one in London that summer in Hyde Park, their memorial for Brian Jones. If they didn't do one in the States, they would look selfish, turning their backs on a so-called obligation to the community.

So, they announced their free concert would happen in San Francisco—not as originally hoped in Los Angeles—but not in Golden Gate Park. It would be at a location yet to be found, with less than one week to go. Their glorified road manager actually turned down one place, which had all the necessary infrastructure, because of "aesthetics." Mick called asking for ideas. I suggested he call the person who in the end found Altamont, fifty miles east of San Francisco. It was an auto racetrack with no facilities for big crowds, much less for a gigantic rock concert.

The day of the concert, December 6, I went to a waterfront pier to catch a helicopter ride with some of the Dead. I was having second thoughts. It was a gray, grim day—not great helicopter weather as far as I was concerned—and I had no ride back. I thought it over and went home. I had missed Woodstock and I would miss Altamont. The next day, the Sunday *Examiner* headlined page one "300,000 Say It with Music." The paper made Altamont seem like what they already had decided it would be: "Woodstock West." They mentioned a murder, but brushed it aside.

When I got to the office Monday morning, Greil was on the phone. He was grim. Something terrible had happened. Ralph called, leaving an urgent message. The Hell's Angels had murdered someone in front of the stage, a black kid, Meredith Hunter. Then John Burks, my managing editor, walked into my office. He laid out a plan for wall-to-wall coverage — our writers had been there, people were calling to help, photographers were already bringing in film. Altamont was in our backyard and was our story to do if ever there was one.

The problem was that this could lead to our placing the blame on the Rolling Stones, particularly Mick. The staff was keenly aware of my relationship with him. So how did I want to handle it? The pressure was not subtle. I had a choice, and I didn't have a choice. Mick meant a lot to me, the pleasure of his company, the bragging rights of knowing him. He would expect me to be protective. But perhaps, with time, it would be less painful, and he would understand what I had to do.

That was possibly the defining moment for *Rolling Stone*: Were we to aspire to the high standards and principles of honest journalism? Or something less, which I knew would be corrosive to our hearts and minds? I asked them to give me a few minutes. I sat alone in my office and stared at my picture of Daniel in the lion's den and at the banned *Beggars Banquet* cover on my wall. I didn't think what had happened was any more Mick's fault than that of others involved in the tour, but I got up, walked into the editorial department, and in a clear voice, that Greil remembers to this day, said, "We are going to cover this thing from top to bottom. And we are going to lay the blame. Let it bleed."

We reported, assigned, and rewrote from every angle: an eyewitness account of the murder, interviews with the musicians, some of the Stones, the promoters, Bill Graham, the Dead, the San Francisco hippie leaders, the Hell's Angels, everyone involved, including lots of concertgoers with their painful stories. We found the family of the eighteen-year-old kid who had been murdered by the Angels. The piece took up seventeen pages in the magazine, an astounding piece of reporting and reading. I was proud. We wrote responsibly and drew conclusions from the facts. But it was dark, dark, dark. I knew Mick wasn't going to like it.

No one was innocent in this one. The Rolling Stones had the ultimate say on everything, but failed to use their power methodically and with due diligence. Their tour manager had run the show; he was arrogant and an amateur, a fatal combination. He in turn relied on the advice of the local rock managers, especially the Grateful Dead's, who recommended hiring the Hell's Angels for $500 and free beer. There was the Haight-Ashbury hippie leadership poking into everything, as if they were trying to enforce kosher laws. Bill Graham was the only person who could have put Altamont on properly but refused because he once had a fistfight with the Stones' tour manager and a falling-out with Mick. Ralph Gleason, in *Rolling Stone* but especially in the *San Francisco Chronicle*, had been pushing a story line of the Stones as "greedy" versus the new paradigm of free for the people. The "community" was having its say and driving the anti-Stones narrative as much as anyone.

The Stones brought to any situation an energy which sent out whips of electricity that disturb the force fields of people and places. It was chaos and disaster. Whose fault? I think everyone was to blame; everyone behaved poorly, immaturely, and in haste. There was a collective guilt: Vietnam was coming home and violence was the new zeitgeist, and there was no getting out of its way. No one's karma was good enough to save that day.

A few weeks later we were doing a piece on the aftermath of Altamont and asked Mick for an interview. He sent me a telegram:

Dear Jann,

You want to ask me many questions about Altamont, which I would normally be only too pleased to answer and have indeed answered to many other people. However, unfortunately rightly or wrongly we no longer trust you to quote us fully or in context. I hope our friendship can flourish again one day.

M

THAT WAS OUR last issue of the sixties.

For the blue meanies, the antifun police, and the haters, Altamont marked the end of the sixties, which meant the end of youth rebellion and its challenge to social and political authority. But it wasn't. It wasn't the end of anything except the end of the innocence; it was a course correction, a warning to get real. So, we got real.

CHAPTER 15

HELTER SKELTER

"Jann is going to Los Angeles next week for a few days and frankly we are all looking forward to taking a breather."

— LETTER FROM JANE WENNER TO MY FATHER

THINGS WERE STARTING to get busy. I hardly had time to take drugs. Mostly. We crowded into the printer's loft, desks jammed together, shelves filled with stacks of back issues, a long wall of clipboards with manuscripts, schedules, ideas, printers' galleys, and page proofs. Three large bay windows looked out on Brannan Street, a back alley, an abattoir, and bail-bond offices. We lived with the fumes of molten lead and burning black ink.

To put the darkness of Altamont behind us and celebrate the new decade, we put John and Yoko holding a dove on the cover. The headline was "Man of the Year." He and Yoko had celebrated their marriage with a "bed-in" for peace, started a WAR IS OVER billboard campaign, and announced a peace festival for the New Year. It would be in Toronto, where they had been meeting with Prime Minister Pierre Trudeau. They would call me every week with their latest news, making us their paper of record. In February, we ran a terrific cover of Little Richard by Baron, with a series of photos inside showing him in performance, shirtless, sweating, but with immaculate makeup. In the interview, he talked about how he wrote "Tutti Frutti," "Long Tall Sally," and "Good Golly, Miss Molly" while washing dishes in the Macon, Georgia, bus station.

We were running well-reported music pieces, profiles, and interviews of new stars and old bluesmen, R&B hitmakers, and the occasional jazz artist. I wanted to push us in other directions as well, into cultural and social issues. I was working on the premise that fans of the music we covered shared a range of concerns, broadly related, that could be seen through the lens of that music.

Charles Manson, along with members of his family, had been indicted for the Tate-LaBianca murders. But was he an innocent, hippie victim of persecution by the fascist LAPD? That was a widely held view, and one that I wasn't certain of, either way. I thought *Rolling Stone* had an obligation and an opportunity to find out and to answer the question definitively. Jerry Hopkins had taken a leave of absence to write the first biography of Elvis, and the Los Angeles bureau chief position was open. I looked for someone to fill it who could also start a Manson investigation. I landed on a San Francisco State journalism graduate who was a prizewinning general assignment reporter for the *Los Angeles Times*, David Felton. I interviewed him at my father's house in Los Angeles and after an hour agreed to match his annual $15,000 salary. A few months after he started I learned why his nickname at the *Times* had been The Stonecutter.

By MARCH 1970 we had forty-seven people on the masthead. We crossed the Rubicon and moved out of the printer's loft, which we had physically outgrown. We had emotionally outgrown it as well. The second floor of that two-story pink building contained the spirit and youthful energy I had put into creating *Rolling Stone*. It was a nurturing place to be, away from the crosscurrents of the music business, Haight-Ashbury, the revolution, and other wolves at the door — including rent-collecting landlords.

But it also stood for — and made me and our staff internalize — what we had to leave behind: volunteerism and amateurism, the hippie-dope laissez-faire, and a seat-of-the-pants fragility. I didn't see that at the time. I was just barreling ahead with my eyes wide and eager to see the world.

The new offices were on the top floor of a renovated redbrick warehouse in the South of Market district, a mix of old residences and apartments, grocery stores, bars, and light industry. Our building, 625 Third Street, was situated between a branch of Wells Fargo Bank and the MJB Coffee Company. When you move to new offices, you start spending money. Everyone needs a new assistant, typewriter, or overseas phone privileges. There were bills for all that Xeroxing and office supplies, electricity, water, watercoolers, and, of course, rent. I was oblivious to all that; I was the worst offender. I convinced a totally straight adult, Dan Parker, who worked at Garrett Press, to come with us. He handled the printers, production, shipping, and all sorts of logistics. He was the in-house grown-up.

Jane and I moved, too, into a sweet little house with a large backyard and garden with a goldfish pond on a cul-de-sac off upper Market Street. That house was the first one that Jane fully decorated. She got a high-backed couch that she covered in pillow ticking and a French country dining table. Our hi-fi system was a KLH portable record player that packed up like a suitcase. Boz always thought it shameful that I had such a cheap system, given my job. I also had a 1956 Fender Esquire, which Jane and Boz had given to me for my birthday. We bought a Rover, the poor man's Jaguar. It came with an eight-track. I would throw in the new Traffic album or *Got Live If You Want It!*, fire up a joint, and arrive at the office with bloodshot eyes and in a good mood.

When we moved to our new offices, I decided to start a new magazine, *Earth Times*. There was no general alarm sounding about a climate crisis in those days, but the message of the first Earth Day in 1970 got us thinking very seriously about the environment. It was the same newsprint, quarter-fold format as *Rolling Stone*. By the third issue, we were attacking big oil (Standard Oil, later a part of Exxon). It was solid work and, had it been sustainable, might have become a meaningful player in the battle. But I didn't have the publishing smarts or the money for it, and we shut it down. I had a feeling, though, that I would bring it back another day.

RICHARD NIXON SENT U.S. troops into Cambodia. Ralph wrote in his column, "There is no effective way to react logically to the presidential horror show of Cambodia. The logical steps are useless, and we know it...Goebbels' Big Lie Caper is as cool as a freight train and as subtle as a crutch compared to 'We are not in Cambodia.'" National Guard troops killed four students on the campus of Kent State University in Ohio. This was a national emergency. Neil Young wrote, "Tin soldiers, and Nixon coming. We're finally on our own. This summer I hear the drumming. Four dead in Ohio."

We were another wartime generation, a country that watched live television imagery that became numbing — blowing up, gunning down, napalm burning Vietnamese peasants; the truncheons and the gas swirling up around city streets filled by black people marching for their freedom or rioting against hopelessness. Paratroopers were being sent to our cities to support police and the National Guard came into our schools. These were our fathers and our brothers in government uniforms beating and killing blameless people.

I came of age with my country in flames, at home and abroad. Nixon came along and mobilized fear and hate into a national political movement. He started the War on Drugs. Every last bit of it was racist. The men I believed in were assassinated, shot down like dogs. This was not what we'd been promised. This was not the American Dream.

WE DECIDED TO crash a special issue titled "A Pitiful, Helpless Giant," from the phrase that Nixon used to warn America about what lay ahead if Americans continued to challenge institutional authority. The cover showed a student atop a car waving an American flag at a San Francisco demonstration. It was a photo from a portfolio left with Bob Kingsbury by a student from the San Francisco Art Institute who was looking for freelance work, Annie Leibovitz. She was twenty years old.

Allen Ginsberg sent me a long poem, "Friday the Thirteenth." It was his State of America, a corrosive mini-epic. That issue was the perfect place for it: "Growth rate trippers, Hallucinating everglade real estate developers. Steak Swallowers zonked on Television, Twenty-billion-dollar advertising dealers. Lipstick skin poppers. Syndicate garbage telex heads."

During the demonstrations at the Capitol, Nixon left the White House around 4:30 a.m. with his valet and a few Secret Service men and went to the Washington Monument. He talked for an hour with students who were spending the night there in sleeping bags. I had our reporters track those students down and put together a vignette of Nixon, rambling and repeating himself, trying to defend himself to a blind world. Apparently, he was drunk.

I was in New York when my mild-mannered assistant and office den mother, Gretchen Horton, suggested I get back to the office because there was discontent brewing, at the center of which was the managing editor. I flew back to find him circulating a petition demanding that I cede editorial control of *Rolling Stone*. We had a photo of Bob Dylan, without cap but in gown, receiving an honorary doctorate from Princeton. I wanted to publish the picture; I thought that kind of establishment recognition of Bob was an important indicator of how youth culture was changing American society and how the establishment was beginning to acknowledge Bob as a great American poet. The managing editor thought it was trivial, so I told him it was time for him to hit the road. Which he did. I got rid of his loyalists, kept Ben Fong-Torres and Charlie Perry, and started putting together a new staff.

I decided I would be the new editor.

DAVID DALTON, ONE of our early writers, was fully into the hippie ethos, well versed in all matters cosmic. He had a connection to Charlie Manson through Dennis Wilson, the handsome, troubled Beach Boys drummer. David and his wife were living with Dennis, who had gotten to know Manson through some of his girls, whom Dennis had picked up hitchhiking. He told David, "Charlie's cosmic, man. He listens to Beatles records and gets messages through them." Dennis mentioned "Piggies," "Rocky Raccoon," and "Helter Skelter." Dalton's cousin was Sharon Tate's best friend and was convinced that the Manson family were a bunch of falsely accused hippies. The mood in Los Angeles was paranoid, because every house in the hills was a potential target for knife-wielding, drug-inflamed hippies. Dalton thought Manson was innocent. I put him on the story with David Felton, who had already started our Manson reporting. Felton had the skepticism and the factual standards of a newspaperman. This *Rolling Stone* duo was an award-winning journalist teamed with a dyed-in-the-wool hippie, and together they began to investigate the twisted saga.

Through Manson's music manager, who wanted to hustle his record, Dalton and Felton arranged a meeting with Manson in the Los Angeles County jail. In the interview room, Charlie, dressed in blue prison denims, was on his feet, animated like a dancing wizard, laughing, sobbing, and grabbing his crotch. Felton remembered the sound of his half-inch fingernails clicking across the table. Manson spoke about "Helter Skelter." The *Rolling Stone* duo spent two hours with crazy Charlie. When they left the jail, they had a fight. Dalton was certain of his innocence. Felton thought he was a con man, full of self-serving bullshit.

The next day they had an appointment at the district attorney's office with one of the prosecutors on the case. Felton had arranged it through his old colleagues at the *L.A. Times*. The D.A. showed them the evidence the police investigators had dug up, including the coroner's photographs of the crime scenes and the bloody bodies. It was sickening. In one photo the words "Helter Skelter" were scrawled in blood on a door. Felton felt a cold hand on his back. He now knew for sure that Manson was guilty. Dalton needed no further convincing.

Dalton was terrified. He had come in for the meeting from the Spahn Ranch, where he and his wife were staying at the invitation of the Manson family for some friendly reporting. His wife was still there. In his panicked imagination the oddballs, runaways, and petty criminals at the ranch turned into menacing homicidal maniacs. He was sure the family had a finely tuned "psychic hive vibe" and would soon be onto him. He hitchhiked there, staged a screaming fight with his wife, and chased her to the main road. They flagged down a Mexican kid driving a truck full of cantaloupes who took them to the nearest town.

The two Davids had one more fight: Who would write the opening? Dalton had written one with a cosmic overview, tap-dancing about the inevitable conclusion: Manson's guilt. Felton had rewritten it, and they had come to an impasse. I brought them up to San Francisco. We sat at the round table, passed around a joint, and were able to resolve it. I made Felton the principal writer.

The problem was that Felton was painstaking. I now knew why they called him The Stonecutter at the *Times*. I made him stay in the San Francisco office so I could supervise him, pulling the story out of him at the rate of five triple-spaced typewritten pages a day. I refused to pay him or allow him to leave the office, except for the occasional shower, until it was done. The story ran twenty-two pages in the magazine. We had waltzed into a divisive story in the white-hot national spotlight. It was deceptively sophisticated journalism. The news-breaking interviews with the district attorney and Manson were done as short stage plays. We had never done something with that level of craft. I was the editor on the piece, but my input was largely limited to hounding Felton to write. We tried to nominate ourselves for the Pulitzer Prize and were told we were ineligible because we came out every other week, not weekly. But we had set the template for what *Rolling Stone* would become.

WE WERE RUNNING out of money. The costs of the move and the increase in daily operational spending were budget busters. We had spent a tiny fortune buying full-page ads selling *Rolling Stone* subscriptions in a half-dozen big-city newspapers. Postal workers went on strike the day before the ads appeared, so no one thought about mailing anything, let alone subscription coupons, with money. We had been living on large up-front payments from our new national distributor, which had doubled our print run and printing bills. They were sending us advance money as if we were selling at least half of what we were printing. We were growing, but not that fast. Suddenly the checks stopped and we were in big debt.

Cutting back on pencils, pads, and postage — and renegotiating our lease and sitting on big bills — was not going to be enough. I called the three people in the record business with whom I was closest and asked them to advance money against future advertising. Gil Friesen, of A&M, with whom I was forming a strong friendship, Clive Davis, and Jac Holzman all came through within days. We were no sure thing. It was a sign of faith that came when I needed it.

We skipped an issue for the only time in our history. I scheduled a staff meeting about cost cutting and David Felton gave me a memo with his suggestions. "Tell them the usual brief shit, bad times in the early days. Role of Ralph Gleason (make it clear this time). Vision of rock culture. Solution to Generation Gap. Growing number of enemies shows we're doing good. Try to paint a murky picture of a threatening world. Suggestions for further savings: Calls home should be limited, collect if possible. Whereas each man now calls his wife, one wife could be called and she could call the others. Persons working here for six months or less should use third class or bulk rate. Stamps on return envelopes can be steamed off." I realized I was headed nowhere on this one.

Looking for a big investor, I met Arthur Rock, the man who coined the term "venture capital." He later became one of Steve Jobs' earliest backers. Arthur, a severe-looking man seemingly without emotion, wasn't interested, but he had a friend who might be. The name Max Palevsky didn't mean anything to me, but Arthur had backed a company Max had started, Scientific Data Systems, which designed advanced computer systems for NASA and the Defense Department. In 1968, Max and Arthur had sold SDS to Xerox for close to a billion dollars, at that time the largest acquisition in the history of American business.

Max lived in a Spanish-style mansion dominated by modern art in the wooded hills of Bel Air, not far from Elizabeth Taylor. He looked young, with a full head of hair (not his). He spoke loudly, laughed loudly, and was loudly opinionated. I liked him. Max was a difficult guy — he was on his way to his third marriage when we met — and he didn't have that many friends. Jane and I were quickly taken into his small circle and spent weekends at his futuristic compound in Palm Springs, stayed at his apartment at the Sherry-Netherland in New York, and sailed with him in the Mediterranean.

On my twenty-fifth birthday I got a check for $200,000 from Max, valuing our company at between one and two million dollars, for his share in Rolling Stone, depending on how much we earned over the next two years. We were out of the woods by then and not only didn't need his money, but never spent it. Max's business advice turned out to be more destructive than helpful. He insisted that we hire someone to run the business instead of me, which I was fine with, but it resulted in two short-lived and expensive hires, including a very pleasant young exec from Walt Disney who was a hopeless fit at Rolling Stone. At the same time, I had just begun the first serious expansion of the company, a small book publishing division, Straight Arrow Books.*

Alan Rinzler, hired to run the book division, was a godsend. He arrived from New York with his wife, two kids, and a big brown poodle, settled them in the Berkeley hills, and set up shop at Rolling Stone just as money got tight. Our plan was to start an independent book company built on Rolling Stone stories and writers. Alan was a brash New Yorker, all hustle, intelligence, and good intentions. He became a confidant and helped me figure out how to run a business. His first memorandum to me was titled "Progress Report and Cosmic Memo #1." It was a relief to have someone I could rely on. We were doubling in size each year. It was a lot of change to handle and hold on to, and I needed help.

---

* Straight Arrow Books was in business until 1975, with its own payroll and offices, and published nearly a hundred titles, including Rolling Stone writers, major biographies of James Dean and Jack Kerouac, a scholarly history of the Israeli Army, The Art of Sensual Massage, and The Connoisseur's Handbook of Marijuana. The last two were our biggest sellers.

CHAPTER 16

JOHN LENNON AND HUNTER THOMPSON DROP BY

HI, HI. SO, the thing is, you see, that we, John and Yoko, too, are in San Francisco, and we're coming to see you." It was Yoko on the phone, speaking in her staccato whisper. It was late spring 1970. Twenty minutes later, John Lennon was striding down the hall in a green military shirt. I was nervous, trying to be in the moment. Something about him seemed without guile. Suddenly, he was standing next to me. Everyone was up from their desks, dead silent, at a standstill. I showed John and Yoko around and introduced them to the staff one at a time. Meet John Lennon. The real living, breathing John Lennon.

John had brought me *The Primal Scream*, a book by Dr. Arthur Janov, a psychotherapist who treated patients in group therapy by trying to regress them to infancy and scream the pain out. John had inscribed it:

Dear Jann,

After many years of searching — tobacco-pot-acid-meditation-brown rice-you name it — I am finally on the road to freedom and being REAL + STRAIGHT. I hope this book helps you as much as it did for Yoko + me. I'll tell you the "true story" when we're finished.

Love, John + Yoko

We had lunch at Enrico's, a sidewalk bistro in North Beach where I was a regular. John was a constant talker. Yoko would punctuate his sentences with a "Yes, yes" or some little bit of emphasis. I was uncomfortable with the harsh way that John refused an autograph seeker: "Can't you fucking see that I'm eating?"

John had never seen *Let It Be*. Jane and I took them to an afternoon showing in a nearly empty theater, sitting together in silence. The movie so obviously forecast the Beatles' impending breakup — you could see them coming apart right in front of your eyes. John said nothing. When we walked out, the four of us stood on the sidewalk, arms around each other in a huddle. John cried, and then all of us joined in.

We had a great dinner at my favorite Italian restaurant, Adolph's, just two couples out on a Saturday night. Yoko had spent some childhood years in San Francisco, so we drove around and did a lot of sightseeing. The next weekend we visited with them at their rented mansion in Beverly Hills. They lived in one room hung with weavings, incense burning and candles lit. John agreed to give me the interview I had been asking for when "primal" was over. He was ready to tell his story of the Beatles.

The ads from record companies kept rolling in. More ad pages meant more editorial to produce, more interviews, more reviews, more photos of undressed people rolling in mud or sitting in front of shacks in the woods. In July, twelve Canadian National Railway coaches, the Festival Express, left Toronto for Calgary on a weeklong trip carrying the Grateful Dead, Janis Joplin, the New Riders of the Purple Sage, and Delaney & Bonnie — 140 musicians to play festivals and gigs along the way. We sent Jonathan Cott and David Dalton as our lucky editorial team. "Janis," they wrote, "was the presiding spirit of this journey, the bacchanalian Little Red Riding Hood with her bag full of tequila and lemons, lurching from car to car, like some tropical bird with streaming feathers, defying the sun to interrupt our revels for another day." It was a bacchanal on steel wheels, a rock and roll fantasy that was about to run off the rails. Janis and Pigpen would soon be dead.

IN ADDITION TO chronicling the musicians and artists in the Bay Area, we felt a responsibility to report on the counterculture. They were not the laid-back artists but more like the angry neighbors next door. There were battles on many fronts: civil rights, sexual freedom, Vietnam, drugs. Even clothes, hair, and music were under attack by the Establishment. Unbelievable when you think about it — fucking haircuts.

I was looking for a proper response, one that would be both moral and effective. I thought "Off the pigs" and "Amerika" were nonsense. What could you achieve by killing an innocent bystander with a home-made bomb? No amount of violence could be mustered that could bring down anything other than those who were themselves the agents of violence. I believed in a revolution of culture and consciousness.

Ralph Gleason was my ally. To me, he was the conscience of *Rolling Stone*. "Violence is still bullshit," Ralph wrote in one of his best columns. "I do not believe in it when the police do it, nor do I believe in it when the so-called revolutionaries do it, whether they know or not which way the wind blows. Trashing some little old lady's ribbon shop is no revolutionary act. Positive action is better than negative action. Winning the grape strike by positive action was better than blowing up the homes or warehouses of the growers.

"I have heard some of my longhaired friends say they are 'the new niggers.' Long hair is being discriminated against viciously and heavily, therefore they know what it means to be black in a white society. This is bullshit too, and worse, it is pretentious. It serves you ill, oh my brothers, to say it. Frustration runs rampant, paranoia strikes deep. We are all victims of it. We are wasting our strength and precious time."

• • •

Jann Wenner
Rolling Stone

Your Altamont coverage comes close to being the best journalism I can remember reading, by anybody. When I cited it to a friend who teaches at UCLA's journalism school he said he'd never heard of *Rolling Stone* ... and that sort of says it all I think, except maybe to speculate that the trouble really isn't with print, but with the people who control print. And that's an old bitch, too, so fuck it. Anyway, *Rolling Stone* makes McLuhan suck wind. It's a hell of a good medium by any standard, from Hemmingway to the Airplane. People like Kunkin [*L.A. Free Press*] and Krassner [*Berkeley Barb*] never came close to what you are doing ... don't fuck it up with pompous bullshit; the demise of *Rolling Stone* would leave a nasty hole.

Sincerely,
Hunter S. Thompson
Woody Creek, Colorado

That letter showed up out of the blue. I was, like all of us, a huge fan of his book about the Hell's Angels. He had balls and could write like a bastard. I wrote back and asked if he would write about Terry the Tramp, who wanted to quit the motorcycle gang and had committed suicide. Hunter considered Terry to be his only friend during the year he had spent with the Angels. He replied, "I could write a decent thing about him as a freak-symbol of an era he never quite understood. What do you have room for? A short obit or a long, rambling truth nut? Let me know quick — if you need it quick — and also say what you'll pay. I'll write the fucker anyway, if there's room, but I tend to bear down a little harder when I smell money." After a few more thoughts about money, he continued, "Shit ... I sound like a pawnbroker here (or a speed dealer) but there is no point my zapping off a huge chunk of esoteric madness that nobody can use. I've done that all too often, and it gets old…Ok for now…and in any case, keep *Rolling Stone* on its rails. We are heading into a shitstorm on all fronts."

The letter and the language made me wonder. What do I have here? Hunter said he was currently running for sheriff of Pitkin County, Colorado, where he lived, just outside of Aspen. In a long, long letter back, he explained that he was serious about the election. He and his posse had a proposition on the ballot that would officially rename Aspen "Fat City." I asked him to write about running for sheriff: "Your story in *Rolling Stone* should be part of the larger effort to get everyone to register in 1972."

"The dropout, head mentality," he wrote back, "is a maddening thing to work with; they don't know Kent State from Kent cigarettes, and frankly they don't give a fuck. But I'll get a decent piece out of this scene — for good or ill."

Hunter came to San Francisco to see me for our first meeting in the summer of 1970. I had expected him to be at the office around two o'clock, just after breakfast, he said. He showed up at four, making what I later realized was his typical, carefully put together entrance. He was a big solid guy, a few inches over six feet. He wore Converse white sneakers, Bermuda shorts, and a rayon shirt patterned in interlocking red circles. Most notably, he had a head full of silver hair in curls, cut in a fashionable lady's bubble style.

He mumbled something to the effect that his name was Hunter. I got up, shook his hand, and sat down while he swung a leather satchel onto my desk and began unpacking it with a clumsy deliberateness, punctuated with grunts and the occasional "Aha!" He wanted me to notice every item he deemed necessary to have on hand. He had two six-packs of Budweiser, a bowie knife in a leather case, a hammer, a bottle of Jack Daniel's, a pipe, and an air horn screwed to an aerosol can, along with other daily needs such as a carton of Dunhill Red cigarettes, a Zippo lighter, a plastic case of Tar Gard filters for his cigarette holder, magazines, and notebooks. Also, a black, heavy-duty police flashlight that doubled as a billy club. And emergency road flares.

Hunter was sorting through what he would need for our meeting and what to put back when he hit the button on the air horn, which shrieked for about three seconds and scared the piss out of me, and then suddenly stood up and yelled "Ye gods!" He settled down and pulled off the wig he was wearing. He was shaved totally bald.

We talked for two hours. He spoke rapidly, in a low mumble. You had to listen carefully and closely, like trying to understand a foreign language. Hunter had no particular place to go that afternoon; I was exhausted. We agreed on a deadline of the end of September for his Aspen sheriff story.

I had no idea what was coming down the tracks.

I LOVED JANE but didn't have the time to be in love. *Rolling Stone* came first. We both knew that. I also struggled now and then with a sharp emptiness if I met a beautiful young man. It was a powerful and unmistakable desire that I didn't have, nor could I summon, for Jane. She must have known this ever since I had met Robin that summer on the Russian River. Both of us knew the elemental power of sexuality. We had agreed, with little explicit discussion, to stay together. When she learned that I had seen Robin again, there was sadness and sorrow. There was regret. But there was no explaining it away. I promised, and meant it, that it was over. Something had been altered in a way we didn't discuss.

Then along came our new friend, Sandy Bull, a guitarist who played Middle Eastern instruments. I'd been a fan of his back in Berkeley. He had a folkie cult following until he became a junkie. I met him after his release from Mendocino State Hospital. We did a story on him, became friendly, and Jane took him under her wing. She seemed to gravitate to people who needed help. I thought nothing of it. I liked Sandy. He was quiet, boyishly shy.

Jane and I were heading for England to attend the wedding of *Rolling Stone*'s London bureau chief, at the country home of his bride's family. Jane asked if Sandy could come with us, and a bit reluctantly, I agreed.

He would keep Jane company while I was busy. From there, we were on our way to Ibiza, off the coast of Spain. I flew down from London; Jane and Sandy took the train across France and through Spain. I had no patience for the extra days of travel but knew it was a mistake. Although it was in the back of my mind as a possibility, I naively didn't think they were sleeping together.

Ibiza was a major hippie stopover, with drugs and full-moon parties on the beaches of the nearby island of Formentera. A friend had a finca, a white stucco house, down a red dirt road among fields of cactus. There were no toilets. You found a spot in the cacti during the day. The setting was memorialized by Joni Mitchell in her song "California": "I caught a plane to Spain, went to a party down a red dirt road. There were lots of pretty people there, reading *Rolling Stone*, reading *Vogue*."

I read on the internet that "the party was at a house Jann Wenner had rented. Joni played dulcimer and sang. It was a blissful afternoon," but I have no memory of it. The song was so singularly evocative of that time and place, plus her affectionate mention of *Rolling Stone*, that I have forever kept it in my heart. Joni goes on to sing, "They said 'How long can you hang around?' I said a week maybe two, just until my skin turns brown, then I'm going home to California."

I would, too. How long can you sit under the blazing sun and smoke pot? It was my first vacation since starting *Rolling Stone* and I needed the break. I only made one call when I found a phone in town, having just heard of Jimi Hendrix's death, to make sure we were doing a cover. It was time to go home. Jane wanted to stay on. She and Sandy would take a cruise ship to Turkey before returning. I was in no position to throw down with suspicion or accusation. And off we went, apart but together.

HUNTER'S FIRST PIECE was "Freak Power in the Rockies: The Battle of Aspen." The silver-mining town in Colorado that had become a resort for skiers was now also home to urban dropouts, well-heeled hippies, and drug dealers. Hunter was one of those "dropouts," raised in

Louisville, Kentucky, who had arrived in the late sixties after writing gigs in Puerto Rico, Brazil, Big Sur, and San Francisco. The year before, the Aspen newcomers had nearly elected their own candidate for mayor, with Hunter as campaign manager.

Hunter's platform, which he laid out in his *Rolling Stone* piece, was "1) Sod all the streets at once...rip them up and use the asphalt to build a giant parking lot on the outskirts of town; 2) Change the name of Aspen to 'Fat City' to make it painful for land developers to sell, because you couldn't easily sell Fat City Highlands like you could sell Aspen Highlands; 3) Control drug sales and erect stocks in the center of town to punish dishonest drug dealers; 4) Forbid hunting and fishing to non-residents; 5) The Sheriff and his deputies would never be armed in public; and 6) The Sheriff's office would savagely harass all those engaged in any form of land rape."

Once we published the article, the idea that "the hippies" were trying to take over a wealthy ski town became catnip to the national press. Soon the newspapers and networks — even the BBC — were covering it. The flames were fanned; both sides went right to the wire. The images of Hunter, shaved bald, cigarette holder in hand, and with the American flag wrapped around his shoulders, were powerful and spoke to powerful ideas. In the end, he lost by thirty-one votes. Aspen didn't get a new sheriff, but I realized that, in Hunter, I had a fellow traveler.

HENDRIX WAS THE first star of the new rock era to die from drugs, at twenty-seven years old. Janis Joplin, also twenty-seven, died two weeks after Jimi. Brian Jones had mysteriously drowned in his swimming pool outside London a year earlier. He too was twenty-seven. Soon enough Jim Morrison would also flame out at twenty-seven. Ron "Pigpen" Mc-Kiernan, the blues voice of the Grateful Dead, would shortly die at twenty-seven. Robert Johnson himself died at twenty-seven. Maybe it had to do with the deal with the devil when they were at the crossroads.

Janis was recording in Hollywood when she was found in her hotel room with fresh needle marks in her arm. With Janis, there was a lot of hurt. I first saw her in a hole-in-the-wall club near Berkeley. Her voice had blown me into the back wall. Through the backstage social life at the Avalon Ballroom and the Fillmore, Janis found out who I was and usually would start yelling at me about something — a bad review or an item in "Random Notes." Most of the time she was drunk. We had some ups, but mainly downs. She was profoundly vulnerable. When she died it wasn't a surprise, but it was sad.

We printed the famous Jim Marshall photo of her in her dressing room, eyes focused in the distance, a sad expression on her face, holding her bottle of Southern Comfort. The cover was also a Marshall photograph, Janis with a twinkle in her eye, a fur hat tilted back, her hair flowing. She was smiling.

Jerry Garcia told Charlie Perry, in a piece in that issue, "Janis was a real person. She went through all the changes we did, on all the same trips. She was like the rest of us — fucked up, strung out, in weird places. Back in the old days, the pre-success days, she went out after it hard, harder than most people do, or ever conceive of doing. She was on a real hard path. She did what she had to do and closed her books."

ANNIE LEIBOVITZ'S FIRST cover shoot was Grace Slick. The inside portrait of Grace and Paul Kantner in bed, playing with their new baby, China, foreshadowed Annie's trademark reportorial style: finding a casual, personal moment that had the power of unexpected intimacy. Annie would barrel into the office, six feet tall, wild hair, with the energy and enthusiasm to do anything we asked. She had been a painting major and bought her first camera two years earlier. Annie was a military brat, her father a career Air Force officer, her mom a dance instructor. She was the third of six children. No one could have imagined the light within.

Jon Landau took over the record review section with his typical gravitas. His opening move was a 5,000-word manifesto, "The State of

Rock," followed by his first lead review, a look at new records by the Temptations, Sly Stone, and Ike and Tina Turner. Jon was an R&B fanatic. We understood that we had a special relationship and responsibility to what was still thought of as "colored" music. Even more than sports, music was going to be an equalizer, a driver of integration. Rock and roll was black popular music, and we were its acolytes and advocates. Ralph demanded that we be nothing less. He had told me something Louis Armstrong had said: "There are only two types of music, good music and bad music."

Charlie Perry, on top of the dope beat, crafted one of my favorite sections, Letters to the Editor. I titled it "Correspondence, Love Letters, and Advice" because I wanted our readers to interact with the magazine, not just comment on individual stories. They got it, and Charlie curated it. It was witty, silly, and affectionate.

Ben Fong-Torres recommended we hire Paul Scanlon, who had been a classmate of his at San Francisco State. Paul had gone from sports editor of the school's *Daily Gater* to the *Wall Street Journal* local bureau, then via the draft to Fort Ord, where he edited the *Fort Ord Panorama*. Paul edited our staff writers and recruited new ones. I had found someone with the same sensibilities and standards I had, with a greater knowledge of reporting and writing, great taste, and, as far as I could tell, someone who wasn't particularly bothered by my ego. A year later I named him managing editor. Paul became my right-hand man through the next five years, what came to be called "The Golden Age of *Rolling Stone*."

CHAPTER 17

LENNON REMEMBERS

WHEN JOHN AND Yoko got back to London, soon after their visit to me, they recorded his first solo album, *John Lennon/Plastic Ono Band*, through the rest of '69. I got letters from him, addressed to me in "San Franciscow, Californiar," with the *W* of my last name illustrated as butt cheeks. Inside one was a postcard of a dominatrix spanking somebody with a horse crop, wishing us all Merry Christmas. Another letter read, "From a man wot once met Elvis." That one had a page torn from a porn paperback on which he had written, "This is John and Yoko's Christmas Message." He would be in New York in early December for the release of the album, and ready for our interview.

There was so much in the Beatles' history that we knew, but in fact, we knew very little. They had lived in a well-guarded world, and now a clumsy and awkward breakup was under way, with no explanation other than who might have had the idea or said it first. I made a list of songs that I was curious about how and why they were written. "A Day in the Life" — who wrote what parts? What does this image refer to? How did the McCartney and Lennon partnership work? I made handwritten notes for questions on a yellow legal pad, a habit I picked up from my dad.

Annie, who had little experience with something so important, offered to travel on a youth fare and stay with friends. She begged for the chance and agreed that I would own the negatives. Deal! When I met her at the San Francisco airport, she was carrying nearly a hundred pounds of equipment. She turned down my offer to help with it. Yoko told her that she and John were so impressed that I had let someone like her — she was still in school — shoot them, when they were used to the most famous photographers in the world. They didn't treat her like a kid. Right away, John put her at ease, just as he did me at our first meeting.

John and Yoko referred to themselves in the third person as Liz and Dick — Elizabeth Taylor and Richard Burton — whenever I went out with them. One day they were in a loft with a small camera crew making *Up Your Legs Forever*, a Yoko project in which they filmed more than three hundred people's naked backsides from the waist down. I was having lunch with Tom Wolfe, and brought him to the studio, dressed to his toe tips as usual. Annie was there, shooting. Tom declined to strip; I would only do it with my underpants on. I'm the one in the navy-blue jockey shorts.

Our interview took place in the paneled boardroom of Allen Klein, who now managed Apple Records in addition to Phil Spector. "Oh, you've got notes and all that. Well we have to get right to it, don't we? Give me the paper to doodle on. Where to start? Don't be shy."

John took charge. It was to be more about what he wanted to say than what I wanted to ask. I didn't expect the intensity of his responses, his anger and bitterness about so many things, from childhood and the teachers who didn't recognize his talent and potential genius to the rejection that had been laid on Yoko by his fellow Beatles, the fans, and the popular press. John spoke in argumentative, sometimes harsh tones. I think it came from his Liverpool upbringing. He could veer quickly into anger. He needed to fight back, to be paid attention to. He also had an unerring sense of humor, the sharpness of it overwhelming any need to be polite or kind.

John talked about his early days in London when the Beatles and the Stones ruled the nightlife; his ongoing friendship with Mick; meeting Bob Dylan; his LSD trips; songwriting with Paul; his favorite songs; vacationing with Brian Epstein, their gay manager; his love for the poet Chuck Berry. There was also a lot of myth shattering. "The Beatles tours were like Fellini's *Satyricon*. We had that image, but the tours were something else, whores, junk, orgies." But what got the most attention was what he said about Paul. They were in a battle for control of the Beatles business, with Allen Klein facing off with McCartney's in-laws, the Eastman family, father and son, both tough entertainment lawyers. John was respectful of Paul's talents and the partnership they had shared. But it was a public divorce, and he had some pretty nasty stuff to say.

John was putting out his first solo album, an extraordinary revelation about himself. No one at the time made an album that intimate. Certainly no one so famous would dare to. It was painful in many parts, chilling and disturbing. To best understand the interview, you should listen closely to that album…and vice versa. The album was stunning. One of his greatest works. He was on a mission to tell the truth. Throughout his life, John had a desperate need to be a truth teller. He never had been allowed to say what he felt when he was a Beatle, and having kept so much of it hidden, had had enough. He was ready to explode, unleashed through therapy and his new album. He explained in the interview that he had stopped writing about outside situations and stories, and now wrote about himself. He was in search of his truest self, and in search of peace and love. The interview, along with the album, was an epitaph for the Beatles and their special world, one that we had all wanted to live in:

> The dream is over
> Yesterday
> What can I say?
> I was the dream weaver
> But now I'm reborn
> I was the Walrus
> But now I'm John
> And so dear friends
> You just have to carry on
> The dream is over

In the interview, he said to me, "I'm not just talking about the Beatles, I'm talking about the generation thing. It's over, and we gotta—I have to personally—get down to so-called reality." What a dream it had been. But if it was a dream, why has it never been forgotten? How many end-of-the-sixties moments were there going to be? The last question I asked was "Do you have a picture of 'When I'm Sixty-Four'?" He replied, "I hope we are a nice couple living off the coast of Ireland, looking at our scrapbook of madness."

Annie had a wonderful session with them. John wore bib overalls with a small American flag sewn on the front. He looked like a working-man, especially with the round wire-frame glasses, the kind that were issued by the British National Health Service. When we got back to San Francisco I looked at Annie's contact sheets. She had many good photos, but nothing stopped me until I got to a sheet of head shots. It was just one frame—I saw it immediately. He is thinking. It's very private. There is no mask. It's a mystery. She had been using one of her cameras to take a light-meter reading; he gave her a quick look and, in that moment, she snapped the shutter for the aperture test. It was an accident, a simple twist of fate.

I called the interview "Lennon Remembers," after the memoir that had just been published, *Khrushchev Remembers*. I liked the direct echo with Lenin and couldn't think of anything better. Because of his anger at the time, he focuses on the dark side. He is describing the inside of a never-seen, sealed-off world. Imperfect and incomplete as the interview was, it stands as Lennon's memoir of the Beatles. The piece hit front pages. The End of the Beatles! *Satyricon*, Lennon Claims! I Don't Believe in Beatles Says Lennon; I Broke Up, Not Paul—banner headlines for days in England, splashed on every newsstand, and throughout the world.

Paul was hurt the most. In a later *Rolling Stone* interview he said, "I sat down and pored over every little paragraph, every sentence. And at the time I thought it's me…That's just what I'm like. He's captured me so well. I'm a turd." I had an awkward relationship with Paul for years because I was the handmaiden to this "last testament" of John's, where he defined what he thought should be Paul's legacy. I'm sure John would have liked to take back some of what he said. He started calling the interview "Lennon Regrets." But it was all truth, his truth, and to read it is to know that and to know John Lennon.

Rolling Stone was more visible than ever, once again because of John and Yoko. We published the interviews as a book the following fall, against John's wishes. I had the clear right to do so. I suspect John had not expected the blowback from the interview. He had hurt and disparaged people he knew and who had helped him. Later he said, "It's just me shooting my mouth off. I'll say anything. I can't even remember it."

To refuse the wishes of someone who had conferred an unquantifiable recognition on us, through the status of his own legitimacy, tore me apart. We had been given a sanctified role in a sacred ritual called the Beatles. It made me sick to feel as if I was "betraying" John. He accepted it but wouldn't talk to me. His relationship with *Rolling Stone* remained, which was a comfort. He signed off his later letters to me with "Lennon remembers!" It was playful and I took it as a sign of reconciliation.

Although John had been angry, we remained allies, stayed in touch, and worked together till the end. He sent me a letter thanking me for the magazine's later support in his immigration battles.

Dear Jann,

Got yer note. Re/read it on the 7th! Am leaving for the snow on the 8th. You're reading this on the ... 10th/11th? (in S.F.)?

...A simple twist of f.f.f.faith!

we're pretty much lost in Babyland...

thanx for the immigration,

lennon remembers!

love y dove

hi to jane

happy new now!

John

We had done the interview in New York City, December 8, 1970. Ten years later, to the day, John was dead.

CHAPTER 18

PUTTING TOGETHER
THE HOME TEAM

I WAS RUNNING THE editorial department from my corner office, which had redbrick walls, a large red oriental carpet, a potted palm in one corner, my postal sorting desk behind me, Bank of England armchairs at my round oak table, a tufted leather sofa I had bought on a trip to London, and a red IBM Selectric typewriter on a side stand. I looked out my window at a ten-story brick steam tower with a crack down the side, top to bottom, a constant reminder that San Francisco was yet to have another "Big One."

I wanted to turn *Rolling Stone* into a journalistic force, not just the "Bible of Rock and Roll." Hunter and I were discussing what he should do next. We had a natural affinity, and *Rolling Stone* was a once-in-a-lifetime ideological and editorial fit for him. We didn't have to talk about it; we were going to work together from then on.

I also wanted to bring Tom Wolfe into the fold. I saw him for lunch every time I was in New York, reveling in his hilarious stories of reporting and his wicked comments on the literary world. I hired Boston-based Timothy Crouse, a graduate of Harvard, where he had been the editor of the *Crimson*. He had been in the Peace Corps for two years and was now at the *Boston Herald*. Not that we needed a music writer in Boston, but he was a dogged reporter, first-class writer, and loved music. Tim's first cover was James Taylor and the Taylor clan, "The First Family of Rock."

Baron's portrait of James, an especially handsome young man, signaled the beginning of a New York state of mind at *Rolling Stone*. We opened up an office at the corner of Park Avenue and East Fifty-Sixth Street, five floors above an odoriferous Japanese restaurant. Jonathan Cott had moved back from London, settled into the new office, and was writing regularly.

We ran an interview with legendary labor organizer Saul Alinsky, in which we asked him about the Youth International Party. He said, "Jerry and Abbie couldn't organize a luncheon, much less a revolution." We published dueling open letters from Timothy Leary and Eldridge Cleaver, both in exile in Algiers, their alliance broken on the rocky shores of Cleaver's espousal of violence and "the revolution." I saw those pieces as a part of our mission. I believed there were bullshit people out there with bullshit notions about violence as performance art. It was quicksand, and our readers needed to be steered away.

We put Muhammad Ali, who had refused the draft, on a cover. We profiled David Harris, who had been student body president at Stanford and a high-profile antiwar activist. He had married Joan Baez and just returned from a twenty-month prison sentence for his refusal to be drafted. These were the people I wanted to celebrate. Ones who were in real-world struggles and paying real-world dues.

In my new york travels I ran across Paul Morrissey, who was part of Andy Warhol's inner circle and Andy's principal filmmaking partner. The Warhol scene in general was plastic anathema to us nature-loving San Francisco hippies, but seen in his natural habitat, New York City, Warhol made sense. He was the real deal. He had just started *Inter/View*, which he wrote was modeled on *Rolling Stone*. Andy and Paul had just released *Flesh*, starring Joe Dallesandro, a former juvenile delinquent who was married but earned a living as a hustler. This was the Joe of Lou Reed's "Walk on the Wild Side." I had met a New York writer, Dotson Rader, who was a friend of Tennessee Williams and Norman Mailer, and had just written a book about hustlers. He was delighted to do a profile, as much about Warhol and the scene at the Factory as about Dallesandro. Annie did a cover portrait of the shirtless star with his baby boy, Joe Jr., in his arms.

Warhol and male hustlers, indeed the whole gay sensibility, were off-limits then in rock and roll. Rock was macho, a guy's thing, guitar slingers. Bands came on like outlaw gangs who would burn down your town when they arrived. The Rolling Stones, despite Mick's costumes, were the model of the rock and roll band as a macho gang. It took a while for things to change.

I FIRST VISITED HUNTER on his home turf in the winter. I was a good skier, and Arthur Rock, the severe-looking venture capitalist, had invited me to be his condo guest. Hunter's wife, Sandy, was a blonde, like a surfer chick, with a pretty smile and endless patience, and they had a little boy, Juan, with a bowl haircut. They lived thirty minutes from Aspen in Woody Creek, a homestead Hunter had named Owl Farm, where he had two Dobermans, Lazlo and Weird, and three peacocks in a cage on his front porch. I didn't know their names. The living room had a plate-glass window from which you could see the peacocks and distant mountains of Snowmass. Hunter's leather-upholstered chair with a high back sat in front of a weaving of a lama hung on the wall behind him. It was his throne. A fire would blaze at night, which Hunter would feed with glee. He had a stereo system with towers of twelve speakers each. Flames and loud music would be at full tilt as we would talk through the night with our heads full of acid.

The main hangout was the kitchen, where Hunter would start his day, sometime between two and four thirty in the afternoon, when the East Coast feed of Walter Cronkite would be broadcast. Hunter sat in a high chair at the counter, photos, clippings, letters, notes, and drawings pasted everywhere — around the door, on the window frames, in the spice racks. The most important notices or reminders were on the refrigerator door. The War Room, in the basement, where he wrote, was an unorganized storeroom of files and boxes of his work that Hunter had rigorously accumulated.

One idea we discussed was to wrap up the Battle of Aspen, what had happened and what we learned. The phrase "freak power" and Hunter's colorful language made it seem like something less than serious, but his analysis was on the money: "It's a hard thing to figure out. Does Freak Power really have a future or will the old Nazis win in the end? Maybe we should just give them their rotten fucking system, and let them sink with it. But the really ugly possibility is that they might take us all down with them when they go. The question is not whether we should work within the system...but whether we can afford to ignore it. The terrible truth is that the fuckers are capable of doing terrible damage to us all before they go."

Hunter had started an assignment set in the Mexican American community of East Los Angeles, for *Scanlon's*, a magazine that had folded. I asked him to finish the story for *Rolling Stone*. The LAPD had murdered a respected journalist, Ruben Salazar. Hunter had found his way into the story through a wild man lawyer he knew from Aspen, Oscar Acosta. During the Salazar trial, Oscar had subpoenaed and deposed all one hundred Los Angeles County superior court judges, trying to prove bias. Hunter reported it well, and wrote it vividly but soberly. While composing it, he had taken an assignment to write a quick few hundred words on the Mint 500 motorcycle race in Las Vegas for *Sports Illustrated*. He took Oscar with him, and Oscar became Dr. Gonzo.

Hunter came to San Francisco and stayed at my house, supposedly writing the Salazar story. At that time Hunter was a reasonable houseguest; no disruption, because he slept until noon. I got back from the office one afternoon and he handed me fifteen pages of double-spaced manuscript on thick goldenrod paper. He said he had started playing around with something other than the Salazar piece and was having more fun writing it than anything he had ever done. He wanted to know what I thought. It was the opening of *Fear and Loathing in Las Vegas*. It was sharp and insane. "We were somewhere around Barstow on the edge of the desert when the drugs began to take hold..." I showed it to David Felton, who was then working with me on Salazar. He thought it was genius. I said "Go," as long as he got Salazar done first, which he did.

Tom Wolfe was in town and I invited him over to the house to meet Hunter. The two of them were great fans of each other, *Hell's Angels* and *The Electric Kool-Aid Acid Test* were almost companion books, yet these men had never met. Hunter of course gave a mini-performance simply through the ritual of his arrival, and Tom was in his full costume, all white, hat to spats. Hunter threw an awkward hug around Tom. They grinned and smiled like two excited boys. Each had met one of his heroes.

A few weeks later, Hunter sent a note: "Dear Tom... You worthless scum-sucking bastard... I just got your letter from Rome, you swine. Where the fuck do you get the nerve to go around telling those wops that I am crazy? You thieving pile of albino warts; when I start talking about American writers and the name Tom Wolfe comes up, by God, you are going to wish you were born a fucking iguana... What else can I say except to warn you once again, that the Hammer of Justice looms, and that your filthy white suit will become a flaming shroud!"

A pure Hunter compliment.

GROVER LEWIS, AN older guy at thirty-seven, showed up one day on assignment from the *Village Voice* to do a piece on us. He ended up not writing a word about the magazine itself; instead he produced a sociologist's field report on the various social strata of our employees, from the switchboard to the corner office. An excellent, funny piece that the *Voice* never ran. An old boy from Texas, Grover had graying hair and a raspy smoker's voice. He wore wire-rim glasses with lenses so thick that his eyes appeared to be swimming, and you could never make full eye contact.

I hired him. Grover was a craftsman and stylist, and instantly had senior status. He started off with a *New Yorker*–like visit to Barbra Streisand, a story she hated. He went on the road with the Allman Brothers. He spent a week on the set of *The Last Picture Show*, the era-defining film by Peter Bogdanovich with Cybill Shepherd and Jeff Bridges at their sexiest. With that one piece, Grover set the new standard for movie-set reporting.

Grover discovered a student from San Francisco State, Tim Cahill, who had gotten his master's degree in creative writing. He was a star college swimmer from Waukesha, Wisconsin, a big cuddly kid, six foot plus, who was easygoing but when pushed didn't back down a step. He began as a junior jack-of-all-trades. One of his beats became Jesus Freaks and cults. For one piece, Tim hung out on Sunset Boulevard and got recruited to join homeless and runaway kids in a Christian cult, staying for a week and then escaping. He ended up covering the Jonestown Massacre in Guyana for us.

We also hired Chet Flippo, from Fort Worth, Texas, who had served in naval intelligence before he got a master's in journalism at the University of Texas. He started as a staff writer and became our New York bureau chief two years later. He would become our man with Dolly Parton and Willie Nelson and our overall senior statesman in Nashville.

Our first full-time female editorial employee was Sarah Lazin. Her starting salary was $5,000 a year. Sarah was twenty-four years old, had a head of barely tamed brown hair, and she was tough. She was raised in a small town in rural Dutch Pennsylvania and went to New York University, where she got a master's in history. After graduation she lived on a houseboat in Kashmir with her boyfriend. She was fluent in Italian and ended up in Rome, translating, transcribing, honing her administrative skills, proofreading, and using a computer (of which we had zero, having only gotten our first electric typewriter).

I interviewed her and got the full rundown on her European travels, her musical favorites, and her past LSD use. I used to ask about those things to get a sense of the person. I wanted to work with people who had the same cultural experiences as the rest of the staff and were pulling in the same direction. I asked Sarah to meet with Paul and Grover, as she would be working most closely with them. She and Paul fell in love at first sight. There was a brief attempt at discretion, but eventually they moved in together. On her first working day, she had to transcribe one of the live-action tapes that Hunter had made in Las Vegas.

Our first female contributing editor was Robin Green, a twenty-four-year-old Brown graduate who majored in American literature. Her job interview with me was preceded by a box she had sent along with her writing containing home-baked chocolate chip cookies and copies of Marvel comics. Robin, it turned out, had been comic book legend Stan Lee's secretary. She wrote a story-idea memo about the wacky, wonderful world of Marvel, in which Lee personally identified with his characters and acted out scenes for his illustrators. I assigned the piece, and it was so great that we put the Hulk on the cover ripping apart the *Rolling Stone* logo. Robin was relentless. I made David Felton her editor, and he took her under his editorial and personal wing.

OUR NEW LONDON office was on a noisy street in a three-floor walk-up, a couple of rooms without noticeable heating. But we had a great crew, and installed a new bureau chief, Andrew Bailey. He was a solid reporter — unlike the other English writers we had tried to use. Andrew was also responsible for keeping our British edition going, selling advertising to record companies and editing local news. Chris Hodenfield worked out of the London bureau, along with a young sportswriter and talented "full-time freelancer," Bob Greenfield. I would pitch in editorially when I was there. One day, on a visit in 1974, I had lunch with William Burroughs. He said little, and we didn't connect. (My charm, such as it was, didn't work on him.) However, he agreed to do a conversation with David Bowie.

Andrew visited San Francisco every year and swept up the unattached women. That he seemed like an innocent boy was the key to his success. The accent worked magic, too. He was outgoing, got to know everyone, and easily joined the *Rolling Stone* family. At first he stayed at our house, but he was too social for us to handle. His office nickname was Bedroom Bailey.

Another occasional visitor to San Francisco who became part of the home team was Phillip Frazer, from Melbourne, Australia. Phillip was a handsome lad and took one of the female staffers with him back to Oz. He had founded a music magazine *Down Under* in the late sixties, but his natural love was politics. He launched *Rolling Stone* in Australia, our first and longest-lived foreign edition. It rose to become equivalent in status to *Rolling Stone* in the U.S. We had a brief run with a Japanese licensee around that time, until he was busted for shipping quaaludes to Japan in our editorial pouch. We also had one going in Mexico called *Piedra Rodante*, Spanish for *Rolling Stone*.

CHAPTER 19

THE HOUSE
ON CALIFORNIA STREET

I WAS IN NEW YORK to accept a National Magazine Award from the American Society of Magazine Editors. The ceremonies were in the ballroom of the Plaza hotel. The other winners were *Vogue*, the *Nation*, the *Atlantic*, and *Esquire* — the grown-up magazines. *Rolling Stone*, still a hippie newspaper in San Francisco, won for its stories on Altamont and Charles Manson. They said we had "formula-free and effective journalism," and balls: "The judges particularly admired the integrity and courage of the magazine in presenting material that challenged many of the shared attitudes of its readers." Eager to learn as much as I could about the magazine world, I had lunch with William Shawn, editor of *The New Yorker*, at his regular table in the Algonquin Hotel. He was a quiet man, but we connected, talking about how to handle writers. We were opposites; he let writers take as long as they wanted, never gave a deadline, and would keep them on retainer endlessly. He told me bits and pieces about working with Truman Capote, J. D. Salinger, and James Baldwin. On another trip, the *New York Times* managing editor, Abe Rosenthal, took me to lunch, toured me around the city room, and had me as a "guest of honor" at the daily page one makeup meeting.

I also met Henry Grunwald, another of the great modern editors. He was Henry Luce's successor, the new master of *Time*. In my opinion, his was the most important magazine at the time in America. *Time* shaped how most of the country thought, and Washington knew it. Henry was Austrian by birth and accent, an intellectual, a stocky man. He was our earliest booster in the national press.

I had written a letter of scalding outrage to "Mr. Grunwald" in March 1969, well before we met, accusing *Time* of stealing our groupies story "without any acknowledgment of the quotes you lifted directly... and the names, the people, the ideas you bald-faced thieved." In that same issue, they also had written about the overnight stardom of Johnny Winter, crediting his discovery to "an underground newspaper." My letter concluded with this bit of chutzpah: "Why don't you come clean and admit it? And if you can't do that, why don't you take out a subscription for yourself. It will do your head a lot of good. And you'll be reading your stories two or three months before they appear in your own magazine."

Two months later, *Time* ran a piece on us, our first national press, which credited us with the groupies and Johnny Winter stories. They called our readers "youngsters." Unbelievable. The piece ended on this note: "The notion that life, and even work, can be fun, pervades *Rolling Stone's* airy offices. 'We've reversed the priorities,' says Wenner. 'We have a good time first and a viable business second.'"

THAT SUMMER JANE and I drove to Aspen to spend a week at Owl Farm. It was Hunter at his best — relaxed, sipping whiskey, the Dobermans at his feet as we sat on the front porch, the mountains spread out in front of us. We would smoke weed from a tobacco pipe, but no other drugs. Jane and Sandy sat in the kitchen and talked or headed into town. Hunter spoke normally, thoughtfully, colorfully. We shot guns at targets, not exploding cans of gasoline. That would come later. *Fear and Loathing in Las Vegas* was half done. We talked through the plans to finish, edit, and publish it. We settled on two parts, back to back, to celebrate our fourth anniversary in November. We pondered the next move once *Vegas* was wrapped and spent gentlemanly evenings at the bar in the Hotel Jerome, run by Hunter's great friend Michael Solheim. We discussed politics and getting out the youth vote — eighteen-year-olds had just been enfranchised. We decided he should cover the war in Vietnam.

Annie Leibovitz was hard at work, tagging along on assignments like the Streisand profile or reportorial assignments like Jesus Freaks. After her rookie home run with Lennon, she had gotten noticeably better, developing a feel for covers and the special sauce that made a premeditated image simple and compelling. We had a story on Jethro Tull by Grover Lewis, who had on his desk a sign that read, "I don't write no rock and roll." Annie shot lead singer Ian Anderson in whiteface. He looked like a startled mime as a raggedy doll. It was sophisticated and gave *Rolling Stone* style on top of the swagger. There was another thing Annie brought us: the emergence of a feminine energy and point of view in what was an all-male shop, one about to become very macho. Annie worked as hard and intensely as any of the writers.

JANE AND I found a two-story restored Victorian, a very formal home, on the edge of Pacific Heights. Joan Didion, who came by whenever she was in town, used it and a bit of our life there in one of her novels. She called it "the House on California Street," like the title of an old-fashioned novel or a World War II spy movie. The place took on a presence in our lives, a third spirit with its own personality and needs. Francis Ford Coppola and his family lived around the corner. I purchased the lithographs of Chairman Mao when I visited Andy Warhol at the Factory in New York. The full suite of ten different color schemes was hung on one wall in the dining room, next to a large potted palm and a pinball machine. In the front parlor were various pieces of modern Italian furniture and a large oil painting by Richard Diebenkorn, which I had bought for Jane. With her eye for design, she was in decorating heaven, including the shopping and the schlepping. She also was happy with the life of ease.

The house was grand in appearance, in a way that we were not. We were still kids in our midtwenties but were becoming older in our life and our choices. We became even more social. Jane was now the center of a salon for the talent that had built *Rolling Stone*. She managed friendships for me while I worked. She charmed the people we wanted and was an elegant housemother for our visitors.

The library, with big sliding-glass doors that opened onto a large garden, was the hangout, with floor-to-ceiling bookshelves and a sound system with McIntosh amplifiers that glowed lime green when they warmed up. We had one of the early wall-size television screens, the kind with a cabinet-size projector on the floor. We watched movies and played a lot of drug-fueled Pong into the early morning hours. At one of our dinner parties, David Felton showed up in a friar's cassock and Annie came dressed as a nun. David once arrived with a tank of nitrous oxide so big he wheeled it in on a handcart.

Sometimes it seemed that Annie virtually lived with us. She was becoming a big factor at the magazine and Jane was her creative director, muse, and traveling companion. They drove back and forth to Los Angeles in Annie's Porsche on some assignment two or three times a month, amassing a large collection of Polaroids of the California Highway Patrol officers who wrote them many speeding tickets.

Art Garfunkel moved to San Francisco to make his first solo record and we soon began a weekly tennis game and a gab fest at the post-match juice bar. He talked in curlicues and long, winding metaphors. I started out as a partisan on Artie's side in his long and tortured relationship with Paul Simon. As the years passed, I got a far more nuanced education on that partnership. Artie remained a lifelong pal.

FROM OUR FIRST issue, *Rolling Stone* had taken the implicit position that there was nothing wrong — and so much right — about smoking pot. Our coverage of it was extensive, amusing, and positive. We, in so many words, openly advocated for marijuana use. Cocaine was a different animal. We reported the dangers and the damage. We knew too many people using it. I had first tried it at a record business convention in early 1968. Bob Krasnow, who founded Blue Thumb Records and was our first advertiser, gave me some. I had forgotten about it, but at some point it began showing up in little paper packets. It was fun.

My mother was deep into her bohemian life by then. Once, when she was staying with us, she made herself an omelet with pot for breakfast before flying back to Hawaii. By the time she got to the airport her plane had left, so she returned to our house and slept until the next day. I didn't mind getting her pot, but I did mind being called "man," as in "That's cool, man." She crossed a line, though, when she joined a cult in the East Bay called Morehouse, a commune dedicated to "the study of pleasurable group living." She was totally taken with the leader, a real estate hustler, and how "he played his life game." She became his right hand. It was based around polysexuality. The whole thing creeped me out. With anyone else, I might have accepted it, but this was my mother, and it made me crazy. I also sensed a good story. We assigned it to Robin Green, and in addition to all the sexual action, she discovered that the unpaid communards were renovating fixer-up houses that were being sold at big markups.

My sister Kate was married and living in Cambridge, Massachusetts. I never saw her and rarely heard from her. My other sister, now named Merlyn, was living the hippie life in Hawaii. Before that, she had been living a mile from our childhood home in Marin, caring for one of the elders of the hippie scene, the manager of Quicksilver Messenger Service, Ambrose Hollingworth, who was in a wheelchair after a crash in his VW bus. He wrote an occasional astrology column for *Rolling Stone*. Denise Kaufman was Merlyn's best friend. My mother was trying to seduce Merlyn into joining Morehouse. There was a branch in Honolulu, where my mother, her new guru, and my sister took acid together.

My dad and his wife were living in Brentwood in Los Angeles after moving back from St. Louis. He was now in real estate, raising money from investors to buy mobile home communities in Arizona. He was bringing in good money, which was apparent in his lifestyle. I finally asked if I could invest in one of the parks. It was called Mountain Gate Partners, and turned out to be the only one that went south.

I had no time to be a dutiful son, being so full of myself and the important things I was doing, the important people I was meeting, and the important drugs I was taking. My dad was a good-hearted, generous man who had gone out of his way for me as I was growing up and took care of me until college. I owed him. I visited him every trip I made to Los Angeles.

I never once thought about displacing my father, or outdoing him, or competing with him. He got used to my minor fame and fortune, except once, when he and his wife came to visit us on California Street. I had been up into the early morning hours again — blame it on the blow — and took my time getting downstairs to greet them. It had been over an hour, and my dad was furious. He was insulted. He carefully and coldly gave me a lesson I needed, the one called "Who the fuck do you think you are?"

CHAPTER 20

A DAY IN THE LIFE

I N THE FOURTH-ANNIVERSARY issue, we published a letter from a reader whose plea was prophetic:

> Upon reflection on your politics and content I've decided that your coverage of the music scene encompasses much more, and I have a request, a suggestion. I've spent a lot of energy in the last two years dealing with my sexuality and am writing from a state of mind where I am quite comfortable and proud of being a homosexual male. My own personal development and the growth of the gay movement are very important to me. It's another subculture — perhaps less visible than others — but certainly coexists as significantly with the rest of this incredible country.
>
> It's depressing to me to see that our "enlightened" brethren are often just as ignorant and prejudiced as their fathers. I have come to trust your journalism and request that some attention, whether documentary or editorial, be paid to gay people who are struggling for some peace, along with everyone else.
>
> Your outrage at inhuman marijuana laws has been evident — and many thanks — but are you aware that *castration* can be committed on some victims for certain homosexual offenses in California? And that most states have insidious prison sentences for homosexual behavior?

I could lead a full life without dope, but not without sexual
expression and yet how rarely is anyone concerned that millions of
people live with this oppression, from government, from institutions,
family and "friends" as a fact of life? Where are our priorities?
— Kurt E. Johansen, Minneapolis, Minnesota

Other than a report we commissioned on Stonewall in 1969 and a piece
about the Cockettes, the hippie drag review in San Francisco, he was right; as
busy as we had been fighting the war in Vietnam, the War on Drugs, and on
behalf of racial justice, we hadn't covered gay rights or touched gay culture.

ONE OF THE people who showed up at the office was Yale professor and
legal scholar Charles Reich, an odd duck, middle-aged, long straggly hair, and
sandals. He had just written a bestselling book, *The Greening of America*,
about how young people were leading the country into a social and spiritual
revolution. It was a powerful intellectual rationale for my generation, which
gave him a good deal of fame and celebrity. I had no idea that he was gay.

Reich was a Grateful Dead fanatic who considered Jerry Garcia close
to a prophet. I was a lapsed Deadhead. He suggested that he and I interview Jerry. On a sunny afternoon, Reich, Annie, Jerry, and I sat on the front
lawn of Jerry's home overlooking Stinson Beach. Jerry was the kind of person everyone naturally gravitated to. He had a bemused tolerance for all
who came around, so no matter how far out there Charlie got, I figured it
would be okay. I did the first part of the interview. Once Jerry brought out
the pot, which was strong, I lost my concentration. I had been sitting in the
sun with my shirt off, forgot to put it back on, and got burned and bummed
as I listened to Charles ask him all kinds of spacey shit about acid and consciousness. But the interview turned out fine. We published it in issue 100
with an oddball Annie cover of Jerry laid upside down on the beach.*

---

* It was published later by Straight Arrow Books as *Garcia: A Signpost to New Space* and is
still in print.

THIS WAS A typical *Rolling Stone* issue then: Grover Lewis and Annie went on the road with the Allman Brothers. Annie took the classic portrait of Gregg and Duane sleeping with their heads nestled, sitting on a bus. Grover had to handle a request from Gregg to carry his cocaine stash through a security checkpoint. Jon Landau took on the sad task of writing from the funeral of Duane Allman, who had died at age twenty-four after riding his motorcycle into a truck. Bob Palmer, the sax player of the jazz-based rock band the Insect Trust, and one of the best music writers ever, filed from the mountains of Morocco about the hash-mad trance musicians of Joujouka. Bob Greenfield interviewed Federico Fellini; Ben Fong-Torres visited Ike and Tina Turner at their home and came back with a too-intimate profile of Ike's bad taste in decorating, cocaine ("He doesn't know coke from Drano"), and women (Tina called his recording studio "the whorehouse"). Tim Crouse meticulously chronicled Sly Stone's suspiciously erratic appearance at Madison Square Garden and equally erratic hotel room life, and Ralph Gleason was trying to persuade our readers to register and vote in the upcoming presidential election.

OUR PRODUCTION MANAGER, the most thankless of jobs, was Cindy Ehrlich, a very funny and level-headed woman who lived with a fine-arts potter, Ron Nagle, who was also our in-house carpenter. She managed the mechanical details of grinding out the magazine on deadline. She would come to work dressed as a nurse. Cindy asked if I would pay for a small in-house newsletter, and out came the *Corporate Giggle*. It was sharp office gossip. I was not off-limits; she reprinted an item from *Women's Wear Daily* not calculated to win me fans in San Francisco: "Wenner forsook his usual three-piece Great Gatsby suit for the Bob Dylan millionaire rock star look of jacket and bell-bottoms." Fair enough, but how about "Jann and Jane (*Rolling Stone* Arbiter of 'good taste') seem or/are still allegedly making a go of it…buying a house…take a cruise…good luck, J & J!"

Rolling Stone was still a family. There were now fifty of us, a mix of people in their twenties and thirties who were in tune with the easygoing spirit of San Francisco. Everyone was a friend of someone who already worked there, and it created an easy, binding homogeneity. The fact that we all felt we had a serious task gave us cover, an excuse for our craziness and our special bubble. We partied and there was a lot of sleeping around. We were young, hormones on fire, and drugs bountiful. The *Giggle* told all.

Laurel Gonsalves joined us in 1970 in our first office at Garrett Press. Her father was a tuna fisherman and had put his two girls through college. Laurel's degree from Occidental was in science, and she had started her career at the Salk Institute. When Jane and I met her she was working for Steve Miller's manager. Laurel was a smart, capable woman who understood me. She took over as head of advertising, such as it was, record company ads coming in over the transom plus a smattering of classifieds. She built it into a small operation, with salespeople in New York and Los Angeles, pushing into high-fidelity and musical-instrument advertising. We got Fender, Gibson, Panasonic, Acoustic Research, and the campaign featuring the guy holding on to his chair with his long hair being blown straight back by his speaker system. That was our first beachhead outside the record business and gave us more substance and security.

Laurel oversaw the tricky and somewhat ideological decisions about what advertising *Rolling Stone* found acceptable and what we wouldn't print. She wrote up a series of guidelines. "It's not that we prohibit pubic hairs, or that peace signs absolutely rip off our culture, or that calling two women 'easy pieces' can never be done, but doing it all in one ad makes for bad taste." She forbade advertising by the tobacco companies who were insistently knocking at our door, sex-based dating clubs, hard-core porn, bootleg records, and abortion referral services. She relented on abortion services as long as they had a legitimate reference and if we gave equal free space to Planned Parenthood. Laurel was unrelenting on rejecting Army recruiting ads. When I first put her in charge of advertising, she told me, "I didn't know you had to sell ads. Don't advertisers just call up?"

The money was coming in and we were growing, so I never paid much attention to the financial statements. We didn't do planning or budgeting; we had no controls in place except for the honesty and conscientiousness of the staff. I got a report on income and spending each month, but too late to do anything about it, so I rarely looked at it.

NINETEEN SEVENTY-TWO WAS the year of the Jesus Freak. Hunter was trying out the idea of doing a regular column and sent me an example of one:

> URGENT MEMO
> To: *The entire staff*
> From: *The Sports Desk*
> A recent emergency survey of our field sources indicates a firestorm of lunacy brewing on the neo-religious front, so called "Jesus Freaks." During the next few months we will almost certainly be inundated, even swamped, by a nightmare-blizzard of shlock, gibberish, swill and pseudo-religious bullshit of every type and description. We can expect no relief until autumn.
>
> The following measures have been now put in place:
>
> 1) The mailroom will be paralyzed with wave after wave of pamphlets, records, warnings and half-mad screeds from persons and/or commercial organizations attempting to cash in on this grisly shuck. We have already made arrangements to establish an alternate mailroom to handle our serious business.
>
> 2) We expect the main elevators to be jammed up by a never-ending swarm of crazies attempting to drag huge wooden crosses and other oversized gimcracks into the building. To circumvent this, we are even now in the process of installing a powerful glass cube electric lift on the exterior of the building. The ground floor door will be disguised as a huge packing crate in the parking lot. An armed guard will be on duty at all times.

3) We expect the phone lines to be tied up almost constantly by hired and/or rabid Jesus Freaks attempting to get things like "Today's Prayer Message" into our editorial columns. Raoul Duke, the eminent theologian, has prepared a series of recorded replies for calls of this nature. Any callers who resist automation can leave their names and numbers, so that the Rev. Duke can return their calls and deal with them personally between the hours of two and six a.m.

HUNTER STOLE MY McIntosh amplifiers. He had been staying with us again, working on *Vegas*, and took them when he went back to Aspen. He also walked away with a typewriter from the office and left a note for my assistant: "Stephanie — I stole a typewriter. Check with Jann before you call the cops." When he got back to Aspen, he sent a note: "J — Max [Palevsky] just left. For Christ's sake don't send any more of your friends out here to hang around the house and beg for drugs. It makes me nervous and besides I have work to do, H."

I decided not to send Hunter to Saigon. He might have done brilliant writing from there, but he instinctively was not a war correspondent. He liked guns, not war. He was a politics junkie and operated in the nexus of politics and culture. We negotiated a deal to move him to Washington, have him write election coverage in the magazine, pay his travel expenses on the campaign trail, and publish it as a book. Hunter wasted enormous energy haggling with me and his agent, Lynn Nesbit, who also represented Tom Wolfe. Hunter's expenses for Vegas were considerable for me at that time, and I at first refused to pay for the rental of the Cadillac convertible that was central to the narrative. His response: "Do you expect me to cover the American Dream in a goddamned Volkswagen?"

CHAPTER 21

FEAR AND LOATHING
IN LAS VEGAS

UNTER'S VISITS TO the *Rolling Stone* offices were performance art pieces. There was a round oak table outside my office, in the middle of the editorial department, which served as a conference spot. Hunter would arrive in late afternoon, set his satchel down on the table, and unpack it as people gathered to watch him. Everyone would stop work to talk a little with the Doctor, as he liked to call himself. Hunter and I set up a gag to play on the editors. He had purchased an authentic-looking hypodermic needle big enough to use on a young adult elephant. It was a trick. The needle invisibly retracted as it appeared to be plunged into the skin.

I arrived very late to work after a night with Hunter. As the editors gathered in my office to discuss the day's business, I threw up my arms and exclaimed that they would not believe what he was up to now. I wouldn't believe it if I had not myself seen it, but he was extracting juice from a grapefruit with a giant needle and injecting it directly into his belly. I left it at that and went on with the meeting.

Hunter showed up later that day, unpacked all his stuff on the table, fumbled around until he had a maximum audience, and then plopped a grapefruit on the table and put the elephant needle next to it. He said nothing. He took his good time getting to it, playing it innocently and letting the suspense build. Finally, he put the syringe in the grapefruit, extracted the juice, and plunged the needle through his shirt into his stomach. He took a breath, then jerked his head back and screamed out in agony and horror. There was full silence; people's mouths dropped, the editors squeezed in closer. Hunter rolled his head back, then forward, and slowly opened his eyes as if waking from anesthesia, rolled them from side to side, taking in the horrified audience, and broke into a loud, satisfied cackle.

HUNTER WORKED IN long bursts of energy, awake until dawn or, too often, two dawns. To keep him on track, he needed companionship, what editors call hand-holding, but in Hunter's case it was more like being a junior officer in his war. He required his creature comforts, which meant the right kind of typewriter and a certain color paper, Wild Turkey, the right drugs, and the proper music. It was important to keep people away from him. He had friends, fans, and groupies — not one of them helpful. Hunter found the Seal Rock Inn, a motel at the far end of San Francisco on the Pacific Ocean, above the giant rocks where the seals and tourists gathered. It was just far away enough to do the trick. Finishing *Fear and Loathing in Las Vegas* had now become a siege.

As well as finishing *Vegas*, we were trying to move him and his family to Washington, D.C., in November to cover the 1972 election, so I was simultaneously juggling two deadlines, two heinous negotiations, and two logistical dramas with my very indulged, speed-swallowing star writer, whom I liked enormously. He left a letter for me before going to Aspen on the eve of the deadline for *Vegas*, with instructions on how certain holes in the manuscript could be filled:

> The central problem here is that you are working overtime to treat this thing as Straight or at least Responsible journalism... whereas in truth we are dealing with a classic piece of irresponsible gibberish. You would be better off trying to make

chronological sense of *Highway 61, The Ginger Man* or *Mister Tambourine Man* or *Naked Lunch*.

No doubt the holes and kinks should be filled, but for some reason I can't work up much zeal for the job. Maybe after 12 or 20 hours of sleep I might think differently, but I wouldn't count on it. I am not in much of a mood, right now, to act grateful for any editorial direction. (I am not seriously opposed to any cutting or editing, but don't expect me to get wired on the idea of adding big sections I didn't feel like including in the first place.)

Anyway, I have worked myself into such a stupor of crazed fatigue that I can't even sleep — and when I went into the office today, your business manager was ready to have me arrested for stealing this typewriter. So I think it's time to go home. I'm in a massively rotten mood, trying to stay awake until plane time — seeing double, feeling bugs under my kneecaps.

Anyway, I'm at the end of my wire — a bit on the wrong side of the edge, as it were. But I think the campaign and book contract shit is settled which is a pretty big step.

Fuck this — I'll send another chunk of Vegas II when I get back home. But let's not worry about it. We have enough and 90% of it is absolutely right — on its own terms.

And that, after all, is the whole point.

Hunter suggested that Ralph Steadman, a Welshman, illustrate *Vegas*, so we sent the manuscript to him in London. Two weeks later a large mailing tube arrived with fifteen black-and-white ink drawings that came to define *Fear and Loathing in Las Vegas* as much as the words. There were Gila monsters drinking at a bar, craps tables with lizards making bets, obese police chiefs swilling drinks, Dr. Gonzo vomiting into a toilet and being electrified in a bathtub. I loved the portrait of Hunter in his wraparound glasses, cigarette holder, Hawaiian shirt, shorts, and tennis shoes, on tiptoe, carrying his satchel.

"One thing I want to add up front in 'Vegas,'" Hunter wrote to me on deadline, "is a set of directions on how to read it . . . what music to play at top volume, what drugs to eat (read only between 2–6:00 a.m., etc.). Do I have time to get this in?" We framed *Vegas* as an event and ran full-page ads in the magazine announcing its coming publication. The Steadman drawings were on two consecutive covers. We knew it was as classic as anything in contemporary literature.

HUNTER WAS NOT all laughs. The most painful thing was how he treated Sandy. We would be on deadline, with him in Woody Creek in the War Room in the basement, into an all-nighter, or maybe two in a row, highly strung on speed. I would hear him on the phone screaming at Sandy, cursing at her in a rage, about getting him "some goddamned ice, stupid," or more paper. It was cruel and abusive, tough stuff to hear. I wanted to tell him to stop but didn't feel it was my place. He never physically harmed her — he was a big man, she was slight — and she accepted it, I guess. It made me cringe.

We had spent a lot of time together in the year since Freak Power, and our families were close. We spoke about our goals and all the possibilities for *Rolling Stone* — what it could do, what we could do with it. Hunter wanted to become my partner. We never tried to create a formal agreement because we both knew that his loose-cannon proclivities would blow that up and everything along with it. I might have come home one day to discover that he had bought the Cadillac Hotel in Pueblo, Colorado, with a loan secured by me. Hunter would remind me of the partnership between Briton Hadden and Henry Luce, who together founded *Time* magazine in 1923. Hadden was one of the most influential journalists of the twenties, invented the *Time* style, and was an icon of the Jazz Age. He died at thirty-one. Luce took him off the masthead and barely mentioned him again.

Hunter was shaping the editorial department by the force of his charm and personality, extraordinary talent, and energy. He was an inspiration and a leader. People wanted to write with a little more snap and color and wit. Everyone realized how deeply reported his stuff was and how essential the accuracy and the integrity of facts were for him. Everyone wanted their work to be important like his, about important things.

We wanted to collaborate on where *Rolling Stone* was going with political coverage, to have our voice heard in the national conversation and learn how to use the power of our readers to make America a better place. We intended to politicize our generation and wrest this stirring force away from the fake politics of the revolutionary, and the too hip and apathetic. That was the mission we chose and defined. I would keep a careful eye on his interests, and he would do the same for me. That was our understanding. It lasted for a lifetime, even when we weren't working together. Hunter was in the DNA of *Rolling Stone*.

CHAPTER 22

THE BEAST STIRS
IN BIG SUR

A T THE END of 1971, I brought all the editors and staff writers from London and the East and West Coasts together for a gathering of the tribe in Big Sur, at a motel that hadn't been upgraded since the mid-1950s: worn-out shag rugs, tiny bars of paper-wrapped soap, aluminum room numbers nailed on every door. I called them all editors, implying the sense of responsibility each one had for the whole. Four of them — Ben Fong-Torres, Charlie Perry, Jon Landau, and Jerry Hopkins — were the original crew from the first year. Ten of them had come from daily newspapers, the basic training ground for good reporters. They had come to *Rolling Stone* for a higher bar, a greater sense of purpose, and their freedom.

The actual business conducted there has long been forgotten. I went around the room and asked everyone to discuss their current assignments, what they had ahead, and their ideas for the magazine. I took everyone to dinner at the fern-infested landmark, the Nepenthe Inn. After dinner, we all went to Esalen hot springs. Annie made everyone take off their clothes, line up, and look out at the sea. The photo was a moonlit portrait of the bare-assed boys who ran *Rolling Stone*.

Hunter was stopped at 4:00 a.m. that night by the California Highway Patrol. Somehow, he passed the roadside alcohol-aerobatics tests.

He dropped me a note a few days later: "I can't figure out what the fuck makes me think the Big Sur gig was such an unquestionable success, but as far as I am concerned, it was. (Except for Felton, that treacherous little bastard. Why not send him down to open a Lima bureau and then stop payment on his expense checks? That would sure as hell teach him a lesson.) On balance, I think we somehow managed to chop the Great Croat Knot. Sorry we didn't get a chance to talk more, but what the fuck? The important thing was to croak my Hate Trip & that worked out. I feel definitely up about things now, and I was impressed with the general style and tone of the crowd you've managed to put together. Whatever problems we have now seem minor."

THE NEWEST HIRE at Big Sur was Joe Eszterhas, who carried a buck knife. He had emigrated from Hungary to Cleveland at age six with his family in 1950. His father had been a newspaper editor, and no one in his family spoke English. Joe went to Ohio State and was picked as the College Journalist of the Year. He started work at the *Cleveland Plain Dealer*, where he was a police reporter, a feature writer, and an occasional front-page columnist.

Paul Scanlon had spotted a wire story in the *San Francisco Chronicle* about a biker riot in Cleveland, and through the grapevine heard about Eszterhas as a possible writer. Joe was a total stranger to us. We didn't know then that he had come by our office in San Francisco a year earlier to buy all our back issues. The mail room staff thought he was a narc. Paul gave Joe an assignment, three thousand words on what we would call "The Biker War at Polish Hall." It came in three days later, beautifully written. Joe, with his first *Rolling Stone* byline, was in heaven. Ours was the journalism he had fallen in love with. Unbeknownst to me, Hunter sent him a letter that expressed, in his fashion, high praise: there was "at last another cheap journalist" who could write about motorcycle gangs.

Paul then asked Joe to write a piece on the first anniversary of the Kent State killings, which Joe had covered at the time. He wrote an emotional and cathartic narrative that got us excited about the possibilities of bringing him aboard. A week later he showed up in a paisley shirt, an imitation-leather jacket from Sears, Roebuck, and bell-bottom jeans. Paul insisted we hire him. He had found a home.

I don't know whether it was on the Innocence & Arrogance spectrum or on the Foolhardy Courage & Mighty Righteousness one, or some combination of the two, but we decided to have Joe take on San Francisco's number-one federal narcotics agent. It was Joe's debut as a full-time *Rolling Stone* writer. The agent was at war with the local drug lawyers, who were also the local rock-group lawyers. Like all good narcs, he was a bad guy. We put him in a mug-shot-style photo on the cover. We caught him crossing the line, and he was fired.

THE ONE-HUNDREDTH ISSUE had my Jerry Garcia interview on the cover, and inside were interviews with Francis Coppola and Stanley Kubrick. Ralph wrote a letter to our readers about how proud he was of the landmark occasion, what it meant to him, and what he thought it meant for the world. I felt it was also a personal letter to me, a pat on the back in a way but mostly a reminder of how serious what we were doing was and to not fuck up. It was like sitting down with Ralph back in Berkeley, when he would pull on his pipe and in his wise man's voice say, "Well, Janno..." Ralph wrote, "Everything changes. *Rolling Stone* is going through changes now, some of which are visible and some of which are invisible, even to us. It is predicated on honest intentions, on the belief that music is central to our time, and that the great musicians are, in the culture, more than any other recent times, the true shamans, the religious and secular spokesmen, the educators and the poets. Music is the glue that has kept this generation from falling apart in the face of incredible adult blindness, and ignorance and evilness."

CHAPTER 23

FEAR AND LOATHING ON THE CAMPAIGN TRAIL

I WENT TO STAY in Washington with Hunter and Sandy, who was pregnant again and for the second time would lose the baby right after birth. It was just weeks before the New Hampshire primary. I arranged a meeting with Frank Mankiewicz, George McGovern's campaign wizard. By the time Hunter and I arrived in Chevy Chase, a fancy D.C. suburb, at Frank's large colonial house, we had gotten ourselves totally baked. It was a version of a beginner's high: giggles almost impossible to stop, and when you look at the other person, the laughing takes off again, even worse. All the way to the paneled front door, where Frank welcomed us. We stared straight ahead. For two hours, Frank laid out for us his state-by-state strategy in the run-up to the July convention in Miami. Thanks to that private briefing and his own fine instincts for politics, Hunter called the race correctly through the whole campaign.

Hunter's first piece from D.C. before he hit the campaign trail was several thousand wandering words on gambling, the National Football League, and free-form paranoia about politics and political journalism: "I feel the fear coming on, and the only cure for that is to chew up a fat black wad of blood-opium about the size of a young meatball and then call a cab for a fast run to that strip of X-rated film houses on Fourteenth street, peel back the brain and let the opium take hold." That was Hunter's first National Affairs report. The piece was called "The Million-Pound Shit Hammer."

HUNTER SHOWED UP in snowy, freezing New Hampshire. Tim Crouse had asked me if he could help Hunter cover the campaign and, now and then, find a story for himself. Tim had proven he could do exquisite rock star profiles and was clearly a dogged reporter and skillful writer. I said yes, on the condition that he would be second fiddle to Hunter and serve as his assistant on the deadline battles that were certain to be ahead. So, Tim also turned up in New Hampshire. Of the seven people on the McGovern press bus, two of them were from *Rolling Stone*.

Hunter loosened up on the campaign trail. In March he filed "The Banshee Screams in Florida." We met the Boohoo, "a mescaline-crazed heckler" whom Hunter had found in a bar and to whom he lent his press credentials for the Sunshine Express, the whistle-stop train for the Democratic-establishment candidate, Senator Edmund Muskie. Hunter also introduced "Zang!," a new exclamatory figure of speech similar to "Zounds" but spoken on speed. Another Hunter word I cherish is "Cazart," which I translate as "Stare in amazement, but it is a done deal."

I HAD A new blowup with Bill Graham. The first one, in 1968, was over a headline I wrote for a story about the Dead going to Rome, "Pigpen to Meet Pope." Bill called *Rolling Stone* trash for that bit of fun and pulled his $50-an-issue advertisement. Now he was closing the San Francisco and New York Fillmores and had turned the announcement and the final concerts into grandiose, maudlin, and self-serving events. He said he was getting out because of how greedy everyone else in the business had become, how much the artists wanted, how much the agents demanded, and so forth. He used his press conference to tar and trash the music business, a business that had made him very rich. Everybody was to blame except him. He used to give away free apples at his shows; I guess that was breaking the bank. But even though he was shutting down the low-profit Fillmores, he was still the biggest concert promoter in the United States.

Tim Cahill did an even-handed investigation of Bill's empire and the disparity between what he said and what he did. We titled it "Bye, Bye Miss American Pie, You Sleazy Cunt," both a reference to his claim that rock was dead and an homage to his well-known use of crude language. Bill had only three speeds: outrage, egomania, and humble pie. He called me, screaming, "Listen to me, mister, you motherfucker. You're a dead man. I've only said that to one other person. He was my sergeant in the army, and he's dead." Over the years I had watched him get abusive but never challenge anybody tough. He was a bully. I proposed an official sit-down with the large-size Tim Cahill and me for Bill to present his side of the story. He brought an assistant and a tape recorder with him, and for two hours we heard Bill talk about himself with virtually no interruption and no discussion of the facts. And that was it. I was still alive and never had another problem with him.

Annie's next assignment was David Cassidy, the teen idol who filled arenas with screaming girls, a wonderful tradition in popular music. The stars were androgynous, pretty but not threatening. David was the heartthrob of the television show *The Partridge Family*, a new version of *Ozzie and Harriet*. I often thought that some subjects were too plastic, too middle-of-the-road, or too pop to be in *Rolling Stone*. The *Partridge* music wasn't great, but the show was well within our franchise as a chronicler of popular culture.

David posed fully naked for the camera. We ran the most provocative shot on the cover, cropped just below a shadow from the line of pubic hair below his belly button, the reality of the full photo left unspoken but obvious. With this very act, David killed his suffocating image and ended his life as a trapped teen star. Tony Perkins wrote us a letter asking for a print of the photo, saying it would be from one "former androgyne to another."

The other main features in the Cassidy issue were a profile of Tammy Wynette and an interview with William Burroughs ("We're all black centipedes at heart, so why worry about it?"). That issue had another long, hilarious dispatch from Hunter as well. What a mix that was. The combination of David Cassidy and William Burroughs was undeniably weird. What is going on in the world when you see those two together? Who did that? Why? That led to one of my favorite cover headlines of all time, written by David Felton: "Naked Lunch Box."

I WAS HAVING the time of my life with the good Doctor Thompson. McGovern called him Sheriff. Hunter was always using some form of speed; he would talk at enormous length and leave me weeping with laughter. He once told me — and later wrote — he had discovered that Senator Muskie was using the rare South American drug ibogaine, which enabled the native tribe to remain absolutely motionless for a full two days while maintaining mental alertness. There was a doctor from Brazil aboard the campaign train because Muskie's mind had become paralyzed and at rallies could only see Gila monsters, not people.

Hunter's deadlines were great fun for me, but the art-and-production department, down to five people by the early morning hours, was usually in a foul mood. They didn't get any kicks from Hunter filing at the last minute and felt they were being held hostage to his irresponsibility and immaturity. Finally, they all signed a petition asking for help and posted it throughout the office under the title "Hunter Sucks." Those people had the hardest and least-honored jobs at the magazine; they were the crew that had to absorb all the fuckups, delays, and deficiencies of the creative departments to meet the deadline without fail.

I sent a copy of their "Nobody is worth this shit" petition to Hunter. He sent a gracious apology, restrained in humor. He was humbled by understanding the damage he had done to a bunch of hard workers, the people who were helping him. Hunter didn't change, but his apology and his thanks were persuasive. He was taking over a good part of my life as well. I did not appreciate his phone calls after midnight when I was home and told him to stop unless it was on deadline. I loved seeing him at the office or on the campaign trail. My personal schedule was set to the Democratic primaries and Hunter's deadlines.

The great pleasure was his copy. He would write in great bursts of twisted imagery that snarled and screamed and suddenly switched to a lyrical flight of observation. He developed a structure and rhythm to his writing that underlay — and was obscured by — his flamboyant choice of words. He could contain diverse ideas and odd choices in numerous subjective clauses, pauses, ellipses, and asides — riff playfully and in dazzling runs — and bring it all back home, landing it smoothly.

Hunter was wickedly funny. He sent me a memo about all the reader mail he was getting: "About a week ago I got a letter from someone in Chicago calling me a 'crypto-faggot, bulldog-Nazi, honky-fascist pig.' I can really get behind a letter like that. But most of the stuff is lame. I'm not running a goddamn 'Dear Abby' service here. Anybody with problems should write to David Felton, Bleeding Heart Editor, at the San Francisco office. But I have more important things to do. Politics. Human problems are secondary."

We put McGovern on the cover leading a children's crusade, a drawing by Ed Sorel. I wrote a Letter from the Editor that called McGovern "a wise man to whom we should entrust the stewardship of our society." Hunter was worried about the black ravens that were being sighted in Miami.

Joe eszterhas set up shop in the middle of the editorial department, sat with his feet on his typewriter, pulling on his pipe, either on the phone or reading the daily papers. He changed the day-to-day feel of the place. Joe was a big personality, ambitious, and an obvious talent. He was gifted with an ear for language and an eye for storytelling. He didn't hesitate to make his opinion known about anything. His favorite pejorative was "chickenshit" and his mostly affectionate nickname for me was "Napoleon." He could run roughshod over whomever he cared to. He toughened the staff up. He was an investigative reporter and lifted our game.

Paul saw a wire service story about a twenty-year-old who had gone over the edge in a small Missouri town and killed four citizens in the town square, a showdown between the local longhairs and the town elders, an ancient clash in modern costume. We sent Joe. "Charlie Simpson's Apocalypse," a tour de force, brought alive a time and place in a little-noticed corner of America. Tom Wolfe enshrined the piece in his anthology of the best of the New Journalism.

I had come up with the idea that finally inspired Tom Wolfe. NASA would be sending up Apollo 17, the last mission to the moon. I asked him to cover it for *Rolling Stone*. Only *Life* magazine and Norman Mailer had written about the astronauts, and both accounts had been pure mythology. The true history of the Mercury program was a quintessential American saga, about the test pilots, the nature of heroism, and having the right stuff. Tom went to the launch and dove in. This would be his follow-up to *The Electric Kool-Aid Acid Test*. I would have something to follow Hunter; I would deliver Tom, the great man himself.

AT THE SAME time, I asked Truman Capote to go on the 1972 Rolling Stones tour for a few dates. I wanted to examine something at the very core of what we were about, as a magazine and as a culture, from another sensibility, that of an outsider, someone older and potentially wiser. Truman was the best-known, most recognizable writer in the country, due to *In Cold Blood* and his ongoing guest appearances on *The Tonight Show*, where he would talk in his lispy voice — the gayest man on television. When he joined the Stones tour in Kansas City, he arrived with his own photographer, Peter Beard, and his close friend, Princess Lee Radziwill, Jacqueline Onassis' sister.

In the middle of the night, Keith Richards painted Capote's hotel room door with ketchup, thumbing his nose at the snooty Mr. Capote and the Princess with a not-so-veiled reference to *In Cold Blood*. My friend Marshall Chess had become the Stones' manager a year earlier (I had recommended him to Mick) and was on the tour. He was not a suave guy, in fact he talked and looked like a Jewish gangster. Truman developed a total antipathy for him. Truman stopped by our office on his way home and spoke with delighted disdain about Marshall and the Stones' PR man, also Jewish. He enchanted our editors with his gossip and seemingly unimpeachable insights. As for his piece, Truman had been struggling with writer's block since *In Cold Blood* and couldn't finish the assignment.

We also had sent Bob Greenfield to cover the Stones tour, to stay on it from beginning to end, barnstorming in private jets and trailer-truck caravans across the country. When Bob was on staff in our London bureau the year before, he had gone out with the Stones on a small tour in England. They were comfortable with him and let him inside their entourage, the "Stones Traveling Party," which was both a logistical designation and a state of mind. Bob didn't let anyone on the tour see him taking notes. He was mentally reconstructing everything they said and did.

Mick accused Bob one night at the end of the tour of just hanging around, running wild, and not doing his job for *Rolling Stone*, since he never wrote things down. Bob had been given unlimited access. It was true that Bob was having the time of his young life on a road trip with Keith et al. "Mick Jagger," he wrote, "felt the need to challenge me on this point, rattling the bars of my cage to see who was home. Nothing personal, mind you. Just Mick being Mick (a full-time job if there ever was one). Call it my final exam for personal credentials in a world where he was the final judge of everything and everyone." It was dead-on Mick.

I caught up with the Stones tour at Winterland. It was the group's return to San Francisco after Altamont, and before the show began you could imagine tension in the crowd about the potential for violence. Then the lights went up on the darkly lit stage and there they were, the band beyond compare, in a line, laying down the opening to "Brown Sugar," a driving guitar and horn tangle about interracial sex, drugs, and slavery, "You shoulda heard him, just around midnight." There was no group in the world that had a repertoire as dramatic and riveting, that could stop you in your tracks while also dancing, waving your arms, and shouting. They would not do "Sympathy for the Devil" because of the Altamont legend. I was at the front of the stage, jammed in with fans transported out of their heads. I especially remember Mick, isolated in a red spotlight, doing "Midnight Rambler," slapping his studded belt on the stage floor.

I think the group was at the peak of its power for that era. Mick Taylor had intensified the harmonies and interplay of the guitars. It was potent. The blatant sensuality and imminent danger with which Mick presented himself fused sex and violence, even death.

I MET HUNTER in Miami Beach a few days before the Democratic convention. Phalanxes of cops were in riot gear with space-age face shields and billy clubs, backed up by the National Guard. Helicopters circled over the convention hall day and night, a sound you knew on the television news from Vietnam, the beating whip of the blades, the heavy-breathing rhythm of impending battle. It ratcheted up the tension to full-alert adrenaline. We were at a political convention, a bedrock of democracy, in a war zone.

The convention floor was more madness. Like so much of everything that week, it was disorderly and felt just a few seconds away from sliding out of control, a few flying folding chairs away from a riot. I went down to the floor with Hunter on the first night, as the delegates and the press took their places before the session began. After wandering the hall, taking it all in, we sat down with friends in the California delegation, the largest one, directly in front of the podium, which loomed over our heads behind a thicket of state banners. The sound of the helicopters had receded, but they were inescapable, locked into your brain like distant chain saws cutting down a forest. Sitting in front of the podium, under banks of thousands and thousands of watts of television lights, I felt as if

I was in the pounding, blood-filled central cortex of the nation. Then Hunter turned and put a small bottle in my hand. "Try this." My first hit of amyl nitrate. Rocketman!

I DIDN'T GO to the Republican convention or watch it on TV. Max Palevsky had invited Jane and me on a boat trip in the Mediterranean for that week in August. Neither of us had been to the Continent, so everything seemed "finer" in every little way, from the bed linens to the butter. We boarded the *Lisboa*, which we were told was the third-largest private yacht on the Mediterranean.

We traveled in the last of its mid-century glamour days, when there was lots of money but fewer people with it. We had mud baths at spas; ate in Michelin-rated restaurants; drank Chateau Lafite, La Tour, and Cheval Blanc; and swam at all the beaches in Sardinia and Elba—and dope. Max introduced us to a world of wealth. Two weeks on a yacht is heady stuff, and you soon get spoiled. There would be no turning back.

MEANWHILE, IN THE States, Hunter and Ralph Steadman had returned from the GOP convention. Hunter was in a dark, sour funk. McGovern had stumbled right out of the gate, whereas the Nixon convention was as slick as anything Goebbels ever staged. Ralph's drawings were brutal: Nixon as Hitler with an armband, a mug shot of Agnew, a Nuremberg sign among the state banners, and, most memorably, Nixon speaking at the podium while farting bile out his ass.

ONE OF HUNTER'S hunches that paid off was "The Boys on the Bus," the idea that Tim Crouse should start reporting on the press and how they covered the campaign. We were going to not only cover the candidates but investigate the investigators. Hunter and Tim were well liked on the bus; funny, smart, and *real* writers...and from *Rolling Stone*! Tim profiled all the major players, from the easygoing Walter Cronkite to R. W. "Johnny" Apple, a stuffed shirt who was the chief correspondent for the *New York Times*. *Time* magazine had more than a hundred editors and writers at each convention. It was what big-time journalism looked like. Tim called it "pack journalism."

HUNTER STRUGGLED BETWEEN the shadow and the reality. McGovern polling numbers were twenty-two points behind. Nixon's re-election was a lock. With each new piece Hunter filed, we would pick out a new style of dingbats to use as space breakers between columns of type. Now we chose vampire bats. "It is time," he wrote, "to come face-to-face with the fact that we are a nation of 220 million used-car salesmen with all the money they need to buy guns…Jesus! Where will it all end? How low do you have to stoop in this country to be president?"

Hunter at his most memorable: "It is Nixon himself who represents that dark, venal and incurably violent side of the American character. Our Barbie doll president, with his Barbie doll wife and his box full of Barbie doll children is also America's answer to the monstrous Mr. Hyde. He speaks for the werewolf in us; the bully, the predatory shyster who turns into something unspeakable, full of claws and bleeding string warts, on nights when the moon comes too close…

"At the stroke of midnight in Washington, a drooling red-eyed beast with the legs of a man and the head of a giant hyena crawls out of its bedroom window in the South Wing of the White House and leaps fifty feet down to the lawn…pauses briefly to strangle the Chow watchdog, then races off into the darkness…toward the Watergate, snarling with lust, looping through the avenues behind Pennsylvania Avenue and trying desperately to remember which one of those 400 iron balconies is the one outside Martha Mitchell's apartment…"

CHAPTER 24

TRUMAN AND ANDY, PAUL BOWLES AND UNCLE EARL

TOM WOLFE BROUGHT the latest pages of *The Right Stuff* to the Sherry-Netherland in New York, where I was staying in Max Palevsky's suite. Bernardo Bertolucci was getting up to leave; his *Last Tango in Paris* had just been released into the firestorm over its X-rated content. "What was that lump of white stuff hanging out of his nose?" Tom asked. I told him it was cocaine. I didn't mention that I had indulged as well. "Santa Baranza!" Tom said softly, in mock shock. It was his favorite exclamation. Everybody should have a signature expression. Tom had a great toast, too, which I would use, always with credit to him: "To Fortune, that much maligned lady."

I was going to look at the new pages and send them via the mojo wire (this was what Hunter had nicknamed the portable Xerox Telecopier he carried on the campaign trail) to San Francisco. We were on deadline. I tried to pick my words carefully: "Uh, well, Tom, this is great but this sentence here and…" He looked at me and said, "You can just say 'bullshit.'" It was a big moment. If I could help the man himself make his story better, I must know what the hell I was doing.

DR. HOOK AND the Medicine Show hit number one with their single "The Cover of the *Rolling Stone*," in which the band lamented that although they "take all kinds of pills that give us all kinds of thrills," they just can't get on the cover of *Rolling Stone*.

We put them on the cover. Fair trade.

AROUND THAT TIME, in 1973, I met Earl McGrath, who was to become one of Jane's and my closest friends for all the years to come. Nominally, he owned an art gallery on North Robertson and Melrose in Los Angeles, with an apartment on the floor above where he lived with his wife, Camilla. Earl was in his early forties, the son of an itinerant short-order cook from Superior, Wisconsin. He had joined the Merchant Marine and ended up in Los Angeles. Camilla was from an aristocratic Italian family whose ancestors included Pope Leo XIII.

I was wary of him at first; he was too familiar and frivolous, but he didn't care what anybody thought. Earl loved to laugh, especially at his own jokes, however many times he told the same one. He was a bohemian in his heart but more at home in the world of wealth and art. He had a cast of friends who were nuts in one way or another, talented and funny. If you were a friend of Earl's, you became friends with all of his friends, and he seemed to know everyone: Euro-aristocrats, the lights of café society, actors, writers, the stars of the art scene. He was a favorite on the A-list and the Z-list, too. He had more than twenty godchildren. He took us into his world, and soon we were the closest of friends; it was through Earl that I got to know Ahmet Ertegun.

Earl knew Peter Wolf of the J. Geils Band and brought him to the House on California Street. Jane and Peter did a double take. They had been classmates in the beatnik crowd at the High School of Music & Art in New York. Jane and I were staying at Max Palevsky's suite at the

Sherry-Netherland in New York on one trip, when Earl decided we should have a party. I didn't quite get the full import of it, but Earl had decided to introduce us to New York City, his version of it. I remember Andy Warhol taking pictures with a Polaroid of the beautiful young couple from San Francisco.

Camilla McGrath, her brother, and three sisters had inherited their parents' estate, Villa Reale, near the walled city of Lucca in the village of Marlia. The place was one of the jewels of Northern Italy, with vast lawns, formal gardens, an amphitheater, and a grand villa with outbuildings, all built by Napoleon. We made several summer visits. At the end of our first trip, Earl took us to Milan for a few days, where we shopped for furniture for the House on California Street. Toward the end of his life, Earl was asked what he had done for the Wenners: "I taught them how to be rich."

TRUMAN CAPOTE FAILED to turn in anything on the Stones tour other than six triple-spaced pages mocking my friend Marshall Chess. Perhaps something more was lurking in the brain of the Tiny Terror? Truman could talk. It was easy to fall under his spell as he unspooled his secrets about his famous friends. He would gossip about William Shawn, and how Shawn used to coddle J. D. Salinger. Truman did not like Salinger and had been very jealous of him. While Truman was making a documentary film about death row in San Quentin, he often came by the House on California Street. He was fixated on a baby-faced prisoner, a twenty-year-old member of the Manson family.

I asked Andy Warhol to interview Truman about the Stones' tour. Andy also had a high voice, but his was slow and whispery, and he didn't talk that much. Andy was a lot of "gee whiz." The two of them met on a Sunday. It was a sunny day, so they went to the zoo in Central Park and started chatting. Truman had noticed Mick's ability to go from totally extroverted to totally private almost instantly. Andy asked why he hadn't written the Stones piece. He said the group was fun, but there was nothing to discover. "For me," Truman said, "every act of art is the act of solving a mystery." Truman, however, had titillating bits of debauchery, and Andy pulled them out. On the other hand, Truman thought Mick was not a good dancer or singer (and Bob Dylan's lyrics were "atrocious"). Mick had given our royal correspondent the royal treatment, and he returned it with a bitch slap. Andy and Truman ended up at the Carlyle for lunch, bouncing back and forth about the movies, death row, and skin care. It was the zeitgeist, glimpsed in an overheard conversation between two of its brightest lights.

I called the story "Sunday with Mr. C." It was a stretch for *Rolling Stone*, the world of New York "high" culture. I thought Andy's piece needed more substance, and I decided to add a further chat with Truman as a coda. I went to Palm Springs to do it myself and stayed with him. He had one other houseguest, a strapping guy who he said was his nephew, a former Army paratrooper or something. It didn't occur to me that there might be more to it. Later I was told he didn't have any nephews.

After taping the interview, we went to a tiki restaurant, drank a lot of margaritas, and headed to Oil Can Harry's, a gay disco, my first sight of that world. As we walked to the door, people in line began applauding. It was a hero's welcome for Truman, the world's most famous homosexual since Oscar Wilde or Alexander the Great. We were seated at a VIP table right on the dance floor. Men kept asking Truman to dance. He turned them all down, pretending I was his date. Over Truman's objections I left him alone for five minutes to take a stroll through the club, which was neither interesting nor sexy. I wasn't bothered or worried a bit about being seen at a gay club; Truman was my beard.

ALICE COOPER WAS barnstorming the country on his chartered plane, with the usual good dope and bad weather, hangers-on, managers, and a *Rolling Stone* writer. I didn't like the piece that came in, and in a coke-fueled burst of too much energy decided I would interview Alice by phone. Over the next three days we talked, as he went from city to city, and I turned that into a new piece. His best line: "I felt it was important to act out violent sex in front of American youth, because they need it. If they listen to what their parents say, they will go crazy." Annie had done a shoot with Alice and Salvador Dalí posed cheek to cheek. My byline was Harry Swift, and my author's bio read, "He is a small, fleshy, often ferocious man, about whom little is known and less is asked."

JANE AND I went to Morocco for a quick vacation. In Tangier, we settled into the Mamounia Palace. The bar opened into a garden courtyard with a splashing fountain and birds singing. You could imagine a sheik sweeping by in his robes or perhaps Humphrey Bogart leaning against a shadowy wall near the door.

Paul Bowles met us at the bar. I knew of him as the author of the mesmerizing *The Sheltering Sky*. He was the last of an era; he had lived in Paris when he was Aaron Copland's lover, was a part of Gertrude Stein's circle, and so enchanted Christopher Isherwood that he named Sally Bowles after him in *The Berlin Stories*. Bowles was a composer who collaborated with Tennessee Williams, Orson Welles, and Leonard Bernstein, and early on had visited the Master Musicians of Jajouka, who would play for days uninterrupted in a hash-trance state. We had published one of the stories he had translated by the Moroccan author Mohamed Mrabet. We met Mrabet with Paul, who I assumed was also a boyfriend, and they gave us more short stories.

Paul hosted us for three days. He had a fragrant blend of hash that was always at hand. His wife, Jane, had died just weeks before we arrived, and Paul told us stories of her long decline, which he said had been caused by their jealous maid, who had planted voodoo herbal potions around their apartment. Paul told us hilarious stories about Truman, Tennessee, and Gore Vidal coming to Tangier, all in their youthful prime. Paul was now in his sixties, thin and gentlemanly. He graciously took Jane and me into a world that was quickly passing.

Later, Michael Rogers would interview Paul for the magazine, a piece that is considered definitive. Michael was another great hire for us. He started at *Rolling Stone* at twenty-one, eager, and curious about the world. He got a degree in physics from Stanford while he pursued writing. He was an outdoors buff, and we skied together in Tahoe. He asked if I would send him to the Sahara desert to watch an upcoming total solar eclipse with other eclipse junkies who were camped there. It would be the longest total eclipse until 2150. I told him okay and to stop in Morocco on the way back to interview Bowles. Michael sent me a letter from there: "Have made it safely to Tangier, following incredible 200-km, 12-hour train ride from Casablanca. Paul has been extremely nice, gone out of his way in everything possible to make a successful interview. I have five hours of tape. Tennessee Williams is staying at the Minzah, in a room right below mine. Last night I went to a dinner at [author] Gavin Lambert's with him. Williams is a great *Rolling Stone* fan, thinks it's a 'marvelous' magazine, loved the Capote interview, and is also of the opinion (from some *Time* or *Newsweek* picture) that you are a very cute fellow.

"The Bowles interview: sex, dope, magic, gossip but in a totally associative, stoned-rap context. I am trying to keep the stoned-rap flavor but make it a fast-easy read…which means does this sentence logically follow the previous? Not as easy as it sounds. I've given up smoking dope for the interim."

MICHAEL READ ABOUT an upcoming conference to discuss the threats to humanity emerging from the new field of recombinant DNA, the ability to combine genetic material from different life-forms, including dangerous bacteria, to make new ones. In other words, genetic engineering was at hand. The National Academy of Sciences turned down our request for a credential. But then Michael's piece on his trip to the Sahara unexpectedly won the annual American Association for the Advancement of Science/Westinghouse Science Award. At the ceremony, Michael was seated with the president of the association, who could hardly say no to his request to attend the DNA conference after handing him the award.

I WAS A terrible science student. I failed frog dissection. But I was fascinated with the diversity of the natural world, and thought if we didn't understand it, we would lose it. For me, science coverage in *Rolling Stone* was not too far a stretch. I saw a story buried in the *San Francisco Chronicle* about scientists who were using a line of human cells, known as Hela, that didn't die and reproduced endlessly. They described them as "immortal." I gave it to Michael. He discovered Henrietta Lacks, a black woman who, while dying of cervical cancer in the "colored" ward of Johns Hopkins Hospital in 1951, had tissue involuntarily removed to use in laboratory cloning and in vitro fertilization. Her cells had been bought and sold by the billions. One of the strongest cell lines ever found came from a poor black woman, a tobacco sharecropper. *Rolling Stone* was the first publication to reveal her identity. The story became the 2010 bestseller by Rebecca Skloot, *The Immortal Life of Henrietta Lacks*. I also hired Tim Ferris, a young UPI reporter who went on to bestsellerdom, to write for us about astrophysics and cosmology.

JOE ESZTERHAS' PIECES were usually sagas of 10,000 words or more. He got into people's shoes and heads, whether they were cops, killer cops, or cop killers. His story "Death in the Wilderness" was the third of our series on lawless narcotics enforcement. A Northern California task force of nineteen men — local sheriffs and federal agents — in a Huey helicopter borrowed from the Army swooped down on a mountain cabin in search of a million-dollar PCP lab. What they thought was the lab turned out to be two chicken coops. An innocent young man in his twenties was shot in the back while his wife watched.

We became known for this style of narrative, long-form journalism. I called those pieces the Big Reads. We had the space, and readers still had attention spans. Cahill, Eszterhas, Grover Lewis, and Paul Scanlon were a great features team, assigning, writing, and drinking at Jerry's Tavern across the street in the afternoons. They gave the office its swashbuckling character. Joe was pretty much the ringleader, the star, and the hothead. He gave Paul and me buck knives and had us each draw blood, mix it, and swear an oath of brotherhood.

HUNTER SENT ME an expense-reimbursement request on which he had scrawled in red ink: "Investigation of Oil Fraud — California and Nova Scotia — all expenses related to secret investigation, $20,099.50." If I had submitted it, no one in the accounting department would have thought twice. With Hunter off the campaign trail, I suddenly had time to build the business.

I FOUND AN experienced "old boy," George Carlton, to take on circulation and work the network of semi-shady people who owned magazine distribution monopolies. I wanted him to tell me how he got this done. He said, "Don't ask." I hired a serious controller from our auditors. It was a relief to have someone buttoned up and reliable minding the spending. I hired one of the big five accounting firms to do our audits and had the whitest white-shoe law firm in San Francisco. I was running the overall company and having endless meetings and lunches in San Francisco and New York with anyone I thought I could learn something from. Eventually I landed on Joe Armstrong, an ambitious and hardworking Texan with a law degree and magazine experience who put together an experienced ad sales team and began to run the overall business far better than I. He was our first real publisher. The oddball way *Rolling Stone* was printed as a tabloid and then folded in half, with a cover on one of the quarter folds, was cooked up to make it fit into magazine racks. It was an awkward and an implicitly downmarket look. As part of the great leap forward, we got rid of it and went full tabloid, which gained us a stunning poster-size cover.

I WANTED TO interview Daniel Ellsberg, who had given the *New York Times* the Pentagon's secret history of the war in Vietnam. He came to stay for a few days, a much different kind of guest at the House on California Street. He had been a Marine. Dan was lost in the clouds, except that he had a serious admiration for himself and his brain power. He was intense to be with. We spent hours with a tape recorder, sitting at a table in the front parlor next to the large indoor palm tree.

We talked about his experiences in the national security machinery, and the corrosive nature of secrets and what they do to individuals, governments, and societies. It was heady stuff that I wanted to get a handle on. He had drunk from the secret cup and then betrayed the priesthood. He disliked no one more than Henry Kissinger. Dan laid out Kissinger's spider web. His critique from that interview is now in all the standard texts on Kissinger.

For the cover, we rendered Ellsberg in profile like a president on a coin, against a field of red. I added this quote from the Declaration of Independence: "Let Facts Be Submitted to a Candid World."

I TRACKED DOWN Richard Goodwin, one of John Kennedy's fabled speechwriters. Dick had graduated from Harvard Law School, had clerked for Supreme Court justice Felix Frankfurter, and went to the White House with Kennedy, on whose behalf he secretly met with Che Guevara in Uruguay. Dick stayed on with Lyndon Johnson, coined the term "Great Society," and resigned in protest against the Vietnam War. I hired him to be the new political editor of Rolling Stone. Hunter still held the National Affairs Desk.

Dick had uncombed black hair, a puffed-out nose, and bad skin. His eyes were bright and intense; his grin suggested that he already knew everything you might say. He knew how power worked, why certain things that you had no clue about had happened. He wove a spell. He was a left-wing liberal, like me, and we hit it off. Before I hired him, I had lunch with Dave Burke, Teddy Kennedy's top guy, and asked about Dick. "Goodwin," he said, "is like an unmade bed." It took a while for me to figure that out. In the meantime, Dick shared the same conspiratorial

At the zoo. Age three, 1949.

My father, Edward Wenner.

The house where I grew up, at the end of Rainbow Road. My father stands in front of the fruits of his labors: the home, the family convertible, and his personal treasure, an MGB, one of the earliest sports cars brought into the United States, 1955.

My mom, Sim Wenner, divorced and with her three kids at boarding schools, began traveling the world. After a few years, she settled in Hawaii. This photo was taken by the airline for its in-house newsletter, 1959.

The Wenners: two World War II vets with their contribution
to the American Dream and the Baby Boom. Jan Simon, Edward, Kate Gilbert,
Sim, Martha Gilbert. San Rafael, California, 1952.

A newly minted boarding school graduate. I was quite the achiever: editor of the yearbook and school newspaper, student body vice president, and an operetta principal. I am on my way to the University of California at Berkeley, 1963.

Within a year, Rolling Stone *seemed like serious business,
and I wore a tie to work each day to reinforce that perception. Jane put a poster
of the Marx Brothers smoking a hookah over my desk, 1968.*

Jane and I worked together every day in the first year, 1968.

Mick Jagger and I hold a press conference to announce that we will jointly own and publish Rolling Stone *in the UK, London, 1969.*

Our first chief photographer, Baron Wolman, backstage at Woodstock, 1969.

I was interviewing John for Lennon Remembers *and romancing Tom Wolfe to write about the astronauts when I introduced them to each other, 1970.*

Charles Reich and I conduct the Rolling Stone *Interview with Jerry Garcia on Jerry's front lawn in Stinson Beach, 1972.*

Rolling Stone *cofounder Ralph J. Gleason backstage with John Lennon at the Beatles' last concert, Candlestick Park, San Francisco, 1966.*

With Mama Cass Elliot, volunteering as "celebrity ushers"
at a George McGovern fundraising concert, 1972.

With Boz Scaggs, while making his debut album, on the porch
of a cabin owned by Otis Redding, Macon, Georgia, 1969.

Backstage in San Francisco with Pete Townshend. He became an RS contributing writer and a steady presence in our pages, 1971.

Earl McGrath, one of my closest friends. "I taught the Wenners how to be rich." Barbados, 1974.

Hunter S. Thompson with George McGovern on the presidential campaign. McGovern called him "The Sheriff," 1972.

Annie Leibovitz, who started at Rolling Stone *while still an art student in San Francisco, did more than 500 assignments for us, 1973.*

In my San Francisco office in typical form:
smoking, talking on the phone, feet on the desk, 1975.

Tom Wolfe on assignment
for The Right Stuff, *Cape Kennedy, 1972.*

Cameron Crowe, still a teenager, reporting for
RS *from the rock and roll road, 1970.*

Jon Landau and Jonathon Cott were on the masthead of Issue Number One, 1967.

Joe Eszterhas came from the Cleveland Plain Dealer *and David Felton from the* Los Angeles Times. Rolling Stone *offices, 1973.*

Ben Fong Torres was the music editor of Rolling Stone *from 1968 to 1977.*

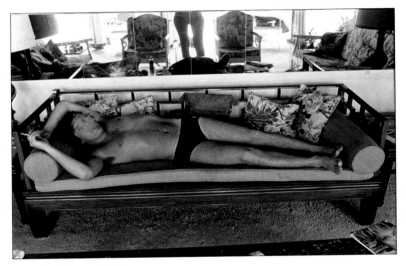

In my Speedo years, Barbados, 1975.

tenor I had with Hunter; we would get the country back on track. Hunter and I paid him a visit at a farmhouse in Maine he shared with Norman Mailer. At the time we were staying at Dick's home near the Harvard campus, where we made a cassette tape of ourselves screeching and howling, as if in the throes of death. When we arrived at the farm at 7:00 a.m. after a hairy overnight ride through the twisting back roads of New England, with our heads full of acid, we put the tape machine, turned to full volume, in the living room and tore out of there until nightfall. We wanted to properly welcome him to *Rolling Stone*.

Dick made his debut in our last issue of 1973, "The Obligation of the Congress to Impeach the President," a title that was meant to suggest the gravity and tone of *The Federalist Papers*. Dick was a dense thinker but had the eloquence one would expect from a presidential speech-writer. His piece was a manifesto, a bill of particulars and constitutional questions, a plainly worded, inescapable case for Congress to impeach Nixon.

CHAPTER 25

A WONDER
OF AMERICAN
JOURNALISM

THE GROUND BENEATH us had shifted. The *Columbia Journalism Review*, the voice of the American journalism establishment, sent a writer out to take a look at us and published an article titled "*Rolling Stone's* Quest for Respectability." I thought the headline was predictably sniffy though undeniably correct.

The piece opened with the tale of Dr. Hook, but quickly got to the premise. "In a very real sense, it has spoken for — and to — an entire generation of young Americans. It has given an honest — and searching — account of one of the deepest social revolutions of our times...*Rolling Stone* spawned a unique brand of long (up to 20,000 words) profiles and essays, splashy graphics and hard-hitting investigative pieces cutting across the underbelly and nerve endings of modern American life. *Rolling Stone* is one of the latter-day wonders of American journalism."

I believed that. I believed it in a way that was taking me over. I was twenty-seven years old. "His success has created an almost mystical worship on the part of some of the staff," the piece continued. "In his office, Wenner seems anything but the embodiment of a counterculture rock publisher. Indeed, in a dark blue suit, neat haircut, red-and-white checked shirt and gold wedding band, sipping Ballantine's scotch, he looks like a slightly mod salesman for Merrill Lynch. His office itself, with the color TV, oriental rug, books and posters could pass for any senior editor's office at *Time* or *Newsweek*. Except in the middle of an interview he finished off the scotch, opened his leather attaché case, took out a small paper bag, poured some white powder on his hand and started sniffing it."

Our editors were virtually all complicit in the use of cocaine. Only Ben abstained, though he had certainly spent enough time with Ike Turner. But editors didn't make enough money to get too deep into that nefarious drug. The complaint I remember is that I would arrive at the office in the late morning with an edit on a piece that was a little too aggressive. I was a skilled line editor, but often choices are purely taste, not obvious. And I didn't edit with a pencil: I used a red pen.

IT WAS TIME to bring more women into the magazine. Marianne Partridge, a twenty-five-year-old "social philosophy" major at Bard College, a gofer for the Southern California bureau of the *New York Times*, had never run a copy desk but said she could do it. She was one of those people who are born to be in charge of something. Marianne was told to hire whomever she wanted but before going outside she should consider our assistants who might qualify. Christine Doudna, who had been hired the summer before, was Joe Eszterhas' assistant. Before landing in San Francisco she had lived in Africa, teaching French at the University of Lagos in Nigeria. Twenty-two-year-old Harriet Fier, our assistant switchboard operator, was moved to editorial. She was a Phi Beta Kappa from Smith, and her father was the chairman of the economics department at Brooklyn College, but more important, she had been to Woodstock. Barbara Downey, a New Yorker who had been tripping out in Berkeley, was hired as a proofreader. Her employment test, given by our production director, Cindy Ehrlich, dressed in her nurse's uniform, was to find typos in *The Queens' Vernacular*, a dictionary of gay slang.

I quickly came to trust Marianne's judgment. She had a strategic view of what I was doing. She was not part of the drug crowd. I made her a senior editor in the fall of 1974, and she started attending the editorial ideas meetings, the first woman there other than Annie. Marianne's first assignment was by Ellen Willis on a rape case. It won awards.

The first cover of 1974 was a Robert Grossman cartoon of Nixon sticking his hand up the skirt of the Statue of Liberty. We hooked up with the children of E. Howard Hunt, the CIA agent who had led the Watergate break-in. One of the sons was a long-haired rock musician. Their mother had died a year earlier in a plane crash, their father was in prison, and three of the Hunt kids lived together in their childhood home, which was being sold. Smart kids, very much of our generation, who told the story of an absent, cold father in the spy business and their new life in the Watergate spotlight. It was perfect for us.

Before we published it, William F. Buckley Jr. invited me to lunch at the Four Seasons. He was godfather to the Hunt kids — barely knew them but was their legal guardian. He wanted me to kill the story. What stuck with me after the discussion about Nixon, politics, and Watergate that consumed lunch was what he said when I asked him point-blank: "Do you believe in the Constitution of the United States?" He looked directly at me and, in that irritating, aristocratic drawl, said, "I believe in America." I understood exactly what he meant, and it gave me chills. We didn't kill the piece. I received a letter canceling my scheduled appearance on his television show.

ON FEBRUARY 4, 1974, Patty Hearst was kidnapped from her home in Berkeley by self-styled radicals who called themselves the Symbionese Liberation Army. They were nine white kids led by a black ex-con named Donald DeFreeze, who titled himself Field Marshal Cinque. He had been in prison for robbing a prostitute. The parallels with the Manson family were very plain.

San Francisco was transformed by the kidnapping. We were a small town in many ways, and out of the blue found ourselves in the unblinking glare of the ravenous national press. The Symbionese Liberation Army had also murdered the black superintendent of the Oakland school system, using cyanide-packed hollow bullets. They were issuing long communiqués and demanded their manifestos be published word for word in the *San Francisco Examiner*, which the Hearst family owned. The negotiations were conducted in the press via open letters and daily press conferences with Patty's stoic father and histrionic mother. It was a total shit show.

There was no trace of Patty for two months, until she was seen on a security camera during a bank robbery carrying an automatic weapon. She announced to the press that her new name was Tania and that she had joined the Symbionese Liberation Army. No one wanted to say a bad word about the SLA; the Hearst paper and the other local media didn't want to upset the kidnappers and endanger Patty. Left-wing activists stayed silent out of their own impotence, ideological uncertainty, and the implicit threat of violence or death against them from the SLA.

I felt that *Rolling Stone* had no choice but to speak out. I was appalled by the kidnapping of a nineteen-year-old college girl and the murder of a public-school administrator. The SLA's manifestos were half-bright, self-serving attempts at the language and rationale of the repressed and the downtrodden. We ran an editorial about the timidity of the press, the pointless violence, and the underlying need to seriously deal with economic inequality. We denounced the SLA, their words, and their deeds.

In May I watched the live television news broadcast of the Los Angeles Police Department surrounding a tiny house in Compton where they had tracked an unknown number of SLA members. The LAPD used up 1,600 rounds of ammo, so much firepower that the house burned to the ground. Six SLA soldiers were cremated, including Field Marshal Cinque. Patty was not one of them; she had vanished into thin air.

CHAPTER 26

FROM ELKO TO EGYPT

UNTER HAD THE idea to have a summit of the best people we had met so far in politics, for the purpose of writing a manifesto and a strategic plan for the 1976 Democratic nominee for president. We thought it could galvanize our constituency and influence the choice of a candidate and the choices that candidate would make. For the meeting location Hunter chose Elko, a gold mining town in the Nevada desert, population 10,000, "the heart of northeastern Nevada." The downtown centered around the Commercial Hotel and Casino, which featured a ten-foot-high stuffed polar bear in the lobby. It was winter, freezing cold. The attendees could slip in and out of town without notice.

Hunter made the guest list and I paid the expenses. As always. The attendees were Dick Goodwin and his fiancé, the historian Doris Kearns; Pat Caddell, the McGovern pollster who ultimately went to work for Jimmy Carter; and the two best organizers in the McGovern campaign, Rick Stearns and Carl Wagner. There were two Kennedy principals: Bobby's speechwriter and deputy attorney general, Adam Walinsky, and Teddy's top consigliere, the aforementioned Dave Burke, a buttoned-up, tough, no-nonsense guy. Everyone assumed that Teddy was the likely 1976 nominee. The subtext of the meeting was the reconciliation of the McGovern and Kennedy camps.

When the group assembled Saturday morning, American flags were posted on either side of the door to the meeting room. Hunter had provided everyone with a clipboard and large spiral notebook (on which he had glued another American flag). He had also given everyone a two-and-a-half-foot wood baton, with a strap at one end and, at the business end, a thick ring of steel, called a "tire checker." It was used by truckers to check with a solid whack the inflation of tires on their eighteen-wheelers, and to deal with any stranger who threatened trouble. Hunter wanted everyone in the spirit of the occasion. It was a serious group. There were presentations about what Americans wanted and would vote for. Hunter tried to achieve a consensus, but this, no matter how high-minded the cause, was a bunch of political guns for hire. Nothing would matter till the new sheriff came to town.

We taped the whole thing. On every cassette, Hunter had written in a red Sharpie "ELKO/A76; Full Moon Conference." After Elko, he stayed at the House on California Street for a few days to discuss what to do with the tapes and the energy of the meeting. We taped our own meeting, too. Those cassettes were labeled "Half Moon Conference." Someone had to listen to them all and draft an Elko Manifesto. Dick was the obvious choice but declined. Neither Hunter nor I had the discipline or commitment. It was a high-level study group but didn't influence the course of the nation. My education was continuing to be a costly one. The tapes went to storage.

DICK GOODWIN SET up our new offices in a building on Pennsylvania Avenue, across the street from the White House. We shared it with a tenant who turned out to be a CIA front. Dick hadn't found a permanent place to live, so Ethel Kennedy loaned him Hickory Hill, the Virginia estate where she had lived with her and Bobby's eleven children. Dick invited me to spend the weekend.

I was reading in bed Saturday night when John F. Kennedy Jr., thirteen years old, walked in and then ran to get his sister, Caroline, sixteen.

To have President Kennedy's kids sitting on either side of my bed was quite a surprise. These were children from a television fairy tale. They were rock and roll fans and kept me up late. They were funny, good kids.

Riding the Kennedy family high, Dick was puffing me up about going to see "my" Washington office. Dick could say the most serious stuff with a twinkle, like he was getting a good quiet laugh out of some deeply evil shit. If you smiled back, then you were part of his conspiracy. He had a good measure of President Kennedy magic dust yet to sprinkle on me. On the way to the office, we stopped at the Lincoln Memorial. I had never been there, and he said he wanted me to read what he considered the greatest political speech ever written, now engraved on the granite walls. With that in mind, and the grandest sense of purpose, I worked my first day in Washington.

Dick had written three brilliant essays for us already; his style was elegant, and it was academic, and it suited the lessons of an American political history he was trying to explain. It didn't resonate easily with our readers. Many of the editors thought of Dick as "Wenner's Folly." He began editing a new section of the magazine called Politics. In the first Politics section, Tim Crouse reported on his visit to George Wallace, who had been paralyzed two years earlier in an assassination attempt. Dick brought in Joe Klein, Bob Shrum, Pat Caddell, Daniel Yergin, and Bill Greider, the *Washington Post* assistant managing editor, whose piece on Nelson Rockefeller was illustrated by *Washington Post* cartoonist Pat Oliphant, who showed the new vice president butt-fucking Uncle Sam. That nearly got them both fired by the *Post*. We had a political "Random Notes" called "Capitol Chatter."

He brought us Jan Morris, who had previously been James Morris, the *London Times* correspondent who had accompanied Sir Edmund Hillary and Tenzing Norgay on the first expedition to summit Mount Everest. Dick brought Jan into the fold to write a sophisticated travel piece about Washington, D.C., which turned into a two-year series of visits to the great cities of the world, now considered her best work.*

---

* *Destinations*, Rolling Stone Press, 1980.

Dick rented a house in Georgetown. He decided to host a *Rolling Stone* Foreign Affairs dinner. About the time the catering bill arrived, an unpleasantly expensive surprise, I got a call from Ethel Kennedy asking me to get her bedsheets and pillowcases back from Dick. He was ignoring her calls. Dick introduced me to Anne Wexler, then in her midforties, formidable, a fast-rising Democratic political operative. She had started in politics in college, ringing doorbells for Harry Truman, and had worked for Eugene McCarthy, Muskie, and McGovern. She was warm, nurturing, and no-nonsense. She took over our D.C. office, in charge of public and political relations. I wanted Washington to read *Rolling Stone*, every office on the Hill and every wing in the White House. That was Anne's responsibility. She became family, another adult in the house.

HOWARD KOHN, BEFORE his fall from grace, had been the star reporter for the *Detroit Free Press*. He was raised on his father's small farm outside Bay City, Michigan. Until he was eighteen, the family had neither telephone nor television. At the University of Michigan, he graduated with honors in history and journalism. He had been investigating heroin trafficking in Detroit, a business that, surprisingly, the *Free Press* generally ignored. He had already identified twelve corrupt cops in his exposé and was preparing to name some of the highest officials in the police department who were also involved — until a man kidnapped him, trying to get Howard to identify his sources. Howard was carrying a gun, there was a struggle over it, it went off, and the kidnapper escaped. Because Howard had not told his editors he had been armed, he was fired. All the cops he named in his original article were convicted, and he won the Detroit Press Club award for reporting. His final story, exposing the top officials, was never printed.

Howard moved to San Francisco, hoping to write for *Rolling Stone*. Both he and David Felton had seen the same wire-service story about a nuclear worker in Oklahoma, Karen Silkwood, killed when her Honda inexplicably ran off the highway into a wall. She was en route to a rendezvous with activists in her union, carrying documents that she had taken from her job at a plutonium manufacturing factory.

We published "Malignant Giant" in March 1975. It seemed obvious that the Kerr-McGee nuclear power company had been spying on Silkwood and following her. There was smoke, but no smoking gun. I sent him back to Oklahoma for more reporting, where he gathered more circumstantial evidence about a possible attempt to poison Silkwood with a radioactive toxin. Howard returned again and again and finally found two management employees who confirmed our story. I put up $10,000 to finance the Silkwood family's lawsuit and printed an appeal in the magazine that offered to match all readers' contributions. The wheels of justice began to turn. One of the best criminal lawyers in the West was engaged. After eleven weeks of testimony in a federal courtroom, the longest trial in Oklahoma history, a jury found Kerr-McGee guilty of contaminating Silkwood's apartment with plutonium and awarded the family $10.5 million.

WILLIE HEARST, PATTY's cousin, and I had become good friends, and being with him and his wife, Nan, another married couple our age, was an oasis of normalcy for Jane and me. He had looked me up to ask if I would write op-ed pieces for the *San Francisco Examiner*, his grandfather's journalistic debut. One Thanksgiving we stayed with Willie and his parents in the Hearst Castle itself. They put us in the "B" cottage — canopied beds, silk-lined walls, marble tubs and sinks, braided cords that rang bells to summon the staff. Willie's dad took us on a moonlit nighttime tour of the castle, told us about the old man, "WR," and his memories of growing up there. Willie's mother, Bootsie, took us swimming in the afternoons in the Neptune Pool, the one with the Greek columns and statues.

SAIGON WAS ABOUT to fall. I wanted Hunter to go; we would never see a story like that again. Getting him there was easy — credentials, travel, a suite at the Continental hotel. Apparently, those were not in great demand anymore. There was all the usual Hunter stuff about typewriters, assistants, and other needs (we assumed his drug requirements would be easily satisfied in Saigon). There was the usual haggling about his expenses and payments. He put more time and thought into his money than anyone I worked with. At first, I thought it was just a game he found amusing. As it went on, it got obsessive and sad. He was generally in debt to a few friends in Aspen, always on the brink with credit card companies, had a big drug nut...but the meager circumstances of his childhood stalked him.

I suggested he take out some life insurance. He brushed it off, but I went ahead and got the insurance and made his wife and son the beneficiaries. It was expensive. After he got back, he started telling people and his college-lecture audiences that I had canceled his health insurance while he was in "the middle of a goddamn war zone." It got a good laugh but the story was patently false. I shrugged it off at first, but as he kept spreading it, I realized that people believed him. I told him to stop or I'd start telling the true story. He stopped, but that allegation lingered.

Hunter got into Saigon at a time when he could hear the roar of the artillery guns getting closer to the city. After checking in with correspondents he knew he became obsessed with the logistics of his own evacuation plan, what the American embassy's emergency code words were, and whether he ought to rent a car and driver to seek out the North Vietnamese commanders. I told him I had no way of making these decisions from San Francisco, that the exit strategy was up to him. Paul Scanlon had a friend, Laura Palmer, who worked for the Associated Press and had written stories for us from Saigon, and she and Paul began working with Hunter to file something on deadline. He did a dispatch that was strong and promising, but nothing substantial — what Paul described as "Hunter warming up." He spent most of his time on the phone talking to Paul about story fees.

Hunter got on a commercial flight to Bangkok before Saigon finally fell. Sandy flew to meet him, and he spent a few weeks there on totally undeserved rest and recreation. He had clothes custom made, and ordered a brass door plaque that read "*Rolling Stone*: Global Affairs Suite. Dr. Hunter S. Thompson." Behind those words was a map of the world and two lightning bolts. That was it. No story. Just that plaque.

ANNIE AND I went to Oregon to visit Ken Kesey at his farm. When he picked us up at the Eugene airport, Kesey saw Annie but pretended he didn't recognize me. When Annie introduced me, he acted confused. He said he thought I was tall and blond, like the Marvel Comics version of Jann Wenner, whom he had seen in *Daredevil 100*, when Daredevil dropped into *Rolling Stone* for a visit. Furthur, the magic bus, still decorated but fading, was parked near the barns. His wife, Faye, put out home cooking, we smoked good pot and spent the night. The next day Kesey had some work to do with his cows, including a few calves, which he roped up and had me cut off their balls. Another first. Kesey and I were on our way to interview the eccentric progressive governor of Oregon.

I asked Ken if he would go to Egypt and write about the mystery of the pyramids, do something we could call a *Rolling Stone* Expedition. He would need a guide familiar with the land and the language. Charlie Perry was not only familiar with many forms of drug use but also spoke fluent Arabic, and I would have a minder from the home office. Kesey and Hunter were old friends and kindred spirits, and I didn't need to find myself being followed by robe-wearing bill collectors from Cairo once this was all over.

When they got back to San Francisco, Charlie declined to put his two cents in on Kesey's manuscript, which we ran as a three-episode mini-saga. Kesey had told Charlie it was more important for a writer to find his personal myth than to relate facts. "Most of the things he has to say about me," Charlie wrote to me, "are, let's say, literature." Kesey was happy and wrote to him: "What does it all mean, Charlie? Probably nothing. But if I were Jann, I'd send out another probe, just to be on the safe side. He's got to keep his finger on the dark vein of the World Beyond, whether he detects any pulse or not. We could beat them to it, Charlie. You choose the wine. I'll chart the channel. Hunter has already volunteered his pineal gland, no strings attached...At the ready, Keez."

CHAPTER 27

FAREWELL
TO RALPH J. GLEASON

PAUL WAS WAITING for me at the offices, looking inexplicably solemn. Ralph had just had a heart attack. It was June 3, 1975. Paul walked me into my office, and I sat on my couch and cried. I phoned Ralph's wife, Jean, who was on her way to the hospital, and asked her to tell Ralph that I loved him.

Ralph was diabetic. I didn't know that meant he had been in a long battle with deteriorating organs, narrowing blood vessels, and failing eyesight; that the daily shots of insulin he gave himself were with painful steel needles; that walking had become difficult; and that what was a battle had become a massacre.

When I was at Berkeley, untethered from college by politics, music, and drugs, Ralph gave me a family and an education. After coming back from London, I had no notion of what to do until he offered me the job that set the stage for the rest of my life. I could never have done *Rolling Stone* without him. Before I first met him, I had read his wisdom about the protests in Berkeley: "The ultimate tragedy is that the older generation will never see how wrong it is, how deeply it has misjudged these youngsters, how sadly it has maligned them and how deviously it has taken refuge in rhetoric and legalities, when the youth have been speaking in plain moral terms. Literature, poetry, and history are not made by a smooth jowl and a blue suit. They are made with sweat and passion and dedication to truth and honor."

Everyone in the office had heard the news and they were keeping a discreet eye on me; Ben had left the office to pick up Cameron Crowe, a promising young music writer he had been using, who had flown in to meet me. "It's not a good day for Jann," Ben told him, but added that I wanted to meet him anyway. Cameron wrote later that he walked in and "there was Jann, looking unlike any photo I had ever seen of him. On that day, he was the oldest-looking young man I had ever seen, a solitary presence at his round wooden table, with a three-quarter-full bottle of vodka sitting in front of him. It was early afternoon."

I remember the office being dark, faraway shuffling sounds, the thick oriental rug, as if the room were being prepared for a séance. Cameron was the youngest-looking young man I think I'd ever seen, hair flopped over both sides of a long face, like a teenage Oscar Wilde. He was nervous and his respectfulness was evident. Cameron was getting noticed in the office for his ability to penetrate the inner circle of a rock and roll band and deliver an intimate story. His reporting and writing were shaping up quickly with Ben's guidance. I thought I should put a hand against his back and give him a little push. I told him I liked his reporting but that he had written "the story the band wanted written, not the story you saw and wanted to write. What did that piece mean to you as a real writer?" I gave him my copy of Joan Didion's *Slouching Towards Bethlehem*. The best writing takes a stand. "Did you take a stand?" It was as if I was channeling Ralph.

Ralph died. He was fifty-eight. It was my first experience losing someone so close. We began work on a tribute issue that was scheduled to have Mick and Keith on the cover, a somber black-and-white portrait by Annie, unlike any cover we had done. Paul and I split up the duties of the issue and brought in Ralph's eighteen-year-old son, Toby, to be part of our labor of love.

It started with Lucille Armstrong, Louis' widow, and Mercer

Ellington, Duke's son. Dizzy Gillespie wrote, "I have been knowing him about thirty years and he hasn't deviated one centimeter from what he sees as the truth — in music, in politics, or any other field of human endeavor." There was a letter from Lenny Bruce. Frank Sinatra called him a "rare and gifted friend." Miles Davis wrote one line: "Give me my friend back." Jerry Garcia, Paul Simon, Robbie Robertson, and John Lennon all paid tribute, too. He had helped them all.

Ralph's closest friend, Mary Ann Pollar, a folk music promoter and activist who was Odetta's best friend, wrote, "He spoke for black people for so many years in places we were not allowed to speak for ourselves and he told the truth. His ability to hear and feel what was happening with black music was a wonder. I understood why he was able to do it. It was his respect. That's why Ralph could communicate with me in a black way...He knew *what* he knew, he knew what he didn't know but could sense and he let you know that. A lot of people know about jazz and black music, but who will serve that music? He served that which he loved. And that is what made him such a great teacher. There is an old spiritual that says, 'Low, low is the way to that bright shore.' To bow low and to serve it, is what opens those gates — and I don't know of anyone else today who stands at the top as Ralph did and bows low."

Ralph was a crusader for justice, and nourished its champions, especially writers and musicians. He saw that struggle in the lives and work of jazz musicians, folk music singers, and rock and roll bands. He saw it in comedians and he saw it in poets. He loved to see the mighty fall. He laughed at folly. One of the greatest thrills of Ralph's life was when the news came out that Nixon had been keeping a secret "White House enemies" list and he was on it. Ralph felt he had been honored for a lifetime of work.

I wrote a sentimental goodbye for the issue. I quoted the last paragraph of his last column, about journalist and activist I. F. Stone — the last thing he wrote for *Rolling Stone*, and as far as I know, the last words Ralph ever wrote: "Stone is the journalist as incorruptible man, honesty personified and as such brings to life an American myth: that the honest journalist is a saint who can save us all by his integrity and his dedication to truth. He is the reporter as poet, Knight of the Holy Grail of Truth. He cares passionately about humanity and about truth, he doesn't expect people to be perfect or truth to be absolute, but he does care. He is a testament to the possibilities left in man, and we need the inspiration he can give us these grim days."

CHAPTER 28

BECOMING BICOASTAL

S OMETIMES AFTER AN issue was back from the printer, I would find a hidden message in it. Different articles would have commonality, a synchronicity that would reveal itself to me. Often it was a mood that was talking, like the person on the cover was trying to tell me something, telling me to figure something out.

The Ralph Gleason issue was like that. I had just met Richard Avedon, and asked Annie to shoot Mick and Keith in his style, black-and-white on a seamless backdrop with no detail, standing alone. We hadn't done Mick and Keith together for the cover in years. It worked: the simplicity and the formality matched the gravity of our treatment of Ralph's life. The man I had respected most was there together with my favorite band, the band that set the template for the modern rock group. The quality of our execution had jumped all of a sudden. Maybe that was the message, just how good it could get if you went all in.

I WAS SPENDING more time in New York; the magazine business was there, as were many of the writers I wanted to work with. New York was more fun than San Francisco. There were places to go; there were parties, small ones, medium ones, and big ones. Earl McGrath convinced

Jane and me that we should sublet the apartment next to his on the East Side, a small place, and it drew us even closer to Earl and Camilla, who were now central to our lives on both coasts. Without my realizing it, Earl had created a circle of friends for Jane and me and a new home in New York.

I was getting to know Ahmet Ertegun, the founder of Atlantic Records, through Earl. He spoke a hip black patois in a deep raspy voice. His eyes were hooded behind green-tinted glasses and he was dressed in coat-and-tie perfection at all times. I didn't know what to make of him, other than he was Earl's great friend and had the imprimatur of Ralph Gleason — two wildly different men. I felt that Ahmet would be in my life for a long time. He rang me in San Francisco just as we were getting acquainted and asked to meet for lunch the next day at Enrico's. He was sitting with a stunning young brunette, whom he introduced as Charlie Chaplin's daughter Geraldine, who spoke only French. For at least half an hour he dragged me through a conversation with her, which he would translate into French. I was about to faint from nervous-boredom disorder.

Finally, with unstoppable laughter, like out of a children's cartoon, he said she wasn't Geraldine Chaplin after all, but some random girl of the day, and I had been played by this hoax, trying to pretend I was some sophisticated cineaste and so forth. It never seemed that funny to me, but Ahmet loved it, thought it was a great prank, and told the story in front of me fifty times or more over the years, bringing himself close to tears each time. I learned to love it and laughed every time.

DICK GOODWIN INTRODUCED me to his ex-girlfriend Mary Gimbel, who was looking to sublet her duplex. Her nickname was Piedi. Born Mary Bailey, she was a Greenwich, Connecticut, socialite who had two children by Peter Gimbel, an heir to the department store family. The old Irish doorman told us about the times President Kennedy had come over late at night. The apartment was on East Sixty-Sixth Street, across from

St. Vincent Ferrer, a Catholic church and priory, where you could see nuns walking about at night. It had a two-story living room, a balcony on the second floor overlooking the great room dominated by a two-story, stained-glass window, and floor-to-ceiling bookshelves with a ladder that moved on wheels. We rented the apartment furnished. It had been done by society decorator Billy Baldwin, with lots of upholstery, patterns, little footstools, and pink-and-blue floral wallpaper. Six months later we bought it. Piedi and her children became great friends of ours and our extended family.

I became acquainted with Lally Weymouth, the daughter of Kay Graham, publisher of the *Washington Post*. She was ambitious, part of the political court of her mother. I was on her list, which meant private lunches at the Four Seasons, dinners at her apartment with Kay and Clay Felker, and a whirlwind of parties. One particular party was at the peak of Lally's reign as the high hostess of New York media society. I was taken aback by the luminosity of it. Gore Vidal and Norman Mailer got into a fistfight. I ended up in a conversation with Kirk Douglas, who, learning that I was from San Francisco, wrote down the number of his son Michael. He was living there, filming his TV show, *The Streets of San Francisco*, and needed friends. Kirk asked me to look him up and I said I would.

DICK GOODWIN HAD run out his time for *Rolling Stone* in Washington, D.C., and wanted to move back to Cambridge with his new wife, Doris Kearns. He had done an impressive job editing the Politics section, but I decided not to evolve the section into a national magazine for Dick to edit. As I had been warned, Dick was indeed an "unmade bed," and he left me with quite a few unpaid bills, kill fees, and other surprises, like Ethel Kennedy's missing sheets.

The office manager in Washington wrote me, "Per your request, I have asked Dick Goodwin for the tape recorder. At first, he said he had no recorder. Later in the conversation he said to tell you that the tape recorder had been destroyed in the line of duty. He said to tell you it had fallen into the tidal basin when he went to interview the Lincoln Memorial." I was furious and was beginning to whip myself up into a lawsuit, over bedsheets, a tape recorder, and unpaid restaurant tabs. Instead, I decided to take my payment in good karma.

ROLLING STONE IN the early seventies had become home to Tom Hayden, the author of the Port Huron Statement, the founding manifesto of the Students for a Democratic Society (SDS). He had grown up in Michigan, the son of an alcoholic ex-Marine who attended the church of the anti-Semitic radio priest Father Coughlin. Tom went to the University of Michigan, where he edited the student newspaper. By the time he got to *Rolling Stone* he had spent four years as a community organizer in Newark, New Jersey; been put on trial as part of the Chicago Seven; and made fact-finding trips to North Vietnam. He had also married Jane Fonda. He wrote a number of articles, including the first major profile and interviews of our new governor, Jerry Brown. Tom wanted to run for United States Senate against the popular but lightweight John Tunney, son of former heavyweight boxing champ Gene Tunney. John was known in the Senate for his work as Teddy Kennedy's best friend.

Tom was shrewd, a born fighter. He had star power and brain power. I believed in the possibility of his election. My involvement in his campaign was supposed to be part-time. I would produce the campaign literature and media out of *Rolling Stone*. The official announcement day arrived, four cities by air in one day. It started in Sacramento, then San Francisco, where I introduced Tom at his press conference. Los Angeles was next; I flew down with him and then went to San Diego. In the end, Tom lost the primary, but not by much. It was a foreshadowing of what Tom had said in one of his speeches: "The radicalism of the 1960s is becoming the common sense of the 1970s."

JANE AND I spent the Fourth of July with Willie and Nan Hearst at San Simeon. It had been seventeen months since Patty had been kidnapped, and she was still nowhere to be found. We were no longer on knife's edge all the time. Willie and I drove down after work very late on Friday. We had stopped in Chinatown and found someone selling illegal fireworks and arrived after midnight at the bunkhouse, where a bunch of the Hearst family and guests were already asleep. Willie and I set off the fireworks. Within a minute we were surrounded by men with their weapons out. They thought we were mounting an attack. Other than that, there were horseback rides, picnics, and swimming holes, another all-American family weekend with fireworks.

NEIL YOUNG WAS on the August cover, in a painting that echoed childhood cowboy mythology, his hair spread out in tendrils from under a wide-brimmed hat. It was my favorite cover and favorite drawing of him, except for the full-page portrait inside by Joni Mitchell, done with the bold strokes of colored marker pens, which had a boyish beauty to it. Cameron did the interview.

DOONESBURY BY GARRY TRUDEAU had become the hip strip. The whole thing seemed square to me, but it was a messenger from one generation to another. I liked Garry, a Yale graduate who was in a frat and took divinity courses. Wholesale and without permission, he took Hunter's alter ego, Raoul Duke, and put him in his strip, and it became one of his most popular ongoing characters.

I told Hunter he could and should stop "Uncle Duke," that it was his literary property, his soul, his livelihood. But Hunter did nothing. He was flattered to be the main character in the renowned comic strip, and I think he feared a popular backlash if he sued. I never said anything to Garry about it, other than to make a few casual digs, and when he asked about doing a *Rolling Stone* cover of Uncle Duke, who in the strip had become the U.S.

ambassador to Samoa, I went along with it. It was the dumbing down of a wonderful creation, what I knew was a literary classic, and a reduction of Hunter himself to the most one-dimensional level. The cartoon Duke overwhelmed the "real" Duke—the real Duke never returned—just as the cartoon of Hunter overtook the real thing and slowly drained his power and life. Garry became a friend and ally, and we did more covers, including another *Doonesbury* cover as a promotion for one of his new characters—Jimmy Thudpucker, a would-be rock star—but Uncle Duke had killed Raoul Duke, our sports editor. Or maybe it had been a mutually assisted suicide.

MICHAEL DOUGLAS AND I first met at his high-rise apartment on Russian Hill, where he was living while doing *The Streets of San Francisco*. We started talking, like lost friends, about growing up, girls, people we knew. He had gone to boarding school like me and had been a pothead hippie at the University of California at Santa Barbara. He was a gas station attendant one summer and had even won the attendant of the month award.

The local establishment had snubbed Michael for being part of an "exploitative" television show and, even worse, for being from Los Angeles. The few friends he had were the cops whom the show celebrated (there were no dirty cops on television in the seventies). The detectives who worked as advisors and extras would usually give him the illicit fruits from some of their busts. We began to hang out, and if his shooting location was near the *Rolling Stone* office, Michael would pop up for a visit, often with a present from the police.

MICK HAD HIRED Annie as the Stones' tour photographer. I didn't like the idea. Annie's style was to move in with her subjects. I didn't want to lose her for that long and was worried about her picking up their contagious habits. I gave her the talk I was obliged to give, which she politely heard out. I knew she was going no matter what I said, and also that I would get photography no one else would have of the greatest band in the world.

That tour was the band's first with an elaborate set. I went to one of the L.A. shows. The houselights would go dark, and the stage, a giant lotus flower with its petals closed, began to come to life, first the lights from inside, then the sounds of instruments tuning up like an orchestra. A translucent curtain hanging over the top of the closed set pulled up and away, and five giant lotus petals unfolded outward to reveal a stage in the shape of a star, surrounded by hanging lights, a set as if you were in old Shanghai. Hanging on to the tip of the front petal as it descended was Mick singing "Honky Tonk Women."

"It was the best show of the tour," I wrote, "no two ways about it. Mick is the Queen of the Hop, cold and calculating. Keith's guitar is the key to the Stones sound. The band's deep strength is the rhythm section, and Keith runs it; he is the musical heart of the band." My last thoughts written on that night were "It is time to remove the curse of Altamont from the Stones and from ourselves. When they played 'Sympathy for the Devil,' it had a Mardi Gras feel. We have seen the best Stones in 1975, ever."

LED ZEPPELIN HATED *Rolling Stone*, and me in particular. Jimmy Page blamed me for the dismissive review of their first album and for supposedly stealing his girlfriend — "an incident with a woman in England" was how he described it — so when we asked for an interview, they said no with animosity. Cameron Crowe had an assignment to cover the Zeppelin tour for the *Los Angeles Times*; we told him if he could get the interviews, he would have the cover story. He got the interviews with everyone except Page. The group still had not made up their minds about a *Rolling Stone* cover and debated it for a few weeks. Finally Page agreed, cursed me, and told Cameron he was doing it for him. Page showed up at the photo shoot with a bouquet of dead roses.

IN THE FALL of 1975 Cameron again came to the rescue. The Eagles had three top-ten singles in a row and were a must-have cover. The idea that an artist would turn us down was not something I could accept. The Eagles were also pissed off about an early record review, thought they had been slighted as a lightweight California band and were not being lionized like the groups that the East Coast "critical elite" were championing. Glenn Frey was always competitive, and Don Henley had an easy-to-scratch bitter streak, so "Fuck *Rolling Stone*" was their instinctive impulse. Nonetheless they also felt they deserved the stature of the cover, that their legacy demanded it. Cameron had just turned eighteen. Glenn and Don had Cameron move in with them for a week to watch them work every night. They wrote "Lyin' Eyes" in front of him. He was their go-between with the magazine, and Glenn told him to just make sure they would look "cool." They hated being called mellow; their goal was to be the biggest band in the world. The story was all everyone wanted, including us. The "feud" was over.

JON LANDAU OFFICIALLY resigned to produce and manage Bruce Springsteen. He invited Jane and me to the debut of *Born to Run* at the Bottom Line in New York. Bruce was playing his guitar from the tabletops and seemed to be having the best time of his life. Then we went to his show in Los Angeles in October, and I came away thinking it was nearly as good as the Stones performance and decided I had to write the story myself. And then Bruce played the refurbished Paramount in Oakland — I remember how loud the crowd was, and turned around to look at the balcony, shaking with the thunderous dancing, and thought about the headlines if it collapsed. Must have been the pot again.

ONE MORNING ON deadline at 1:00 a.m., Annie dropped by with Mick in tow, giving him a tour of *Rolling Stone*. He had been in court in Oakland on some lingering Altamont case and had been accused of deliberately avoiding making an appearance. He said he had used my name in court, explaining that he hadn't been evasive — all the court had to do was call me, since I knew where he was all the time. Out came the blow, and we had a long visit. On another break from the tour, Annie came by and dropped three large rocks of coke on my desk, "a gift from Keith for you."

WE RAN INTO trouble with advertisers — not for the first or last time — after we ran a preview of the new venture from former activist Eldridge Cleaver: "the Cleavers," men's pants with a form-fitting extension sewn onto the front, an exterior pocket for the penis. Eldridge was happy to be the model. Because of the Cleavers, Sears refused to pay for its advertising in that issue, demanding that we cancel its upcoming ads and never mention their name again. I had never thought twice about this kind of thing, but I really learned my lesson when we published some quite unnecessary short story in which a nun gives someone a blow job. That was brought to the attention of the person who was not only the head of the Ford Motors Dealership Association but also chairman of the Bishop's Auxiliary Council for the Archdiocese of Greater Chicago. He sent it to Ford, and all their advertising was canceled. This caused me to reject a story Stephen King sent to us, about a hotel maid who got pregnant licking semen from the sheets of a wealthy guest.

Since Ford had been advertising with us for a year or so, we were able to get an appointment at their headquarters in Detroit. I went with our advertising manager in charge of car ads. After being ushered in, we were told that they did not advertise in magazines like *Hustler, Rolling Stone,* and "others of that ilk." I gave it my most ingratiating best, but groveling wasn't getting me anywhere. So, my ad sales guy starts talking about patriotism and American values, and I begin wondering if this isn't skating where the ice gets too thin. Then he jumps out of his chair and starts talking about being in Vietnam and how he read *Rolling Stone* when he served as a Marine and how proud he was to be an American. Then he turns to me and unbuttons his shirt to his belt, revealing two long, ugly battle scars, and wordlessly turns back to face the Ford executive. He then buttons up, we wrap up the meeting politely, and leave. It was the best ad sales call I was ever on. It worked.

HUNTER WAS NEGOTIATING a book and a reporting contract with me to cover the 1976 presidential campaign when I closed our book company. The issue wasn't money — he would get an outstanding book deal from any publisher — the real issue was whether he had the discipline to spend so much time on the campaign trail and whether he had that much to say about the subject again. Could he possibly meet expectations? Mine? His readers'? His own?

I wrote to him: "This is not up to me now. I've given you the room, the opening, the encouragement, the money, the freedom, the *Rolling Stone* charter, the commitment to space and to your direction of it. Take it and run it; it is your move... We have been doing this together for four or more years now, and I still can't put it on paper." I didn't know at the time that Hunter was in trouble and didn't want to admit it.

CHAPTER 29

✍

THE SCOOP
OF THE SEVENTIES

HOWARD KOHN CAME into my office with his ex-brother-in-law, David Weir, a long-haired guy with wire-rim glasses and a Fu Manchu mustache. They shut the door, sat at my desk, and told me they had met with someone who had just spent several months hiding Patty Hearst. They had come from the offices of Michael Kennedy, a radical-left lawyer who made his money as a defense attorney in big drug cases. I knew Michael and knew he was legit. They had met Jack Scott, a basketball coach from Oregon, who had been radicalized by Vietnam and become an advocate for exploited black athletes. Right after the Los Angeles shoot-out, Patty Hearst and two other survivors showed up at his apartment in Berkeley, desperate. Scott and his wife agreed to drive them across the country and hide them in a farmhouse in rural Pennsylvania. Scott was ready to tell the story.

I met with all parties to agree on the legal and moral parameters of what we were embarking on. I was going to live in two worlds new to me, where no mistakes were allowed and any fuckup would be a disaster. We were in possession of evidence about the location of federal fugitives wanted for murder. We were also sitting on what would be the biggest news story in the world and had to hold on to the information and the reporting of it with extraordinary secrecy. I didn't know whether the

FBI might find out and come after us. The first thing I told the "boys," which is what I called Howard and David, my very own Woodward and Bernstein, was that only the three of us would know about what we had until we decided otherwise.

Patty, now calling herself Tania, had told Scott about her kidnapping, captivity, and conversion. He had offered her the chance to go back to her family and she had angrily refused. He hid Patty and the other couple, and kept them in money and food throughout the summer. After months of recovery and simple living, the tensions among the group over their revolutionary dogma caused them to split up, and in the fall, Scott drove Patty back west, dropping her off in Las Vegas. She had been missing for a year and a half. He never saw her again. We got as much as we could out of Scott. We talked with people who could confirm his story, visited the farm, and kept him under wraps. We sat on the story for most of the summer, waiting for the missing pieces, another source, something we might have missed.

It finally seemed foolish to try to keep this secret any longer, so I set an absolute date when we would go to press. I had to start widening the circle of secrecy to bring this off, first bringing in Paul Scanlon. I was sure he would say nothing, and his inclusion was a great relief. The wheels started to turn; Sarah Lazin, as head of research, was "read in." She was going to have to fact-check and verify a story with one source. She lived with Paul, so that was a plus. As we got closer, we had to bring in our art director, designers, typesetters, proofreaders, our press people — each at the last possible minute and in a compartmentalized way so that they wouldn't talk about it with each other, if that was possible in such an intimately staffed office. Howard and David slept in my office for the deadline.

I flew overnight to New York to arrange for the public release of the story; Paul called everyone together in San Francisco to ask them to hold the line, which they did. We hired guards at our printing plant in St. Louis so no copies would leak as they came off the presses and were put on trucks in sealed boxes.

NBC News agreed to break the story first thing Monday morning with a half-hour *Today* show opening segment. They showed up in San Francisco over the weekend to film Howard and David in my office, with a six-foot blowup of the cover behind them. We sent out notice of a press conference at our offices on Monday morning.

A few months earlier I had decided to take the entire San Francisco staff away that very weekend for an overnight gathering in Big Sur, a party, a thank-you, and a morale builder in the *Rolling Stone* tradition. By sheer luck, it would also keep everyone incommunicado and out of town for the weekend, as it became, thanks to sheer numbers, harder to keep the story secret.

Then, as if out of nowhere, Patty was arrested by the FBI in an SLA safe house in San Francisco on the Thursday before our Big Sur weekend and Monday publication. She had been missing for nineteen months. She was photographed with her hands cuffed and raised in defiance. She refused to say a word. By the next day, correspondents and cameras from the four corners of the earth were in San Francisco. But beyond the details of the capture, they had nothing to report. She wouldn't say a word. They had *nada* until Monday, when we released the exclusive account of Patty's secret year on the run. It was titled "The Inside Story."

All three networks opened their evening news with the cover of *Rolling Stone*. We broke open the champagne in my office. Front-page banner headlines about our scoop ran in every newspaper in the United States, and most of the world. It continued like that for five days and nights running. I wasn't at the press conference on Monday. The personal publicity didn't mean that much to me, and it was someone else's turn. Jane and I stayed in Big Sur on Sunday night and got a good sleep and a quiet day in the sun before driving back.

It had been a raucous, late-night Saturday in Big Sur. Howard and David had made it down in the afternoon, brandishing a copy of the new issue that no one had seen yet. I gave a garrulous talk to the staff assembled in the pool, thanking them, praising them, bursting with pride and joy. I was carrying on about marching on the Hearst Castle, a scant hundred miles down the coast. Ventana, the resort we had rented, had interconnecting spas and a large Jacuzzi pool between the men's and women's sides. Behavior there was quite respectable, though I was taken a little by surprise to be sitting with my new secretary, who was topless. When Jane and I checked out, the manager thanked us — Ventana had just opened, and we had taken over the entire place — and complimented me on how well-behaved the *Rolling Stone* staff had been. But one thing puzzled him: Why, in so many rooms, had the mirrors been taken off the walls and laid flat on the coffee tables?

Even as the tsunami passed, we had to get to work delivering part two of "The Inside Story," which we had already promised our readers. We had a lot of reporting done, but the arrest required a lot more. The smart thing was to announce we were putting the second part off by one issue. That story had to do with Patty's return to California, her involvement in a bank robbery and the killing of a bystander, her capture by the FBI, and the months of secret negotiations with Patty's father. We had a lot of sources, including her boyfriend during her last months in hiding. It was a complex story, one I found more interesting and more ambitious.

Other than Watergate, it was the scoop of the seventies.

HUNTER WAS NOT going on the road to cover the 1976 elections. Most of the national press were copying what they had learned from him, the new paradigm. I wrote to Richard Avedon, suggesting that he cover the campaign for us by producing portraits of the candidates. He invited me up for lunch to his apartment above his photo studio on the Upper East Side. Dick had a well-combed mop of salt-and-pepper hair, and was a handsome man, petite. We knew enough people in common that we could gossip easily. He was beyond charming, and I liked him enormously.

Dick was legend in the magazine world and acknowledged one of the masters of modern photography. He knew all about *Rolling Stone*, which surprised and pleased me, that someone of his intellectual and aesthetic caliber appreciated our quirky and passionate efforts. Working for *Rolling Stone* for a year appealed to him in somewhat the same way it had to Tom Wolfe; as an enormous canvas, freedom, and a shared fascination with America. And we were a pretty hip place to be published.

Dick proposed a variation on my idea. He thought we should commission him to do portraits of the broadly defined American establishment, not just presidential candidates but union leaders, businessmen, and generals as well. He wanted to have an entire issue and total control, not just choice of photos but of subjects, copy, and the cover. These were nonnegotiable requirements. I said yes. No guts, no glory. It would be another watershed for us. *Rolling Stone* would decide who was the Establishment in our country. An entire issue of photography by Richard Avedon. We began work in January and called it "The Family."

PART THREE

THE EMPIRE

CHAPTER 30

THE BIG APPLE

RALPH GLEASON, OUR historical and spiritual anchor to San Francisco, was dead. I had lost my interest in the ethos of San Francisco and its fading hippie orthodoxy. New York was where I belonged. Jane wanted to come home, and I think she sensed we had exhausted our possibilities in San Francisco. Jane never learned to drive. She never left her heart in San Francisco. I took little convincing. Two-thirds of the company were located in our converted warehouse in San Francisco and the rest were packed into two floors of a small office building in New York. We needed to be in one place, and I needed to be in one place.

National magazines were based in New York. The talent I needed lived in New York. What I failed to see or anticipate was how New York would change both me and the magazine, and how powerful and all-consuming the city would be. Ambition was in every breath of New York air and every bite of the apple. Ambition was the sustenance that was necessary for staying alive.

DICK GOODWIN HAD asked me if I would like to meet Jackie Onassis. I loved the formality of referring to her as Mrs. Onassis, which is how I met her, not as the gauzy, public fairy tale. She lived at 1040 Fifth Avenue, just a block north of the Metropolitan Museum, in an apartment that overlooked the reservoir in Central Park. The elevator opened into the foyer of her apartment on the fifteenth floor. On the table I noticed a silver serving tray that had been given to the president, with his name surrounded by the engraved signatures of his cabinet and colleagues, names I knew, the legends of Camelot. I wanted to remember everything I saw: pictures, books, the chairs, the curtains. How did someone of such extraordinary fame and mystery live? The apartment was restrained, light and bright, elegant, with a view out of every window. Most of all I remember Mrs. Onassis, with her soft, whispery voice that communicated her delight at something you had to say, and her smile, which felt like the sun shining on you.

She asked question after question, about me, about Jane, about *Rolling Stone*, about Hunter, about music. She was so interested, and you wanted to tell her everything and how important and serious it all was. Dick was anxious to talk about the political magazine he and I had been thinking about. I thought taking me up to Jackie's was Dick's way of setting the hook. I learned later that this meeting was Jackie's idea, for her own reasons.

When I went back to San Francisco, she wrote to say, "Call when you come to New York in March. It would be nice to see you again and we can discuss everything. Jackie." She would send notes on her pale blue stationery, signed in blue ink with a flared *J*, asking me to see a writer or suggesting something to read. One afternoon she wanted me to meet Uri Geller, the Israeli psychic. I went to her apartment to watch him bend a spoon and then locate gold jewelry that Caroline had hidden in a bookcase.

We met when she was forty-six and I was thirty; she was barely a year older than me when she was in the White House. We started to meet for lunch in New York, often at a very stuffy restaurant called Quo Vadis with faux Roman décor. It was impossible not to be dazzled by her and by being with her. The way she spoke, the gracefulness of her movements, and her smile were distracting, and you couldn't take your eyes off her. It was sometimes difficult to be fully present in a conversation. She knew that, of course, and kept her guard up. She was frank about it, and that tiny bit of intimacy started to break the ice. On top of her love of the arts and the intellectual life, she liked to gossip, and she was tough. And funny. And kept a tight watch on her kids.

By 1976, NEW YORK CITY had become firmly incorporated into the *Rolling Stone* worldview. One cover showed Paul Simon, taken by Annie, standing in the window of his apartment with his view of Central Park. The profile was titled "The Odysseus of Urban Melancholy," and was a good look at how deeply neurotic Paul was. One of the photos in the piece was of Paul at a table at Elaine's, sitting with a group that included Lorne Michaels, Chevy Chase, and Jane. She was decorating our new apartment, and Paul became her shopping partner.

It was the nation's bicentennial year. Jane stayed in New York for the fireworks and I went to stay with Willie Hearst in San Simeon and watched the ranch hands set off fireworks which they tucked between their legs. *Time* put out a special issue to celebrate America's two hundredth year by picking two hundred "leaders of tomorrow." I was on the list, the youngest one.

ROGER BLACK, AN outgoing and jolly kid in his early twenties from West Texas with no training and no credentials, became one of the magazine's greatest art directors. Roger's passion was typography. He understood the nature of type, not just on a design level, but the emotion a given typeface could convey, what message could be implied. He gave *Rolling Stone* a look that reflected our early attempts at classic design, but which was far more sophisticated and felt new. There was no room left for the hippie potpourri that had been so much a part of our early years. He commissioned a type font that was unique and exclusive to us, *Rolling Stone* Roman. The serif face was integral to the look, the identity, and the philosophy of the magazine. The new, cool thing was *sans serif*; any typeface stripped of formal detail. I thought it was good for highway signs, airport restrooms, and manuals for microwave ovens; generally, it was forbidden at *Rolling Stone*.

I ASKED AVEDON HOW he got to be so good. He said it was because he had the opportunity to shoot nonstop when he started out at *Harper's* and worked for Diana Vreeland and Bea Feitler. They were equally relentless. They would not back down until they got what they wanted. I applied that wisdom to Annie, who continued to work regularly for us. Bea, who joined us to work with her, tutored Annie and made her confident about her place and work in New York. They became lovers.

TWO YEARS EARLIER, Hunter had traveled with Teddy Kennedy for a possible profile and went with him to listen to a speech Governor Jimmy Carter gave for Law Day at the University of Georgia. Carter's plainspoken thoughts about the justice system — from failed drug laws to inhumane prison sentencing and how his understanding of justice was driven by the writings of Reinhold Niebuhr and Bob Dylan — had a big impact on Hunter. When it became clear that Carter had a good shot at the presidential nomination in 1976, Hunter wanted to have a say but didn't want to go back on the campaign trail. He turned in a 10,000-word "Rude and Wistful Tales from the Bowels of the American Dream with Notes, Nightmares, and Other Strange Memories."

Once he started writing, finding a riff he loved, Hunter was unstoppable. Nearly every phrase and sentence had a clear — to me — purpose. He wrote with rhythm in mind. He would describe someone as "cackling like a hen full of amyls," or as crazy as "three iguanas in a feeding frenzy." I loved it. Hunter's best subject was himself, but he did finally get around to how special he thought Carter was and his day with him at the governor's mansion. We put Carter on the cover, a drawing of him as a prophet in white robes, and called it "an endorsement, with a great leap of faith by Hunter S. Thompson." After that, we were virtually an official part of the Carter campaign, and they treated us as such.

THE DEMOCRATIC CONVENTION was scheduled for mid-July at Madison Square Garden. We weren't covering it — we had the Avedon photo project in the works — but I wanted to have a party. Jimmy Carter was the *Rolling Stone* candidate. By tradition, the nominee in waiting does not appear in public before his acceptance speech, but I had an inspiration: "In honor of the Jimmy Carter Campaign Staff, *Rolling Stone* invites you to join us, Monday, July 13." Blue-and-white engraved invitations went out to about four hundred people, and I expected about two hundred to come.

We rented a brownstone on the East Side that had been turned into a conference center. When I arrived, people were already waiting on the street, and inside it was full. I had invited the cast of *Saturday Night Live* to come, which is when Jane and I first met John Belushi. It was so crowded that I couldn't get across the room; I kept getting called to the door to deal with people trying to get in. We were told by the fire department that absolutely no one else was allowed in. My strapping first cousin Steve Simmons and I stood outside trying to keep order, but by now the entire block was shut down with people waiting to get in. I waved at Kay Graham, sitting on the hood of a car with Warren Beatty, but there was nothing I could do.

The next day, I was surprised to see a full-page story in the *New York Times* and another in the *Washington Post* about our party and about the block party outside, listing the celebs who didn't get in and those, like Paul Newman, who did. It was said that getting in was "like trying to storm the Bastille," except when Walter Cronkite arrived, and "the crowd parted like the Red Sea."

I ASKED THE staff in San Francisco to assemble outside my office and told them the news: we were moving to New York. We were a major-league franchise now and would be deserting our hometown fans and family; the factory would be shutting down. I spoke to sad and long faces, hiding my own excitement, trying to do what I could to be comforting. I hadn't fully appreciated what a move to New York would do to the staff if we uprooted and moved so far from where our lives and ideas were grounded. Nor did I understand how much it would change the direction of the magazine. I was wearing a three-piece suit.

IN SEPTEMBER, ELTON JOHN finished his U.S. tour at Madison Square Garden, an extravaganza featuring flying bananas. He was doing the next cover and wanted to get a few things off his chest. "There is nothing wrong with going to bed with somebody of your own sex. I think everyone is bisexual to a certain degree. It's not a bad thing to be... I just think people should be very free with sex; they should draw the line at goats... Nobody has had the balls to ask me about it before. I would have said something all along. I don't want to shove it over the front pages, to be on the front of newspapers with my tongue down somebody's throat. That's appalling."

I wasn't comfortable "outing" someone. I called him up to get his explicit acknowledgment that he was sure he wanted to do this. I didn't know him, though he was a thorough reader of our magazine. He said he wasn't worried about the consequences.

In the Elton issue we also ran a piece by John Dean, the former White House counsel for Nixon, who had turned in a ballsy and serious piece of reporting on the GOP convention. Steadman went with him, and I passed through Kansas City to visit with the newest *Rolling Stone* reporter on the job. John flew back to California on the same flight as Pat Boone, Sonny Bono, and a cabinet secretary who was trying to explain to those around him why the GOP wouldn't get the black vote: "I'll tell you what the coloreds want. It's three things: first, loose shoes; second, a tight pussy; and third, a warm place to shit. That's all." Right after we hit the stands, a *Washington Post* reporter tracked down the postconvention travel of all the cabinet secretaries to see who was on a

California flight with Dean and identified Secretary of Agriculture Earl Butz as the man with the loose lips. It became a national scandal, and he was forced to resign.

AVEDON'S "THE FAMILY" turned out to be a landmark in the history of magazines, a museum-style photo exhibition in a single issue. Ronald Reagan, Gerald Ford, Hubert Humphrey, Jimmy Carter had quickly agreed to a shoot. George Bush, head of the CIA, was eager to help. Nixon was a no, so we shot his secretary, Rose Mary Woods, as his stand-in. One portrait was of the man who turned out to be Deep Throat. There were corporate, union, money, and media heavies. We showed George Wallace in his wheelchair. Avedon liked his expression in one picture, his hands in another shot, and cut each one in half to assemble the final photo.

I HAD AN itch to start a new magazine. By then I thought I knew what I was doing. I was half right. Someone had suggested a magazine about backpacking. I loved hiking and camping, and skiing in the mountains. If you considered the idea more broadly, you could see that the easy availability of travel, sports technology, and affordable equipment had become new staples in our lives. Adventure and nature travel were now within reach of everyone. I took this formulation another step: if you liked being in, playing in, and exploring the natural world, you were likely committed to protecting it. Presto: the environmental magazine I had wanted to start years ago.

I kept hearing the word "outdoors" as the potential title for such a magazine, but I didn't like the way it sounded and there seemed something prosaic about it. One weekend Willie and I were in a jeep, off-roading through the Hearst ranch at San Simeon, talking about my new magazine idea, and I was babbling along about the joy of being outside. Eureka! "Outside." Willie completely got what I was talking about, mixing the fun stuff with a sense of purpose and being part of something important, larger than yourself. I asked him to be the editor. He was a bit of a scatterbrain and eccentric for sure, but he was smart, he had a degree in math from Harvard, was trained in the editorial process, and knew how to charm and lead.

He would be leaving the family business, which surprised a lot of people, but it was the best thing he could have done. Willie didn't want to do the day-to-day managing or copyediting, so we hired Terry McDonell to handle the nuts and bolts. Terry was a strong editor, and leaned toward articles by his friends and heroes, like novelists Tom McGuane and Jim Harrison. He had been at UC Berkeley on a football scholarship, quit, and gone to Tehran and Beirut with camera in hand. He showed up for his interview with us riding a Ducati 305, wearing cowboy boots, Levi's, and one of those insufferable corduroy jackets with elbow patches. I commissioned Michael Rogers to write an editorial statement of purpose for *Outside* and to come up with names and descriptions of departments and story ideas throughout. He was the architect.

Jack Ford, son of the president who was just leaving the White House, joined us as a spokesperson. He, Willie, and I launched the first issue with a party at the Explorer's Club in New York. We were a pretty natty threesome. We did another launch party the next day in Chicago, and the Lincoln Continental limousine carrying us had posts on the front bumper for small flags. There were two American flags in the trunk, so I requested they fly them. We had a good laugh with Jack. I also had to laugh when I got a memo from Willie, which he signed, "Your faithful employee, WRH3, Son of son of citizen."

JANE AND I looked at a handful of possibilities for *Rolling Stone*'s headquarters, all in midtown Manhattan. One, an older building on Madison Avenue where William Paley had his early CBS offices, had a quasi-spiritual appeal for me. Another finalist was a modern glass skyscraper with a staggering view down the length of Central Park. That appealed to my ever growing sense of grandeur, and it was hard to walk away after seeing it. In the end I signed a lease for four floors in the Squibb Building at 745 Fifth Avenue, at the corner of Fifty-Eighth Street, overlooking Central Park, across the street from the Plaza hotel, and next door to the General Motors Building. When I was a kid in New York, it was the building that had FAO Schwarz, the best toy store in the world, on the first floor.

Our December cover at the end of 1976 was by Maurice Sendak, the illustrator and writer of *Where the Wild Things Are*, a painting of children decorating a Wild Thing with Christmas ornaments and holiday trimmings. Jonathan Cott interviewed Sendak for months, another of his amazing adventures in the land of geniuses. Cott had the widest knowledge of music and culture I had ever run across — from Gregorian chants to Thelonious Monk. I believed his instincts would take us someplace special, so I was willing to go with his arcane curiosity.

He suggested Sendak do a *Rolling Stone* cover at Christmas that was an icon of childhood and innocence. We made it into our official Christmas card. The last time we had done one, five years earlier, Annie shot tattoo artist Lyle Tuttle, inked head to toe, with Christmas lights strung on him. Both were wonderful.

CHAPTER 31

JOHN BELUSHI, INCOMING

JOHN BELUSHI ENTERED my life with the crash of a door, a broken chair, and maybe pots flying out of the kitchen cabinets. When we were living in San Francisco, he would fly out after an *SNL* show, sleep at our house for two days, delight any other visitors, guests, and editors who were around, and then fly back to New York for the next show. He showed up out of the blue on New Year's Eve 1977 with acid and tickets to the Grateful Dead all-nighter at Winterland.

In New York, our doormen, who loved John, would send him up to our apartment unannounced at any hour. One early morning he was downstairs asleep in the lobby. Jane and he would walk her dog. John would always oblige strangers with a spontaneous samurai show. I became a good friend of John's, and we would go off on our own adventures. He used to say I had a voice that could "march troops across Czechoslovakia." It lifted you up to see John and Jane together, how much they laughed and how much fun they had. They were brother and sister with their private language, happy to welcome you into their world.

John had the week off after the election, and he and Danny Ackroyd wanted to drive to the Jimmy Carter victory party in Atlanta and then through the "New South" to our offices in San Francisco. Danny would write about the trip. On the way to Atlanta they spent the first night at the hotel in Philadelphia where Legionnaires' disease had killed a dozen guests. They checked in wearing gas masks and ordered room service with their gas masks on. They stole a bath mat for me. The next night they were in Atlanta hanging out with Jimmy Carter's kids and a thousand revelers in the Omni Hotel's giant ballroom, presenting themselves as *Rolling Stone* reporters, and of course the crowd ate it up. The next morning, they hit the road ("the slab") for the run to the West Coast.

I was at home in San Francisco, happily sniffing, sipping, and smoking, when sometime after midnight the phone rang: "Hello, Mr. Waynur," the man said in a thick Cajun accent. "My name is Solomon Perez. I am the sheriff of Plaquemines Parish in Louisiana. I have in custody two gentlemen who say they work for you." I had to tell the truth but also avoid liability for whatever John and Danny had done. I didn't know if they had wrecked a car or burned down a hotel. "They are, uh...writing an article for us. As freelancers. They are not my employees. What is the problem?"

"There has been an accident. The vehicle they were driving hit a man earlier this evening. We don't yet know what will happen, but the man is in the hospital. These gentlemen were driving eighty miles per hour... And Mr. Way-nur, I must also tell you that upon searching their vehicle we found what we suspect to be narcotics."

I asked to speak with Danny. John would be useless. Danny told me it had been dark out, he didn't see the man come from their side of the road, "he bounced off the hood and went completely over the car." He wanted to explain about what the cops found in their car, about what they scored at Carter headquarters. I told him not to tell me details over the phone and to give me a few hours to find a lawyer for them in Louisiana. I had been totally jolted out of a stoned, slow-motion state, and now had to deal with a manslaughter case, probably worse because of the drugs. I didn't know what to do. The sheriff came on again. "Mr. Way-nur, these are fine boys you've got here, but we can't allow people to be coming into our parish..." Then Danny is on again and he's laughing. Then he passes the phone to John, who is also laughing. I had been had. They were fucking pros.

I walked into the editor's office they were using when they got to San Francisco and found John circling words with his black marker in our highly prized (and pricey) research department dictionary. I threw up my hands: "John, goddammit, don't mark up the dictionary!" He looked up, ripped the marked-up page out of the book, and said, "Okay, no more marks."

ANNIE ARRANGED THE five members of Fleetwood Mac on a mattress, sharing the same bed. Yet another brilliant cover. In real life, as they poured out in detail to Cameron Crowe, they had all swapped partners, an emotional and sexual explosion set off by a powder keg of blow during the ten months it took to record *Rumours*, one of that era's great records. That album, along with *Hotel California*, the Eagles' masterpiece about Southern California, and Jackson Browne's *Running on Empty*, defined those years. Cocaine had a stranglehold on the music business. Drugs were the coin of the realm, enabling bad behavior, bad relationships, and lapses of judgment all around. If you hung out with musicians, especially at night, there was going to be cocaine. A studio or a backstage dressing room was certain to have lines laid out on an overturned plate. If not, you waited for someone to offer you a bump. Of course, you began to ask for it, to search it out, and that became a kind of game, which had humiliating and pathetic aspects, faking friendships or scrounging for a line from someone you didn't really know or like.

Coke kept the party going; you could drink more, and you could talk more, although it's true what Jimmy Buffett once told me: "After one o'clock in the morning nothing is worth saying or listening to." Jimmy and his wife, Jane, lived in Aspen, where I first met them. Jimmy had been a reporter for *Billboard* in Nashville before his songwriting took off, so I took to him immediately. Don Henley lived two stones' throws from

Hunter in Woody Creek, and Glenn Frey was across the canyon. I was in Aspen for many rodeos with this crowd. The very first was a proper dinner party that featured a silver tray of neatly arranged lines of coke passed around every half hour. Fabulous!

The epitome was a party one New Year's Eve. Jane Buffett had rented Aspen's chicest Italian restaurant, carefully made out a seating chart for the big-name rock and roll and movie crowd. The traffic to the bathroom had been so heavy that nearly every plate of food went untouched. Don Henley's beautiful and frightening song "Life in the Fast Lane" was the classic that enshrined this era definitively. You were in the land of poor choices.

In JANUARY 1977, I was back in New York. Michael Douglas met me the day after the Carter inauguration and announced that he had fallen in love while he was in D.C. with a princess, Diandra de Morrell Luker. She was nineteen, he was thirty-three. She was blond, beautiful, and had been raised in Spain. Three months later they were married in a small ceremony in Beverly Hills. I stood with Jack Nicholson and Warren Beatty; we were Michael's close friends — not exactly the most innocent company, nor a particularly promising omen.

By the time I got back to Manhattan a few weeks later, Belushi was in the hospital after breaking his leg falling off the stage while performing a samurai skit. He insisted I come straight to the hospital from the airport and would not accept a no. When I got to the room, I found him lying in bed, his leg in a cast suspended by wires. He reached up into the top of the cast and pulled out a vial of coke.

NEW YORK AT night was a world of its own that you could put together in many ways. There was always something to do that was close at hand and generally irresistible. Dinner parties were in; going out was in. It was an exuberant time, and Jane and I got swept up in it. Earl and Camilla

McGrath had moved to a large apartment across the street from Carnegie Hall. Once or twice a week they would have a dinner party. They both cooked sophisticated Northern Italian food and hired waiters to serve. Earl had joined the Rolling Stones to run their record company, so Mick and his cohorts were regular guests.

Every weekend we went to the NBC studios in Rockefeller Center and watched *Saturday Night Live*. Lorne let us stand with him on the studio floor while the show was being broadcast, and we could wander freely around to wherever a sketch was being done or in front of the stage with the band. Following every show, an after party would begin at some secret location where cast and friends would stay until dawn.

Our apartment was a quiet spot, sort of. Belushi was a regular. Mick was an occasional late-night drop-in. And Bobby Neuwirth. Lillian Hellman once was a guest. Our steadiest visitor was Johnny Pigozzi, a young French-born Italian who had just graduated from Harvard. Johnny was thin, tall, had a head of dark frizzy hair, and spoke English without regard to the rules of grammar. This was funny and authentically eccentric. Jane had met him on a boat trip down the Nile. Pigozzi, who never touched an intoxicant in his life except breakfast tea, lived with us on and off for a year; we were his pied-à-terre. Sabrina Guinness and her Filofax of rock stars was a steady presence, and Stephen Graham, the madcap youngest son of Kay Graham, usually worked the night shift.

JACKIE ONASSIS HAD a dinner party to welcome Jane and me to New York. Guests included William Styron and his wife, Rose — they were Martha's Vineyard regulars with Jackie; Pete Hamill, the *Daily News* columnist; and Annabel and Mike Nichols. In the middle of the sit-down dinner, Mike asked if anyone wanted to see his imitation of Irving Lazar; he pulled up his pant leg and put his black eyeglasses on his bald knee. It was fall-down funny. Mike was incomparable, generous, and a genius.

CHAPTER 32

OUR TENTH ANNIVERSARY

CLAY FELKER STARTED *New York* magazine the same year I began *Rolling Stone*. He was a founding father of "the New Journalism." He was gracious about, and accepted without protest, Tom Wolfe's move to *Rolling Stone*. Rupert Murdoch launched a hostile takeover of Clay's magazines. Clay had diluted his company's stock and had some snaky partners who were happy to sell him down the river. Murdoch threw him out. I met Murdoch when he first arrived in New York. He asked if I would sell him *Rolling Stone*. He seemed then an engaging, intelligent publisher who looked like Yoda but of course turned out to be the Sith Emperor.

I assigned Gail Sheehy, Clay's romantic partner and one of his star journalists, to write "The Showdown," a 15,000-word saga about Murdoch versus Felker, admittedly from Clay's point of view. I indulged in a burst of headlines for it: "A Fistful of Dollars, Featuring the Good, the Bad, and the Ugly. A Spaghetti Eastern." We announced ourselves to New York with the best piece on the biggest New York media story of the year. We were now center ring.

JANE AND I rented a saltbox-style wood-shingle house with low ceilings on Further Lane, on the town line between East Hampton and

Amagansett. The house was one of five of the same colonial-era style clustered together on the Tyson Estate, which overlooked double dunes and wide beaches on the Atlantic Ocean. Further Lane was a country road through potato fields and apple orchards. The estate belonged to the dowager Carolyn Tyson, whose husband, James, had been forbidden from the property after being caught peeping through the windows of tenants. Jackie Onassis had grown up on Further Lane, right down the road, and told me that East Hampton was the best summer place in the world.

Lorne Michaels and his girlfriend, Susan Forristal, had rented a rambling white house in East Hampton; Chevy Chase and Michael O'Donoghue had the house across the street from them. Paul Simon was just down from us. John and Judy Belushi were in a bay cottage nearby. Lorne's was generally the center of the action; just about everyone had some kind of drop-in privilege. Jane and Susan were becoming close friends. We called her the Whisper Girl, because of a deodorant commercial she had done. We had a weekly barbecue. Dick Avedon spent one weekend and woke us early in the morning with the news that photographer Peter Beard's windmill home in Montauk had burned to the ground in the night; we drove out to see the smoky ruins where we had had lunch a few weeks earlier. Dick was thrilled, since he had just bought the land next door. One summer, Paul was dating Carrie Fisher. I was developing a crush on her — we met for lunches in the city, on top of the social life at the beach — until one night I came home to find a Princess Leia doll with pins in it on my pillow.

WE WERE ONLY a few months away from moving into our new Fifth Avenue headquarters. I assembled managers, department heads, plus the people who would be staying in San Francisco to run *Outside*, for a weekend meeting and get-to-know-you in East Hampton. We rented a large house with a dozen bedrooms and a swimming pool with a ten-meter diving board. It also had a large statue on the front lawn that wound up in the pool by the end of the weekend. I had my six-year-old redheaded niece, Megan, who was on a summer visit, at my feet under the table during the meetings. John Belushi came each day. He would make an entrance crawling on his hands and knees, and cracked up the meeting with his imitations of me. He delighted everyone and made them feel special about being at *Rolling Stone*.

These were young adults, neatly dressed in polo shirts and Bermuda shorts, sitting properly on folding chairs with loose-leaf notebooks in their hands. This was not the "Make love, not war" crowd. This was a "Make money, make more" group. I think all but a few of the thirty people understood that I had big plans and a mission for *Rolling Stone*. I was thirty-one, a boyish figure with a judge's gavel in his hand.

I WAS APPROACHED TO do a Thanksgiving prime-time television special to celebrate the tenth anniversary of *Rolling Stone*. I had only a vague idea of what I was doing. I thought it would be great to stage a private concert by the Rolling Stones at some remote and exotic spot, maybe an island. Mick met with the producer I was assigned, who told him that they couldn't do any new material, it all had to be greatest hits. Mick politely walked away from that, and I was embarrassed and worried. Then I got John Belushi and Danny Aykroyd to agree to do a few Hunter and Jann skits, and that got turned down because the producer didn't think they were well-known. I brought in David Felton and Ben Fong-Torres to help write the show, but they got frozen out in favor of writers from *Laugh-In* and *The Smothers Brothers*. Mick asked me how come I didn't ask Lorne to do the show; we weren't on Lorne's network. That's the way this cookie crumbled.

Jimmy Webb, the boy genius who wrote "Up, Up and Away" and "By the Time I Get to Phoenix," had been hired as the show's musical director. He would not have been my pick; the sound of "Up, Up and Away" didn't fit my sense of what was appropriate for *Rolling Stone*'s birthday party, but Jimmy and I hit it off in about two minutes. We were long-lost brothers...and discovered how much we had in common, including the daily little bottle of blow. We went off into our own world in the recording studio, producing tracks for the show. I would sing on some, and Jimmy on others. I was staying at the Beverly Hills Hotel, but spent most of the time at Jimmy's Spanish mansion in Encino, where he lived with his seventeen-year-old wife, Patsy Sullivan, who would have six kids with him. Jimmy and I survived the blow and our two families became close friends.

It was too late by the time I found out that the producer of the TV show was someone who had won an Emmy for *The Barry Manilow Special*. He hired a choreographer to blow our budget on the pièce de résistance: a medley of dancing to a mash-up of Beatles songs, culminating in "Birthday" as the nod to *Rolling Stone*. Jimmy Webb and I had recorded all the tracks. I sang "Back in the USSR" rather well (or so I thought), but they refused to use my vocal, I think out of spite. It was my anniversary, after all. One bit that came to characterize the whole show stands out: for "Strawberry Fields Forever," they came up with a bunch of Las Vegas dancers in strawberry costumes parading and prancing around like a Fruit of the Loom ad. We had proposed the Beatles medley be a symbolic portrayal of the big cultural events of the decade, but instead we got dancing strawberries... Lucy at Caesar's Palace with Diamonds.

The letters about the show that came in were both fun and angry. David Felton demanded that he respond to our readers. "First off, the fact is the powers that be at *Rolling Stone* have no one to blame but themselves. *Rolling Stone* could have conceivably killed it at any time, but it would have cost the magazine a million bucks and forced the editor to give up his limousine service for a year. *Rolling Stone* blew it, what more can I say? Except it probably will hurt *Rolling Stone* more than the viewers, readers, or rock and roll; and secondly, sometimes it's hard to tell a ship is sinking when all the rats stay on board."

WE MOVED INTO our new offices on a Monday in the middle of August. On Tuesday, Chet Flippo walked into my office to tell me that Elvis had died. We had already closed an issue the week before; it was sitting at the printer so we wouldn't have to put out an issue as we moved in. The issue was devoted to New York, with articles about the world we thought we were moving into, and we had an original cover of Bella Abzug that Andy Warhol did for us. The news of Elvis's death was our equivalent of a five-alarm fire. We had four days until deadline. The staff hadn't even had a chance to unpack their files when they were called in for an all-hands-on-deck. We would have to do a new issue from scratch, in an office we didn't know our way around, on equipment we had never tried, with half the staff never having worked with the other half.

Chet went straight to the airport for the next flight to Memphis. Ben flew to Los Angeles to meet Elvis's ex-bodyguards, who were ready to talk about his last days. We got on the phones for tributes, prepared discographies and a filmography, a profile of Colonel Tom Parker, and a visit to Tupelo, Mississippi. Jackie called to say that Caroline Kennedy was flying down to Memphis with Pete Hamill, and would I like her to write a piece about going to Graceland, seeing the mourning, and meeting his ex-wife? Caroline saw Elvis in his open coffin and spoke with Vernon, Uncle Vester, Aunt Delta, and Grandmother Minnie.

In August the city is hot and muggy, and our air-conditioning wasn't working, so the windows were left open and we could hear a sax player through the night, twenty-three floors below on Fifth Avenue. It was a long four days and nights. We found an old fan-club picture of Elvis, painted it in pastel tints for the cover. I wanted to show him in his youth, full of promise and beauty. Bruce Springsteen wrote, "Elvis was as big as the whole country itself, as big as the whole dream. He embodied the essence of it." We were proud of the issue, and proud of our performance. We had game.

MY FIRST VISITOR at the new office was Jackie, who brought me flowers. I nearly burst my appendix trying to be nonchalant. Welcome to New York, indeed. I hardly needed a key to the city; our block was Fifth Avenue and Fifty-Seventh Street, the crossroads of Manhattan. We had views of the

Plaza hotel, Central Park, and could even see the George Washington Bridge on clear days. The Squibb Building was one of the older office buildings that had smaller floors as it rose higher and windows that opened, with terraces along the Fifth Avenue side. We had taken four floors, joined together by stairs in an interior atrium. We had interior walls of glass brick, and light throughout. The *New York Times* did an architecture story on it.

CHARLES M. YOUNG had won our first College Journalism Award when he was a student at Columbia Journalism School. Chuck was a preacher's kid, as was Chet, who was running the New York bureau and had hired him. Chet had a drawl and was quite a cool character well liked by all. Chuck was what they used to politely call a "nonconformist" in high school, a young man on a lifetime crusade against hypocrisy and authority. He brought his crusade against "the man" to *Rolling Stone* and expected me to be his Dean Wormser, which I wasn't. I think he thought a bit of conflict was healthy for both of us.

Despite the reputation he tried to cultivate, Chuck couldn't help himself: he was fun to be with and absolutely likable. He was a talented writer and reporter. And a wit. When he was in charge of "Random Notes," he once produced a section in which every item was about Mick Jagger. One of his first cover ideas was controversial: the editors knew I didn't want to do the Sex Pistols, but Chuck had rallied them to his cause and the righteousness of being bold, embracing the new, and giving the kid a shot. It was legitimate news, and Chuck would write a first-class piece, but it was not a slam-dunk cover, and if we did it, we would put our imprimatur on the group. I went for it.

I LOVED THE TIME I spent with Jackie. Being in public, even walking, was like being in the inside of a beautiful and shiny sunlit bubble. People watched her, made way for her. She seemed to enchant them. The force was strong. We had many lunches. She didn't talk about history, or art, in academic or intellectual terms (though it was obvious how knowledgeable she was), but in an experiential sense, about her reactions, how something or someone made her feel, and what it was like to be at an event or a place, the thrill and the fun of it.

She was a gossip, and I heard some rarefied stuff. She liked to hear about rock stars and movie people and whoever was in the news. She would talk about Ari and trips to Skorpios, but little about the White House and Jack. Lots of Teddy, occasionally Ethel, but never Bobby. She didn't open up those parts of her life, and although I think she would have, I didn't ask. The press had made her life unpleasant and she was bitter about that, although she was great friends with many writers and some journalists. We talked about her kids a lot. She had forbidden John, still in his teens, to take a job as a water-sports instructor at a Caribbean beach resort. She knew exactly where that was headed. She was a proud and protective mother.

Jackie, Caroline, and I once went to a movie screening and its after party at Tavern on the Green, in Central Park. I was photographed walking in with Caroline on my arm. I was asked for my name and told them I was no one in particular and moved on. The next day the New York City tabloids — and the *San Francisco Chronicle* — all carried the photo, with the headline "Caroline with Unidentified Mystery Man."

WITH EVERYBODY IN one office, it was unmistakable how big the whole enterprise had become. Editors, the art director, designers, and the photo department had an entire floor, with private offices and assistants. Two floors were totally devoted to business operations. There were table-size Xerox machines and a switchboard that did all kinds of tricks like conference calls and had a feature called "executive override," which allowed me to interrupt and listen in at will to anyone's phone call in progress. I tried it once and it creeped me out. It was a long way from the printer's loft a block from the city jail.

The energy grew as people saw how many people were working together, and they were inspired and challenged to step up their game. The implied message was that you had to not just carry your weight but get really good at what you did, or you wouldn't fit in. It was a chain reaction, a burst of energy that would need to be controlled and focused. We were gaining strength with every issue. It felt big. It was real in a way it hadn't felt before. It was serious.

We had become an essential voice for a generation. We had done 254 issues of remarkable journalism, photography, and design. We would celebrate all that and decided that we should do an issue about ourselves. The Tenth-Anniversary Special. We would show what a good magazine we had learned to produce. It was the first time we ran a glossy cover and used the oversized magazine format with trimmed edges and a staple — more or less a real magazine, on high-grade polished newsprint.

The issue was driven in great part by Roger Black, who redesigned and refined the *Rolling Stone* logo for the occasion, the first time since 1967, when I had whisked away the unfinished drawing in a haze of pot smoke from Rick Griffin. Roger convinced me that we needed a modern logo that signaled what the magazine had become but still respected the time and place of its origins and cultural roots. The idiosyncratic shapes of hand-drawn lettering were made into proportioned letters, all the while retaining the slant, the swashes, and strength. The cover was red and white, the first use of red in a way that made it our signature color. He hit a level of finesse that was exquisite, centered it around a cover-size *X*, the Roman numeral for ten. This would be the new *Rolling Stone*.

The heart of the tenth-anniversary issue featured our two North Stars, both with an elegiac piece by Hunter and forty-eight pages of Annie Leibovitz's photography. Plus, choice valedictory writing by Chet Flippo and David Felton about their personal histories with *Rolling Stone*. Felton called his piece "Lifer." The breadth and depth of Annie's work was a revelation. By that time she had shot fifty-eight covers since 1970, and perhaps double that number of assignments, portraiture, and reportage on musicians, politicians, actors, and writers.

CHET'S STORY BEGAN, "I will never forget the first glimpse I got of *Rolling Stone*. I was in the Navy and my buddies and I had discovered dope and *Rolling Stone* about the same time; we sat out on the fantail of a Navy destroyer smoking and reading the first issue and marveling that finally there was a magazine which covered everything we were interested in. *Rolling Stone* was, as Ralph J. Gleason once said, 'a letter from home.' A transitory home, a home for the soul, a storehouse of everything meaningful to me." Chet had written me a long, rambling letter from the ship pleading for a job; it listed twenty-five story ideas and a summary of his life history and philosophy. I remember keeping the letter, it being such a classic artifact of the era, and damned if it didn't pop out of the filing system after he came to work.

Hunter did something quite brilliant, and from the heart. His idea was to search for his old friend Oscar Zeta Acosta, the Chicano lawyer and activist on whom he had based the character of the three-hundred-pound Samoan attorney in *Fear and Loathing in Las Vegas*. Hunter had seen the warrior spirit in Oscar and a soul mate. He was smart, didn't really mean anyone harm, but was also angry and a danger to others and to himself. I had taken acid with him a few times. He had returned to Mexico, where he disappeared in 1974. He was most likely dead, the victim of violence, probably a drug deal where he stepped out of, or over, the line. Hunter's wasn't a physical search, but a search of his memory for Oscar and who he was, what his inability to survive said about him, us, our times.

"A screech owl the size of a chow killed two of my peacocks on the front porch. The antique winch-powered crossbow that Steadman sent over from England was seized and destroyed by Sheriff's deputies and a man named Drake was demanding my number from bartenders at the Hotel Jerome because he claimed to have a bizarre message for me from the Brown Buffalo, Oscar Zeta Acosta. Then Sandy came back from the store with the mail and the latest issue of *Newsweek*, the one with the photo of Caroline Kennedy rolling Jann through the door of Elaine's on that custom built, cut-glass dolly from Neiman Marcus." That was the prelude to receiving strange news of Oscar and a drug deal on the high seas.

"Fear and Loathing in the Graveyard of the Weird: The Banshee Screams for Buffalo Meat" was full-out craziness, but its understory was his love for Acosta, a never-to-be-sung hero: "Oscar was one of God's own prototypes — a high powered mutant of some kind who was never even considered for mass production. He was too weird to live and too rare to die. We are better off without him. Sooner or later he would have had to have been put to sleep anyway...So the world is a better place if he is now out of sight, if not certifiably dead. He will not be missed — except perhaps in Fat City, where every light in the town went dim when we finally heard he had cashed his check.

> 'To the living we owe respect, but to the dead we owe only the truth.'
>
> — Voltaire"

CHAPTER 33

CHRISTMASES WITH JACKIE

JANE AND I spent Christmas with Jackie and her kids. Peter Beard and his girlfriend also came. We gave John and Caroline, who were going on a ski vacation, each a pair of red long underwear. There was a tradition in the Kennedy family to always give a gag present as well as a serious one. Jackie gave Peter and me each a copy of the 1978 Gay Men's Calendar.

I WAS CHASING THE good life and the good life was chasing me. I was eating up everything the Big Apple had to offer. We sat with Jackie in her box for the opening night of the American Ballet Theatre. I saw Nureyev dance, and Baryshnikov leap, and the Balanchine *Nutcracker* for the first time. Lincoln Kirstein, general director of the New York City Ballet, took me out to lunch, hoping that I could introduce him to Michael Jackson. There were movie openings, birthday bashes at Studio 54, parties for record releases, art galleries, book signings, and elaborate fashion shows.

Jane and I made our first trip to Barbados. Ahmet and Mica Ertegun regularly rented a large house there on the beach next to the Sandy Lane hotel, on a white sand, palm-fringed bay. David Geffen, who at the time was a vice-chairman at Warner Bros., was staying in Barbados and invited Jane and me to fly down with him on Warner's twelve-passenger corporate jet. That was the first time I had ever flown in a large private jet. Only major corporations or wealthy families like the Rockefellers or the Paleys could afford them. The jets were an incomparable luxury. David said that I was his tax deduction for the trip. Our circulation was now 750,000.

BOB DYLAN WAS putting out *Renaldo and Clara*, the four-hour movie he had made of the *Rolling Thunder* tour. It was a film that existed somewhere near the border of myth and reality. We gave him his ninth cover, his first by Annie, staring straight ahead wearing black Ray Bans. Jonathan interviewed Bob, and both were in great form. He said that "Idiot Wind" was "a philosophy that doesn't have a title and it's driven across with willpower." He said something was "not as weird as it should be. Weirdness is exactness." Jonathan, being an agile student of literature and philosophy, quoted Jewish mystics, French poets, and Dylan's own oeuvre in a game of wonderful one-upmanship and discovery.

I decided to put Donna Summer on the cover of an issue in March 1978. Disco was considered the music of the anti-Christ by many, and the staff was up in arms. I thought the music was strong and made you want to dance, dance, dance. Wasn't that where rock had started? In the end, it was more about one's choice of clothes than anything else, and maybe subconscious anti-gay prejudice. There were other tensions in the *Rolling Stone* gestalt then. I could see them, at least metaphorically, in a gauzy and glamorous Jefferson Starship cover, full makeup, dressed by stylists, hair blowing in the breeze of studio fans. A decade earlier Jefferson Airplane sang "White Rabbit" and spoke to the counterculture dream. Now their lives had gotten complicated by their success, money, and the freedom to have internal creative differences. The culture we had helped shape had been absorbed into the mainstream.

I began to hear that we had "sold out," which had been a sour-grapes gripe I was immune to. But now I heard it in connection with forsaking

San Francisco for the glamour and power of New York. I suppose my own lifestyle and friendships in New York legitimized a lot of that. What Hunter had written about Caroline Kennedy wheeling me into Elaine's was hilarious to me, but it did not sit well with a lot of the people who pay serious attention to such things — including many on the *Rolling Stone* staff.

It was becoming clear that the cultural center of the country had moved away from San Francisco, and the greater part of it was back in New York again. San Francisco, as a new and dynamic city of the arts, politics, and rock and roll, had gone quiet. Rock and roll now included television, movies, and literature; we broadened our coverage accordingly. We even had a rock and roll president, of sorts, in Jimmy Carter. The saga of the hippies was losing its story line, though the relevance of its many concerns — drug use and enforcement, healthy living, care for the environment, sexual freedom, and human rights — was more urgent than ever. Flower power was dead, and it was time to move on. Tim Leary understood it: "We must pray for Jann. He is at the crossroads, either he will go too commercial or not commercial enough."

NINETEEN SEVENTY-EIGHT WAS the year of *Some Girls*, which I thought was the best Stones album since *Let It Bleed* in 1969. "Miss You" was always in the air. Mick lived in New York at the time, and we saw each other often. He was on the June cover in a suit and tie, clean-cut. It looked like a men's clothing campaign. Mick was two years older than me, but I felt he was years wiser. He had learned how to inhabit his celebrity. He embraced it, enjoyed it, and used it to protect himself. We always had fun together. He was rarely not "Mick Jagger." Getting to know Mick was tricky. He could be imperious, especially when he was on tour. He could be unfriendly and cold, and do it with ease. It was gratuitous, possibly a test or perhaps a way of establishing another person's status as a supplicant. Whatever it was, it was deliberate.

In the cover interview, Jonathan asked Mick about dreams, quoting the line "I only get my rocks off while I'm dreaming." Mick's response was a discussion of dreams in the work of "the lowliest rock and roll writer" to the writings of Chaucer and Shakespeare. The interview was one of the most interesting and thoughtful Mick had yet given. He responded to Jonathan's intellectual playfulness and his detailed knowledge of Stones songs. They talked about Mick's attitude toward women, from "Under My Thumb" to "Beast of Burden." He talked about his sexuality, too:

"I really don't like being a soap opera. It really must be some sort of sexual attraction, and I hope I am not being immodest saying this, but when I was a kid I had it... There was always room for the androgynous type. Anyway, all guys have a feminine side. But most girls really don't fall in love with a completely gay guy, even though they like the feminine side showing.

"There is one song that's a straight gay song—'When the Whip Comes Down'—but I have no idea why I wrote it. The Rolling Stones have always attracted a lot of men. That sounds funny, but they are not all gay. And of course, I have a lot of gay friends, but I suppose everyone does in New York City... and what does that have to do with the price of eggs?"

At one point Jonathan said, "You have said you didn't want to be singing 'Satisfaction' when you were forty-two."

"No. I certainly won't."

Mick told me he thought the new design of the *Rolling Stone* logo missed something; something in the spirit of it. He said we had taken "the funkiness" out of it. He was right and I made the changes, restoring some of the swashes and cross strokes based on his intuitive feel for funk.

JANE AND I celebrated our tenth wedding anniversary. We sailed from New York to Southampton, England, on the *QE2*, and checked into the Hotel George V in Paris for a week. Lorne and Susan met us there. It happened that the Dylan tour was in town. We saw him perform on July

Fourth at the Pavillon de Paris. To be an American in a foreign country on Independence Day didn't give me a big burst of pride, but it stirred something that surprised me: humility. How profoundly grateful I was to be an American. Lorne and I were together, taking our places in our world. We both raised our lighters at the concert, swept away by Dylan.

Lorne had tapped into the zeitgeist through the collective sensibilities of his cast, which refracted his own. A natural symbiosis existed between *Rolling Stone* and *SNL*. We did lots of pieces about them — even published a book titled *Rolling Stone Visits Saturday Night Live* — and our cover often featured their cast members or their weekly musical guest. Lorne and I were partners in the larger scheme of things.

WHILE WE WERE in Paris, the latest issue was sent to us air freight, and unbeknownst to me, Patti Smith was on the cover. Annie had taken a portrait of her as a street urchin posed in front of a wall of flame. Despite her new hit single that Bruce had written, "Because the Night," Patti was still a little-known, oddball poet from the Lower East Side, of narrow appeal but loved by our critics. Patti had written reviews and poems for *Rolling Stone*, and her guitar player and musical partner, Lenny Kaye, was a steady contributor. Patti was perfect material for us — outspoken, rebellious, talented, hard-core. She was a member of the family. That cover was one of our classics, and the photo was one of Annie's greats. When a show of Annie's work was put on at the National Portrait Gallery in Washington, D.C., we went to the opening and that photo of Patti was hanging outside as a multistory banner between the Greek columns, next to banners of Alexander Hamilton and Thomas Jefferson.

IN 1978, NATIONAL LAMPOON'S *Animal House*, *Midnight Express*, and *Up in Smoke* were hit movies, all on the heels of *Saturday Night Fever*, which had sprung from a *New York* magazine article. Therefore, if you knew about the "youth" generation, drug smuggling, or ran a magazine — better yet, all three—you could also make hit movies. I thought I should figure this thing out. I never slowed down enough to ask myself or anyone else— Why be in the movie business? I hadn't grown up on movies nor was I a movie buff, but opportunity knocked, and it looked like fun.

Of the four studios that made offers, I chose Paramount. Barry Diller and Michael Eisner were men I liked. I had a "development" deal to deliver three original scripts. They gave me an office and one of their vice presidents to work with, a stiff young man named Jeffrey Katzenberg. I gravitated to two other guys, Don Simpson and Craig Baumgarten, both on the fast track and with a taste for blow.

The first projects were titled *Key West*, a drug smuggling caper by Hunter, and *Somebody to Love*, about a rock and roll reporter falling in love with a Janis Joplin–like rock star by Ben Fong-Torres. About the same time, Cameron Crowe was planning to go back to his high school in San Diego for an article. Someone else got ahead of me and made a deal with Cameron for a script that became *Fast Times at Ridgemont High*. I was flying back and forth to Los Angeles, meeting movie people, lunching at Ma Maison, one time with Sue Mengers as we watched Jack Nicholson and Orson Welles eating together two tables away.

I made a deal with Jimmy Buffett for Hunter to stay at his Key West apartment. I wanted him to create a Buffett-like world of happy-go-lucky outlaws bringing in hundred-kilo loads of fine pot. Buffett would have a cameo; some good guys would meet their untimely end at the hands of the DEA, or some heavy-duty Latin Americans, or both. Nicholson would be the evil narc. It was to be a paean to a romantic notion of pirates with hearts of Acapulco gold.

WE REPORTED ON the death of Keith Moon, thirty-two. I had sent my doctor to minister to him one night in San Francisco years before so he could go on with the show there. When he did his skit for our television special, which was about trashing a hotel room, I had told him to take it easy in the rehearsals, but he let it loose on the first take. He tore the set to bits. He had two women with him and stayed locked in his room on the set with them the rest of that day and into the night.

GEORGE PLIMPTON WROTE "Notes from the Battle of New Orleans," the last win of Ali's career. I had been at the fight with my old friend John Warnecke. He had come with some LSD, so I saw none of what happened in the ring. When I went over to Plimpton's apartment to get the manuscript early one morning on deadline, he was at his desk, wearing a silk robe that had "Muhammad Ali" lettered on the back. He was still typing, slugging it out.

IT WAS CHERUBIC Roger's last issue as my art director. He was restless. Roger said he would stay if he got a big raise and I returned to being the hands-on editor. I told him that neither was in the picture. The art director's job was one of our toughest. Roger's social life was consuming; he and his staffers would call up a limousine and head out to hit the clubs, Studio 54 and his favorite, Danceteria. That meant drugs. He was exhausted by the wear and tear of the nightlife. *Rolling Stone* was his magazine, and he knew it. He won the Gold Medal that year from the Society of Publication Designers. Roger suggested, and I agreed, to have his production director, Mary Shanahan, succeed him as art director and hired Bea Feitler as a consultant. The very next issue our formal cover border went to a leopard-skin pattern.

I SPENT LESS AND less time at the office, often tired or hungover when I got in at 11:00 a.m. to begin my day. I tried to make my arrival low-key. Hardworking people were doing their jobs, and I was embarrassed by setting such a thoughtless example. It was an endless parade of nightlife, both in and out. Our apartment was a stopover for quite a few people, and everyone sooner or later would come through New York. We had friends from San Francisco, Los Angeles, London, even Paris, who were more than happy to spend a few days. We also put up *Rolling Stone* writers. Hunter was a magnet for even more guests. I found this note on my desk after one HST visit: "Jann—install a goddamned shower in your guest room. And send me that $5000 at once—or I'll rip your nuts off your body with a plastic fork. Yrs. From the bunker. HST."

I was not a denizen of Studio 54, although Steve Rubell gave me house privileges, including access to the basement. The shirtless guys behind the bar were like a college gymnastics team. It was the place for parties—one of the best was Calvin Klein's sweet sixteen for his daughter. Invites arrived in plastic boxes filled with silver confetti. I would go to 54 for a party, but it was never my hangout. Sooner or later, everyone went there...if you were rich, and/or famous, and/or beautiful.

WE HAD OPENLY embraced pot use and the "War on Drugs" was one of the issues to which I had *Rolling Stone* devote its resources and reputation. This was about our generation, our audience, the people we were responsible to who were getting hurt, sent to jail, having their families damaged, even their lives destroyed. For fucking what? Smoking pot?

We ran pieces attacking the insanity and cruelty of the Rockefeller drug laws; we editorialized against the aerial spraying of Mexican marijuana fields with poisonous herbicides, which would inevitably end up inhaled by United States users. We ran the stories of people stuck in prison. One was a kid who had just graduated from high school in Missouri, been accepted to college, and was arrested with five dollars' worth of pot. He was an only child, and his mother and father were both blind, living on Social Security and a pension. He was sentenced to seven years. His appeal was turned down. These were heartbreaking, soul-crushing stories, but no one knew or seemed to care. The victims of the ill-informed, punitive system had no money and no voice. This was our government in action. It made me angry. We would have to get even busier on it.

RIGHT AFTER THANKSGIVING, Jackie had a birthday party to celebrate Caroline turning twenty-one and John turning eighteen. The party was on Sunday night at Le Club, a small, almost private restaurant on the Upper East Side. I was seated between Ethel Kennedy and Jackie, which I thought was pretty far-out — until Ethel started laying into me about Hunter, whom her son David had been hanging around with in Aspen. Jackie whispered to me, pointing to the gentleman seated on Ethel's right: "That is one of Bobby's oldest friends, and he's the one selling drugs to David."

Before I had left for the holiday, I was offered $12 million to sell *Rolling Stone*. I liked the man who made it, Bill Ziff, who had founded Ziff Davis, a great magazine company. But New York was the beginning of a new era for *Rolling Stone*, and I was having too much fun.

For Christmas we flew to a resort on the island of St. Martin to join Jackie with her sister Lee and all their kids. There were other cousins along, and it was like some legendary Kennedy clan event. I tried to keep up the pace waterskiing and ended up crawling back to the beach every afternoon. No one water-skied in the San Francisco Bay, and I was a long way away.

CHAPTER 34

THE DRY HEAVES

B
Y 1979 WE were running out of money. Again. I still wasn't paying attention to "the bottom line," a cruel and inelegant phrase that was the new American paradigm. *Rolling Stone* was making my lifestyle money, and I didn't have to think about public shareholders. One of my advisors thought we should take a loan for a million dollars, apparently an easy and cheap thing to do. When the bank looked at the books a year later and saw the money we were losing on *Outside* and the overhead on Fifth Avenue, they decided they wanted their money back, pronto. I remember walking back to the office from that meeting, and my advisor telling me I should shave my mustache because I looked "too Jewish." What was I supposed to make of that?

We would have to close down or sell *Outside*. Initially I had been unaware of a magazine from Chicago, *Mariah*, that covered hard-core expedition travel. Now we were more or less competitive with it. The founder was a wealthy adventurer with no publishing experience and was losing money. He bought *Outside*. We had created a first-rate magazine, and its genes were strong. It survived and flourished.

MY MOVIE DEVELOPMENT deal meant I was in Los Angeles for a week every month. Michael Douglas was producing a movie then about the dangers of nuclear power, *The China Syndrome*. He played a journalist exposing a cover-up at a nuclear plant on the California coastline. This was parallel in time and politics with *Rolling Stone*'s investigation of Karen Silkwood's death. Jane Fonda had been developing our pieces about Silkwood for her own movie at the same studio. They put hers on hold and assigned Jane to Michael's movie. When the movie premiered in New York, Michael accepted the praise with pleasure and modesty; I was so proud of him and so happy. We put him on the cover when the movie came out. Annie did a poignant portrait of Michael holding his infant son naked. Michael sent me a letter that stated, "It's amazing how a grown man holding a baby can make a drug magazine look so respectable."

Days after our *China Syndrome* cover, a nuclear reactor in Pennsylvania, the Three Mile Island Nuclear Generating Station, went into a partial meltdown, just like the disaster in the movie. I was in Aspen when the news came. No one seemed to care. It was sunny, spring skiing. We were thousands of miles from the wind supposedly headed toward New York City. Back east there was panic. I was talking to people at the office who wanted to know what to do. What was I supposed to tell them? That I was sending in an extraction team? The nuclear industry hit a turning point, and new reactor construction in the United States began to slow and eventually stopped.

JERRY WEXLER RENTED a house in East Hampton. His wife was less than half his age; he liked young people, being near the action, and coming to Lorne's or our house for the frequent barbecues. It was the suburbs. I used to tell Lorne how much I got a kick out of washing my car, and he would expound on the pleasure of mowing his lawn.

Jerry had just finished producing Bob Dylan's new album, *Slow Train Coming*, in Muscle Shoals. Mark Knopfler was on the sessions. As Jerry played it for me, he narrated it with the benefit of his insights. This was Bob's "born again" Christian album. He gave me his tape. Do not copy; do not share; do not tell.

If you listen to a new album more than ten times, you find yourself falling in love, luxuriating in the emotions that flow from it and the intimacy that comes from knowing each note and where it is going. And when it's all yours and no one else's, it's all the more your private passion. That is not very objective, but it happens a lot, and it always becomes a lifelong love. But then you sometimes get, as they say, too far over your skis. I decided to write the review in *Rolling Stone* — not just any review, but one that would be as rich in scholarly insight and musical notes as our best reviewers', indeed, even better: "Only prophets and those most personally involved are willing to risk definitions. This has always been Bob's special link to his audience." I still am not totally sure what that means. It was his best album in years, but I went so far as to say perhaps his best ever. Ouch. I dove into the failure of economics and politics of the times, my own lack of religious engagement, the nature of Bob's voice. I did single out Mark Knopfler as "easily the best new guitarist in years. My hat is off and eaten." I had a fan's knowledge, for sure. But not the critic's gene. What I wrote should have been sent back and cut in half.

JANE AND I took the Warner jet to Barbados again, this time as guests of Ahmet and Mica. We had rented a house with Diane and Marshall Chess. Annie also came along. Richard Pryor was on the island and hung around our house. The Erteguns had other guests staying with them, including Mick and Bianca. After Thanksgiving dinner, we were sitting around outside, well fed and smoking cigarettes, sipping cognacs, when Bianca asked if anyone had seen Mick. She came around twenty minutes later, asking again. I had noticed that Annie was missing, too. This time Bianca took a seat with us, waiting for her husband, who soon showed up with sand on the knees of his white trousers. Annie followed a few minutes later. Bianca walked out without a word and there was a general sigh of relief. Then she returned with a large pot of water and poured it over Mick's head. It was hilarious. Justice!

When it came time for a Jimmy Buffett cover, Annie shot him in a white suit, standing in the ocean, fully soaked. Chet interviewed him on

St. Barts, a tiny French island in its modest days as an off-the-beaten-path paradise of local French citizens and a floating population of high-end hippies and drug smugglers. Chet gave a little too much attention to the smuggler's paradise part of the story and Jimmy's occasional involvement with the trade. His profile was of Jimmy at his cheeseburger-in-paradise best but got him kicked off the island. He had to wait a few years to return.

HOWARD KOHN TOOK an assignment I had been considering for Hunter. Sonny Barger, the president of the Hell's Angels, had just gotten back from a four-and-a-half-year jolt in Folsom Prison. It would be a great opportunity to catch up with the Angels and see how they had aged. One night Barger's number-two man blindfolded Howard, drove him to Sonny's house, and led him into a pitch-black garage. When the lights were turned on, he found himself in a circle of a dozen Angels in full colors who began closing in on him. He had to swear to keep secrets and tell the truth. He spent a few weeks with Barger and his lieutenants, who drove Lincoln Continentals and Corvettes, their hogs now kept inside except for ceremonial occasions. Howard subsequently found himself in the middle of a police investigation of the Angels, who had evolved from pool-cue-waving Altamont goons into an interstate drug-distribution syndicate. And killers. We had become adept at writing and producing crime stories, partially because of our interest in drug enforcement, partially because we treated them as serious sociology. They were always nonstop reads.

ANNIE AND I were all over the place. Sometimes I was a brother to her but, too often, a scolding father. She told me she felt sometimes like "the bad child." Very little could stand in the way of what she wanted, particularly getting a picture and her travel and studio expenses. As her drug use amped up, her carelessness about spending turned into recklessness. She would not return rental cars, leaving them parked at the curb if she was late for her plane. Her contribution to the magazine was rich and had defined our soul as much as Hunter had. Annie had something in nearly every issue, photojournalism and high-quality provocative portraiture, stark or tender. She could knock it out of the park. By this time, a *Rolling Stone* cover conferred iconic status. For record companies, it was gold. The fact that you were going to get a portrait by Annie was an extra incentive that got us anyone we wanted.

I had to reckon with Annie at home as well. She and Jane hung out at the apartment, taking cocaine and talking simultaneously to each other nonstop. There was no interrupting, and no one listened to anyone. To Annie, Jane was beautiful, sophisticated, and had exquisite taste in art, architecture, and design. Annie wanted to absorb all that. Annie was also in love with Jane, though I didn't know that at the time, nor would it have even occurred to me.

One of Annie's great covers at that point was Bette Midler posed as a pinup on a bed of long-stemmed red roses when Bette had her Oscar-nominated turn in *The Rose*. Annie's assistants spent a day picking off the thorns. Avedon sent me a letter complimenting Annie for one of the best covers of a magazine he had ever seen.

WE HAD GONE through a nearly complete turnover in the staff since we migrated east. I decided it was time to have another editorial conference, or perhaps someone said it was time we had a party on the company tab. This time it was in Sag Harbor, not Big Sur. The macho culture was done and gone. I tried to have a meeting one morning after breakfast, but there were too many people, and too many hangovers, to get anything said or settled. People brought musical instruments, and I brought a few guitars and amps as well. The nightlong jam was the weekend's highlight. The fun level was so high that everyone wanted a reprise at the annual Christmas party. Thus were born the Dry Heaves: Jon Pareles, our music editor, who would leave for the *New York Times*, on keyboards; Kurt Loder, who would leave for MTV News, on lead guitar; Tim White, who would leave for *Billboard*, on drums; Chuck Young, who stayed, on bass; and me on rhythm guitar. Plus, other staffers who wanted to sing and play had their slots. I would issue repertoire and schedules as formal memoranda. There were nighttime rehearsals in the office conference room. Peter Wolf came up to offer us advice, which was that we should all be in coats and ties. Thus were we dressed for our big night.

We took over the New York City club Austin City Limits. The place was packed with staff, spouses, squeezes, and significant others. The highlight was "Gotta Suck Somebody," a Dylan parody written by Ben Fong-Torres:

> *You might like acid, or you might like grass*
> *You might like tits or you might like ass*
> *You might like getting down at Studio 54*
> *You might know Steve Rubell and sail right through the door*
> *It might be the roadie*
> *It may be the boss*
> *But you're going to have to suck somebody*
>
> *You may know Paul Simon, you may know Elaine*
> *You may know Jann Wenner, you may even know Jane*
> *You may have home numbers for Ahmet or for Clive*
> *You may know the cast of* Saturday Night Live
>
> *Might like Rick Nelson, or Rickie Lee Jones*
> *Might like the Styx, might like the Stones*
> *Some people are suckers, some people get sucked*
> *Some people suck blood, some people just suck*
> *But you're going to have to suck somebody*

As the set began, Annie came in with Mick and sat in the front row. I was taking myself very seriously and was very focused. I was going to ignore him. I wasn't going to fall apart. When I took a brief break, Mick came over to me and offered a piece of advice: "Shake your ass."

CHAPTER 35

ASLEEP AT THE WHEEL

I TURNED THE EDITORIAL department over to Harriet Fier, once the girl at the switchboard in San Francisco, and named her managing editor. I had liked doing it myself, but it wasn't the same anymore. We had a new crew, all good, clearly, but not my family. Upstairs in our Fifth Avenue offices, on the twenty-seventh and twenty-eighth floors, I had a triumvirate of business guys — Kent Brownridge, Jim Dunning, and Claeys Bahrenburg — whom I liked working with and who could run the company. They were young, hard charging, and knew what they were doing. Finding businesspeople who were on my wavelength had bedeviled me in the past, but these guys were having fun at *Rolling Stone*. They were living it, breathing it, and making money.

SHOW BUSINESS WAS calling. The Beverly Hills Hotel was saying come stay with me. I knew nothing about screenplays, had never read one before. I had my drug-smuggling project with Hunter under way and met with Michael Mann, Oliver Stone, and Paul Schrader. None of them wanted to do my outlaw-hero adventure. They wanted dark, dark, dark. I wanted a happy ending, and they wanted violence. I sent my two original scripts to Michael Douglas for his thoughts, knowing he would be both honest and gentlemanly. He was thus, unfailingly. In so many words, he said each script would need to be rewritten from scratch. The movie business seemed so full of anxiety on so many levels, the stakes and judgments were personal and painful. No one would ever tell you no, they would just leave you hanging. In New York, people to whom you sent a manuscript were happy to be the first ones to say no.

I started to look for other ideas. Jonathan Cott and I wrote a post–*Star Wars* update of *Alice in Wonderland*, which hadn't been remade since the Disney classic of 1951, engaging with all the changes in technology, cultural sensibilities, rock and roll, and psychedelic imagery. How about the Jim Morrison story starring Matt Dillon? I took one last shot. I found a romance about a high-end New York bachelor who falls in love with a brassy Brooklyn taxi driver, called *Going to the Chapel*. It had been written with Bette Midler in mind. She agreed immediately. It was a vehicle for her and for whatever hunk she wanted opposite her. Bette's agent wanted $1.25 million, but Eisner was only willing to pay her $750,000. They wouldn't compromise. Finally, I gave it to Meryl Streep. Jonathan Demme was ready to direct it. She said yes; Paramount said no; I said goodbye.

HOLLYWOOD STRUCK AGAIN with a quasi-biographical comedy, *Where the Buffalo Roam*, about Hunter, starring Billy Murray. It was well meant but hopelessly bad, and our review called it "utterly devoid of plot, form, movement, tension, humor, insight, logic or purpose. The cultural revolution of the Sixties is reduced to a Three Stooges movie." Billy did an amazing job of capturing Hunter's physicality in each tic, step, and outburst. Hunter loved nearly every minute on and around the set — how could he not enjoy such an apotheosis? — even when he realized the buzzards were circling. There was a minor character actor playing me — he'd once played a wimpy Mafia kid trying to become a hit man — and in one scene I was shown putting golf balls in my office.

I HAD AN OFFICE at home, where I would do my reading and entertaining through the night. I would get to bed immediately if I heard the rumble of garbage trucks. My lunch spot was the ground-floor boîte of the Sherry-Netherland hotel, a block from the office. The Café Bar was small, old-fashioned, and discreet. Over the years I put away a boatful of grilled bay scallops there. Back in the office, I had a small refrigerator where a bottle of iced Polish vodka was always ready. I smoked Sherman cigarettes, the long kind wrapped in brown paper that came in hard red boxes. I would set a bottle on my desk, send down to the Capri Lounge for an order, and work away the afternoon.

The Capri Lounge was now open five days a week by popular demand, not only on deadline. The lounge was a darkroom located behind a double set of interlocking circular doors that opened on one side as the other shut to keep unwelcome daylight and visitors out. Inside was a convivial space for dabbling and dealing in drugs, particularly middling-quality blow. It was our camera room, now a relic of the past, run by two very well-liked guys we had brought with us from San Francisco, Patrick Cavanaugh and Tim Reitz — bearded, long-haired, down-to-earth, and lovable. We had an in-house dealing operation, an unofficial, off-the-books perk available to all staff.

JANE AND I were thirty-four years old, and we wanted children. We had stopped using birth control, expecting that sooner or later she would get pregnant. At the time we were staying in on the weekends, ordering Chinese food, and watching movies on laser discs, a hot new technology that preceded DVDs, and there were ample opportunities to conceive. We consulted a fertility specialist, passed the tests, and were given thermometers and calendars to calibrate our sex life. Most of our friends in New York did not have children at the time, but my longtime pals Ned Topham, John Warnecke, and Willie Hearst were all new dads. I couldn't pass a stroller or a child in Central Park without a longing smile and a wave hello. I liked to talk to kids of any age. I knew how to bring them out, that the secret was not talking down. I wanted children and was not willing to grow old without them.

UPON MY RETURN from La-La Land, I had to take a hard look at the magazine. I had been gone a year. There were no general assignment reporters on staff, just extremely talented music and entertainment writers. I found the magazine missing excitement and energy; there was nothing provocative about it. It was a quality magazine about music and movies, but other than the occasional good read (Gabriel García Márquez from postwar Vietnam, a *Rolling Stone* interview with our own writer Tom Wolfe), nothing rattled the rafters. Our campaign reporting was conscientious but predictable. Reagan's upcoming victory seemed predestined, and his impenetrable charm masked an unknown but grim reality that you could feel in your bones. Nothing good would come of this.

A letter from a reader in Kansas using the exact words and phrases from one of our record reviews said, "Peter Herbst's review of CSN, with its *a-melodic ramblings*, was far too *moralizing* and *intellectualizing* — so *disconsolate* and so full of *solipsism*. Herbst's *attitudinizing struck me as quixotic, albeit morosely*, in an *almost frighteningly dolorous way*. Come on, Peter, stop being *cloying*: *incomprehensible* only has six syllables — you can do better than that."

I was trying to think through how to broaden our scope, how to be more general interest, to start covering science and television, to reformat, get back to social and political issues. It came down to Harriet. As delightful and as hardworking as she was, the X factor was missing. I hated letting her go. I liked her, and she would have been fine as a features editor if I hadn't overpromoted her. I told her at the end of September, despite my reluctance and some resistance from friends. "Dear Jann," Harriet wrote me the next day, "I had the time of my life! I remain your friend, fan and loyal employee always. XXX H." She went on to become editor of the Style section at the *Washington Post* for years.

The Christmas cover was by Avedon, Dolly Parton dressed in a very skimpy Santa Claus outfit. It was commercial, fun, and just a few hairs short of *Playboy*. The magazine had become unmemorable and weak. Newsstand sales were slumping, a sign of danger, since those sales were the readers voting yes or no. It hadn't been a very good year.

CHAPTER 36

THE DREAM IS OVER

ECEMBER 8, 1980. John Lennon shot and killed.

Of all the people to bear the news to the nation, it fell to Howard Cosell, while calling a *Monday Night Football* game on ABC. He was the rough-edged sportscaster who had stood up for Cassius Clay as he transitioned to Muhammad Ali. The news was so improbable that it was beyond belief. Jane and I were stunned. Is it real? How could this happen? What should we do? I needed to talk to people who might help me. I called Jean Gleason, Ralph's widow. I got hold of Greil Marcus. They were understanding, but what could they do? I called Annie to have her go to the Dakota, where John had been gunned down, even though she didn't want to. It was all I could think of. In the early morning hours, when the phone calls stopped, I walked across Central Park to the Dakota, where several hundred people stood vigil in the winter air. I stood there trying to absorb the awesome and frightening reality that such a man, a towering man, an irreplaceable genius of my times, to whom I owed a deep personal debt, had been murdered, and that I, and perhaps all of us, were in scary, dark waters. My mind was filled with waves of sadness for Yoko and her son. And there I stood for hours.

The next week was gloom and solemn purpose. Nothing else mattered. John Lennon had been murdered. He was gone, this great man at the center of everything I believed and everything I was. Why does a man who writes of love, an artist who stands for peace, get shot down on his doorstep? What kind of world? What kind of madness or sickness? I went into the office each day, obviously badly shaken. The staff was quiet and respectful, probably pretty worried about me. We had to put out an issue. John and Yoko had just released a new album, *Double Fantasy*, their first in years, and they had been at work with Annie and Jonathan on a *Rolling Stone* cover story, like old times. We had great new photographs and what had become his last solo interview. John and Jonathan had spent nine hours with each other. I was determined to do the most beautiful tribute issue of all time. Everyone knew that we had to rise to an occasion that seemed unimaginable. The last line of our introduction read, "It's hard to believe our luck has gotten this bad." I insisted on being hands-on with every bit of it.

I stayed in my dark office listening to *Double Fantasy*, sinking deeper into mourning and sorrow. I felt dulled out, depressed, as I quietly worked on copy, approving layouts, taking phone calls, receiving people. I didn't speak with the reporters who called looking for a quote. Or book publishers trying to buy the rights to *Lennon Remembers* for a quickie reprint.

Jane Pauley, with whom I had become friends through her husband, Garry Trudeau, asked if I would be a guest on an NBC News special they were doing the night after the murder. I said I didn't want to go to a TV studio and look as if I was trying to generate publicity for the magazine, but if she wanted to come to my office that afternoon to tape an interview I would do it. When I watched the show that night, because of the way it had been lit, I looked as if I was sitting in my den by the fireside talking about John's personal and generational impact. At one point, Jane asked me if I thought John and Yoko deserved credit for ending the war in Vietnam. I'm not sure what she expected, but I didn't hesitate. "Yes. Absolutely. There were many factors that ended the war, but John and Yoko were one of them."

The next day Yoko called. She had been watching. She wanted me to come over to the Dakota. I had not seen her or John in person for ten years, even after Jane and I ended up in New York, living only ten minutes apart. John had been passing me messages through Jonathan during the past two weeks as we were gearing up to help them launch *Double Fantasy.*

A vigil was still under way outside the building, and I walked through the very place of his death and went up to her seventh-floor apartment, where I was asked to remove my shoes. There were beefy off-duty cops at the door and inside as well. It was hushed. No television was on, no newspapers were in sight. Yoko was under siege. She didn't know what would happen next. She gave me an account of the killer calling out John's name and then the gun coming out, how she and John had seen him there in the afternoon when they'd left, and what it had been like at the hospital. Sean scampered through to say hello and shake hands like a grown-up. She had John's glasses with dried blood on them. She wanted me to look at them and hold them.

Yoko asked for ten minutes of silence around the world on Sunday at 2:00 p.m., New York time. There were mass gatherings in Liverpool and London and cities across America and around the world. The largest was in Central Park. Jonathan came to my apartment and we walked over together. Over a hundred thousand people had assembled. The band shell was empty but for two stacks of speakers, a portrait of John on an easel, garlands of evergreen, and a single wreath. His softer songs played: "In My Life," "Norwegian Wood." The sun broke through for "All You Need Is Love," and the clouds reappeared for "Give Peace a Chance." Yoko had asked that radio stations around the world be silent for ten minutes. The helicopters flew away out of respect; there was not a noise of any kind among the hundred thousand people I was with. It was profoundly peaceful. You could feel John's spirit moving. After ten minutes, the meditation ended with "Imagine." As Jonathan and I walked back to the office, it began to snow. I felt older.

In our special issue we ran a portrait of him by Annie, sitting on the windowsill of his apartment in a black leather jacket, channeling his lifetime hero, Elvis. Annie also shot a photo of John and Yoko, with John naked, curled up in fetal position around Yoko. They had told Annie they wanted that picture on the cover. It was unimaginably powerful, an echo of their *Two Virgins* photo, and now something like a foreshadowing of death and rebirth. It said all there was to say, and I decided there would be no headline or words. I didn't like the idea of an advertisement on the back cover either and pulled it, at some cost, replacing it with the lyrics to "Imagine" in my own handwriting. The cover received wide recognition as one of the top ten magazine covers of the twentieth century, one of the best of all time. It is Annie's most famous portrait. Novelist Scott Spencer called it "the *Pietà* of our times." The picture and that moment in history became one and the same.

Just before we went to press I wrote a small note to John, promising to watch over Yoko and Sean, and had it taken to the printer, where, at the last minute, it was hidden in the binding, where the pages were stapled together, of two million issues. That was my secret, although Yoko somehow got wind of it twenty years later.

John and Yoko had kept watch over *Rolling Stone*. Now those days were gone.

CHAPTER 37

FUCK THE NRA

TERRY MCDONELL MOVED from Livingston, Montana, to New York to become my managing editor. He arrived the week before John Lennon was shot, read the situation wisely, and backed away while I put out the memorial issue as a spiritual ritual. A take-charge guy, Terry knew exactly how to run a magazine and liked to endlessly tinker with budgets. He also had a vision of what he wanted in his magazine. I moved up to the executive floor while someone else, who didn't particularly need my help, ran my shop. It would be my year of living desultorily.

Terry liked fiction, so we had Joe Heller, Richard Price, Tom McGuane, Robert Stone, J. P. Donleavy, and Kurt Vonnegut writing for us. Terry was not a rock and roller; Terry liked hanging out at Elaine's.

YOKO LEANED ON ME as she built a new life. My first piece of advice was to get rid of the off-duty cops and security inside her apartment. They were a horrible reminder that made the apartment an unpleasant place for her to live in and for Sean to grow up in. The Dakota was always a creepy building, the set for *Rosemary's Baby*, and to get in now you had to walk past the scene of the murder. The hallways and the elevator were dimly lit, with ornately carved dark wood. Inside Yoko's apartment was a world of Dalís, Magrittes, and Egyptian sarcophagi. The shades were shut, blocking the views of Central Park. At one end a kitchen and family room were filled with Lennon memorabilia; at the other was the "white room," the living room with the white piano on which John composed "Imagine."

WHY WAS JOHN LENNON killed? Why was he dead? I had to make his death stand for something, to have some good come out of it. I assigned Howard Kohn to take a look at why Americans owned more guns than any other country in the world. He turned in an investigation, which I made into a cover story with giant type — THE NRA: INSIDE THE GUN LOBBY — with a photo of John Lennon. Howard discovered an organization run by a self-perpetuating board for the interests of gun manufacturers, for their own personal financial gain, and to advance a broad right-wing agenda. And so began my education in one of the most intractable problems in American politics. I later discovered I had earned an NRA Marksmanship award when I was fourteen.

There were two small antihandgun groups in Washington, D.C., fighting as much with each other as against the gun lobby. I decided to start my own group. I hired Jimmy Carter's deputy director of the Environmental Protection Agency to start the Foundation on Violence in America. Friends chipped in with big contributions. I was surprised to find out that it was not so hard to ask people for money if you had a righteous mission. In a way, it was an honor. I commissioned Peter Hart, the Democratic pollster, to conduct a study on the public's attitudes and ideas about violence. I thought I could mobilize a unified campaign to alter the perceptual and political environment, and hopefully change the debate. One of the key questions asked was who the respondents thought would be the best spokespeople on handgun control. In the past we had heard only from clergymen, movie stars, senators, and victims. But far and away, the people we asked said it was the cops on the beat or local chiefs of police that they would trust on this subject. I had not expected that.

The question then became how to bring the police into an alliance with us former draft-dodging, long-haired potheads. I got Ed Thompson, editor in chief of *Reader's Digest*, to join my effort, and together we went around promoting our common cause to old and young, conservative and liberal alike. I met the New York City police commissioner and the San Jose and Atlanta police chiefs and the superintendent of the Chicago Police Department, an old-school cop with a buzz cut. These men knew that the NRA stuff about self-protection was pure bullshit. The police chiefs joined our board. We convened our first summit with the handgun groups, where Peter Hart presented our findings, his analysis, and our plan to make the police the spokespeople for gun control. I had no idea what I was up against.

THE FIRST MENTION of U2 in *Rolling Stone* was a small profile in our music section by Jim Henke, a native Clevelander who had taken on the duties of music editor. It was a bylined story from Coventry, England, where he interviewed their front man, Bono Vox, at a local club gig: "'I don't mean to sound arrogant,' the loquacious Vox tells me, 'but even at this stage I do feel we are meant to be one of the great groups. There was a certain spark, a certain chemistry that was special about the Stones, the Beatles and the Who and I think it's also special about U2.'"

On the other hand, our critics didn't particularly like Queen. The group's drummer, Roger Taylor, sent us a letter decrying "your peculiar 1970 time-warp attitude coupled with an innate, congenital miscomprehension of rock and roll...the pseudo-political political slant and the personal dishonesty that you continue to peddle in your outdated, opinionated, down-home rag." The letter was written on an airline motion-sickness bag.

Stuck for a cover idea, I came up with the inspiration of doing a dead rock star, namely Jim Morrison, a breakthrough concept at the time. Since the *Apocalypse Now* soundtrack and the million-selling biography *No One Here Gets Out Alive*, by Jerry Hopkins, one of *Rolling Stone's* founding fathers, Jim Morrison was hot again. The headline, which I wrote — though others may claim credit — lives in infamy: "He's Hot, He's Sexy, He's Dead." The same issue had a photo essay on gay rodeo cowboys.

MTV's GURU AND founder, an ex–disc jockey, Bob Pittman, and his wife, Sandy, took Jane and me to dinner one night at the Quilted Giraffe, the first of the ultraexpensive, over-the-top gastronomic restaurants in New York. I felt awkward because it was like corporate entertaining; the wives didn't know each other, and I barely knew Bob. He had a motive, which was an offer to purchase *Rolling Stone* in exchange for 25 percent of MTV. I saw it as a cultural and musical mismatch. I declined.

The movie *Rich and Famous* was released that summer, in which a famous writer, played by Jacqueline Bisset, falls head over heels into an affair with a hunky *Rolling Stone* reporter. This to me was a vast improvement over Shelley Duvall as the daffy *Rolling Stone* writer in *Annie Hall*. Our only other prior movie cameo was in *Looking for Mr. Goodbar*, in which Richard Gere snorts cocaine off a cover of *Rolling Stone*.

Paul Simon and I threw a bachelor party for Lorne right after Labor Day. Lorne was marrying Susan. We took over the Friars Club one night, trying to be like old-fashioned show business guys. Lorne liked to quote studio moguls. We got Henny Youngman to emcee, and the guest list was comedy Grand Central Station. It was the last time I saw John Belushi. He had just finished a new movie. John was fit and healthy, but there was jealousy in the air among the colleagues he had left behind at *SNL*.

THE ROLLING STONES were back — Mick and Keith had resigned themselves to a new truce — rehearsing in rural Massachusetts, getting ready for their first tour in three years. They were nineteen years into their career. Annie shot a great cover of Keith wrapped in a scarf, the skull ring prominent on his hand and looking scary overall. Bill Graham, who was managing their tour, called me up, pissed off because, he said, we had chosen that photo specifically to make Keith look like a junkie. They played three nights in New York; Tina Turner opened. I decided to stand in the pit, crushed among the fans, and went nuts. Bob Palmer wrote, "They were rocking harder than I have ever heard them rock before. Was it *meaningful*? Did it have *cultural relevance*? Was it the *rallying cry of a generation*? It wasn't about cultural relevance; it was about stomping the joint down to the bricks." I thought it was no longer a roadshow for the apocalypse. I saw generational relevance — maturity, that rock and roll can grow up.

WE HAD OUR first piece by P. J. O'Rourke, "Lessons in Modern Manners." It was a hilarious guide to the etiquette of cocaine, just exactly how dumb, greedy, craven, hypocritical, sneaky, sex-crazed, sex-disabled, incoherent, babbling, and selfish you could get in a blizzard of "Aspen indoor lift lines." How to invite people to go to the bathroom with you and not invite others, how to introduce your dealer … is he your friend? Your employee? "Is it polite to refuse the offer of a hit of cocaine? It's hard to know because it has never been done."

I always called him O.J., a silly reference to the golden football great. He grew up in Toledo, Ohio, where his dad was a car salesman. He ended up with a master's in English from Johns Hopkins and got swept into the student protests. He was dressing full preppy when we met, when he was editor of the *National Lampoon*. Like all comedians I've known, he had a compulsion, a sort of nervous tic, to have a flow of one-liners. Our luck was that he was a terrific wordsmith, too. We immediately hit it off, and Terry recruited him to leave the *Lampoon* to join us.*

---

* Many collections of P. J.'s *Rolling Stone* articles were published, several of which, *Parliament of Whores*, *Republican Party Reptile*, and *Holidays in Hell*, hit the bestseller lists.

JACKIE TOOK A job as a book editor. I started giving her first look at our books, starting with a coffee-table book about the Beatles. Andy Warhol would do the cover; we would have exclusive rights to Avedon's famous solarized portraits. She couldn't sell it to her new bosses at Doubleday, a reliable but musty Book of the Month Club–type publisher. When the book was issued by another house she wrote me a letter. "It is the most beautiful book and don't think I won't show it around here and grind a few noses in the dust...And your front-page *NY Times* Book Review! I am happy for you, the father of it all. Congratulations. And do give me another chance. It should be easier next time."

I gave her a proposal for *The Ballad of John and Yoko,* a collection of our articles and interviews with them, which they did buy. When I turned in my preface to her, it was perfunctory, essentially lifeless. Jackie wrote me a letter back:

Dear Jann,

I understand how painful it is for you to write about John Lennon. That is why, I believe, your preface is so distanced... You don't have to use the word crusade, but you did crusade for him, on his immigration fight, which was a crusade against injustice. You are crusading against violence now...It helps people who mourn to be able to do something for the cause of the fallen, not to have let them have died in vain, even though you may feel a deep weariness and despair. You mustn't, in your preface, abdicate a leadership that has meant a great deal to people. As a friend, I want this preface to show what you have stood for. Nothing will be served by self-effacement. With the reserve I respect in your piece, could you permit a flash of personal feeling to show? In no more than a sentence could you say something to the effect that you loved his music, his point of view, his fight, that you were his friend?

CHAPTER 38

GOD HAS
HIS HANDS FULL

EAGAN PUT US back in the national affairs business. The three-term governor of California was also the first media creation sold to us as president, one who embodied the myth of a benevolent small-town America. Meanwhile, he would begin to dismantle what was a progressive tax system that helped build the great American middle class in favor of huge cuts for the rich.

Both Hunter and Jon Landau had recommended we hire William Greider. The assistant managing editor of the *Washington Post*, Bill had already created a scandal for the Reagan administration in his interviews with David Stockman, the whiz kid Office of Management and Budget director known as "the father of Reaganomics," who admitted that supply-side economics was "just a Trojan horse to bring down the top tax rates." Bill was also the man who coined the term "Nader's Raiders."

It took a while to woo Bill. He was in his midforties, had two kids and a powerful job at a hugely influential newspaper. He had gone to Princeton but was no Ivy League gentleman journalist. He was about social policy and the cost of living, not politicians and dinner parties. He was an advocate for the people, democracy, and unions. He took ideas well, but not direction, and he was a prickly man to edit. Bill did not wear expensive suits, polish his shoes often, or visit his barber. He stayed with us for seventeen years.

The first of his two big pieces before the 1980 election was on income inequality, "Brother, Can You Spare a Million?" Bill took on both parties for not telling the truth about how wealth, and therefore political power, had been concentrated among relatively few people in America. His second piece was about the rising role of religion in American politics, how the fundamentalist preacher Jerry Falwell "tells us that God has chosen Ronald Reagan and George Bush as divine instruments." Under the cover of cultural war and religious morality, the rich would get incredibly richer and the poor a lot poorer.

JOHN BELUSHI DIED in Los Angeles in March. No one was shocked that it was a drug overdose; John did everything in excess. We all had taken drugs with him. The surprise was how scared his death made us, how easy it was to see that happen to you or someone you had known. It badly spooked Hunter. I had very occasionally tried sniffing heroin; one time it was in the early morning hours with someone who was found dead the next day.

It was sad, it was disappointing, it felt inevitable. We flew up to Martha's Vineyard on a small plane through stormy weather for John's burial. It was an Albanian Orthodox service in a small wooden church. He was in an open coffin. I spent a few minutes looking at John, thinking about him, talking to him, both with love and anger. Danny Aykroyd rode his Harley and led the hearse to the grave site. It was just his family and a few dozen friends and colleagues. We stood in the cold, a light snow falling, watching the casket lowered as James Taylor stood with his guitar and sang:

> If I had stopped to listen once or twice
> If I had closed my mouth and opened my eyes
> If I had cooled my head and warmed my heart
> I'd not be on this road tonight
> Walk down that lonesome road, all by yourself

John's tombstone reads, "I may be gone, but rock and roll lives on." There was a large memorial for him the next day at the Cathedral of St. John the Divine in New York City. As he had promised John, Danny played a recording of "King Bee" from the pulpit.

John told me that Albanians — he was 100 percent Albanian — were the most quarrelsome people in the world, and he definitely got whatever he wanted, but his heart was big. John could be abusive, and a lot of people couldn't handle it, but those who did loved him. Don Novello, the *SNL* comic known as Father Guido Sarducci (who covered a papal tour of the United States for us), closed our tribute issue to John: "It was a joy to have known him, and an honor to be his friend, and we all know now that God has his hands full."

HENRY KISSINGER WAS one of the central villains of those times. I had been hoping that the articles of impeachment against Nixon would include the secret bombing of Cambodia, but too many people were complicit who would have to be charged, and it was dropped. Steadman had done an image of Kissinger as Godzilla, breathing fumes, clutching a rolled-up document in his claws labeled "Peace with honor." Dan Ellsberg had excoriated him in our interview. Now we commissioned William Shawcross, a tall, gangly Brit, to review Kissinger's memoirs. Willie's father had been the British chief prosecutor at the Nuremberg trials. After an Eton and Oxford education, Willie, who was just my age, had become an international activist and journalist. He had written *Sideshow*, a book that exhumed and fully laid at Kissinger and Nixon's feet the secret bombing and destruction of Cambodia, one of the most inhumane acts in American history. We published Willie's critique as our lead feature in May. It described a group of sick, mad people who had carried out a scheme of cold butchery.

OUR MUSIC STAFF was impressive. We essentially had our pick of any music writer we wanted, although I had lost a few stars over the past fifteen years. Jim Henke had come aboard, along with Chet Flippo, Kurt Loder, Paul Nelson, Mikal Gilmore, Chris Connelly, Michael Goldberg, David Wild, Dave Marsh, Tim White, Fred Schruers, Jancee Dunn, Jenny Eliscu, Kim Neely, Jon Pareles, Daisann McLane, Anthony Bozza, and, soon, David Fricke. Henke was a music-loving son of an amateur musician, who had joined our copy desk from the *Cleveland Plain Dealer*. He ultimately returned to that city to be the head curator of the Rock and Roll Hall of Fame. On first impression he was a nebbish, but in fact he was a nerd, focused on one thing: rock music. Later on we added Andy Greene, Patrick Doyle, and Brian Hiatt to our rather talented lineup of music writers.

Paul Nelson was a man of literature, from Dashiell Hammett to Warren Zevon. He wore a snap-brim tweed golfer's hat, spoke with a downbeat Midwestern drawl, and always had a cigarette between his lips. His early claim to fame was lending his Woody Guthrie records to Bob Dylan when he was in college in Minnesota, which Dylan never returned. Paul ran the record review section, gave it a serious book review tone, and was himself a fine profiler and meaningful critic. One of our all-time best.

Chris Connelly was a scholarship product of New York's private schools, with lawyers as parents. His mom took him to hear Martin Luther King speak at the Lincoln Memorial in 1963. He answered our ad in the *New York Times* for a part-time receptionist and was hired because he had a "good phone voice." Reception was on the editorial floor, and he was the ever cheery mascot type who got to know all the editors and started getting assignments for "Random Notes." Finally, he took over the section and ran it for three years. We had a great interviewer then in Nancy Collins. She was an outspoken blonde who specialized in unabashedly asking for the intimate details. Among others she did John Travolta, Jack Nicholson, and Bette Midler, people I knew, who shocked me with the stuff they told Nancy.

AT LONG LAST I had to go head-to-head with the record business. The issue was home taping and the impact that new technology was having on their profits. Record sales had declined considerably, for which the industry blamed people who taped borrowed records. They began lobbying Congress to enact a federal tax on sales of blank tapes and cassette recorders. Our role was to advocate for the interests of the music fans and the musicians. I believed the sales slump was about a cyclical downturn in the vitality of the music and the too high prices for records that were becoming less desirable as they were rushed out faster and faster.

The industry had closed ranks around a doomed misunderstanding of its dedicated, devoted customers and the changing technology. David Geffen, whose label was being distributed by Warner Bros., didn't buy that line and told the *Rolling Stone* reporter, "Home taping exists and that's that. It will always be around and there's nothing we can do. When a company starts complaining about home taping taking away sales from new acts, it's usually trying to make excuses for the lousy job it's doing in the A&R department."

A few days before we went to press with "The War on Home Taping," David called and asked me for a favor. He had just been put in charge of the record industry's war on home taping, and could I take his statement out? It was too late, I explained, and would cause a rebellion from my staff of journalists, one that would blow up in my face and his. He had directly undercut his new position, and his statement was a "smoking gun." The bill stalled in Congress. He could not understand that my sense of personal and professional integrity should prevail over doing him a favor. Our once close friendship never fully recovered.

By then records had become one of our smallest advertising categories, probably not even profitable due to the deep discounts we gave to the music business, because I thought record ads were a part of what our readers looked forward to, a form of news and part of the general purview of the magazine. But that purview by then had grown to include automobiles, beer, Marlboro men, Sheik and Trojan condoms, Zales diamonds, and double-page spreads of the pecs on the Bowflex exercise man.

WHEN REAGAN INVADED the tiny Caribbean island of Granada to stop communism's latest attempt to undermine American freedoms, we sent Hunter, despite his failures in Saigon and Zaire, hopeful that this was an assignment, limited in scope and with zero hardship, that he could do easily. Terry McDonell wanted to handle it, but as soon as he told me that Hunter had done a tape with a taxi driver that would be the basis for the piece, I knew we were sunk. We both wanted Hunter back at his typewriter, but nothing worked, no matter how easy we tried to make it, including a carte blanche column where Hunter could unleash any screed he wanted, which he wanted to call Asshole of the Month.

Terry's two-year commitment to me was up. He was a strong leader and had strong ideas, like me, only there was too much butting of heads, which killed the fun. So, he left, and we stayed good friends. Terry returned to work for me some years later as editor of both *Men's Journal* and *US Weekly*.

CHAPTER 39

DIAMOND RASH, LIMOUSINE ELBOW

MICHAEL DOUGLAS SENT me a strip-o-gram for my birthday. The editors crowded into my office to cheer on the uncomfortable moment. I was thirty-six and by any measure an adult, with a wife, a career, and responsibilities.

In our first issue of 1983 we reported on a new piece of equipment only available in Japan, the $1,000 compact disc player, with the headline "Will the Compact Disc Make the LP Obsolete?" Our main feature in the next issue was "Is There Death After Sex?" Three hundred people across the U.S. had died from what was being called the "gay plague," and half of them were in our hometown, New York City. We spoke to every scientist and researcher at work on it. They thought it might be spread by unsanitary food handling. Another long piece of reporting was a narrative and analysis of how the NRA defeated the handgun-control forces on a California ballot proposition, 4.7 million to 2.8 million votes. That was despite the killings of a California mayor and a city supervisor by handguns, not to mention John Lennon and failed attempts on Ronald Reagan, George Wallace, and the pope. Outspent, outmaneuvered, outgunned.

ANNIE LEFT. SHE had reached the end of her rope—physically, emotionally—and her survival instinct was receding. Drugs had leached her strength; this big, powerful woman was barely able to execute assignments without a wide berth for scheduling, sobriety, and sudden disappearances. She didn't care what she spent, where her equipment was, who had her negatives. It was a mess, which I tried to handle, but she was out of control. One day I got a call that Annie had been taken to a hospital uptown near Harlem. She almost died there. She was laid out, barely conscious, on a gurney that had been left in a hallway on a busy floor. No one was paying attention. Jane showed up just after I did. Annie was losing her color fast. Jane started yelling at the attendants and doctors passing by, and refused to be quiet until finally help came. I called Annie's parents to ask them to take over, and her brother Philip came right away.

After she recovered and cleaned up, Annie never touched drugs again. She took up a large contract shooting for *Vogue* and *Vanity Fair*, and did memorable advertising campaigns. She is now considered the world's greatest living portrait photographer. Annie had done nearly five hundred assignments for me in her decade as chief photographer, not to mention how she chronicled and shared Jane's and my life.

We have stayed lifelong friends.

ONCE ANNIE LEFT, I started offering more assignments to Avedon. We got along extremely well; Jane and I saw a lot of him and his companion, Renata Adler. We had vacations together in St. Martin, and spent the most old-fashioned Christmas ever at his house in Montauk, when it had snowed nearly two feet. Dick was drawn to gifted people, including those in rock and roll, and he liked sexy. He was eager to do Prince, who specialized in sexy. Dick did a portrait of him in a purple overcoat, wearing white lace gloves, a leather neck collar, and softly licking his upper lip. Eddie Murphy and Boy George also showed up at Dick's studio to get the treatment—a setting, a look in the camera, a magnetism that Dick knew how to conjure with the plunger in his hand as he stood next to his big box camera. Dick rarely took more than two or three photos once he had composed and lit the subject.

He took assignments from us for another ten years, and we ran the portfolio of his American West project. Working with him was always some kind of whirlwind from which you absorbed the forcefulness of his ambition. He was endlessly seductive but blatantly manipulative whenever it served him. I was a cheerleader until one day I wasn't, but I still find myself in thrall to him, perhaps because I saw a lot of myself there.

WE BEGAN A cartoon series about Nancy Reagan's life in the White House by James Pendergrast, recently of the U.S. Navy, who did the witty drawings on our letters page for years. He brought our attention to her medical issues like "diamond rash" and "limousine elbow." Bill Greider started bringing guests to lunch with the editors in New York: Jesse Jackson, Gary Hart, Jerry Brown, Walter Mondale. One was California senator Alan Cranston, the majority whip and a friend of my mother's during her days in Democratic politics. I was bringing up Barry Diller, Calvin Klein, and David Geffen to meet the editors. "The Gay Mafia." And Norman Pearlstine, the editor of the *Wall Street Journal*, who knew more about rock and roll than most of our staff.

HUNTER WROTE ONE of his least-known but best pieces, oddly enough centered on a divorce trial in Palm Beach. I had despaired of Hunter being productive again. I told Terry he was over-the-hill and couldn't report anymore. But before Terry left the magazine, he came up with the idea of Hunter covering the Roxanne Pulitzer divorce trial; he told Hunter that I had said he was washed up. That made Hunter nuts, ranting about showing me, and he started making expense account demands. We were giving Hunter this "big story" as a challenge.

"There is a lot of wreckage in the fast lane these days," Hunter wrote. "Not even the rich feel safe from it, and people are looking for reasons. The smart set say they can't understand it and the dumb snort cocaine in rich discos and stomp to a feverish beat. The stomping of the rich is not a noise to be ignored in troubled times. It usually means they are feeling anxious and confused and they act like wild animals."

Hunter worshipped F. Scott Fitzgerald. A reading of *The Great Gatsby* quickly reveals the language and the techniques that Hunter absorbed. In fact, he once had typed out the whole novel to help him understand how it worked and how Fitzgerald wrote it. He gave his son, Juan, the middle name Fitzgerald.

Hunter was right for that territory, the search for the American Dream, just substitute cocaine for bootleg whiskey: "There are hideous scandals occasionally — savage lawsuits over money, bizarre orgies at the Bath and Tennis Club or some genuine outrage like a half-mad, eighty-eight-year-old heiress trying to marry her teenage Cuban butler — but scandals pass like winter storms in Palm Beach and it has been a long time since anyone got locked up for degeneracy in this town…The penalty for forgetting your place can be swift and terrible. When word got out that I was in town asking questions about the Pulitzer divorce trial, I was shunned like a leper."

This was not Fitzgerald's famous "the rich are different from you and me"; it was pure Hunter: "Palm Beach was becoming a place where price tags mean nothing, and the rich are always in heat, where pampered animals are openly worshipped in church and naked millionaires gnaw the brassieres off the chests of their own daughters in public."

I found it impossible not to laugh out loud when I read his stuff. Hunter had found his voice, his métier, his song. The subtext here was plain if you wanted to see it. Cocaine. The drug was everywhere in the eighties. It didn't matter where you went or whom you knew: someone had it and would give you a hit, as if they were buying you a drink, my new friend.

Cocaine's destructive powers were less known than the sly gags that

Johnny Carson would slip into his shows. Hunter barely tried to be discreet; he was a connoisseur. He also knew the dangers. "Welcome to cocaine country," he wrote while at the trial. "What is a judge to make of two coke fiends who spent $441,000 on miscellaneous and unknowns? It suggests a genuinely awesome rate of consumption — like thirteen grams a day. The numbers are staggering, even in the context of Palm Beach. Thirteen grams a day would kill a whole family of polar bears."

The last scene is Hunter, moved to Palm Beach, cruising the oceanside at dawn in a red convertible, with a bottle of champagne, a head full of bogus cocaine, and two beautiful lesbians sitting in the front seat, talking to each other in French. My favorite line of the whole piece: "What's wrong with incest anyway? It takes 200 years of careful inbreeding to produce a line of beautiful daughters, and only a madman would turn them out to strangers."

RICHARD GERE AND his Brazilian girlfriend, Sylvia Martins, a painter and free spirit, were our standing houseguests for the summer. He was filming *The Cotton Club* in the city and showed up every weekend furious about something Francis Coppola had done. I went to the set one night with him and sat in a trailer with Francis, who was directing his movie on a dozen video screens hooked up remotely to the cameras and smoking too much dope. On weekends Richard liked to mosey around in his underwear and would sit in the pool, where they would become nearly transparent. He asked me one day if I was homosexual, because it was perfectly okay with him. His brother was. I said no, as casually as possible. Senator Cranston came to stay with his wife, whom he didn't seem to be too interested in. Luckily, Richard and Sylvia were there, because it was a stiff weekend. Jane said it was like having her parents visit. We had a big back lawn and a regulation croquet set. Richard was a gung ho player. We mixed up a lot of Bloody Marys and got Cranston onto the field. He turned out to be an aggressive, competitive player, and beat all of us. Alan took me aside at one point to talk about a "confidential" campaign matter. He said he was thinking ahead to the general campaign (he withdrew after three primaries) and wanted to know if I would do concerts for him and raise money from ticket sales that would go unreported. The lesson I learned about politics was how easily I said yes.

That summer I also took up ten-speed road racing, and every weekend headed out to the Montauk Lighthouse. I was one of those people in a yellow/green/orange jersey, Lycra stretch pants and cleats on their shoes, bent over steadying the nose of their bike six inches from the back tire of someone in a line of other riders. Kent Brownridge, then our circulation manager, was an international competitor on the senior circuit, and initiated me into the sport. Soon we had the *No Mas* Club, with a few of the office twenty-somethings, who rode every weekend. I could climb some tough hills.

PETE TOWNSHEND WROTE a lengthy essay, "A Discourse on Mick Jagger's Fortieth Birthday," and sent us a picture of himself holding a lit candle with "Happy Birthday Mick" written across his chest. Pete was both a friend and a fan of Mick's. He explored how you could be one or the other or both, as well as his personal attraction to Mick. "He was wriggling like an eel, the first time I ever laid eyes on him, face to bum, having heard all about this splendid animal from the girls at my art college...He is still very beautiful in my eyes; much has been said of his androgynous attraction, and I suppose my own response to his physical presence confirms all that. Jagger is such a charismatic person that he could easily make you forget his looks...Is Mick Jagger really the ruthless, conniving, duplicitous, scheming, evil-touched, money greedy, sex-mad, cowardly, vain, power hungry swine that his biographers and newspaper hounds have made him out to be? Incredibly, many journalists also feel they have a privileged relationship with Jagger. He is so courteous and gentlemanly."

THE ORIGINAL ROLLING STONE, McKinley Morganfield, born on a plantation in 1915, died at sixty-eight years old. He grew up to become

Muddy Waters, the originator of the electric blues band and, to my mind, the grandfather of rock and roll. Keith called him "the code book. He was more than a singer, a writer, or a guitar player. He was the hoochie-coochie man." Marshall Chess remembered meeting him when Marshall was eight years old; his father had founded Chess Records and discovered Muddy. Bonnie Raitt, who toured with him frequently, said there should be a giant statue of Muddy in Chicago, like the great Buddhas in Thailand, with his eyes closed and his beatific smile. Muddy's first hit song was "Rollin' Stone."

STEVE JOBS LAUNCHED the Macintosh in a burst of advertising, magazine covers, and an Orwellian-themed Super Bowl commercial in 1984. He came to my apartment one night with Pigozzi, who took a telling Polaroid of us. Steve was a head taller, but both of us were dressed in jeans and with hair to our shoulders. We shared cultural and spiritual touchstones—he was an LSD and Dylan devotee, as passionate and even deeper than I was, from San Francisco. He didn't have much interest in print, and I didn't care for computing machines. Steve made a speech at the annual Magazine Publishers Association conference soon after we met, telling them that print was dead and computers would destroy their businesses. He was twenty-five years early, but he was right. I would see him now and then on social occasions but he made himself hard to get to know. He was always respectful to me.

If we didn't have anything obvious to put on the cover, we could always come up with a reason to do the Beatles. They would usually sell more copies than anyone else. Thus, we had a Beatles cover every year. One, from February 1984, was for a story about early fans who remembered seeing them for the first time on *Ed Sullivan* in 1964. We were breathlessly covering a twenty-year-old television show.

CHAPTER 40

THE HALL OF FAME

I GOT A CALL from a woman I didn't know on behalf of Ahmet, asking if I would be interested in joining a committee for a new organization he was starting: the Rock and Roll Hall of Fame. The motley crew Ahmet had assembled included his ex-partner Jerry Wexler, the gray-bearded rabbi of rhythm and blues; Noreen Woods, his longtime assistant, who was dating Ben E. King, the former Drifter who cowrote and sang "Stand By Me"; and Bob Krasnow, the hot-tempered president of Elektra Records, who had advertised Captain Beefheart in the first issue of *Rolling Stone*, and the man who gave me my first taste of cocaine. Ahmet's instinct also led him to a shrewd lawyer, Alan Grubman, who didn't know Jerry Lee Lewis from Jerry Lewis. Susan Evans became our executive director. Seymour Stein was designated president. Seymour was a music-mad kid from Brooklyn. At age fifteen he went to work for *Billboard*. He was quite the character in the New York demimonde — gay and married with kids — both an impulsive child and a bona fide elder, having signed the Ramones, Talking Heads, and Madonna. Nuts. Selfish. Frustrating. But in fact, lots of fun. I quickly discovered that this board was window dressing for a speculative television show. I persuaded Ahmet to get out of that deal and go for the history books, a nonprofit institution for rock and roll music equivalent in status to the Academy Awards or the Baseball Hall of Fame.

I soon began to take the lead, careful to be deferential to Ahmet's instincts and intuition for what was right. I was surprised by how immature and unsophisticated many of the record executives were when they would join us for meetings. We began visiting cities that had expressed interest in having the Hall of Fame: Philadelphia, Chicago, Memphis, and Cleveland. We could barely get a response from New York City because it didn't need another cultural attraction, let alone one as amorphous as a music museum. Memphis' big inducement was free round-trip airfares. Chicago's mayor welcomed us with a speech quoting the "words of the immortal Bruce Springtime." I personally liked Philly; they offered us a Greek-columned building on the University of Pennsylvania campus. Our last stop was Cleveland.

IN 1986 WE rented the gilded grand ballroom of the Waldorf Astoria to hold the first black-tie dinner to honor those who had founded rock and roll when they were teenagers on the fringes of American life. Portraits of the honorees hung from the balcony. I wondered what hardscrabble guys like Little Richard, Chuck Berry, or Jerry Lee Lewis, who had never made big money off their talent, would feel like, coming into a formal celebration in this place, seeing their image on the wall, being honored for their way of life.

The first meetings about who would be the first ten inductees had been filled with reminiscences and stories of how our lives had been blessed and shaped by them. Making the decisions was an act of love as much as scholarship. Who were truly the Founding Fathers? Which early executives were significant? We chose Sam Phillips, who owned Sun Records, and Alan Freed, the DJ who coined the phrase "rock and roll," loved it, played it, and brought it to the world. Ahmet knew those guys, they had been his friends and rivals. Ahmet introduced the first dinner saying, "Rock and roll has generally not been taken as seriously as popular art, but it is a direct outgrowth of American musical traditions, especially black traditions. The artists who planted the seeds have received little recognition. Those of us who know where this music came from have an obligation to acknowledge and honor them."

It was the most extraordinary reunion one could have imagined, the young men who had together ridden an outlaw circuit — chased and shut down by segregationists, cops, politicians, parents, and preachers. James

Brown and Ray Charles — perhaps Ahmet's greatest artist — were there. The Everly Brothers and Elvis Presley's widow and daughter (who accepted the honor from John Lennon's kids, Sean and Julian) came, as well as the widow and daughter of Buddy Holly. The first inductee was Chuck Berry. Keith Richards came shuffling and mumbling to the stage in a black tuxedo jacket. He admitted to stealing all of Chuck's licks and then ripped off his jacket, revealing a leopard-print jacket. Chuck duck walked to the podium to receive his award.

WE DECIDED TO locate the museum in Cleveland. The city obviously wanted us and offered us $25 million to build it. Ahmet told us at the time he thought it would in the end cost $100 million, which it did. No one on the board really wanted to be in Cleveland, once a dynamic big city — now best known for the Cuyahoga River catching fire from its industrial waste — but they needed us. When we flew out for a visit, a delegation, including the governor of Ohio and the presidents of the local Fortune 500 companies, met us at the airport and gave us a tour of the city. At every stop crowds of people were carrying banners and waving signs. At lunch they presented a petition signed by over 750,000 Clevelanders who wanted us to come. I overturned all objections to the city, and Ahmet went along with me.

Ahmet had already decided on our architect. There was no competition, bidding, or process. He wanted I. M. Pei, who had recently finished his glass pyramid at the Louvre. I. M. was not a rock and roller; he was seventy. He was a slight man, born in China, dressed in tailored suits, soft-spoken, an old-world gentleman. He had designed the John F. Kennedy Library, so I called Jackie to find out whether she thought I should work with him. She said, "If I had to choose one person in the world to be stranded with on a desert island, it would be I. M."

On matters rock and roll, we had to bring I. M. up to speed. Ahmet and I began taking him to concerts, starting with something easy, a Paul Simon show. Then we graduated to the loud stuff. We took I. M. and his wife, Eileen, to Graceland, one of the kitschiest places on the planet, with our wives, Susan Evans, and Seymour Stein along. We flew on to New Orleans to continue our musical education. Ahmet's Louis Vuitton suitcase, custom made for eight pairs of shoes, got lost, and a limo driver had to wait for it at the airport all night. We chartered a small bus and toured the slave plantations at the very roots of American music. That night we all went to Tipitina's, where Ahmet and I got drunk — continuing I. M.'s lessons in rock and roll. The Peis watched us with polite amusement, as if nothing unusual was happening. After we got back to New York, I. M. told me he had figured it out, the music and what the building should be about: "Energy." This was 1985. Ten years were to pass before the doors opened.

MICK JAGGER BEGAN his acceptance speech at the annual induction ceremony saying, "We're being rewarded for twenty-five years of bad behavior." I had begun the evening, our third dinner, on a serious note, dedicating the night to Roy Orbison, who had died the month before, the first person to go to rock and roll heaven after being inducted. A very plastered Phil Spector, bopping along to "Be My Baby," was escorted onto the stage by his three beefy bodyguards. He mumbled something and then his bodyguards picked him up off the floor and almost lifted him offstage. Jon Landau, who was sitting with Bruce, had maxed out on vodka and had to be helped out. Little Richard was next up, to induct Otis Redding. They were both from Macon, Georgia. He ran onstage singing "I Can't Turn You Loose," stood at the podium, and did a medley of other Otis hits.

Pete Townshend did the honors for the Stones: "They are all alive. We all know who they are. Why do we have to induct them?" He mentioned how much he owed each of them, but that "none of those things were practical, wholesome, or useful." Pete addressed the rumors that the Stones might reunite and go back on the road: "If it weren't for the vast sums of money they'd make, they might not bother at all. Or at least Mick wouldn't." That was perfectly aimed. "I got so much from the Stones. I had no idea how much of it was secondhand." His conclusion was eloquent and simple. "Guys, whatever you do, don't try and grow old gracefully. It wouldn't suit you."

The last inductee was Stevie Wonder. I got goose bumps guiding him across the stage. He took off his dark glasses, revealing his blind, useless eyes, a startling, intimate, and vulnerable moment, and asked everyone to close their eyes "as I take you through the experience of my life. The sound of hearing many different voices from many different cultures." As soon as the assembled stars returned to the stage and got to their microphones, Stevie took control and led the multitude on a nonstop, fifteen-minute medley of "Uptight," "Satisfaction," "Ain't Too Proud to Beg," "Respect," "Be My Baby," and finally "Lucille." Mick Jagger and Little Richard tore into "I Can't Turn You Loose," and concluded the Stones' set with "Start Me Up." Bruce took center stage and sang one of Orbison's greatest, "Crying," and then Tina Turner, backed with everyone, did a chaotic but stunning version of "River Deep, Mountain High." We had blown the roof off the Waldorf ballroom, and then moved to Phil Spector's penthouse, where he was hosting a party, still jumping and adrenaline-pumping, to assess the ruins. I wobbled out at 4:00 a.m. on Bruce's arm.

WE DECIDED TO hold one Hall of Fame induction dinner in Los Angeles because we were inducting three West Coast groups who had kicked over the beehive: Creedence Clearwater Revival, Sly and the Family Stone, and the Doors. In addition, we were inducting Cream and Van Morrison. It was a big one. Robbie Robertson had come with me and Jane to the previous year's dinner for the first time and called me the next day, not to tell me how much fun he had had but how sloppy the show was. I told Robbie to stop bitching. Why didn't he help? We worked together for the next twenty years, the basis of a great friendship. We brought in Joel Gallen to film and produce the show, and we put the all-star jam to rest, as we were now primarily inducting groups instead of solo artists, so each group had their own mini-set.

Etta James kicked it off with "At Last." Eddie Vedder inducted the Doors and sang in place of Jim Morrison. Bruce, having attended for six years in a row, inducted Creedence. John Fogerty refused to play with his original bandmates, so Bruce and Robbie sat in with Fogerty for three Creedence classics. I was watching from the side of the room with Bob Dylan; he was hiding in a hoodie. George Clinton inducted Sly, who briefly appeared onstage in his own hoodie and said, "See ya soon," and walked off. The big moment, actually a pretty teary one, was the reunion of Cream, who hadn't spoken to each other for more than two decades. Eric said, "If the three of us can be together again, then anybody can be together again. I saw a lot could be gained by coming here tonight. I've been reunited with two people I dearly love."

IT TOOK TEN years to build the actual Hall of Fame. In the first place, I didn't really know what I was doing, and I was the one who knew the most. I got my personal attorney, Ben Needell, who was a real estate expert, to negotiate with the city of Cleveland and help me oversee the design and construction.

The deal we had made with Cleveland stated that they would raise the money, and the New York–based board would have full control over all creative elements. It was either a marriage or a suicide pact. I. M. Pei gave them a plan for a $100 million architectural landmark. Meanwhile, Cleveland's political and corporate honchos handed the project off to their tourism board, and it all went wobbly. I had pissed off record executives on one side and pissed off government officials, especially the new mayor, on the other. The local newspaper, the *Cleveland Plain Dealer*, was ready to blow it all up. The designated local leaders wanted to turn the relocation of sewage pipes on the proposed site into a faux groundbreaking ceremony. The key to making it happen was persuading Albert Ratner, the patriarch of a real estate family and one of Cleveland's most generous philanthropists, to take charge of their end. A charmer, but no bullshit. With him as my principal partner, we got the thing built. The Who played the entire rock opera *Tommy* at Radio City Music Hall as a benefit for the Hall of Fame and gave us a check for $1 million.

YOKO DID ME a great favor when I was finding it difficult to gather collections for the Hall of Fame. Artists had seen how memorabilia collecting had become big money; Bob Dylan, the Stones, and McCartney were sitting on private warehouses. Yoko put together a press conference where the two of us stood next to John's *Sgt. Pepper's* uniform on a mannequin as she announced she was sending it to the Hall of Fame. It was one of the most iconic artifacts in all of rock and roll history and sent a message about how serious the museum was.

WHEN WE FINALLY broke ground, on June 7, 1993, everyone held a shovel sprayed in gold paint. Chuck Berry was given the honor of the first dirt. There he was, Johnny B. Goode, the true father of rock, blessing a monument to his work, his genius, and what he had done. I wondered what he was thinking. Pete Townshend, Billy Joel, and Sam Phillips also were there. Two years later, on September 2, 1995, the day arrived for the grand opening of the Rock and Roll Hall of Fame and Museum. Cleveland already boasted an internationally respected museum and orchestra, but now the world's attention was focused on a city that would henceforth be known as the home of the Hall of Fame, the flagship of one of America's greatest cultural achievements. We had come through for them. I had delivered our end of the bargain with the city and felt an unexpected pride in that. The glass façade that rose seven stories sparkled. It was a pyramid-shaped tent, much like what I. M. had done at the Louvre, but on a grander scale and with a tower that supported structures shaped like trapezoids or circles, suggesting an old-fashioned turntable.

WE CUT THE ribbon on Labor Day weekend and followed with a five-hour live concert at Cleveland's enormous baseball stadium; Bruce, Bob, Aretha, James Brown, et al. It was a bluebird day, a small cloud occasionally floating over the Hall of Fame sited at the edge of Lake Erie.

"Cleveland, look what you have done!" Yoko shouted from the stage. She envisioned what John might have thought of all this.

I had decided to try a Kennedy-style speech: "Why does the world watch what we do here today? Because music speaks all the languages of the earth, and it's calling out, saying, 'Are you ready for a brand-new beat?' The music crosses boundaries of race and religion, nations and generations. This building must remind us of that power. This music unites and inspires, it lifts us up, whether it's a kid listening to the radio in his bedroom or jamming in a garage or in a bar band or in front of vast crowds in giant stadiums. For many of us, that blend of voice, instrument, and rhythm has been a voice for our souls, for emotions and ideas that we couldn't fathom within us, and it will be our voice long after we are gone." Then came the Marine jets in a flyover.

Scissors with two-foot-long blades were brought out, and we cut the ribbon. Yoko was on one side of me, Little Richard on the other. Jane and my kids were sitting in front. I took Ahmet on a tour of the building, which he hadn't seen under construction or with the exhibits and the artists' collections in place. The Stones, the Who, and many others had come through with big collections. We had Jim Morrison's Cub Scout uniform, and the Eagles had sent us a satchel of hundreds of room keys they had saved from years on the road.

We stopped at the entrance to the main exhibition hall. To our right was the ten-foot stack of Fender amps with large horns mounted on top, drivers that triple the audio output. The rig was donated by the widow of Quicksilver Messenger Service's John Cipollina. He was a relatively obscure figure, but I insisted on having it on display. I had spent many a night in front of those amplifiers in San Francisco. At the entrance it announced the Ahmet M. Ertegun Exhibition Hall, the main room of the museum, his name permanently honored at this shrine to his life's work. When the weekend was done, I found a note from Ahmet: "Thanks to you, it's all come true."

CHAPTER 41

THE BONFIRE
OF THE VANITIES

IN 1983 I asked Tom Wolfe to write something big about the current state of New York City. He came back to me with an outline for the first half of a novel, which he said we should publish issue by issue on deadline as he wrote it over the next year — just like Charles Dickens had done in Victorian London. But of course! Tom was doubtful that he could write something that long and wide open without an enforceable, institutionalized set of deadlines. I would be the enforcer. He called me about a week before the first deadline to tell me he couldn't make it. This was our supersize summer double issue with a dozen pages inside scheduled for the splashy debut of *The Bonfire of the Vanities*. I spoke in my most reasonable adult voice: "Tom, that would not be possible. There is nothing else. I will go to press with twelve blank pages that say on each one 'With the compliments of Tom Wolfe.'"

"Janner, I need to change Sherman McCoy. I don't want him to be a writer anymore. I'm going to make him a bond trader."

"No! You can't!" I knew, whatever the merits of the idea, this would mean at least another six months, even a year, for Tom to research this change. "Nobody is interested in Wall Street anyway. People identify with the lifestyles of writers." Ha!

Throughout the summer I would pick up the next installment of

Bonfire from Tom, either driving to his Victorian house in Southampton, where he was doing the writing, or meeting him halfway at the local airport, where I would review the new copy on the hood of a car before shipping it into the city. It was a hot summer, but only once did I see Tom in less than full, beautifully tailored dress, and that was while he was finishing up typing something at home and didn't have his tie on. Tom was equally meticulous about his writing, and I doubt that I altered more than a few sentences in the total sum of what he wrote that year.

Every chapter was polished, filled with utterly delicious description, and funny as fuck. There were characters like Leon and Inez Del Ponce, Park Avenue millionaires; the crusty municipal judge Myron Kovitsky; the Harlem reverend Reginald Bacon; and the wealthy Jew Arthur Ruskin, whose fortune derived from running charter flights for Arabs to Mecca. Ruskin was married to an Italian hottie, Maria, who was the mistress of the also married Sherman McCoy. Sherman lived in a sixteen-room Park Avenue duplex. Chapter by chapter, Tom was unfolding a tale of vanity, deceit, and ambition among the top dogs, bottom dogs, wild dogs, and mongrels of mid-1980s New York City. In November we got to Sherman McCoy's fateful wrong exit off the freeway into the Bronx. I was floating all over town, needless to say, having New York's finest not just in one issue but for a year. I felt very much the editor of the moment, playing the hottest hand in the game.

MY FIRST RESPONSE to a shot at movie stardom was no. Aaron Latham, our Texas-born writer, had created *Urban Cowboy,* in which John Travolta gave a riveting star performance. The director, Jim Bridges, was coming off *The Paper Chase* and Michael's movie, *The China Syndrome.* Now the trio of Latham, Bridges, and Travolta wanted to do a movie about health clubs as the new singles bars. To justify this peep show at hard bodies in Lycra, the hero of the story, Travolta, would be a *Rolling Stone* reporter who falls in love with exercise coach Jamie Lee Curtis and must choose between his love and his profession, yadda yadda. The script called for Travolta to have a boss, his editor. They quickly talked me into trying a screen test. I booked a seat to Los Angeles on Regent Air, an all-frills 727 with private cabins and a lounge with a bar. I wasn't nervous about the test. My heart wasn't set on it, it was just another wacky thing coming down the road. The test took place on the soundstage where Orson Welles had filmed *Citizen Kane* and the lot where David O. Selznick had made *Gone with the Wind*.

Stevie Nicks was staying in the suite next to me on the penthouse floor at my hotel, and late one evening music was coming through the wall. I invited myself over and hung with her, guitar great Waddy Wachtel, and a few others, singing and jamming until the early morning. When I woke up, I had the part.

My first day of shooting at the end of June was at a French bistro on upper Madison Avenue in New York. The police had closed off the block, and Aaron and I were sitting, smoking, at a sidewalk table when Debra Winger walks up to us, stands right in front of me, and starts yelling about how I am always fucking over actors in *Rolling Stone*, and now they are going to fuck *me* over. She was furious that Jamie Lee got the part, not her, and was here for revenge on Bridges and Travolta. I'm supposed to be "settling," concentrating on the part, and Bridges freaked out, afraid Winger's outburst could spook me and shut down the day's production.

ONE NIGHT JUST before we started, John and I were trying to get a feel for how we would interact with each other on camera playing Adam Lawrence, star reporter for *Rolling Stone*, and Mark Roth, his boss and editor. He wanted to tell me whom he had decided to base his character on: Warren Beatty. Warren, whom I knew and liked, was a cipher, an observer, in no way a reporter. But I didn't want to risk messing with whatever fiction John had created for his character. Maybe I should have; maybe it would have been a better movie, but it was too late by that point. Why do reporters need to be so curious about things, want to uncover unknowns, and be guided by some assumed mantle of morality that requires a willingness to put principles above friendship?

I HAD MOST OF the summer off, staying at the beach, waiting for September to start principal photography in Los Angeles. They needed me for five weeks, as I was in a lot of scenes. I gave up ten-speed bicycle riding on the weekends in favor of driving the Ferrari I had bought from Jimmy Webb. It had a California vanity plate, SKATE. From my house it was a twenty-five-mile round trip to the Montauk Lighthouse on the highway, which was empty at 6:00 a.m. on Sunday mornings. I could get the Ferrari up to 110 miles an hour for a few seconds but had to let it drop quickly to 70, which was plenty on a two-lane road. The Bridgehampton racetrack had been officially shut down, but there was some fast shit going on there — no questions asked, such as experience or safety training — and off I went. I knew you had to take a slow lap to get the tires warm. It was a mile-long circuit with two straightaways leading into three hairy turns if you were taking them fast.

I took up this new passion with the same lack of caution I brought to everything else I did. Most of the time I had some experience with what I was doing, but racing cars wasn't one of them. Maverick had yet to articulate "the need for speed," but I was feeling it. Sure enough, one afternoon my car came off the track at 80 miles an hour midway through a sweeping turn, did a full rollover, and landed upright with the roof on the passenger side crushed into the seat. I had a roll bar and a racing harness, so I was able to walk away. It had taken a second at most, and I could visualize it all. My life didn't flash in front of me, but I had definitely used up one of those nine lives.

JANE AND I were focused that summer on having a baby. We kept temperature readings to track her ovulation cycles and used fertility drugs to enhance the process. We were leading a generally quiet life at home, and sex — which never felt scheduled or utilitarian — took place within the world of miraculous intent. Jane came with me to Los Angeles in the fall while I was shooting. We stayed at Michael Douglas' house while he was in New York filming *Wall Street* and staying at our place in East Hampton. Ned and Cathy Topham lived a few blocks above Michael. It was a godsend for Jane and me to have our old friends so close. On weekends we stayed at Michael's place in Montecito. Travolta invited us to his home north of Santa Barbara, a gracious, old-world, colonial-era ranch. He was a meticulous host; someone had taught him the gracious manners of the old world. His nearest neighbors were the Reagans.

THEY BUILT A replica of the *Rolling Stone* editorial offices, right down to the frills of my daily life. There were backdrops outside the fake windows with views of Central Park. Jim and Aaron were watching me carefully. I didn't know what to think. I was in my pretend office, getting ready to pretend to be me. I sat at "my" desk and tried to puzzle this out, whether it had some meaning, and whether it was deep or shallow. It felt like my office all right, but all I knew was that it was full-out weird, a set crawling with maybe fifty crew. I was beyond any kind of control over the situation. I basically had two kinds of scenes in the movie. One was talking with or scolding John in my office; the other was talking with or scolding John on the phone, from my office, or my apartment in the middle of a party, once when I was hungover. No kissing, no painful goodbyes, no deathbed.

John had told me he thought the secret to acting was to be still, not gesture with your hands and body but to communicate through the eyes. Think it, feel it, let the camera see it. And that's pretty much how I approached my role, trying to get an intense stare. I had to remember my lines, pretend that Travolta was not a movie star, and still be real. John was, I soon learned, a very generous actor. He was the last person in the world who needed more screen time. He helped you by feeding you easy-to-understand looks and lines. He pulled you forward.

There is a lot of waiting around while making a movie, but when it comes time for your two minutes on camera, with fifty people on set, all silent, every eye focused on you, something changes. You feel a flash of heat, a moment that flips your switch on, so that in those two minutes you put everything you've got into being the best possible you. Because you are playing you — or some version of yourself that you've made yourself become in character — you have to bring it with everything you've got, all at once, for keeps, in front of the entire crew and God. I loved it.

My last day of filming involved my only scene with Jamie Lee Curtis, the lass in Lycra, where I pulled her aside in a courtroom to let her know that John was blameless for what had happened and that he still loved her. When the cameras started to roll, I pulled her into my arms and kissed her passionately while dipping her as if she were Rita Hayworth. This was taking a chance, but the set broke out in cheers, and Jim Bridges loved it. I was done, except for something Jim wanted: each principal would put on exercise clothes and do an aerobic hip grind, which would be shown when their name came up in the end credits. Being close to my heaviest then, and given the bodies of everyone else, I didn't want to do this and said so. But I would have been the lone asshole, and school spirit demanded it, so I took off my clothes and gave it my awkward best, wearing a tight *Rolling Stone* T-shirt, no less. I knew that scene would haunt me.

Perfect to me was a promotion campaign for the magazine. The title of the movie was rendered like our logo. The movie was a big release, but a bust. The idea that it was about journalism was transparently false; my script notes had been quietly ignored. The story had such utter nonsense as Travolta barging into my office wielding a baseball bat and then smashing my desk to bits. I have never personally heard or even read about such a thing in the history of journalism.

I settled back into my real office — real views and real people — with a feeling that I had changed. The script had written Mark Roth to be a tougher and ruthless version of myself. I started behaving that way at the office — no nonsense and that's final. I was surprised that it not only worked, but I enjoyed it. I had another trick I had learned in front of the cameras: that if you pretended to believe something, then you could make someone else believe it as well, just by sending it through your eyes.

WE RANG IN the new year of 1985 at Basil's, the waterfront bar on the boutique Caribbean island of Mustique, all private houses and one small hotel, a discreet setting for the upper-crust Princess Margaret crowd. We sailed down on a boat with Earl and Camilla McGrath to celebrate with Mick and his wife, Jerry Hall. Mick and I went to the beach and had afternoon drinks every day. He has a default mode of distance and detachment, a method of self-protection to immunize him against the dangers of fame. But in the sunshine, the holiday season, and the safety, all that fell away, and being with Mick was like hanging with the neighborhood kid who was your best pal. We would take the boat out for a sail in the daytime and hold court at Basil's by night.

Mick at his core is a working musician. The Stones had broken up, though no one knew that, not even them. Mick told me he was tired of the tours: they were like "drug circuses." And at the heart of this was Keith. Mick said on their last tour Keith had wanted to take on the leadership of the band. Keith called an all-hands-on-deck meeting and showed up two hours late. Mick said it was *Spinal Tap*.

CHAPTER 42

THE GIFT OF GOD

I WAS ON THE cover of *New York* magazine, which was a big deal. It was a photo of this startled, chubby face underneath the headline "Wenner in Wonderland," framed in a mock cover of *Rolling Stone*. I was now on the receiving end. At first it's stomach-tightening. I suppose you build up expectations that are inevitably too high, or, having made it to your lofty position, you think you are a fairly faultless fellow. Reporters for some reason delight in turning up dish, dirty dishes if possible. It's spicy and shows what tough guys they are. On your first read, all you see is anything negative. "Jann Wenner desperately wants to be famous; he's erratic...humiliates staffers; eats off other people's plates..." You skim past the praise for the achievement that deserves such attention. The writer couldn't resist a story about my getting a nosebleed during a lunch with Jackie Onassis. "The magazine he launched in 1967 for $7,500 is now seventeen and both of them are fat and happy." You want to bitch about that? And being on the cover?

Because I had just come back from Hollywood and fancied making another movie, the article dwelt a bit on my big-screen potential. My favorite quote was this: "'You know what I'd cast Jann as, if I were making a movie? You know what he reminds me of?' says actor and producer Michael Douglas, who is Wenner's best friend. 'A cold-blooded hit man.'"

I HIRED BOB WALLACE to be my new managing editor. He had graduated from Stanford with a degree in literature and was working at the infectious-disease lab at Stanford Hospital, inseminating chickens for genetic studies and hanging out with Koko, the signing gorilla. He lived next door to local R&B disc jockey Phil McKernan and had been friends with Phil's son, Pigpen, the blues voice of the Grateful Dead. He spent a year as a subject in a marijuana, alcohol, and Valium study at the veterans' hospital in Menlo Park. It was the perfect resumé. He came to *RS* as a researcher in 1975.

For eight months our writer David Black chased down the first victims of a strange fatal and unknown disease spreading among gay men, first in one city, then in another. Being in New York put it right in our face. We wove a narrative among the politics and fears of the gay world, the epidemiological investigations that were launched like a police dragnet, and the complex world of medical research and experiments. Larry Kramer and Dr. Anthony Fauci were the main characters. "The Plague Years" ran for two issues, long and enormously compelling. It was the first major national piece on AIDS that I knew of outside of medical journals. We won the award for best reporting that year from the American Society of Magazine Editors.

NOW THAT ROLLING STONE was solidly on its feet and running a marathon, I reasoned that I ought to use my knowledge and the team I had put together to do another magazine. I didn't have a new idea for one, so we landed on an orphan in distress. *US* had been founded by the New York Times Company to compete with *People*, the most financially successful magazine in history. The *Times* didn't have the stomach for frivolous journalism and sold it to a smaller magazine outfit, which also couldn't make inroads against *People*. So, we bought it.

On my first visit to our new magazine I met with everyone on the editorial staff privately for quickie interviews. I fired them all the next day. Somehow this ended up in my later mythology as getting on the public address system and firing them en masse. Can you imagine "Attention. You are all fired, every last one of you. Leave now"? I brought along one editor from *Rolling Stone*, Chris Connelly. I didn't want to raid *RS*, so we built a smaller and wholly new staff in an office a few blocks from the United Nations. I packed up my favorite tchotchkes and moved. Within the year we were putting out solid, respectable profiles of show-biz celebs and flashy four-color photography. (*People* was black-and-white.) We plodded our way to profitability, but I couldn't figure out how to break it big. We were running a distant second to *People*, so we left it on the back burner. And there it sat simmering.

It took us many years to figure it out, but when we did, we hit the jackpot.

ROLLING STONE HAD evolved into a mainstream magazine with afflu-ent young readers. We announced our new guaranteed circulation rate base: one million copies every issue. The fashion advertisers filled our pages with Kate Moss and enough nipples on hot guys to make the mag-azine look like the men's underwear section of the Sears catalogue. Rec-ord clubs had become big advertisers with expensive, heavy-paper inserts. We had maxi pads, birth control pills, and Crest toothpaste. Not to mention Apple, Microsoft, and Intel.

But many potential advertisers still thought we were a countercul-ture magazine stuck in the sixties. We had picked up some major accounts but couldn't get the kinds of higher-level meetings we needed to explain that we weren't about hard drugs and group sex. The iconoclastic advertising wizard Jay Chiat — he was Steve Jobs' main man, and a good friend of mine — told me to call Pat Fallon, the founder of a small agency located in Minneapolis that had just been named advertising agency of the year by some authority or other.

The campaign Fallon came back with was simple: "Perception/ Reality," two-page spreads with an image evocative of the sixties facing a parallel image of a current icon. For example, a flower-power-painted VW bus versus a convertible sports car; a plate of hash brownies versus a carton of chocolate Häagen-Dazs; a condom versus a birth control pill; loose change versus an American Express card; a furry rodent versus an Apple mouse. We had nearly ninety different examples over five years. My favorite was a photo of Bob Dylan versus the same photo of Bob Dylan: some things are eternal. It was sophisticated and witty, with a clear and easy-to-understand message that we were as contemporary as ever, based on easy visual proof. There was also a deeper and subtler message, the hidden persuader: not one of the images from our past mocked that past, disowned, discredited, or denied it. In fact, the ad celebrated our past and we embraced it. It was a message about integrity and the importance of our history.

I WAS AT LAST trying to curtail my drug abuse. One step would be to shut down the in-house cocaine supply, but I couldn't make this happen while I was still such a good customer. I thought somehow it had to be interfering with Jane's and my ability to conceive a child. Cocaine was now a wrecker, an intruder, a disruptive and demeaning presence. Someone would pull out a little bottle with a spoon attached by a little chain to the cap or unfold a packet, and I would wait impatiently for the next line and, of course, the next drink.

So, I decided to stop. I stopped buying. I would still accept the offer of a line, but the less you used, the more obvious and unpleasant the side effects: the teeth grinding, the runny nose, the impatience and anxiety, and the nonstop jabbering. As the weeks and months went by I never missed it, never craved it, never went out of my way to get it. As the years went by, I got to hate it. One thing for sure is that you can't hang around with people who use it all the time. It's a different world. It's like sitting next to someone who is drunk, sloppy, and repeating themselves. It's time to excuse yourself, politely but unequivocally. I was actually saying no to people who offered it. Was that even possible?

Hunter, of course, was a problem. We had already discussed his alcoholism and addiction, not a confrontation but in a thoughtful and honest conversation. I offered to pay for treatment. Hunter was polite and firm; he had thought about it and didn't feel he could or would change. He felt that this was a key to his talent. He said that if he didn't do drugs, he would have the mind of an accountant. The abuse was already taking a toll on his gifts, but that was only a part of his calculus. It was just too late, and he knew it.

The Good Doctor was irresistible. People loved Hunter. He was a Kentucky gentleman, old-school, polite, charming, and welcoming. He enjoyed being surrounded by friends, football-betting buddies, big-time drug users and dealers, and fellow writers wanting to touch the hem. They were all groupies in one way or another. I suppose I was, too. I became friends with most of them, all very decent people, if a little off-kilter sometimes, and almost without exception helping themselves generously to the blow and the bourbon. One by one, each of them told me how to handle Hunter in order to get him to write. Ha!

I loved being with Hunter, but now the hangers-on and the blow made it embarrassing and uncomfortable. It was humiliating to be with him. Hunter knew I didn't like being around him on that basis. He would not leave his house without having his stash and Deering grinder with him. One day I was sitting at home and he walked in, waving his arms and shouting, "Look out. *Eeeek!* Here I come. The Cokey Monster."

IF I WERE asked if I could do it again would I still have used all that cocaine, I wouldn't hesitate. No. It was a waste of money, energy, and precious time.

I WAS THIRTY-EIGHT YEARS old and wanted a family, so we decided to adopt. There are requirements, rules, and red tape. At the end of June, accompanied by Jimmy's wife, Patsy Webb, one of Jane's best friends and the well-practiced mother of five boys, we flew to Atlanta to pick up a five-week-old boy with a head of black hair flying out like Beethoven's and big blue eyes, Alexander Jann (we started with Zachary as the middle name, but the kid looked like me) Wenner. I asked Michael Douglas and Richard to be his godfathers. Earl McGrath had twenty-six godchildren and told me no more, but agreed to be an honorary godfather.

I loved being a dad. I would have Alexander in my arms at any chance or stand with the old-fashioned carriage under a tree and watch him delight at the leaves twinkling in the wind. Friends with their babies were showing up at the house, and slowly our social life began to center around people who traveled with baskets and diaper bags. I felt different and became different, clued in to a secret dad society, one both tender and macho. You're proud, which is a wonderful thing to be. You are now a part of the eternal chain of life, the great miracle of creation.

Yoko was trying to reemerge in the world. She was a naturally paranoid and superstitious person. She threw numbers, consulted I Ching, and read tarot cards. She was prone to conspiracy thinking. She was trying to find something that would explain her fate. I'd regularly visit the apartment and have a meeting and a meal, watch Sean at play, and get to know her boyfriend, Sam Havadtoy. Sam was Hungarian, a young decorator and artist who had been working for John and Yoko. He stayed in the background in official matters. Yoko and I disagreed about raising Sean. She was putting him in the public eye, taking him as her escort to events, one time dressed in a child's tuxedo. I didn't think that was healthy. Her first big public act was to restore a run-down meadow in Central Park, across the road from the Dakota, which she and John used to walk through every day. It would be renamed Strawberry Fields. It was a renewal of hope. Michael and I went to the opening.

At one point that year, one of John and Yoko's former assistants approached me. He had stolen John's diaries and wanted to sell them. "You are at your life's turning point," I said to him in the gravest possible manner, one I didn't know I had. "You can either return them or for the rest of your days carry the curse of being the man who stole from John Lennon. You will be outcast." He returned them.

NINETEEN EIGHTY-FIVE HAD turned out to be a good year. We were on the front lines of the magazine business, still one of the most influential mediums in the country, along with television and newspapers. We were hitting a mark of quality, consistency, and originality in our articles and design that beat the pants off everyone else. The year-end issue was two hundred pages, a hefty and healthy baby.

And Jane and I had a baby boy. We stayed home that Christmas for the first time in years, put up a tree, and watched Alexander crawl around through the toys, trying to make sense of them. It finally felt like an old-fashioned Christmas. The only snow fell from heaven.

IN 1986, YOKO decided to do a tour of Europe with her band and asked us to join her. I couldn't go, but Jane met her for a few days in Budapest and Vienna. When she got back home she was in an unusually perky mood. She said she had decided to stop smoking and using drugs. This was wonderful news, but suspicious. Turned out she was pregnant with our child, after nineteen years.

We moved. Jane found a brownstone just off Central Park West, which was being sold by the estate of Perry Ellis. He had restored its original woodwork, put in parquet floors, and added fixtures from the Savoy Hotel in London. We were turning our backs on one life and moving on to another. We were forty, and we were a family. Jane's body grew with our child; the glow of health burnished her cheeks.

MICHAEL MANN, WHOM I had met during my movie-producing career, was doing a new television series as well as *Miami Vice*, and asked me to have a reccurring cameo in it. *Crime Story* was going to be filmed in Chicago, starring a former organized-crime detective who wore a diamond pinky ring. All my scenes would be with him. I would play his boss. It was going to be NBC's big show for the new season. I had to be in Chicago to film just two weeks ahead of Jane's due date, so I had a long-distance pager to wear on my belt in case, and flew off for a few days on the set. Michael was there to supervise my debut. The director of that episode was Gary Sinise, a fine actor who later turned up as Tom Hanks' best friend in *Forrest Gump*. Unlike the movies, where you settle into a slow pace, filming two or three script pages a day, television is an assembly line where the next shot is always ready. Season two was set in Las Vegas, so I had to get a different haircut and began to travel west. I played the Justice Department's deputy attorney general, Kennedy era.

Jane's contractions began at dawn. I watched the caesarean delivery from the doctor's side of the mini-curtain, spellbound by how they pulled out various organs and laid them on her stomach to make room for the baby to come out. It was a boy. When we got back home, Alex was all dressed up and jumped right into the carrying basket. My father had come to town to be part of the unexpected miracle. Sister Kate thought this was a blessing for her, as it was also her birthday. It was Lorne's birthday, too, and Lauren Hutton's. Lauren presented us with a chillum carved from an animal horn as a gift for the baby. To the new child Jane gave the name Theodore, which means "gift of God."

CHAPTER 43

YOKO
AND THE GORBACHEVS

IN 1987, I went to Moscow with Yoko. Mikhail Gorbachev assembled a three-day international summit about nuclear disarmament and invited dignitaries from around the world. We got on an Aeroflot jet in Washington with Democratic senators, retired generals, bishops, and scientists. Reagan had forbidden anyone from his administration to attend. Gregory Peck was seated in front of me and Bill Moyers behind me.

We checked into a recently built convention-style hotel, the Cosmos, with a five-story-high statue of Yuri Gagarin, the first Russian in space, as its centerpiece. The lobby was filled by delegates in medal-laden military uniforms and old bearded men in black robes with Greek crosses hanging around their necks. The dining room buffet was boiled beef, overcooked steak fillets, cabbage, and steamed potatoes. The Soviet lack of refrigerated railcars and trucks meant no salads or fresh vegetables in the winter, only what could be pickled or buried.

We took the overnight train to Leningrad to meet with the Lennon Club, fans and musicians, college students and hippies, who gathered without permission as a prodemocracy and music discussion colloquium. Never in their furthest fantasies would they have imagined that John Lennon's widow would show up in their midst. Afterward we had our only good meal in Russia, and went back to Moscow carrying cassettes and mimeographed pamphlets.

The Soviet Union's biggest pop star, Stas Namin, invited us for dinner. He was the grandson of Anastas Mikoyan, who had been one of the highest-ranking officials under Stalin, Khrushchev, and Brezhnev. Stas was in his late twenties and lived with his wife and mother in a one-bedroom flat in an older Moscow building. He explained the music business in his country: there was one record company and one concert company, both owned and run by the state. You could only make a record with their approval, otherwise you were underground. I could not eat his mother's cooking, and slipped it into my jacket pocket. On another night we went to a dinner at Yevgeny Yevtushenko's mini-dacha in the Moscow suburbs. It felt like a party for college professors. We had been publishing some of his poetry.

The high point of the trip was lunch inside the Kremlin and a speech by Gorbachev in the presidium of the Supreme Soviet. It was his personal plea for nuclear disarmament. He spoke about a meeting with Reagan in which Reagan discussed a nuclear treaty in terms of a movie he had seen about an invasion of aliens from outer space. Gorbachev said to the audience, "Imagine negotiating about intercontinental ballistic missiles with the president of the United States, who only understands Hollywood movies." I was seated next to Dr. Andrei Sakharov, the nuclear physicist who had designed their hydrogen bomb, won a Nobel Prize, and whom Gorbachev had just freed from exile in a Siberian prison camp. He had false teeth made of metal.

I stopped in a massive, ornate men's room, on the way to the closing luncheon, and stood at a row of urinals peeing with a group of Orthodox bishops in their long robes and ceremonial headgear. The banquet had buffet tables of fresh vegetables. I brought Yoko to meet the Gorbachevs, who embraced her. Mikhail told Yoko how much he admired John's peace crusade and his music, and Raisa sang a few lyrics from the song "Woman." That was worth the trip.

WE SAID FAREWELL to Andy Warhol in an issue with Woody Allen on the cover, two artists who defined the times in New York. I had known Andy a little over the years, mainly from parties and the Factory when we worked on projects together. It felt like stepping into a fairy-tale world, Andy in Wonderland. When his diaries were published, most of his references to me were about how fat I was getting. Andy fell head over heels in love with one of the star salesmen in our advertising department, Jon Gould, a handsome twenty-five-year-old preppy from a proper New England family. They were constant companions, but after a few years living together, Jon died of AIDS. I sent a long letter to his parents hoping to ease their feelings of shame, but never heard back.

ANNIVERSARIES AND BIRTHDAYS have a power that has to do with the resonance of history, especially a shared history. Or maybe survival itself deserves celebration. But it's the kind of thing that advertisers go nuts for, those special editions of magazines called "keepers."

In that case, I figured we should have three twentieth-anniversary issues. The first was in April, "Rock and Roll Style," with David Bowie on a gold cover. Herb Ritts did a portfolio of him jumping around in an unzipped motorcycle jacket. We also ran a fascinating narrative history of our era told through the artifacts — the costumery and the rites — of rock and roll, by Chet Flippo's wife, Martha Hume: "Blue-suede shoes and high-heeled sneakers, raspberry berets and leopard-skin pillbox hats, short shorts and bell-bottom blues, Venus in Blue Jeans and the Devil with the Blue Dress On…" From Elvis to the Eagles, black leather to cowboy fringe, Elton to Ozzy, diamond chokers to chicken chokers. In June we focused on live music for our second special issue, the twenty greatest shows of the previous two decades. The cover featured a photo of a moment I remembered from Monterey Pop in 1967: Jimi Hendrix on his knees, doing an incantation of sorts, a voodoo priest bringing the flames from his burning guitar. The third anniversary special, the real one, was to come in November. It would be ambitious, and I had been at work on it for a year.

WHEN I STUMBLED into magazines, I became enchanted by the world that could be created just by how they looked. The design of the thing could say as much as the words you chose to print. Believing that the art director was my essential partner in realizing my vision for the magazine, I had kept my eye on a guy who had been the art director of *Texas Monthly*, Fred Woodward. He had turned a smart journal of regional politics and culture into a national voice by virtue of his design.

Fred was born and raised in Noxapater, Mississippi, population 500. He first saw three-year-old *Rolling Stone* when he was in high school and began writing his name in the "psychedelic" style of our logo. When he went off to college, Mississippi State and then Memphis State, he started in journalism, then moved to physical education, then political science, and finally to graphic arts, where he set his sights on the magazine he loved, *Rolling Stone*. I offered him the job he had wanted all his life. He stayed for fifteen years. Fred would win more design awards for *Rolling Stone* than did any other magazine in the United States and was considered by his peers one of the greatest magazine art directors of all time.

THAT ROLLING STONE survived and prospered was due in large part to our talent, but also to the music and culture of San Francisco whence it came and values that had been shaped by that time and place. But some were trying to say that we were a generation full of sound and fury, signifying nothing. They wanted us to believe that what we stood for and had achieved was shallow and powerless stuff. I wanted to call bullshit on that. The twentieth-anniversary issue was a stage to stand on and affirm our beliefs. We would undertake an assessment of the past two decades. We turned to the artists, writers, poets, actors, politicians, visionaries, and social leaders we had identified who we thought spoke to our generation. We asked them to talk about those times, what they meant, what they stood for, what had happened, and what they saw ahead.

Bruce Springsteen said, "Because of the naiveness of the era, it's easily trivialized and laughed at. But underneath it, people were trying in some sense to redefine their own lives and the country they lived in, in some more open and free and just fashion. Certainly, the music I've done in the past five or six years is a result of those times and values. In the end, I realized rock and roll wasn't just about finding fame and wealth. Instead, for me, it was about finding your place in the world, figuring out where you belong." Dylan said, "To me and to others like me, rock and roll was a way of life, it was all-consuming."

The interviews were time-capsule material. It was the biggest issue we had ever published, more than three hundred pages and one of the most elegantly detailed, done with the care that might be appropriate to an illuminated Bible. In the Letter from the Editor, I wrote, "*Rolling Stone* at age twenty holds these things dear: high standards in its own craft; rock and roll music and the popular arts it touches; a commitment to stimulating and nourishing musicians and artists; and to have a voice of reason that will be heard in the policies and politics of this country."

CHAPTER 44

MY FATHER'S DEATH

ICHAEL INVITED ME to spend the weekend with him during the 1988 Academy Awards. He was the unanimous favorite for Best Actor as Gordon Gekko in *Wall Street*. He thought I would get a kick out of all the hoopla, which I did, wall-to-wall movie stars for three days and nights. I felt like the best man.

I walked down the red carpet unnoticed in front of a grandstand full of fans. I was collecting another experience, two hundred photographers and reporters who totally ignore you. But the suspense is real. Mikey was up against Marcello Mastroianni, Bill Hurt, Robin Williams, and Jack Nicholson. Jack had already won before, so Michael seemed a shoo-in, but still…And when he won, he walked to the stage looking happy, handsome, confident, a real man and a real star. I couldn't help it and cried tears of happiness. We hit a few parties and ended up at dawn at Jack's house, sitting among his Picassos. Jack said he had been rooting for Michael to win and had been wearing his lucky suspenders to make it happen.

I WAS QUITE HUNGOVER the next day when I met my dad for lunch at the restaurant in the garden of the Hotel Bel-Air. He was subdued, which I thought had to do with my world-class headache. I noticed he only picked at his shrimp salad. He said he was having stomach problems and seeing a doctor. When I got back to my room, my stepmother was on the phone, crying, wanting to know what my dad had said at lunch. She cried more, but wouldn't tell me what was wrong, saying I should talk to him. He had stomach cancer. A month earlier, he and my sisters and all the grandchildren had gotten together in New York to celebrate his seventieth birthday. One day we went down to Annie's studio, where she did a family portrait of *mischpoche*, grandkids and all, our present to him.

I am optimistic. I don't get the benefit of premature and pointless grief, and things have always worked out pretty well. I do not think about, let alone carefully examine, worst-case scenarios until they are at hand and it's too late to do much. (This was decidedly not a good business strategy and cost me a lot over the years.) I didn't believe the luck would run out or the worst would happen. Katie took my father's illness very seriously; she went into research mode, to get an intense education on what we would need to know, so she understood from the start that the odds were very poor. Merlyn was a committed hippie, full of certainties about spirituality and alternative medicines. We met with her "doctors" in New York, which led to coffee enemas. We also sought out the experts, traveling one day to a government cancer research center in Buffalo to find out about enrolling Dad in an experimental project. We flew back in a sardine-size Learjet through a harrowing storm that I thought had a good chance of taking us all. My dad was a good soldier, trying all of this, but he denied the reality of it, even avoiding updating his will.

Dad came to stay with Jane and me later that summer. He seemed healthy. He looked good and happy. He had lost weight, but other than a belt cinching up a too-large pair of pants, he was fit. He was tired a lot, but I discounted that because he was not giving up one bit. I had taken him to a few of his radiation and chemotherapy sessions on my visits to see him in Los Angeles, but wasn't around long enough to see the after-effects. He wasn't playing tennis anymore, and what he enjoyed most was sitting on the floor with our kids in the nursery. I never thought of him as a sick man; he seemed to love every day.

THAT SUMMER BILLY JOEL moved next door to me. He owned a few Harleys. Neither of us had a nine-to-five job, and we became weekday riding buddies. Billy showed me all the back roads and shortcuts in the Hamptons, the best turns and twisties, the straightaways and open roads. We did the Long Island shore and visited the clubs where he'd gotten his start; people always recognized him and were excited to see this true son of Long Island. We would generally begin a long ride with a mid-island breakfast. Billy would throw a shot of brandy into his coffee. Jane and Billy's wife then, Christie Brinkley, were friendly, connected by kids' birthday parties. Billy and I spent a lot of time together. He wanted to be a tough-ass street dude, but was just too intelligent and talented to bring it totally off. He was an extraordinary pop song writer. He loved Gilbert and Sullivan, and we hammed it up, singing duets at parties as after-dinner entertainment.

MY FATHER DIED at the end of the year, a few days after Christmas. I had moved to Los Angeles for the month of November to be with him. He liked to stay home in bed or in a comfortable chair; the weight loss was serious. Merlyn was dealing with his businesses. Kate, the ever dutiful daughter, had moved in, overseeing the bureaucracy of dying and sitting with my father, talking him through the final days of his life, attending to his physical needs and the intimate psychological and spiritual waymarks of imminent death. It's an incredible feat of selflessness to put aside your own emotional struggle at such a moment and absorb the weight of someone else's dying. I tried to pretend this was not happening, to find distractions so I wouldn't have to face it. We put on some semblance of a cheery, normal family and brought out the grandkids, but he couldn't deal with their noise, so we kept them out of sight. I sat Theo with him: "Dad, here is the firstborn son of your own firstborn son."

At some point I thought I should tell him I was gay, because he was on his deathbed and it was time for ultimate truths. But for what purpose? I wasn't looking for acceptance or forgiveness, although I knew he would have been fine with it. Perhaps he already knew. It probably wouldn't have mattered much to him at that point, one way or the other. He knew I had become a success, was well respected, and was married with children. It was everything a father could want.

We took the families for a day at Disneyland, and when we got back found that Dad had checked himself into the hospital. We had a somber Thanksgiving dinner without him. When he returned home I gave him a bath one night. I helped him into the tub. He was naked and frail. I hadn't seen him naked since I was a kid, and now his body had shrunk. I talked softly with him about where he wanted to be soaped. It became a humble, graceful time together, taking care of the old man, now like a child.

It was time for me to go. There was nothing left to do or complete. I needed to get back to New York and away from the death watch. My sisters had been much closer to my dad over the years, and they had already discussed and agreed on what to do. I had asked him to split up his estate between them; I was already set. I only asked for a few pieces of Japanese pottery. He insisted on leaving me his ski house in Utah, which I knew he meant as a nod to my childhood, when he and I would go skiing on weekends. I was the man of the family now. I could feel it coming from everyone.

I sat with him awhile in his bedroom with my sisters. After they left the room I stayed, but there wasn't much to say. I knew this would be the last time I would see him, that this was it. A kiss. I love you. You go to the door and turn for one last look. But what do you do when you turn for the last time and leave your father dying? I wanted to walk away and deal with it later, in my own way. My sisters were waiting, and we hugged it out. They were crying. I cried and started back to New York and my family.

The call came a few weeks later, just days after Christmas. We were on holiday. My sisters said I should come to Los Angeles right away, my dad was near death. When I landed I was taken off the plane ahead of everyone and led into a nearby room that looked like an immigration interview office. My sisters were on the phone; they said Dad was barely alive but wouldn't quit. He was drawing heaving breaths as his lungs began to collapse, struggling to stay alive so that I could say goodbye. He had told this to Katie by blinking his eyes in response to her questions. He couldn't speak but he could hear, so they put the phone to his ear. I had never thought about this moment before, ritualized by so many movies and novels. He was a father with a dutiful and loving son. I said goodbye to him. "I know you are at the end now. I just want to thank you for all the things you did for me. I will love you forever. Everything is going to be okay with us. Your work is done. You can go now."

I think that's what he wanted to hear. It was what I wanted to say. He had done a great job, he had completed his life's work successfully and righteously. And he wanted to hear one last time from his son. My sisters were sitting on either side of his bed. They told me that he breathed for the last time within a minute after we hung up. And they both reported the most extraordinary thing: a light, like a diffuse field of energy, rose out of his body, quietly lifted into the air, and then disappeared.

CHAPTER 45

ALTITUDE ADJUSTMENTS

I NEEDED A HEALTH break and found Canyon Ranch, an oasis in the Sonoran Desert near Tucson, spotted with saguaro cacti, the kind with their prickly arms raised. It was a campus of sorts, with Southwestern-style cottages around gyms, tennis courts, swimming pools, and a separate facility exclusively for the obese, the ghetto. My favorite activity was the daily hike in the nearby mountains, carrying a backpack, running among the boulders on rocky paths up to the pine forests. It was there that the idea for another new magazine began to tickle me. The pleasure of being in nature, having a sweaty challenge, was having a spiritual effect on me. That was one inspiration from the trip, the idea for my next magazine. The other inspiration was going to cost a lot more money.

There was only one plane I was interested in: the twelve-passenger Gulfstream transcontinental jet, which you could stand up in and had beds. Having been on a Gulfstream with Ahmet a few times, I knew that was it. On that first ride I had said to myself, "Someday, son, this will be all yours." After listening to an obligatory warning from Ben Needell, my chief advisor on the "big stuff," I proceeded with the financial analysis and chain of transactions that get you off the ground: what brand, what model, how far should it go, landing cycles, engine hours, avionics, noise abatement, hiring pilots, and how to avoid taxes. This was the money pit.

I chose a Gulfstream II. My passengers on the test flight were Mica and Ahmet. I purchased it in June, and my first flight was alone, sitting by myself above the clouds listening to "Knockin' on Heaven's Door," pinching myself. I kept that plane and then the later model, the Gulfstream IV, for twenty years.

THE STONES WENT on tour. The extended Stones family — the musicians' families and staffs, the security, roadies, and drug dealers, plus writers and the magazine owner with his reporters — would gather for another traveling reunion. The world's greatest rock and roll band was ready to march with a small army. Mick came to the office for lunch to discuss his ideas and ours about covering the tour. I would get the itinerary and figure out my travel plans for the next few months. The *Steel Wheels* tour was a tipping point into a new era of live music. They had created a show big enough to fill a football stadium. The stage was a postindustrial erector set from a quasi–*Blade Runner* future, with ramps, staircases up several levels of the structure, elevators, and a runway with plenty of space for Mick to dance and prowl on. The modern tour had arrived.

BOB PALMER TRAVELED to the mountains of Morocco to revisit the Jajouka, where the Master Musicians would play for days, from dusk until dawn, stoned out of their minds, as hundreds, perhaps thousands, of dancing tribesmen surrounded them. Palmer himself leaped into the bonfire and came out unharmed. P. J. O'Rourke went to Islamabad and Peshawar in Pakistan. The Soviets had just surrendered Afghanistan to the American-armed mujahideen, and the stupidity and folly of it all was plain. P. J. said the CIA would be better off if they had used a decoder ring. Howard Kohn went to Medellín, Colombia, to take a look at the cartels that were running the city with savage violence from their marble-covered mansions with helipads on the roof. They had made the DEA look like Keystone Kops. Incredible reading.

Everyone had a war correspondent. It seemed only right that *Rolling Stone* be on the front lines of the battle for peace, so we hired Larry Wright to be our "peace correspondent." He went to Berlin, where the Cold War had been fought, and then to the International Women's Peace Conference. He also attended a Reagan/Gorbachev summit. He sent peace reports from each front.*

Our best piece of journalism in 1989 was on the *Exxon Valdez*, the tanker that had gone aground in Prince William Sound in Alaska, spilling eleven million gallons of crude oil into a wilderness bay. It was the most important environmental story of the year, and I felt we had to do it. We contacted a former reporter for the *Baltimore Sun*, Tom Horton, who had gone on leave and was living in a fishing village on a marshy island twelve miles out in Chesapeake Bay. After we told him we weren't looking for *Fear and Loathing in Anchorage*, he said he wanted $5,000. We offered him $10,000 for 10,000 words. He went to Alaska, where he stayed in small fishing towns and indigenous villages, talking with local officials and the executives and cleanup crews sent in by Exxon. After four weeks he returned through New York, where we met him for the first time. We published his "Paradise Lost" at 32,000 words, a tour de force on nature, man, and the modern world.

THE STUPIDITY AND injustice of the drug laws and all the machinery that came with it, prisons flooded with people whose "crimes" had no violence or victims, was making me crazy. I wrote a Letter from the

---

* Larry ultimately left us for the more staid world of *The New Yorker* and won a Pulitzer Prize for his reporting on Osama bin Laden and Al Qaeda.

Editor on a full page bordered by a heavy black box. "The War on Drugs has been lost. Despite decades of incarceration and interdiction that have cost billions of dollars, there are more drugs and blood on the streets than ever before. Our courts and prisons are crowded beyond capacity, crime is rampant at home and governments abroad are under siege...Like Vietnam, this is a quagmire. We are in a war tearing apart the fabric of our country. There is no light at the end of the tunnel. It is time to admit we are wrong. Perhaps we can behave as a kinder, gentler and more mature society." It would be another thirty years.

LEONARD BERNSTEIN HAD finally agreed to a sit-down with Jonathan Cott. In the distant past Jonathan's father had dated Lenny's sister Shirley. He never gave a long interview but had loved the one Jonathan had done with Glenn Gould. Bernstein had a two-packs-a-day cigarette habit, and coughed and wheezed as he jumped and skipped around while making his points, a spellbinding wizard. They talked from 4:00 p.m. to 2:00 a.m. He died of emphysema less than a year later, just before we published what would be his last interview. The photos were by Avedon and Henri Cartier-Bresson.

JANE WAS PREGNANT again. We had bought a new house on Further Lane, a dozen driveways west of our ocher-yellow mini-villa, a modern house in the manner of the great Mexican architect Luis Barragán, wildly out of the shingled-saltbox style that ruled the local vernacular. We wanted to live on the ocean. Jane had to have it. Getting more and more pregnant, she would go by herself to the new house, sit in an outdoor chair, and look at the ocean and wait. In early August we had the new baby, a third son we named Edward Augustus — Edward in honor of my father, and Augustus because we wanted a kid to call Augie but who would become Gus, a name that recalled someone who might be the gas station attendant in the old comic strip *Gasoline Alley*. When Jane had the baby, the brothers came to visit, Alexander dressed like a proper five-year-old lad and Theo in his bumblebee costume. There were lots of little Alexanders around. I had discovered a few Theos but absolutely no Guses. Except for Keith Richards, whose two daughters were Alexandra and Theodora, and his dad, Gus. As if, he would always say, nicking the name of his band wasn't bad enough.

CHAPTER 46

~

THE KING
AND QUEEN OF POP

MADONNA WASN'T GOING to give it up to a regular reporter. We thought first of asking Norman Mailer to do the piece, but in retrospect that could have been an ego train wreck. She agreed to Carrie Fisher. (Carrie said she was our "lower-budget alternative.") To my knowledge this was the beginning of the modern era of the celebrity-interviews-celebrity subgenre of journalism. To my knowledge, it's also the only one that ever worked, because Carrie was a skilled writer. Otherwise, you generally go deeply vapid when professional egocentrics talk at each other. On the cover we called it "Big Time Girl Talk."

Madonna was focused, obsessive, and not terribly flexible. She offered us a portfolio of pictures by her friend Steven Meisel, a tribute to the photographer Brassaï, who chronicled the nocturnal demimonde of Paris in the twenties and thirties. They did the woman who loves other women; a butch mistress surrounded by pretty-boy transvestites; a bordello queen drinking champagne from a glass between her feet. You get the picture. We ran ten pages of them, plus the cover of her as a corseted Dietrich in satin heels, straddling the back of a wooden chair. The ladies began with a discussion of their failed marriages. They talked dildos, blow jobs, finger fucking, and the nature of their belief in God. What does Madonna want in a man? "Smart, smells good, confident." And she doesn't give head although she loves getting it. The sex talk belied what in fact turned out to be a conversation between two women determined to control their own lives.

MICHAEL JACKSON WANTED to have dinner with me. He was now being managed by a friend, Sandy Gallin, and one of them thought it would be a good idea if I interviewed Michael for a cover. Dinner was my audition. We met at Sandy's house in the Hollywood Hills, in an all-white, wall-to-wall-carpeted living room. A small table was set for two, and there was Michael, who had brought along his own chef. We traded gossip about famous people we both knew, to break the ice. Michael reminded me of Andy Warhol, a soft voice, sometimes a whisper, with a lot of "gee whiz," saying little, asking a lot, and listening closely. I tried to establish myself as trustworthy, which meant telling some not-too-private confidences in a way that signaled I was sharing a privileged indiscretion, not betraying a trust — that its value was fun, not dirt. Michael wanted to know about *Rolling Stone*, all about my background and my life.

I ran into Michael a few weeks later at Irving Lazar's annual Oscar party at Spago on Sunset Strip. I had flown in from four days of hard skiing in Aspen, changed into black tie on the plane, and arrived pretty wiped out. I ended up sitting next to Michael, small-talking away, deal-ing with people interrupting, wanting to say hello, when Madonna came in. She beelined for us and sat on my lap. My quads were quite sore from the slopes, and she was a bony and hard-muscled piece of work. I was sandwiched between the two of them. She had performed the *Dick Tracy* theme song at the Oscars and arrived in her stage costume, which included elbow-length white satin gloves. She was dying to take them off, so she gave them to me. I asked her to autograph them. Maybe this would be good for the Hall of Fame. They remain in my files, in a moisture-free sealed envelope.

The Jackson interview was on for June, and we set a date to show up for a weekend at the Neverland Ranch. Michael wanted to know if it would be okay to do it at night, no lights on, just the fireplace and candles. I began my research by taking Diana Ross to lunch. She said she couldn't help me; she barely knew Michael. The story about her discovering the Jackson 5 was made up, as was the idea that she had mothered him at Motown. Her last memory of Michael was when she tried to visit him a few years earlier at his house. He kept her waiting two hours, and she left.

I took a few weekdays off to prepare. I listened to the Jackson 5 catalogue, studied the solo records, read books and articles about Motown and the Jackson family, and filled a legal pad with notes and topics, which I would synthesize into my interview. Michael was not my natural territory, but once you start to dig into a story, the process of reporting becomes a series of challenges, minor discoveries, and sudden understandings. I was having fun. Then Michael said he was "too nervous" to do it, but he would make it up to me. I was disappointed but not surprised. The more I learned, the harder it was to understand why he would want to do an interview in the first place. He was not self-examining; he had an insular life and no friends. Everything was no deeper than the surface. Meanwhile I had gained some insight into Michael Jackson and his hermetic empire. Everyone knew his favorite companions were young boys, yet Michael left the public impression that he was asexual, a fairy, like Peter Pan.

Michael Jackson did make up for canceling. He invited Jane and me to the wedding he was hosting for Liz Taylor and the truck driver she had met in a rehab clinic. The first glimpse of Neverland was like arriving at a mini-Disneyland. The first guests I saw were Nancy Reagan chatting with Merv Griffin. The wedding was held outside, underneath an elaborate chuppah that looked like a one-story-high wedding cake. Michael gave away the bride. It was impossible to hear anything because of the helicopters. A paparazzo parachuted into the wedding. I sat at a table with Marianne Williamson, who officiated. Herb Ritts took a portrait of Jane and me. We looked glamorous.

After the wedding Michael invited me to tour his private amusement park. We got on a mini-train that took us to another part of the property, another world that had rides, attendants on duty, a merry-go-round, and a Ferris wheel. It was nighttime. It looked wonderfully American. No one was there. It was like the Twilight Zone. He had a movie theater in its own separate building with a candy counter, popcorn, and refreshment bar, lit but unattended. It was almost a regulation-size theater, and when we went inside he pointed up to the glassed-in rooms in the balcony where he said he liked to bring young cancer patients, lie in bed with them, and watch the show.

OF ALL THE critiques over the years, the one that got me most angry was that we ignored rap. It was a false accusation but struck at our foundational principles, especially the implied racism. We believed and acted upon the conviction that music was color-blind, and our coverage of the blues, R&B, and soul had been deep, wide, and brilliant. I was not a fan, but we covered rap more than anyone else, with greater depth and quality. Rap was not my world. But it was undeniably in the traditions of rock and roll, poetry, political rebellion, and popular culture, which we were responsible for covering. The idea that it was not my personal preference was not going to stop *Rolling Stone* from embracing the music and its cause.

Tom Wolfe, of all people, was the first person who ever told me about rap music. He liked to go to Harlem and the Bronx to watch the crews battle it out, and he was writing rap lyrics of his own. We began with a three-page profile of Kurtis Blow, which was followed in the fall by a four-page roundup on Grandmaster Flash and various other groups on Sugar Hill Records. One year later we gave Grandmaster Flash a featured five-star review, outranking Aretha, Warren Zevon, and Donna Summer in the same issue. We first ran a big profile of Run-DMC in 1985, and within months of their big hit with Aerosmith, "Walk This Way," they were on the cover. The advertising department fought that one as "not our audience," but it was central to our mission.

N.W.A. defined gangster rap with *Straight Outta Compton*. Our writer, Alan Light, met with them at their new suburban office-park headquarters. They were feuding with ex-members, facing court charges of violence against women and protests about their misogynous lyrics. Controversy and chaos surrounded them, a world of feuds, gangs, crews, drugs, violence, and murder. This was not peace and love; this was about a place that didn't get the benefits and largesse of belonging to the middle class. If you had any doubt about the reality of that world, you hadn't heard "Fuck Tha Police." Why would people feel that way? Maybe we should ask them?

Alan Light, the unfazed newbie we had put on the rap beat, had started as an intern with us when he was still at Yale. We also sent him out with L.L. Cool J, clearly on the other end of the rap spectrum, a performer raised in a solid Queens family and one of the first MTV rap stars.

Ice-T had put out a song called "Cop Killer" and was under heavy attack from the Bush White House ("sick and obscene") and Governor Mario Cuomo ("ugly, destructive, disgusting"). He was facing record-chain boycotts, and police organizations were putting pressure on Time Warner to recall the record. As Alan and Ice were getting out of his Rolls-Royce to get some Chinese takeout, a fan shouted out a "Good luck." Ice replied: "Do I look like I give a fuck?" Our new photographer, Mark Seliger, dressed him up for the cover in a police uniform, with gun, badge, and billy club.

WE HIRED ANOTHER young writer, who had abandoned his last name in college before he turned up as an intern. Touré was raised in Boston, his father a pillar of the local black community. He'd had a subscription to *Rolling Stone* since he was fourteen, immersing himself in the weekly installments of *The Bonfire of the Vanities*. Hip hop was hitting its platinum era, and Touré found himself in a whirlwind of assignments. Suddenly he was with Jay Z and Beyoncé, riding in private jets and hanging in all-night $1,000-a-chip poker games. Touré was a good writer fresh from the factory, and I never heard a whiff from him or anyone else about racism. Later he told me the only time he felt impacted by race at *Rolling Stone* was when he didn't get the assignment to review Radiohead.

On one Christmas cover we dressed Snoop Dogg as Santa, adorned with gold chains and smoking a red-striped candy cane. Jay Z dressed up like a proper businessman for his first cover.

WE MOVED TO our fourth and final world headquarters, a modern thirty-five-story office building with Thomas Hart Benton murals in the main lobby. In this land of skyscrapers, we took the second floor, about the size of a football field. Its attraction was that it had floor-to-ceiling plate-glass windows, a dramatic architectural gesture on that level only. It let sunlight flood through the interior spaces and gave us an intimate relationship with the city and life on Sixth Avenue. Our offices had views of a pocket park with sculptures and cherry trees that blossomed white in spring and were wrapped in Christmas lights in winter. If it was raining, the taillights of the Sixth Avenue traffic would shine like a nighttime scene from *Miami Vice*. We were directly opposite Radio City Music Hall, its deco letters lit bright neon-red at night. Another side took in Black Rock, the granite-clad skyscraper of CBS. Time Inc. was kitty-corner across the street. We shared our block with Warner Communications at 75 Rockefeller Plaza. Our buildings abutted and connected so I could walk directly to Ahmet's offices.

I liked the feel of open space for collaborative conference rooms, office villages, and other kinds of new age stuff. At some cost we opened up the ceiling and exposed lighting and air-conditioning ducts as well as the concrete beams that supported the floor above. All the private offices except mine had glass walls. I had offered staffers cloudy glass, but everyone wanted to see through and be seen. I had walnut wood walls installed, put in sliding-glass shoji-like panels, and hung two Fernand Léger paintings.

The *US* staff moved in with *Rolling Stone*. We were now 300 employees, putting out two magazines, each with circulations of over a million. To see all of it together, not separated into different floors and buildings, was a lot to behold. I would walk around the office at night, when everyone was gone, trying to soak it in, to inhabit it, to breathe in the air.

RICK GRIFFIN, THE poster artist who drew our original logo, died after he was thrown off his Harley. He was forty-seven and had four children. We quoted Jerry Garcia — Rick had done four Dead album covers — who said, "I've spent a lot of time trying to recall some sense of the psychedelic maelstrom, trying to draw it, and play it musically. I thought Rick brought more of it back from that uncharted area of the mind than anybody I knew."

The news came by phone that Bill Graham had died in a helicopter crash — it had hit high-voltage lines flying in severe weather — the flight a typically hubristic decision on Bill's part. I had no love for the guy. It had been like that since we first met, when I was a nineteen-year-old student who had dissed him in the college newspaper. I had tried, but he came off as phony and crude. He was an angry man. But he had made an inestimable contribution to the live-concert business and many San Francisco bands. Ahmet and I flew out to San Francisco for the day, bringing Ron Delsener with us, and went to the services in the city's richest synagogue. It was a strange homecoming for me to see the people I had known from way back, with whom I now exchanged nods, handshakes, and long hugs. The hippie vibe was still strong. These were friends I had left behind. I sat behind Jerry Garcia, who I was very happy to see and who had my undying affection. He had gotten older, grayer. So had everyone else. Bill had made it to sixty.

CHAPTER 47

BLUE HIGHWAYS

I N 1992 HUNTER reappeared with a rambling outburst of violent behavior, "Fear and Loathing in Elko," set in the small Nevada desert town where we had held our secret political summit a decade earlier. It begins with a memo to me about the weather in Woody Creek, his breakfast of ham and eggs and whiskey, topped off with a ball of black opium for dessert, reminiscing about the good old days: "We were poor, Jann, but we were happy. Because we knew tricks. We were smart. Not crazy, like they said. Ho, ho. Who knows why? Some people are just too weird to figure. You have come a long way from the bloodthirsty, beady eyed newshawk that you were in days of yore. Maybe you should try reading something besides those goddamned motorcycle magazines, or one of these days you'll find hair growing in your palms."

Suddenly Hunter wakes up and sees a ghost on his TV set, Supreme Court justice Clarence Thomas, whom he met one dark and stormy night years ago in the Nevada desert. The justice was at the side of the road hitchhiking, having just rammed his car into dozens of dead and dying two-hundred-pound sheep, which were lying inert like on a battle-field. Hunter, of course, gives him a lift to a motel where Clarence is running a ring of hookers.

I was back on the phone and the fax with the Good Doctor, laughing, spinning, and giggling at every new gag or insult, slander or evil twist of language. We were like kids in our clubhouse, with a secret language, secret codes, and giant printing presses hidden in the woods.

Skiing and backpacking reawakened my love of big skies and the wonder of nature. Their absence from our daily lives raised serious issues about our capability and commitment to the stewardship of the planet. That the inhabitants of big urban centers no longer lived with the nighttime stars and had no sense of our place in the universe worried me. It was the same impulse I'd had with *Outside,* which I missed and tried to buy back. The man who'd bought it said there was no price, it had become his life. My new iteration would be about men's lives within the context of adventure and achievement, with the same reportorial strength as *Rolling Stone,* along with travel and adventure service. It would look like part of our magazine family, a brother magazine. We wanted to call it *Arrow* or *Atlas,* but focus groups indicated that those names made people assume it was an archery or geography magazine. The business side wanted to call it *Men's Journal,* so they could sell ads more easily.

I hired away the editor in chief of *Outside,* John Rasmus. He had been a journalism major at Boston University and for ten years had run the post-Wenner *Outside.* John had made the magazine a constant award winner. When he joined us in New York the economy went into recession, tanking magazine advertising. I had no intention of backing off. We used the time to make prototypes and test our ideas. We put two years into planning the first issue of what we figured would be a new men's quarterly.

It was a hit. It was the same size as *Rolling Stone,* with a glossy cover, better paper, classic design, and gorgeous photography. The first issue, whose cover featured a kayak pulled onto the beach in an isolated cove, had a profile of Wayne Gretzky by Don Katz. Jon Krakauer did a brilliant profile of the solo free climber Jeff Lowe as he faced his demons on the face of the Eiger. I remember holding my breath when I read it. P. J. O'Rourke weighed in on deep-sea fishing off Margaritaville.

There were car racing schools, desert golf courses, the eight best lower-back exercises, how to build a dream cabin by the sea, full-suspension mountain bikes, multisports watches. I loved it. It was a further opportunity for my bone for adventure. Gil Friesen and I bought a small company called Overseas Adventure Travel. In the very first year, *Men's Journal* won an American Society of Magazine Editors General Excellence Award.

I was cooking up a trip with the boys, a transcontinental motorcycle ride from the George Washington Bridge to the Golden Gate. We called ourselves the Bridge Club. They were all Harley-Davidson riders. The co-captains were MTV founder Bob Pittman — a preacher's kid with one glass eye who was now the CEO of Six Flags — and Sheldon Coleman of Wichita, Kansas, whose family's company, Coleman Stove, had been snatched away in some tax-advantaged maneuver involving insolvent savings and loan banks. Sheldon now owned Big Dog Motorcycles, a shop that customized Harleys. Bob and Sheldon worked out routes that avoided interstates and kept us on the blue highways and beautiful roads through small towns.

Rounding out the crew was my Amagansett friend Michael Cinque, who owned a wine store; Rocky Hill, Bob Pittman's bruiser brother-in-law; Lanier Hurdle, Bob's "cuddin" from Mississippi; Chris Kennan, preppy descendant of diplomat George Kennan; Bob Millard, a Wall Street genius; Woody Johnson, heir to the Johnson & Johnson fortune, who had bought the New York Jets and later became Trump's ambassador to the Court of St. James's; and John Pannone, a prison guard from Connecticut. Tim Mooney, an Aspen skiing buddy, and Gary Wagner, a Harley mechanic, would follow us in a rental truck with tools, three spare bikes, and the luggage. Gary was also packing heat. I thought it would be a great story for *Men's Journal*, so we also brought along Jon Krakauer.

After a slog to our first overnight stop in Pittsburgh, the country opened up into Ohio, forests, rural hamlets with grocery stores and old-time, two-pump gas stations that came into view around the curves of the two-lane highway. There were stops for speeding tickets, and after the first few, the pack broke up into faster and slower riders, strung out between our day's destination and the chase truck. Every morning we got the road map, taped it on our gas tanks, and headed out until the lunch rendezvous, with luck at an outdoor barbecue joint. Indiana was endless fields and the slow march of rotary watering pipes. Now and then you would spot a lone, neatly kept white Victorian or a cluster of houses around a wooden church with a steeple. One breakfast was in a combination restaurant and bowling alley. The other patrons were the small-town elders on a coffee break, a dozen or so gray-haired women with their men, in bib overalls and work boots, at separate tables. I expected we might get some crosswise looks, but the vibe was, Howdy, and what can we do for you? The check for five break-fasts was nine dollars. I gave the waitress a twenty, and she came running out the door after us with the change. It's a trivial memory, but within her gesture was the goodness of an older, smaller America.

We spent one night in Yankton, South Dakota, hometown of Tom Bro-kaw.* A reservation had been made at a pizza place, but everyone wanted to go to the Chinese joint. Would Yankton have better Chinese than pizza? The motel we were in only had a phone at the front desk, so I asked the man-ager to change our dinner reservation. By that point in the trip no one had shaved, hair was an unwashed mess, and everyone was rocking a bandana around his neck or forehead: Don't fuck with these guys, they're hard-core. The clerk gets on the phone with the restaurant owner: "Hank, I got a group of executive bikers here…" Later that night, as we slept, three genuine bad guys showed up to steal our bikes. Gary drew on them, and they left.

We rode to Wyoming over the Black Hills of South Dakota. Less than a mile into a long seven-thousand-foot-elevation mountain pass — in June — hail came pounding out of the sky, marble-size stuff. It doesn't hurt you, thanks to your helmet, leathers, and rain gear, but it's death to ride on.

---

* Brokaw later became a regular contributor to *Men's Journal*.

You go slow, you clench your butt, and you try to loosen your grip. Wyoming is stunning open country, a land of endless horizons and empty two-lane roads with neither fences nor barriers to wandering livestock.

Part of the thrill of a motorcycle is the openness, the constant and urgent awareness of your surroundings, the rapid changes in temperature, wind, geography, smells, and the sound of the engine. Especially in the no-helmet-law states. We were a self-contained group of men who found, for that week, a communal life with little structure other than the road. The nights were for storytelling about the day's ride, not about yesterday's problems or tomorrow's worries. Going 100 miles an hour into a long turn, or 45 into a tight one, clears the mind of anything not in that split-second moment. You don't have a care in the world except for the wind shutting out every noise in that curve save for the scream of the engine, the noise of hell on your tail.

We found a motel outside of Cody and decided to wash our bikes. I pulled my Yamaha FZR1000 out of the chase truck. I let Mooney take my Harley and got on my crotch rocket for the rest of the journey. It gave me the same intense feeling as a high-speed flyby on skis. I couldn't resist dropping behind my Harley-riding companions, only to sneak up behind them and blow by at 110 miles an hour. It's like standing still and a tow truck passes five feet from you at 40 miles an hour, a truck you didn't see coming. That'll frighten anyone.

The visit to the Buffalo Bill Museum in Cody stayed with me. I had expected something corny but instead discovered detailed dioramas of the Plains Indians. The curators had installed a Lakota teepee village, mannequins of women cooking, children playing, men tanning skins, getting ready for a hunt, their weaving and clothes and tools for daily life. These were people we had wiped out, whose humble and deeply spiritual civilization we destroyed. After riding for days, thousands of miles through a bountiful, beautiful, and unpopulated land, I asked myself, Why hadn't there been room for all of us? What had we done?

There were two days left; we had made about three hundred miles a day, which is six hours on a hard seat, into the wind, hot, with the noise and vibration of the engine. There was still a lot of desert to go before the farmlands of eastern Oregon. Once we got to the California border, the freedom of the West and the notion that you were some kind of cowboy were yesterday's news. The Golden State is a land of multilane highways, helmet laws, and the California Highway Patrol. My sister Merlyn and her family met us on the Marin side of the Golden Gate Bridge with champagne and plastic glasses. We crossed the bridge single file, giving high fives to the tollbooth collectors. We shot right through San Francisco to the airport and parked our motorcycles in a hangar to be picked up and shipped east the next day. The irony of getting back to New York on a jet in four hours at forty thousand feet was not lost on me. I was ready to go home and take a bath.

CHAPTER 48

BILL CLINTON AND THE THREE STOOGES

W HEN I STARTED the magazine, at age twenty-one, the average age of our readers was also twenty-one. Now I was forty-six, and our readers were in their midtwenties, now in the middle of the baby boom generation. To celebrate the twenty-fifth anniversary of *Rolling Stone*, I thought that instead of one rhinoceros-size special issue, we had enough of a historical record for three, and laid plans for "The Great Stories," "The Great Interviews," and a final in November, the actual anniversary, "The Great Photographs." And what an opportunity for a party.

We had published approximately 5,000 major features. Multiply that by an average length of 5,000 words (which may be understating), and we're talking 25 million words. The number-one and number-seven books on the bestseller lists at the time were by Bill Greider and P. J. O'Rourke. We chose thirty stories to focus on. I didn't think excerpting them was very imaginative or fulfilling, so instead, I asked the writers of each selected story — basically all our legends, major and minor — to write about how they found the story and got it into print at *Rolling Stone*. These would be true tales of journalism, which in and of itself would be a tale of our times.

Larry Wright was speaking for our second generation of staff when he wrote in his essay that he had grown up reading "Thompson, Eszter-has, Cahill, Crouse, and Flippo—those literary hellcats who brushed aside journalistic convention and social taboos to get at new ways of telling the truth. One accepted a *Rolling Stone* assignment knowing that not only must it be the final word on a subject, but it must be freshly seen and powerfully told. The magazine presents the writer with a challenge to exceed himself."

The first two anniversary specials, the stories and interviews, were all-type covers. We went back and forth on what picture to put on the third, the photos. We couldn't decide which photo of whom should have pride of place on the cover, so we took Elvis' gold tuxedo into the studio and shot it. The simplicity of the gesture, the choice of the artist, the symbolism of the gold—power, wealth, and seduction—and that the suit was empty made a powerful statement. Each of the three anniversary issues was a masterpiece of magazine art. We had successfully curated our vast archives and added a modern spin, a new historical understanding, to each piece of writing and its subject. Every page, from small details of lettering and folio lines to callout boxes, reflected craftsmanship.

The criteria I had set forth for *Rolling Stone* stories from the beginning were these: It had to be about something interesting and important, and not duplicate what you could get elsewhere; you had to report the hell out of it, meaning be passionate and get involved; and you had to write it well—long if necessary—and accurately in every detail, and in the end tell the truth about what you think.

Hunter put it another way: "Wrong... That is the word. That is what it was like to write for *Rolling Stone* twenty years ago. It was Wrong, or at least it looked that way. And that was the terrible joy of it. On some days you could even *get paid* for being Wrong. And let me tell you, on some days that was serious Fun... I remember one particularly ugly night down in Jann's basement on Ord Court when we got so excited about the Salazar story that we stabbed each other with scissors and locked Jane in the garage with a pack of mongrel dogs."

Bill Greider laid down his credo: "We don't ever want to lose our youthful sense of optimism. The trick for the nation is how to become wiser about the world without becoming cynical, how to look at ourselves more honestly, without losing our faith in the future. Whatever the topic, that is the theme of my work in *Rolling Stone:* the need to get smart about things without losing hope, to be honest about the nation's condition while remaining optimistic about our possibilities."

DESPITE HAVING CROSSED paths with Jerry Brown for twenty years, I didn't think he had a clue who I was. Jerry wasn't a touchy-feely guy, but he was tapped into philosophical and political insights about our times that were farseeing. Brown, the governor of California, was running against the governor of Arkansas, William Jefferson Clinton, to be the Democratic candidate for president.

Bill Greider had been following Clinton and concluded that he was a mixed bag, a man of impressive political skills and a grasp of complex policy issues, but it wasn't clear what he stood for. I myself was a Jerry Brown man and wrote in a Letter from the Editor, "His political message is right for the long run. His brilliance is thinking inventively about the possibilities for the future. Jerry has consistently stood for values that matter most to our readers."

Jerry was using our offices as his convention headquarters. He had accumulated enough delegates to get a prime-time speaking spot, on the condition that he would use it to endorse Clinton, who now had it sewn up. The issue remaining for him was whether he would in fact endorse Clinton. Jerry arrived in town on the Amtrak, without a press corps. He denounced delegates who sat around eating tubs of giant shrimp and said he would spend a night in a homeless shelter.

Working in the office with Jerry were his top aide, a mysterious bald man, Jacques Barzaghi, and Dick Goodwin, who was consulting on his speeches. When Jerry continued to refuse to endorse Clinton, Dick and I decided to have an intervention. We all met for a "frank exchange of ideas" in my office. It was the old half-a-loaf argument. Dick was throwing American history and progressive political theory at Jerry, and I was telling him that he would be run out of the Democratic Party for years if he bolted like a brat who couldn't get his way. He wouldn't give us an answer.

I went down to Madison Square Garden with Jerry to watch him speak. Since he wouldn't endorse Clinton, he was denied a prime-time spot and was technically seconding his own nomination, but he still got all the balloons falling and signs waving. I watched all this from the podium. Jerry had been building to this for months. He was sweating, breathing fire, a Jesuit Moses in front of the apostate Democrats, who had sold their loyalties to the special interests and had betrayed the people. I agreed with Jerry but thought his gesture was impetuous and useless. I didn't walk offstage with him. Clinton was coming up, and I had the best seat in the house.

I had a drink with Clinton's press secretary, George Stephanopoulos, the next day. He reminded me that *Rolling Stone* had picked him in 1990 as the hot up-and-coming staffer on Capitol Hill. I wanted to reassure him that we supported Clinton and expected him to give us a long interview with the candidate forthwith.

The appointment with Clinton was set for two weeks later, in Little Rock, Arkansas, at the governor's favorite barbecue spot, Doe's Eat Place. I thought it should be a summit meeting with our wizards, Bill Greider, P. J. O'Rourke, and Hunter, a *Rolling Stone* version of *Meet the Press*, or, as Hunter would later call it, *The Three Stooges Go to Little Rock*. (It was more like *Greider the Guru*, accompanied by his two shit-kicking sidekicks.) On the flight down we dubbed my plane *Rolling Stone One*. We had dinner the night before at the Capital Hotel with James Carville. Greider came in a wheelchair, having twisted his knee just before we picked him up. He was on painkillers. Hunter was drinking, smoking through his Tar Gard filter, and sweating; P. J. was working on his questions overtime as the serious-minded lone *Rolling Stone* Republican.

Doe's was what Hunter called an "artificially degraded replica of a standard-brand Southern diner." Hunter was never not the showman, and on our lunch meeting table he laid out a laser pointer, a plastic fetish wand, and a battery-powered, undulating rubber hand. P. J. placed a yellow legal pad in front of him, with pages of neatly written detailed notes, plus files of reference material next to the pad. It was as if he was the prosecution lawyer in court. Bill Greider was at his coolest, laying down a slim reporter's notebook and a pack of unfiltered Camels.

Clinton came in wearing shorts. He was in his late forties, a young man to Greider. He was quite at ease, just another day of the work he loved. Hunter brought along a saxophone reed, which he presented as a gift. I began asking about his generational moment, the sixties and Vietnam. The context here was that George Bush had been a World War II hero, and was defined by that. Clinton was the first baby boomer ever to run, and he was defined by his refusal to fight in Vietnam. Clinton said he understood all this and mentioned a lady he met on the campaign who said to him, "You've got to go in there and redeem the sixties generation."

Greider wanted to discuss people's sense that the government wasn't working for them but for the rich and powerful, that they were becoming deeply disillusioned with their political leadership. P. J. had his agenda, and asked about what percentage of total tax revenues in relation to the gross national product was being spent on government programs instead of by individual choice, and so forth. P. J. then proceeded to bite into his tamale, whereupon Clinton advised him to shuck the paper wrapper before eating. The response to this wonky, right-wing challenge didn't really matter much. Clinton gently, expertly, smothered P. J.'s facts with his own.

Hunter was strangely, unusually quiet. He thought we were going to have a high-level political parley, at the end of which we would deliver the *Rolling Stone* vote. He asked Clinton about his views on the Fourth Amendment, prohibiting unreasonable search and seizure, particularly using it to defend drug cases. I was surprised by the intensity of Clinton's response about what drugs had done to his brother. George Stephanopoulos had certainly warned the candidate about Hunter and prepared him to shut Hunter down. "Most of the people in the drug culture are profoundly disconnected to the rest of the country," Clinton said. Hunter realized that this was not going to be the moment of communion he had envisioned. The respect and fondness that both George McGovern and Jimmy Carter had for Hunter was not going to be there. In fact, it seemed as if Clinton not only didn't care about Hunter's support, in a way he didn't want it. Hunter was the Sister Souljah of the drug generation; Clinton hadn't grown up on *Fear and Loathing in Las Vegas*. Bill Greider asked how the economy would benefit working men and women, unions, and the middle class, and what loyalty Clinton felt to all the lobbyists and fat-cat money that was coming into his campaign, especially the backing of Goldman Sachs. Clinton said his only motives were out of his deep concern for the direction of the country. He was impressive.

The brain trust wrote up their own impressions of the day, the interview, and the candidate. P. J. was absolutely funny, like a late-night monologue, one great riff and one line after another about politicians. In the end, he said he came from "a long line of Republicans and had a monkey in a blue blazer and green pants" on his back and couldn't possibly endorse him. "If your life is so screwed up and pathetic that you think even a politician can make it better, go ahead and pull the donkey lever."

Greider and Hunter both landed on the willingness and the need to fight the greed and corruption that Reagan had unshackled. Hunter's bottom line: "He is a high-stakes gambler and he can take a punch better than anybody since Muhammad Ali. We have nothing to lose except fun and the joy of watching a serious brawler go to war with the greed heads. Why not? Let us rumble."

Greider was more nuanced, and nailed the central issue: "People are hopeful for him because after a decade of deceitful manipulation, Clinton seems real. His great vulnerability, I fear, is his sense of cautious moderation. If he is truly a great leader, Clinton will be made bold by the crucible, and his presidency will steer America toward the radical reforms it wants and needs."

Clinton spent two and a half hours with us, after which he left for the governor's mansion, where Mark Seliger was set up for the cover shoot. I hopped into the back of Bill's car for the ten-minute ride. He must have forgotten I was along, because when he got out of the car he was in a foulmouthed rage at one of his waiting staffers. Inside the mansion, Mark had set up a diorama of the White House as his set for the cover shot. Clinton changed from shorts and short sleeves into a coat and pants. He came down from his bedroom and handed me a bunch of ties to choose from. He looked at my choice and said to me, "Does it say 'Leader of the Free World'?"

The next day, back in New York, the papers and the evening news all reported that Clinton had canceled the day's campaign activities because of a hoarse voice. The only new video and photos the networks and newspapers had to show was a close-up of him out for his daily jog, wearing the *Rolling Stone* T-shirt I had given him. What a shrewd motherfucker.

Clinton was a baby boomer, a year younger than me, and the first "young" person to run since John F. Kennedy, when I was fifteen years old. Clinton's youth gave me a feeling of purpose, the idea that what we did editorially would count, not just raising alarms and pissing in the wind against Reagan policies. Now we would have the wind behind us. That feeling of centrality began to affect everything we did. It all became more real.

In my Letter from the Editor, I told our readers, "You cannot let this opportunity drop out of apathy or laziness or some sophistry about how politics doesn't really matter. Clinton and Gore are men who came of age in the sixties and whose sensibilities and value systems were formed then. They have the civil rights movement, the cultural revolution, and rock and roll in their blood. Once in office, their greatest task will be to rebuild people's faith in themselves, our native sense of optimism and self-confidence. This election will give our generation the chance to renew our politics and to reconcile our deeply held values with the realities of government."

FOR OUR TWENTY-FIFTH-ANNIVERSARY party we took over the Four Seasons restaurant to stage a seated dinner for four hundred guests. Junior staffers wearing *Rolling Stone* sweatshirts escorted couples in under umbrellas. It looked like the Academy Awards, a head turner to see one well-known face after another from all kinds of surprising places walk in. I was swept up in the reunion. I had invited all the old hands who had thrown in with me. At my table were Tom and Sheila Wolfe, David Bowie and Iman, Don Henley, Ed Bradley with Kathleen Battle, Walter and Betsy Cronkite, and Annie Leibovitz. Jane sat between Hunter and John Kennedy. Fran Lebowitz and Jonathan Cott, my college pal since I was eighteen, were at Jane's table, too. Keith Richards and Eric Clapton were wearing tuxedos.

The gathering spoke to the many things that *Rolling Stone* had become and represented. It was the start of the post-Reagan resurgence of Manhattan, its liberal politics and culture ready to return to power, shining in candlelight that reflected off the rippling beaded curtains, catching the sparkle of diamonds and silver balloons on long ribbons. Did Jay Gatsby do it better?

There were numerous toasts. Bob Wallace spoke on behalf of the staff of *Rolling Stone*, past and present: "Jann has shown us that, while you can't stay forever young, you can be childish for the rest of your life." He also wanted to correct the record about my being short: "Jann is not short. It says so on page three of the company manual."

Hunter was the last speaker, in black tie, wearing the medallion given to him by Oscar Acosta. It wouldn't have mattered what Hunter did; he looked the soul of mischief. He said he thought he was being censored because I wouldn't let him present a gift he had brought along for me, a four-by-four-foot portrait by Mark Seliger, with my arms folded, very serious. Hunter had put an aerosol can of gold paint in front of it and shot a bullet at it, exploding the paint and leaving a hole in my forehead. He gave a sweet toast. Hunter was pretty sentimental; he called *Rolling Stone* "our creature," and raised his glass not only to all of us, but to Jack and Bobby Kennedy, Martin Luther King, and Oscar Acosta.

Billy Joel got up with his wife, Christie Brinkley, a diamond choker around her neck, to sing "Happy Birthday" à la Marilyn Monroe. A cake was brought up. Hunter had Jane under one arm and his other arm around me. The three of us sang "Happy Birthday" and blew out the candles.

CHAPTER 49

A VISIT
TO THE WHITE HOUSE

JANE AND I went to Washington, not for the music or the galas — there were seventeen official balls at which the Clintons would show up — but to witness the inauguration. It was sunny and cold. We had great seats, front and center, on the steps of the Capitol. Jack Nicholson sat next to us. He had a portable ashtray, with a lid that closed so he could slip it in his pocket. How cool! Marines kept stopping by to pay their respects to Jack. It took me a few minutes to put it together: *A Few Good Men* had just been released with its volcanic "You can't handle the truth" soliloquy. He was a hero to leathernecks everywhere. I asked Jack why he had come; he said, "I'm a Democrat." When I repeat that, it sounds unremarkable, but it had a world of meaning to me. I had spent a lifetime following and supporting the good work of men like FDR, Truman, JFK, Johnson, the great civil rights champion, and Jimmy Carter, the peacemaker. I was with my fellow Democrats.

I STARTED SKIING REGULARLY in Sun Valley, often sharing a condo with John Kennedy. Sun Valley is a small, nonglitzy town, a great place to raise kids, and the skiing is world-class. Jane came out to check out real estate and landed on Broadford Farm, a hundred-acre homestead with pastures, cottonwood trees, and the Big Wood River running through it. The house had been built of logs in 1890. It had been the city hall and jail when the silver mines were operating.

I WAS IN THE middle of another magazine launch, *Family Life*, like *Men's Journal*, funded with *Rolling Stone* profits and staffed and managed out of our office, and once again with the oversized format and the classic look of *Rolling Stone*. We would be a family of magazines, generational, because the new magazine would be about having kids, parenting for the baby boomers... such as myself, again.

The idea for *Family Life* came from Nancy Evans, whom I had met at a party at Caroline Kennedy's. She was working as a book editor with Jackie. We were predisposed to hit it off, and we did. She was good-looking, smart, knew what she was doing, and suddenly we had another beautiful magazine. My own identity was still about being editor of *Rolling Stone*, but my career was now as a publisher. Magazines were having a glorious run; journalism and social identity were combined in a compelling mix, saying to readers, here's who you are and here's what you think.

Family Life was a joyful thing to work on, playing with all the magic puzzle pieces that go into child-rearing. It was a bit of a playdate for Nancy and me, without the kids around making a mess. It felt like God's good work instead of the standard magazine rat race. But I had rushed in, missing the strategic flaw: you couldn't build a stable, profitable circulation base, because the subscribers constantly turned over as their kids quickly aged out. I sold it to Disney, which merged it with their similar title, *Family Fun*, and got my investment back.

A GROUP OF US piled onto my plane at the end of the summer for a trip to see U2 in Dublin. The idea came up at lunch, and the next day we left. Jane; Tom Freston; his lieutenant at MTV, Judy McGrath, and her husband, Mike Corbett; and Terry and Joni McDonell were the traveling party. Before diving into Dublin, we took a three-day tour of the Ring of Cork. Sabrina Guinness flew over from London to join our entourage, and she brought Bob Geldof into the mix, who took me on a tour of Dublin pubs. The U2 show was the last date (except for New Zealand) of their *Zoo TV* tour, a two-year trek that had grossed over $150 million. They had once used much more simple stages, until they saw the Stones' industrial cityscape for the *Steel Wheels* stage. U2 now had that multimillion, multimedia spectacle of screens, videos, films, rolling electronic ribbons of words and phrases, and live TV. They wanted to be the biggest band in the world. I guess that meant topping the Stones.

The venue for the sold-out hometown show was a racetrack. There was a VIP platform in the back where I stood with Mick and Jerry Hall. To Mick it was clearly competition, and he was making mental notes, a tad sniffy about being copied. There would be a few more rounds to go on this one, the battle of the world's two rock and roll superpowers trying to outdo each other in tours yet to come. Paul McGuinness, U2's shrewd business manager and partner, led us on an after-show crawl under a full moon until dawn.

The next day Bono had an afternoon tea party at his 1830s Georgian mansion on the cliffs of Killiney overlooking the Irish Sea, the last big house built in Dublin before the great potato famine of 1845. Salman Rushdie — on the lam because the Ayatollah Khomeini had issued a fatwa on him, authorizing any Muslim anywhere to assassinate him — was living secretly in the guest house. It was the first time I had met Bono, other than a backstage visit that John Kennedy and I had made. I was captivated by his gregarious charm and how intensely he engaged with you. His wife, Ali, was quite the pretty Irish lass; there was something homegrown and genuine about her. She and Bono were childhood sweethearts.

BILL GREIDER AND I showed up at the White House gate the first week in November, one day short of the anniversary of Clinton's election.

After body scans, and putting our IDs in metal drawers that passed through bulletproof glass in exchange for magnetized passes to be worn at all times, we were taken to the West Wing's drab waiting room, staffed by Marines. Clinton was at a gun-control event with Jim and Sarah Brady just after a NAFTA cheerleading meeting with Paul Volcker and Henry Kissinger.

Interviewing a sitting president was a first for both Bill and me. It was a world away from our tamale summit in Little Rock. Clinton was in a good mood, buoyed by the NAFTA meeting. After a quick tour of the Oval Office, where he showed off his new rug with the presidential seal, he led us into his private dining room, a painting of Woodrow Wilson behind his seat, a bust of Harry Truman on a table. He also showed us his private library, which would become infamous.

I started: "Are you having fun?" I was casually engaging with a man my age, in the prime of his life. I thought, Well, that could be me — I didn't think it should be or that I could possibly do the job, but I identified with him in some root way. We were both custodians of a set of dreams and ideas, mine to my constituency, his to his party and country. I felt I was sitting with an equal, and we were going to get down to business.

He was having fun — sort of. Clinton said he was humbled by how hard it was to translate convictions into policy, but exhilarated to have the opportunity and obligation to try to do so every day. The problem was that, for a number of reasons, he would be the first president since the Civil War era who would be denied a honeymoon period to get his term off to a good start. He had come under immediate attack from the Republicans, abetted by a conservative mainstream press ever looking to stoke a headline fight.

Washington had become hostile, poisoned in part by rich families and businessmen angry about tax increases, the "vast right-wing conspiracy" that was rising from the mud. It was also generational: the culture war was here, with the arrival of a baby boom president, an anti-Vietnam protester, and the old guard hated him. And because leadership also required compromise, he was taking flak from the rarely satisfied left, which is where to some degree Bill Greider was coming from.

Clinton was incredibly knowledgeable about the complexities and trade-offs of policy making. I loved his language about not being able to get stuff done "lickety-split," or that defense cuts were making Europe "nervous as a cat." Clinton's intellect was awesome. He was late for his next meeting with Jimmy Carter and former secretary of state James Baker. When Greider had run through all the policy stuff, I asked my windup question about what he had learned so far and his own sense of optimism. My job was to take the measure of the man emotionally and morally. His response: "All the old rules are still the ones that count. I feel better every night when I go home if I have done what I think is right. I feel better when I throw away the script and just say what's on my mind."

As Clinton was on his way out, Greider asked one more question. He said a guy who had some minor role in the Clinton campaign had called him that morning. He was now very disappointed and told Greider he should "ask Clinton what he's willing to stand up for and die on." Suddenly, the president was one foot from Greider, his face red and his voice rising in a furious rebuke. He was angry. "I have fought more damn battles here for more things than any president in twenty years, and not gotten one damn bit of credit from the liberal knee-jerk press, and I am sick and tired of it, and you can put that in your damn article. I have fought and fought and fought and fought. I get up here every day, and I work till late at night on everything from national service to family leave to the budget to the crime bill. If you convince them I don't have any conviction, that's fine, but it's a damn lie. It's a lie.

"I have fought my guts out for that guy, and if he doesn't know it, it's not all my fault. You get no credit around here fighting and bleeding. That's why the know-nothings and the do-nothings and the negative people and right-wingers always win. Because of the way people like you put questions to people like me. Now that's the truth, Bill."

Clinton started to walk away. I was speechless, as were David

Gergen and Stephanopoulos, who had been at the lunch. Greider didn't back down and didn't flinch. Clinton turned back to him, still mad as hell: "That's why they always win. This administration is killing itself every day. You hold us to an impossible standard and never give us any credit when we are moving forward. We have fought our guts out for them and the bad guys win, because they have no objective other than to win. They shift the blame, and they play on the cynicism of the media. I come to work here every day, and I try to help that guy, and I'm sorry if I'm not very good at communicating, but I haven't gotten a hell of a lot of help since I have been here."

It was a great interview, a personal and political portrait that presidents never give. I was prouder of Clinton than ever. He was always trying to move the ball forward. Word of the blowup got around the press corps, and we had a lot of calls from TV and radio to release the audio. For what purpose? More pointless and trivial controversy? Clinton would have been beaten silly with that tape. It would have been nice publicity for *Rolling Stone*, but I wasn't going to enable stupid denigration by his enemies — on the right or the left.

THE YEAR WAS over. The last cover was Cindy Crawford in a ruffled bikini bottom and well-positioned hands, an homage to Botticelli's Venus, by Herb Ritts. There was a whirlwind of Christmas parties. People were feeling confident. December 18 was Keith Richards' birthday. He took over a restaurant downtown, where I was seated next to Eric Clapton, newly sober, who didn't say a cross word as I put away several too many. The next day it was off to close out 1993 on St. Barts for Christmas and the New Year.

A yacht of some size, the *Midnight Saga*, had anchored in the middle of a bay, where for the third year we had rented the only house on the bay, built by David Rockefeller. The boat had been chartered by Barry Diller and Diane von Furstenberg, and one of their guests was a beautiful blond in a dark blue Speedo, twenty-nine-year-old Matt Nye. We went for lunch on board, at which Matt didn't say much, but my heart felt like a kid's toy compass, with the needle fluttering as I watched him and tried to catch his attention.

Later that afternoon he swam to the beach where I was playing tag with the kids. He was hard to engage but took to the boys and they started building sandcastles. He brought the kids back to the house later but Jane blew him off. I didn't know what to think. I was trying to be nonchalant, but my head was spinning.

CHAPTER 50

THE DEATH OF JACKIE ONASSIS

I STARTED GOING TO Washington, D.C., a lot. With a Democrat as president, it was time to make another push on gun control. A sense of possibility was in the air. Anne Wexler, my former associate publisher, had become a major player due to her long relationship with Bill and Hillary, which dated back to their days together as McGovern volunteers. She took me around the Senate office buildings to meet with gun-control senators. It was a high school civics class come to life, but it was a slog, with a lot of waiting in reception rooms.

ROLLING STONE PUBLISHED a deep, dense presentation about gun violence, a heavy-duty document with gun statistics, the legal history of the Second Amendment, an investigation into the power of the gun industry, and the politics. I wanted to demystify the ideology and propose a solution. The first step would be a public-education media campaign about the risks of gun ownership. Ten years earlier I was recruiting police chiefs. Now it felt like starting over. The difficulty had been that I was a one-man show. The new effort was called Ceasefire. Guns never worked for self-defense; a child killed himself or an adult committed suicide or killed a spouse with that gun kept at home. We did a series of

PSAs directed by Jonathan Demme with Walter Cronkite, Oprah Winfrey, Paul Newman, and Michael Douglas.

IT WAS TIME for a special issue on drugs, "The Phony War, the Real Crisis." The laws, the persecution of young people and black Americans, the so-called War on Drugs, was an abomination of justice and morality. There had been no noticeable backlash to our hard-line coverage of gun violence and the NRA, but this appeared riskier because of the taint of our being druggies. Many people still associated it with shameful, furtive behavior. It's hard to remember that pot use was once considered radioactive. I was concerned that even a reasonable stance on drugs would turn off our advertisers, who would quickly run from anything that associated them with controversy. Our credibility gave us the ability to speak out on difficult issues, but our power to do so was also based in part on our financial success with advertisers. They have their own constituencies and can be fair-weather friends when they need to be. If they said they didn't feel comfortable with "fuck" in boldface headlines, I thought that was fine. That was not a battle of any importance at this point.

Like the guns issue, we combined advocacy with policy, statistical research, and reporting. We looked at what Clinton had done, which was minimal. He didn't want to touch it, and had fired his handpicked surgeon general, Dr. Joycelyn Elders, when she suggested that the time had come to "study" legalization. She had come to meet me at our office, and I was impressed. We reported on the high rate of drug use across the country, and included a plea for legalization from the mayor of Baltimore, Kurt Schmoke, who was seeing a generation of young black men thrown in jail. We profiled the Drug Policy Foundation, the most thoughtful advocacy group, financed by billionaire George Soros, and the Grateful Dead's foundation, among others.

I co-authored an editorial titled "Toward a Sane National Drug Policy." It laid out our position: "A society cannot long afford to have its laws widely and openly broken. The urge to use some form of mind-altering substance is deeply ingrained in human nature. Attempting to legislate it out of existence can only lead us to grant government the kind of power it should not have in a free society. The arguments against decriminalization are outdated, tired and invalid.

"In the inner cities, where the front-line battles of the war are fought daily, the situation is desperate. The disintegration of the family structure, the dire job outlook, inadequate education and government abandonment have guaranteed communities where drug traffic is guaranteed to flourish. Can we let this damage continue? Isn't it time to stop moralizing about drugs and put an end to policies that are destroying the nation?"

Sadly, we were headed into two decades of harsh and severe criminal prosecutions, largely focused on putting young black men into a government-financed private prison system under mandatory sentencing—deeply rooted racism called by another name.

The coauthor of the editorial was Ethan Nadelmann, a professor at Princeton. Ethan took over the Drug Policy Foundation and came up with the idea of medical marijuana as the stalking horse for decriminalization and full legalization. It was a brilliant strategy; he was the general. It took time, and it worked.

JOHN KENNEDY HAD finished his stint as a prosecutor in the Brooklyn DA's office. He failed the bar exam for a second time. Murdoch made it another bleeding-and-feeding frenzy. John sent me a note: "I'm glad you are sleeping better knowing I am on the front lines of the war on crime. Unfortunately, as you probably read, it will be another few months before my righteous force is felt on the streets of Mudville. If not, then how's the publishing world?"

The DA's office was where John was supposed to rub off his patrician heritage and decide whether he liked the law or wanted to do something else. I saw John a lot in those days; I brought him with me onto the board of the Robin Hood Foundation—I had been one of the founding directors — and we skied together, hit the concerts. I went to my first U2 show with John, who left his briefcase, typical of his orderliness, at my house that weekend. When we went to see the Stones at the Meadowlands, I said I'd get the tickets if he'd bring the dope. Once we parked he pulled out a foot-long bong, as if we were going to bring it to our seats. Very John. He had helped get my kids into his alma mater and was their guardian. I was watching over him, in my fashion, at his mother's none-too-subtle request. We had often discussed what he wanted to do; it was assumed he would run for office. I thought he should. He had the common touch, spoke earnestly, and was a compassionate person. In fact, he was polite, funny, and an all-around terrific guy. He also had a temper, was impetuous, and sometimes reckless.

He had asked me to speak at Harvard's Kennedy School of Government. The very serious-looking poster said in big type, "Rock, the Media, and Politics. A public address by Jann Wenner. Introduction by John F. Kennedy." On the plane ride to Boston, John told me that he was thinking of starting a magazine. Soon after we got back, I met with him and his partner in a formal way at my office. The partner did not impress me. I wanted John to understand that magazine publishing was really hard, I wouldn't recommend it to anyone, and I didn't think he should do it. I knew he wouldn't heed my warning. I told him I was aware of the incongruity of it coming from me, and that if he had a strong enough editorial idea, success was always possible. He had good instincts but no experience to back them up. Last, I asked if he was prepared to swallow the exploitation of the family name. It would be sold as *JFK Jr. Magazine*. "Mummie" wouldn't be thrilled, but it was his life now.

I had lunch with Jackie at the end of April 1994. She liked quiet and off-the-beaten-path; otherwise a casual meal could end up as a public show. We chatted about the usual, my latest exploits, John's current plans and current girlfriend, joked about why Caroline and I didn't get married, and her sadness about her sister Lee's anger toward her, how Lee just wouldn't let it go. Jackie had a strange dry cough. I had no idea that she was being treated for cancer. Two weeks later she was dead. Sixty-four years old.

THERE WAS A rosary service and a wake at her apartment with family and a few friends, nephews, and nieces. Her coffin was there. Arnold Schwarzenegger came with Maria Shriver, Caroline's closest cousin. Saying goodbye was always hard for me: the understanding of how final the loss is, the loneliness and sense of abandonment. Jane grabbed my hand tight: "Do not cry. Jackie wouldn't like it." When we left, I knew that I would never see that apartment again, where Jackie had introduced us to her New York.

The next day a mass was held at the church on Park Avenue where she had been baptized. The streets were cordoned off by the police, like a state funeral. We sat with Dick Goodwin and Doris Kearns. Dick had introduced me to Jackie twenty years earlier. I wanted to think of the Jackie I was blessed to have as a friend — she was a serious woman, and she could light up your life — but this was a farewell to one of the most respected and revered persons in the world. Teddy spoke. He said she gave to everyone, whether they knew her or not, "the gift of herself. How cherished were those wonderful notes, written in her distinctive hand on her powder-blue stationery. She graced our history. And for those of us who knew and loved her, she graced our lives." Jessye Norman sang "Ave Maria," and I could not hold back the sadness that had been quivering in me the whole morning, the whole weekend. I looked up and I saw Jackie's spirit rise from her coffin, rising up to heaven.

It was sad to drive past 1040 Fifth Avenue now and realize that Mrs. Onassis was no longer there. She had been the guardian of New York's best self. The enchanted spell she cast was no more and now it was a different city. She was extraordinary, the most exquisite person I had ever met. She was also my private Jackie who had resolutely challenged me to be my best self and put her gentle hand out to me.

CHAPTER 51

MATT

Nirvana was the first cover of 1994. This time they were dressed in pin-striped suits. On their first cover, Kurt Cobain had worn a T-shirt on which he had handwritten "Corporate Magazines Still Suck," trying to appease his own conscience or signal to his hard-core grunge fans that he wasn't *really* selling out by being on the cover of *Rolling Stone*. Talk about troubled souls. The story opened with him in his pajamas, on a mattress on the floor of his poorly lit bedroom, surrounded by naked dolls and teddy bears. He was gaunt and frail, having eaten little for two weeks. The drug use was obvious, though he weakly denied it. His story of growing up was painful.

On April 5, 1994, Cobain put a shotgun to his head, dying of drugs and despair at twenty-seven. Once again, that voodoo number. The editorial staff, probably averaging early thirties while I was now late forties, told me, "Kurt Cobain is this generation's John Lennon." That was an interesting thought on many levels and worth a serious discussion. I let them loose; they produced a brilliant tribute, intimately reported, and another design masterpiece by Fred Woodward.

When Richard Nixon died, he had been on the cover more than Kurt Cobain. He was a central demon throughout my life. His rise in California politics paralleled my childhood. I asked Hunter, Bill

Greider, and George McGovern for their final thoughts. Hunter wrote that Nixon should be wrapped in sailcloth and dumped at sea, 1,000 miles off the coast of San Diego, "so the corpse could never wash up on American soil in recognizable form." Bill said, "What some of us liked the most was the clammy, animal-like intensity he brought to his mendacity. Most politicians will deceive on occasion, but Nixon was a giant. When he felt the need to lie to the American people, he put his whole body into it. Promethean in his energies, steeped in governing experience, this man of extraordinary skills could not escape his own demons and was thus driven by them."

George McGovern had put their long enmity aside during a few late-life encounters, as old warriors can do when the battlefield only sounds distantly: "I bear no malice toward him. May God rest his soul."

I KNEW OF SEBASTIÃO SALGADO from his photographs of Brazilian workers wearing loincloths, in massive open-pit gold mines scaling long, handmade ladders, swarming like ants. It was a stark yet lush vision of unrepentant capitalist slavery. Although he had trained to be an economist, once Sebastião got his first camera, he discovered a more powerful way to study modern society and its burden on the human condition. Sebastião was a balding man, my age and my height. He spoke with the urgency of the saddest man in the world. When you thought it through, you realized he was a sainted person. His artistry, with his depth of compassion, made him the greatest photojournalist of our time.

He came to see me to underwrite his latest project about mass migrations, a specific but little-noted example of the destabilizing powers of climate change. He wanted to take six years to explore the planet and document these suffering and disappearing populations. Would we be his partner in the United States? His first assignment was the Hutu tribes of Rwanda, who were being slaughtered by the Tutsi tribes. Some 900,000 Hutu had fled to a barren lava plain in Zaire, where they were starving in camps plagued by cholera and dysentery. The death rate in the camps was five hundred per day. We gave Sebastião's photographs twenty uninterrupted pages.

It was a lot of money to spend on anything, not to mention printing twenty pages of photos of starving people living in garbage dumps and war zones, but it was my money. The beauty of how Sebastião photographed it made the suffering all the more real, the cruelty all the more painful. It was a duty to publish his work.

HUNTER'S LAST BIG piece of feature writing was a crazed brush he had for a week with polo players and polo culture. I had reached a point in my life, married with kids and running a business, where his need for attention and drugs was more than I was willing to deal with. The story was set on Long Island, right at my front door. I tried to be involved, but this time it was tiresome, repetitive, a weak reminder of times past. I turned it over to my top editor, Bob Love, whom Hunter called the Pyramid, meaning that Bob wouldn't suddenly go upside down on him, like I apparently had. I also recruited two of our aspiring editorial gofers, excited to work with the legendary Doctor Thompson. But Hunter was fucked up and very abusive. He hounded one of them, a handsome kid, calling him "queer bait." They were devoted to him, but he burned them out. I was too old for that.

THE STONES WERE getting ready for their *Voodoo Lounge* tour, a global itinerary based on the best weather for the biggest possible outdoor stadiums. They began rehearsals in July in Toronto, at the end of which they did a club date. Mick invited me up for the show and a late dinner. The next week, I brought my ten-year-old son, Theo, G. E. Smith, and George Stephanopoulos to watch the band rehearse the full show for the first time on the *Voodoo Lounge* stage to an empty stadium, sitting with the Stones' wives and their kids on blankets around the pitcher's mound. The all-time private show.

Mick rented a house at the end of Further Lane, the street where Lorne Michaels and I lived. Lorne had split up with Susan — who had become a terrific friend to Jane and me — and was now dating Mick's assistant, Miranda Guinness, Sabrina's twin sister. Mick and Lorne were also good friends, so it was a week with Mick in the Hamptons. Mick didn't like interviews, but if ever there was the right timing, it was now. I wanted to do something big, and Mick was game to try. He asked me to present the band's Lifetime Achievement Award from MTV at Radio City Music Hall. I carefully explained in my speech how history-making and awesome they were, and at the end, thanked them for the name. I closed with the predictable but nonetheless thrilling "Ladies and gentle-men, the world's greatest rock and roll band, the Rolling Stones." How could I resist? We had given them that title. Mick responded that if it hadn't been for them, we'd be called *Herman's Hermits Weekly*.

Bob Dylan played Roseland, a flat-out rock and roll show, greatest hits with guests Neil Young and Bruce Springsteen. A few days later I visited him backstage after an *MTV Unplugged*. I was on a relaxed basis with Bob and had learned not to shake hands. If you did, he let his hand stay motionless in your palm as if you were holding a dead fish. It was unnerving and would make you all the more awkward being with him. The first thing he said was that he had seen me give the Rolling Stones credit for the magazine's name. Bob said that he and I knew full well that it came from his song. I sputtered out my explanations, but he was adamant about it and gave me a sideways look that let me off the hook a little. I was having a pinch-me moment: Mick and Bob each claiming the bragging rights for the title of the magazine.

I BEGAN MY WORK on the interview with Mick, flying to see them play in San Antonio. As I arrived in the dressing room hallway, Mick shouted to everyone, "Here he comes! Straight from his private jet, it's Jann Wenner. The world's most expensive journalist." I had scheduled time with Keith and Charlie Watts to talk to them about Mick. What did they think made him go, what would they ask him, what should I be looking for? They knew more about Mick than any other living witnesses. Keith told me that the key to Mick was his mother. I wanted to talk to Mick about performing, as well as songwriting and managing, so I sat with him in his dressing room, through his exercises, vocal warmups, and onstage with him through sound check.

We started the interview over room-service dinner in Palm Beach, Florida. Mick was trying hard to please, to somehow dredge up memories and information. He would get impatient, grab my notes and look through the questions, to say which he wanted to skip, what he wanted to answer. We were going through songs, their origins, who wrote what, how things like "Sympathy for the Devil" came together. I was holding back on the personal stuff until he became a little more committed to the process. What we were doing was against the grain for him; he was not an emotional guy, didn't "share" his feelings, was reserved in the very English way, and just found it boring to talk about himself. We picked up again a couple of weeks later in Montreal, in his latest hotel room. The bedroom windows were taped and sealed by sheets of aluminum foil against even a speck of daylight.

I went back to New York, collected Jane and Michael, and brought them to see the show. I had been taken in as a member of the touring entourage and had a laminate with the 3D *Voodoo Lounge* drawing on one side and my name, picture, and number on the back. Mick's party was numbered one through ten, and I had seven. Keith and Ronnie Wood shared a large backstage dressing room, Camp X-Ray, done in oriental rugs, scarf-draped lamps, and a generous bar. It was a general hangout for visiting friends, family members, and a trusted drug dealer or two, a tribe of traveling gypsies. That night I seem to have gotten very stoned and drunk, and Michael had to carry me out of Keith's suite at the hotel and put me to bed. I went to one more Stones show, in Vancouver, and combined it with a ski weekend. I had a guest with me...

ONE DAY THAT summer, Matt Nye, the beautiful young man with the blue eyes whom I had met on our Christmas holiday on St. Barts, showed up at Further Lane. He had given Theo a ride home from a play-date. We exchanged phone numbers and agreed to meet for dinner in the city. I couldn't believe my luck in finding him on my doorstep. I had once run into him at a party thrown by the Buffetts and had dragged out a conversation as long as I could without drawing suspicion. I didn't know much about him, just that he worked for Calvin Klein and had also worked for Ralph Lauren. I assumed, based on his looks, that he was a model.

Matt and I went for dinner back in the city, to a Mexican restaurant, drinking margaritas, sharing our opinions of people we knew in common and our family histories. He was the youngest of ten children from a strict Catholic family in Michigan, only having come out of the closet to one sister and one brother. He was twenty-nine, not a model but a designer. He had been pre-med at the University of Michigan and a pot-head at UC Santa Cruz. He looked like a surfer, dirty blond hair, thick eyebrows, and blue, blue eyes, one of those exceptionally beautiful-looking guys.

We went back to my house and, after some awkward show-and-tell, ended up standing close to each other and had our first kiss. Matt was regularly coming out to the Hamptons and would stay with friends. I rode motorcycles, so it was easy for me to meet him on Saturday and Sunday mornings to find a secluded spot. I was not interested in breaking up my marriage. I had comfortable homes and three young sons that I dearly loved. The marriage itself had lost its mutuality. Neither Jane nor I gave it much attention, a garden left unwatered and unweeded.

Early on, Matt and I established a friendship based on shared equivalence, irrespective of my gilded life. We talked on the phone every day and waited for the weekends to come. We had been seeing each other for two months and our end-of-day call, when we would exchange our daily news, started not going right. Matt wasn't saying much, and I finally asked what was wrong. "Don't you see what's happening?" he said. "I am in love with you." I knew immediately what this meant. I hadn't wanted us to reach that point but had knowingly let it. I said, "I love you, too."

With those words, my life changed. Now as I wandered around the house, I thought about what was truly mine and how much of it was so unnecessary. There was a new silence between Jane and me because I wasn't interested in listening. I was waiting for the next time I would see Matt. I don't know if you would call that lovesick, but the longer it went on, the emotional swing, from feeling longing and desire to concealing loneliness and unhappiness, became a hazardous gulf every new day.

I felt terrible about hurting Jane. As long as my sexual liaisons were discreet and empty of emotional commitment, I wasn't conflicted. It was distracting, and at some level damaging, but it stayed undiscussed and uncertain. I assumed, by this time, that my secret had been well shared. The second oldest profession in the world is gossip. But I didn't want to be open about being gay, and never discussed it with my closest friends or colleagues. The apple cart was balanced. I was loyal to Jane throughout and, as far as I knew then, forever. Now I was risking that and her loyalty to me, but there was no choice. I was in love and would be free.

Matt worked at the Calvin Klein headquarters in the midtown garment district. We would meet for out-of-the-way lunches. Life was about planning to see each other and coming up with excuses not to be home. Matt went to Paris for fashion week. Mickey Drexler, my friend who ran the Gap, said he was going, and would I like to hop on his plane for a few days in Paris? Apparently I was an open book; Mary Mac, who had by this time put in a decade as my devoted assistant, told me that she — and her assistant — knew something was up based on how ear-to-ear happy I looked about going to Paris. Jane didn't seem to care that I was going without her.

I was crossing an ocean just to spend time with this man. We walked and shopped the Place de la Concorde and Boulevard Saint-Germain. Fashionistas were everywhere, but we successfully kept our heads down. Love is giddy and can be reckless. We ate at Les Deux Magots, Brasserie Lipp, and Café de Flore. Paris was familiar to me, and I knew the Left Bank well, but such an intricate city makes every visit seem new. One night we stopped while crossing the Pont des Arts, "the lovers' bridge," and watched the city's lights shine in the rippling Seine. We held each other close. We kissed. I fell in. I drowned.

We made it through Thanksgiving, though I was starting to take chances, holding Matt's hand on quiet streets and park benches, stealing kisses in empty doorways. I was beset by fear of losing him. Someone else was chasing him, another was courting him. Love is strong, and it conquers all, but still you feel fear and watch your flank. I left family Thanksgiving early to be back in the city with him. His parents were visiting, and we arranged for me to watch them walk by on the other side of the street, white-haired older folk in white tennis shoes.

I suggested that we take the plane to Vancouver, see the Rolling Stones, and spend the weekend skiing at Whistler. Matt's brother and his wife were fans, and I asked if they would come. I wanted that closer connection with Matt. I took them all to meet Mick in his dressing room. I wanted to impress his family. Mick and his personal assistant, Tony King, whom I knew from when he worked for John Lennon, figured it out. I was taking a big chance by bringing Matt so openly into my life. I must have wanted people to know. His brother and his wife were gracious. We were asking for their acceptance and complicity in our secret — Matt was not just gay; he was bringing "home" a man who was twenty years older and married with three children.

But I was the one in trouble. Matt and I had never talked any of this through, though as the summer days turned into fall, our time became more intense. The passion was more eager but also more painful. I was trying to find a balance, a way to manage and keep afloat. Matt was headed off to Rio for the Christmas week, and I asked to see him the day before he left for that tropical hothouse. We met for a walk on a cloudy winter day in Central Park. It was empty, and we found a quiet bench. "I've been thinking about this, and I want to know. I've been thinking about crossing the river, and if I do, if I jump to the other side, will you be there to catch me?" Matt said "Yes."

PART FOUR

SETTLING DOWN

CHAPTER 52

PASSAGES

THE SNOW WAS falling in Central Park, quietly drifting in a dreamscape. Yoko had told me that new snow was auspicious, a sign of peace and new times to come. I was spending New Year's Eve in the city, my first one alone, and had gone for a walk to see the fireworks and absorb the sensation of my sudden freedom and new life. The snow was light to the touch on my face.

After Christmas dinner with the family on Further Lane, I had walked down the road to call Matt in Rio. I was nearly crying when I got back. All it took was a question from Jane, and I poured it all out. I hadn't planned what to say or how to tell her, but I had been building up great emotional waves every day until it became inevitable that no consideration other than those emotions would guide me.

If my world was about to open up, hers was about to collapse. I stayed in the pool house and she didn't come out of her bedroom for a few days. She told me to move out; I drove into the city, packed a few suitcases, and checked into a small hotel on Madison Avenue, kitty-corner from the Carlyle, but still enough off the beaten path. Matt kept his apartment, but we got into the groove of life in a hotel. There was an extra suite that opened into ours for the kids on the weekends.

The boys were four, seven, and nine. We had a family meeting at which I told them about Mommy and Daddy not living together and how it wasn't their fault. I had heard that before, but this time I was watching myself from the ceiling as I talked to them. It wasn't déjà vu; it was an out-of-body experience. I was in two places at once. I knew that children of divorce were essentially fine, and that mine wouldn't be the first boys to have a gay man with such a large place in their lives.

Jane stabilized at first. She had friends and money, but she couldn't let go of me. She phoned every day, either acting as if nothing had happened or, if she was stoned, doubling down on her humiliation and rejection. She would unleash anger and abuse as I listened, silenced with guilt.

Had I not made the blind leap, irrevocably burned the bridge, I may not have had the stamina. I didn't think about where I would live, who my friends would be, the business, my reputation, my fear of being a homosexual. But I felt free, unburdened of the compromises and fears of discovery. I had thought everything I had was okay; I had a wife and kids to whom I gave my love, and a sex life I enjoyed. But then I fell into a new love with someone else.

When I got back to the office after the Christmas break, the news was starting to get out.

The very first call I got was from David Geffen, who already had the inside scoop. Then a gracious call from Calvin, who wanted to offer up what he had learned "coming out," a phrase that I hated, especially when used with "of the closet." It seemed a shameful cliché, that dark and stuffy closet. Debutantes "came out." Edgar Bronfman — the Seagram's heir, a good friend and tennis partner whom I met through Michael — called next, didn't ask for details but wanted to tell me what he had learned from his divorce: make no decisions about money or do anything legal until a year had passed and the emotional landscape was less explosive. Mick called. He was speaking as a family man who had been through divorce. The kids were his concern, an area he knew well. His most important advice was "Don't be one of those weekend dads and just buy them ice cream. Make sure you help them with homework."

I had Robbie Robertson on my lunch schedule for the next day, and John Kennedy the day after. I dreaded having to face them. Robbie was totally comfortable with my news. He had certainly seen it all. "Sex is sex," and we were on common ground. John was nonjudgmental, but I could see it made him uncomfortable. I was a big brother and this was a surprise he didn't want. Camilla McGrath called; she was angry, called me "stupid." When Earl — one of my best friends, gay, and devoted to Camilla — first heard the news, he thought I had run off with Jane's best friend, Susan Forristal. Diane von Fürstenberg thought I had eloped with Arki Busson, a flattering thought, since he was one of the best-looking young men in New York and Europe. And Michael Douglas, when we got a chance to talk, asked, "Jannie, why not me?"

I had no intentions of coming out. I grew up in the Eisenhower era, when homosexuality was concealed, feared, and could land you in prison. If you were a confused kid, there was nobody to talk to, there was nothing on television, "gay" didn't exist. The essentials of desire, denial, and discovery are generally the same for everyone. The details change, and they range from triumph to tragedy. There is nothing for me to add to this literature. I thought I had it worked out, had successfully integrated it into my life. I had no problem with homosexuals and was close friends with a lot of gay men but didn't want to live in a society of gay men, to be restricted or defined. The code language and the gay physicality put me off. I was never "light in the loafers." It was too confining and limiting for the places I wanted to go and the things I wanted to see. I liked being married. I liked women, and I liked kids.

Although my internal circumstances were much like those of anyone else going through a divorce, the outside view was, speaking as a newsman, a scandal. And January is always a slow news month. I tried to keep it out of the papers. Jay Leno sent me a telegram to assure me there would be no jokes in his monologue. I knew Rupert Murdoch's *New York Post* was going to bust a gut to get it. One of Murdoch's specialties was naming homosexuals, even outing famous people's schoolchildren. When I asked Barry Diller if he could ask Murdoch, his old boss, to hold back on the story, he said he would certainly try but there was no chance. This was what Murdoch lived for, and a call would make it all the more tempting for him.

I hired Murdoch's own PR guy, who could exercise some control over Page Six, the *Post*'s gossip flagship, which agreed to hold off unless it was reported elsewhere. So, Murdoch's gossip columnist planted the story in one of their London papers and, boom, I'm suddenly a fresh snack for the *Post*. We were stalked by some paparazzi for a few days, but the photos didn't sell. The *Wall Street Journal* and *Newsweek* were the only two that couldn't help themselves and followed the *Post*. The *Journal*'s excuse was that it was a business story, since the control of *Rolling Stone* was at stake, which was not at all true. They went whole hog on page one. *Newsweek* had nothing to add. However, Matt's parents had a subscription, and he had to make the call he had been dreading. Theo came home from school one day and told me, "One of the kids in my class said his dad said they saw in a magazine that you were being gay with some surfer guy."

BETTE MIDLER WAS someone I casually knew and admired. We had scheduled a lunch at Le Bernardin, before I left Jane. Bette was the sympathetic ear chosen by fate to hear the long and winding, scandalous saga. It was the first time I got to let it all out, and Bette was like Florence Nightingale; over a lifetime we became brother and sister.

The stops on my tour of confession and penitence included my wise sister Kate and Ben Needell. Ben by this point was the family consigliere. He watched over not just the legal issues of *Rolling Stone* but my management of it, and now would do me the greatest service by watching over Jane in her hours of direst need. Kate and Ben took me out for dinner and a deep conversation. They thought they could "talk sense" into me. Kate hit the family angle hard, and Ben told me I was "thinking with my dick." Getting angry was useless. I had found my own tentative peace. I told them I knew their concerns were loving, but I was what I was and happy with it.

David Bowie and his wife, Iman, took Matt and me out for dinner and made it a gracious occasion. British society, certainly most of the Brits I knew, had an institutionally inherited or inbred curiosity about homosexuality. David wanted to hear it all, but he kept repeating what an important moment this was for so many people and that I had done something "historic." David finally got me to accept the public side, inadvertent or not, of what had been a private decision. I was moved by what he said, but also thought that this was just one of many times history has been made by thinking with your dick.

JANE AND I alternated weekends with the kids and shared them during the week. Matt filled our weekends with science fairs, sports clubs, playdates, zoos, movies, and dress rehearsals at *SNL*. Suddenly I was going to see the Yankees, the Knicks, and WWF wrestling. The duel over who was the better parent was on, as was who made most use of our plane. Matt and I went to Sun Valley every chance we got, where I had the house and the kids set up in their four-bunk-bed attic. I was reprising my childhood of skiing, waking the kids up before dawn, cold washcloths on the face as required, so we could set out for the first lift up the mountain. John Kennedy was on the long trips, and Gus, then six years old, wrote in the plane's logbook, "John stuffed me in the refrigerator."

John was determined to do his magazine. There was no way I could stop him. Not since Teddy Roosevelt, before television and radio, in the era of the muckrakers, had a political magazine succeeded commercially. A career in politics was his last choice. He wanted to do something on his own, end of story. John felt the responsibility of the many expectations placed on him and honored his family duty, but he leaned into the side of his personal freedom, his desire to rollerblade in the park or bicycle to work.

John engendered loyalty from all sorts of people and had a generous way with strangers, autograph seekers, and pickup touch football players. He became the trustee of my children's trusts and one of their legal guardians. We had great times skiing together. The race was always on. He was strong, and he dominated in the bumps. I had him beat on the high-speed runs. He took to my skiing buddies, happy to just be one of the guys. Being outdoors together was a shared communion. You never expressed it like that, but that's what it was.

John hosted a bachelor party for his first cousin and best friend, Anthony Radziwill, at the Downtown Athletic Club: booze, strippers, college buddies, and Boston Irish. I got a phone message from John that day via the receptionist at work: "Me and Anthony will be there at 5:30. Come down early and work out, sauna, steam bath, massage, weights, etc. Please bring marital aids for Anthony from porn shop and while you are there, buy some for yourself." That was John.

Matt's and my first summer house in the Hamptons, located on an organic farm near the farmers' market in Amagansett, was about three miles from Jane, a modest house tucked against the woods, with a large sloping lawn where we set up a slip and slide with garden hoses for the kids. It was plain and quiet and didn't invite comparisons to the ocean-front estate I had given up for love. Linda McCartney rode into the front yard one afternoon on her horse. Paul arrived a few minutes later. They just had to see for themselves. It's always risky dropping in on people, but as a Beatle you are welcome day or night, and this turned into a reassuring visit. That broke the ice nicely that first summer.

My interest in the new rock acts had faded over the past year — Pumpkins, Peppers, Jam, Cranberries. The music staff was nearly half my age, and I let them make the choices, as long as my constituency — then a bit out of the action for a while — got major coverage when required. I think we were, without being fully conscious of it, making ourselves into a fresh and friendly ornament of pop culture in our choices, our imagery, and our sparkling typographic playfulness. It was not a conscious or deliberate trade-off. The advertising coming in was pushing the ship, like an ocean current that you barely noticed from the deck, moving us ahead in its general direction. At the time there were no socially divisive movements and no war. The protesters of the Reagan years had been empowered and had begun to work within the system to which they now had access.

JERRY GARCIA DIED in early August in a drug-treatment center a few miles from where I grew up. He was fifty-three, had four daughters, and had lost his battle with drug addiction and diabetes. He was blessed with genius, yet remained a humble man. His music was wide-ranging. His picking was clean, smooth, and relaxed. He could also scream and kill it.

Jerry was a guru. He didn't want to be, and did his best to avoid it, but he knew it was there. He was the central figure in the San Francisco ether. The Dead had been a thirty-year show, a religion almost, a tent revival on the road, a spiritual center in Marin. Jerry didn't have a million fans; he had a million friends.

Rolling Stone had evolved its own way to deal with the sad duties of covering the deaths of our musical heroes. We were journalists, but also family and fellow mourners. For Jerry, like others, it meant a memorial issue. Mikal Gilmore once again wrote the obituary, his signature weaving of a personal story within the context of social and cultural history. Mikal had gone to one of the last shows Jerry ever did. He had ended that show with "Black Muddy River": "When the strings of my heart start to sever / Stones fall from my eyes instead of tears / I will walk alone by the black muddy river / Dream me a dream of my own / I will walk alone by the black muddy river…and sing me a song of my own."

YOKO AND SAM were our closest friends in those days. Matt and I spent weekends with them in their house in the Catskills. We would come up with Matt on the back of my motorcycle; some weekends we would bring the kids. Sean was in the girlfriend business and only occasionally around. At the pool they had a chessboard in the lawn with near life-size bishops and queens.

Matt kept his job at Calvin Klein. Calvin had hired him away from Ralph Lauren and put him to work traveling the world, looking for vintage fashion that could be copied or updated. Matt was also designing belts, cuff links, and other accessories. He brought home a steady supply of sweaters and ties. The small group he worked in included Carolyn Bessette, who had begun a secret romance with John Kennedy, which got public soon enough. John and I would laugh about it, compare notes, bitch about our partners' workloads.

John named his magazine *George*, after George Washington. He turned out a damn good first issue with Cindy Crawford dressed up as the first president on the cover, shot by Herb Ritts. Roger Black, my boy-genius designer from the seventies, came up with the format; the whole thing had met the bar. It was real; it was a pro job. John was on the map.

Annie documented my move to the new Fifth Avenue headquarters, 1977.
I was settled into New York, a full-fledged enfant terrible of journalism.

With Jackie Onassis at a Save Grand Central Station benefit, 1977.
She took me under her wing and introduced me to New York.

Mica Ertegun and Bette Midler, lifelong family friends, traveling companions,
and dinner party partners, 1990.

John Belushi. "Jann has a voice that could march troops through Czechoslovakia," 1977.

Michael Douglas became one of the closest friends I ever had.
We were partners in crime, born in the same batch, 1986.

Sailing with Mick Jagger. Earl McGrath in the background. Mustique, 1985.

Joan Didion, Los Angeles, 1987.

Diane von Fürstenberg, New York, 1990.

Jean Christophe ("Johnny") Pigozzi, 2001.

Bruce Springsteen, 2009.

Yoko Ono, in Mustique. We were together at Thanksgiving or Christmas every year, 1990.

John Kennedy in Sun Valley, 1993.

With Bob Dylan at the Grand Opening Concert of the Hall of Fame, 1995.

Jackie Onassis (left) and Jane Wenner (right) on Martha's Vineyard, 1992.

Mick Jagger and Ahmet Ertegun induct me into the Hall of Fame, 2004.

The first induction dinner. Neil Young, Keith Richards, Don and Phil Everly, Chuck Berry, Ray Charles, John Fogarty, and Stevie Winwood, Waldorf Astoria, New York, 1986.

Cutting the ribbon to open the Hall of Fame. Me, Yoko Ono, Little Richard, Susan Evans, Paul Schaffer, along with Cleveland dignitaries, including Governor George Voinovich, 1995.

With Paul McCartney and Ringo Starr at the Hall of Fame's thirtieth induction. Ringo and I laugh about finally meeting each other after fifty years, 2015.

Bono, me, Mick, and Bruce at the Hall of Fame 25th anniversary concert, the greatest gathering of musical talent in rock history, 2009.

With Bill Clinton on board Air Force One, 2000.
I was finishing my exit interview with him for Rolling Stone.

With Al Gore at a fundraising concert I produced
for his campaign at Radio City Music Hall, New York, 2000.

My first interview with Barack Obama in the Oval Office, 2010. Check out my socks.

Annie shot this for a Vanity Fair *feature. I am looking out on Sixth Avenue and 52nd Street. Ward Bennett designed the office, and I was there for nearly thirty years, the office I finally called home, 1992.*

Portrait of Matt Nye, New York, 1992.

India Rose Moon Nye Wenner
and her godfather, Bono, 2016.

Godparents at Christmas. Matt, Noah, Bruce,
Patti, Jude, me, Rita, India, Tom, 2010.

Noah's blessing ceremony. David Bowie,
me holding Noah, Iman, 2005.

Hunter S. Thompson, Alex Wenner, Jane,
me and Theo. Christmas in Aspen, 1992.

Bob Dylan and Gus playing in Idaho
when he dropped by our house, 2002.

Godfather Bruce with Jude. Only known
photo of Bruce in shorts, Montauk, 2016.

Lunch with the McCartney's at our house on the beach. Me with Alex, Jane, Linda McCartney, Paul McCartney, Theo. Theo's nickname happened to be "Beetle," and he had found one in the garden, so we took a portrait with the two Beatles, Montauk, 1992.

Matt and Mick, fishing off the coast of Panama, 2001.

Noah with Speaker of the House Nancy Pelosi in her office in the Capitol, 2019.

An autumn weekend in Idaho, with snow beginning to fall.
Alex holding Jude; Jane holding India; Theo; me; Gus holding Noah; Matt.

Round One: Gus, Theo, and Alex.
Portrait by Annie Leibovitz, 2006.

This was our first try at bringing the full "blended" family together.
It was a total success. Sun Valley, 2008.

Round Two: India, Noah, and Jude.
Portrait by Mark Seliger, 2020.

Freedom. Annie took this for Vanity Fair, *while hanging out the side doors of a van riding next to me past the open fields of eastern Long Island, 1992.*

CHAPTER 53

A VISIT FROM JANE

S EAN PENN WAS a cover boy, again; the opening sentence got right to the heart of the story: "Sean Penn is famous for being an asshole." The piece opens in a fashionable movie-star bar where Sean is sitting at a table peeing into a wine bottle. When he puts the full bottle on the table, he asks for another one and continues peeing in front of our reporter, Chris Mundy. Chris was a kid from Nebraska who majored in writing at Brown before finding himself sitting at a table with Sean Penn urinating. I crossed paths with Sean often. He was difficult but a comrade. He sent me a copy of his *RS* cover, signed "From one asshole to another."

TIM LEARY WAS diagnosed with untreatable prostate cancer in January 1995, and decided to share his dying with our readers. He had always thought of me and *Rolling Stone* as allies, although we never hesitated to take him to task for his follies. Mikal Gilmore was invited for long visits at Tim's house in Los Angeles. Mikal sat with Tim's family and friends, talked with him, pushed him in his wheelchair, and was a witness to the deathbed vigil. Mikal wrote it tenderly. Tim still had a youthful spirit but was now a gaunt, aged man who had once led a rebellion. His last word was "Beautiful."

I DID A CAMEO in Cameron Crowe's big-time movie debut, *Jerry Maguire*. I played Tom Cruise's tough-ass boss. I thought I could handle it, no problem. The trick was finding a steely look in the eyes. The big scene was around a conference table where I fire Tom. The script didn't call for it, but I threw in a few "motherfucker"s, trying my method acting and scene stealing. Tom came right back at me with much better "motherfucker"s.

A LARGE ENVELOPE FROM the White House arrived with an engraved invitation, including embossed protocol and admittance cards. President Clinton invited me to a state dinner in honor of the president of Colombia, to whom we were sending hundreds of millions in drug-war money. I shook hands on the reception line with the brass-ass general who was Clinton's drug czar. I kept my mouth shut. At the cocktail reception, Matt and I went full tourist and took selfies with Secretary of State Madeleine Albright and Attorney General Janet Reno, who was a popular parody on *SNL*. I also ran into Sandy Berger, whom I had gotten to know on the McGovern campaign and was now Clinton's national security advisor. He had just helped negotiate a new treaty between Israel and the PLO. Sandy told me some of the inside dope. The Clinton gang was riding high.

I was seated at the president's table next to the wife of Gabriel García Márquez. It was a Clinton talkfest. He started off with how Reagan had the table flowers placed on a two-foot pedestal to limit conversation, since he was so hard of hearing. Clinton wanted to talk politics; he was a shoo-in for reelection and ran down in detail how he stood in key districts. The dinner was all Bill, and I was conducting an open interview with him, and came off super smart based on Sandy's private briefing. Clinton said he liked Arafat personally, didn't care for nor trust Netanyahu, and the only Israeli the PLO trusted was the right-wing general Ariel Sharon, their foe, but a man of his word.

Clinton won reelection. He was the first two-term Democratic president since FDR. I thought we might have a bright future. However, Newt Gingrich had held on to the GOP House majority and he was born half smart and full mean. And in October, Rupert Murdoch and Roger Ailes launched the Fox News Channel.

THERE WERE AS many politicians coming up to the office as musicians. Dick Gephardt, the former Speaker of the House, came to chat about running for president. Tom Daschle, then the Senate Minority Leader, was about to become majority leader. Bob Kerrey, the eccentric senator from Nebraska, dating Debra Winger, also talked about a run. Chuck Schumer, then a congressman, was a steady visitor. Senator John Kerry would pop by; he was a neighbor in Sun Valley. And Vice President Gore.

The Compassionate Use Act was passed by popular vote in California at the end of 1996, despite the opposition of President Clinton and the governor and attorney general of California. The door was now open for legal medical marijuana. We ran a long piece of reporting, "California's Separate Peace." A half-dozen other states suddenly had similar legalization measures on their ballots. The tide had finally begun to turn; the roach was being passed to a new generation.

U2 WAS IN the final rehearsals for another multimillion-dollar tour, and their plans for the kickoff included the cover of *Rolling Stone*. Then Allen Ginsberg died in the same news cycle. I never met Allen, but we corresponded as kindred spirits and the magazine had published a few of his long poems. I considered him a journalist-poet, reporting in the same language as Dylan on the landscape of the American soul, and I wanted to put him on the cover instead of U2. I announced that decision and we proceeded to assemble a tribute issue. Johnny Depp wrote a personal memory of meeting Allen for the issue. U2's manager, Paul McGuinness, a delightful man who I thought resembled the Wizard of Oz, immediately got wind of this. He called, pushing politely but forcefully, to save his cover. Paul had a great line: "Look, Ginsberg is dead. It's not going to matter to him. But we're alive and it matters to us." I couldn't fight that one.

"WOMEN OF ROCK" was the title of our three-hundred-page thirtieth-anniversary issue. When *Rolling Stone* started, there were only a handful of women in rock; now we had a busload, and commissioned twenty-eight interviews, from Etta James to Queen Latifah. It was written and photographed entirely by women. We chose Madonna, Courtney Love, and Tina Turner for the cover. The shoot took twelve hours and involved seventy hairdressers, stylists, makeup people, and personal assistants. Tina had been on our second cover in 1967.

"THE TRUE STORY of John/Joan" was perhaps the most heartbreaking story we ever ran. It was yet another item I'd seen in a newspaper. In 1967 an unnamed baby boy was surgically turned into a girl, an experiment on identical male twins by an internationally respected but sexually twisted doctor. The apparent "success" of that surgery subsequently led to thousands of similar sex-reassignment surgeries and tragedies. But that first surgery had been an utter failure, and ruined the child's life. He was a boy forced to be a girl. Thirty years later the truth began to come out. John Colapinto, who had already done a tender piece about young men returning to their parents and hometowns to die of AIDS, found the victim after months of unreturned calls and letters. John/Joan told the story of his childhood, growing up certain in his heart and soul that he was not really the little girl they said he was. His surgery was partially reversed, he married, lived in a small town with his wife and kids, but could not undo what had been done to him and committed suicide a few years later.

I HAD A TASTE for stories I thought were important even if only a hundred people might read them. The phrase "the arsenal of democracy" had immense power for me, almost biblical in its imagery, imbued with the historical mission of my country. They were the words of FDR in a speech he gave weeks after Pearl Harbor, in which he was invoking the destiny of America's industrial strength. My awe of Roosevelt was for a lifetime. I wanted to know what had happened to the arsenal, so I sent out Bill Greider to visit the vast storage bases the Army, Navy, and Air Force kept. It was a staggering inventory of weaponry, billions upon billions upon even more billions of dollars' worth of shiny stuff ready to fly into combat on short notice, mothballed for the long haul, or packed ready to be sold to our "allies," once the armaments were outdated by newer technology: miles of this stuff, unending vistas of the mechanics of death. I called it "Fortress America." It was no longer an arsenal of democracy.

I BINGED ON SEEING the Stones for their *Bridges to Babylon* tour. In the middle of the show, a 150-foot cantilevered bridge shot out to make a second stage. If they had played two weeks straight, not repeating one song, you would still recognize every one of them. The new album was silky, reaching out for modern arrangements and grooves with sharp lyrical edges. One of the tracks, "Low Down," had a shout-out to *Rolling Stone*: "I don't want the movie section / I can see for myself / I don't want all the news that fits / Shove it back on the shelf."

MATT AND I had settled into our Central Park West apartment. He loved taking care of the kids. They were allowed to spray-paint their rooms. We had two iguanas, both of them soon dead. We had a two-hundred-gallon tank filled with angelfish, clownfish, lionfish, not to mention some African this and that. It was quite pretty, but every week or so, one would be floating on the surface, deceased. The tank was in the dining room, and not a good mix with meals. Mary Mac gave us a baby shark, which streaked back and forth in the aquarium until one night, while we were all at dinner, it jumped out and landed on the table.

I was getting along with Jane. If we stuck to discussing the kids, it was fine, but wandering off topic was a minefield. We were seeing a counselor; we attended school events together. If she had the kids for holidays, she would be fine; otherwise loneliness and melancholy would overwhelm her. It looked to her like I was on top of the world and that she had no place to go. I felt guilty; it was my fault, my responsibility.

Then the most unexpected thing happened: the doorman rang and said, "Mrs. Wenner is here and would like to come up." And there she was at the door. How do you welcome your ex-wife to your new home with the man for whom she had been forsaken? I could only imagine that if I were her, I would want to pick something up and smash it. But Jane stood there in an overcoat and rain boots for some reason, wearing her blue striped sailor shirt and bib overalls. She smiled from inside her curtain of long hair. The wall seemed to be crumbling. When I asked her why she had decided to drop by, she told me that her best friend, Melissa Mathison, also estranged from her husband, had told her to get it over with and get over it.

CHAPTER 54

THE BEST MAGAZINE IN AMERICA

W E WERE IN the prophecy business: "Killer Flu" was the headline in our first issue of 1998. "In 1918, an outbreak of flu killed 30 million people. Could it happen again? The world's leading experts say it's inevitable." The piece opened in New York City. "Theaters, office buildings and government agencies have been closed for weeks. A few pedestrians hurry by, wearing white face masks in the cool, spring air. Many of those whose jobs involve close human contact — bank tellers, store clerks, teachers and waiters — are gone from their posts. The city's hospitals are full. Bellevue remains open, but patients are stacked on gurneys along the corridors."

ROLLING STONE WAS nominated for five National Magazine Awards. This was a big deal. We won for Greider's "Fortress America" and Colapinto's "John/Joan." We were also nominated for the *Rolling Stone 200*, the Essential Rock and Roll Library, and "Women of Rock," which surprised me because the judges were pretty crusty and didn't highly value rock and roll. And once again, we were nominated as one of the five best million-plus-circulation magazines. We were up against *National Geographic*, *Vogue*, *Martha Stewart Living*, and *Vanity Fair*. This time we won. We were the magazine of the year. The citation for *Rolling Stone* said that we won for "powerful investigative journalism, superb interviews, authoritative entertainment reporting—all in one brilliantly designed package." *Men's Journal* won an award too. There also was an award given for lifetime achievement. Henry Luce had once gotten it; I was the youngest person ever given the honor. Bob Love and I floated back to the office after the ceremony in the Waldorf Astoria Ballroom. He was my top editor then, co-editing "Women in Rock" recruiting staff writers John Colapinto, Pete Wilkinson, David Lipsky, Rich Cohen, Chuck Sudetic, and the editor who became his successor, Will Dana.

In 1998, TOM Wolfe brought me his proposal for a new novel, *A Man in Full*. I didn't feel it would be right for us to try to repeat the *Bonfire of the Vanities* serialization. It would become a trap. But by that point, I had become Tom's editor and agreed to continue to serve, just for the pleasure. We ran three major excerpts when the time came. When the book was published, the dedication page read, "The author bows deeply to Jann Wenner, the generous genius who walked this book along until it found its feet, just as he did *The Right Stuff*, *The Bonfire of the Vanities*, and *Ambush at Fort Bragg*." I was enormously proud. It was a generous and deeply thoughtful thing for him to do. I thought that *A Man in Full* was better than *Bonfire*, with more sophisticated characters and suppler in style. There were unforgettable set pieces—the horse breeding barn, the museum show of homoerotic art, the "suicidal freezer unit" in the Croker Global warehouse. It was another saga of ambition in the big city, Atlanta this time, and by now Tom had ten more years of wisdom and practice.

DISCOVERING THAT I was diabetic had turned me on to the consequences of what I was eating, particularly sugar. It wasn't so easy to get away from this deadly habit: the shit was everywhere, and it was being hawked by Santa Claus for Coca-Cola and by that stupid McDonald's clown, just as surely as Joe Camel was fronting for nicotine. As I was thinking about ambitious, big new stories for us, one precedent that came to mind was *The*

Jungle, by Upton Sinclair, his exposé of the meatpacking industry, which began as a series of magazine articles. McDonald's and all the other fast-food chains had taken over the American diet with their sugar-saturated and calorie-rich menus. Every family in the country ate at those places, supported by an industrial supply chain to process potatoes, meat, and sugar soda water. We had become what I thought of as "fast-food nation."

Economic policies based on low wage growth for workers had taken women out of the home and into the workforce, and no one was left at home to do the shopping and the cooking. Fast food was not a convenience but a necessity, because most Americans had little choice. And voilà, we had the diabetes and obesity epidemics. It wasn't a matter of self-discipline; McDonald's was essential to the modern family. There were hundreds of millions of dollars in television ads showing that clown talking to kids.

We sent a reporter, Eric Schlosser, on the road for a year, to the potato empires in Idaho, Midwestern slaughterhouses, and processing plants; we followed the dead cow from the meatpacking floor to the "Happy Meal." He wrote *Fast Food Nation.** Hamburgers had been a favorite lunch, but it was two years before I touched one again.

PRESIDENT CLINTON WAS set to be impeached in December and tried in the Senate in January. This was being driven by Newt Gingrich, the fat, white-haired, confessed adulterer and Speaker of the House. Cable news had just arrived, and it was all Monica Lewinsky, all day long. Nothing else seemed to matter; everyone had something to say. It was time for a special issue.

We came up with the notion of bringing our extended family into "The Clinton Conversation," interviewing or getting pieces from our curated, homegrown intelligentsia. It was full of fury and outrage. Jon Stewart said, "In the end, something really terrible is going to happen, like some guy is going to put anthrax in soda bottles. We'll look back on these days with a kind of nostalgia, like people have when they talk about nickel

---

* The series of articles became a bestselling book and a movie.

movies; 'Oh, remember the days when all we had to worry about was the president blowing his load on someone's dress?'" We also had illustrators and cartoonists contribute. By far my favorite was by Robert Crumb, the patriarch of underground comix, the creator of Mr. Natural and Angelfood McSpade. He drew the scene of that day when buxom Monica Lewinsky walks into Clinton's private office, bringing him the take-out pizza. Clinton looks up from the phone and says to himself, "Oh dear Jeezus."

WE HEADED TO Sun Valley for the holidays. Arnold and Maria Shriver had a house about the size of the mountain's main ski lodge. Arnold was the gracious host, a cigar in hand, wearing lederhosen suited to the masculine ambience of his grand chalet, with a bar, a billiards room, a great room, and, off to the side, still on the main floor, an exercise studio with his awards and trophies. They had an annual holiday dinner. There were ski instructors, movie stars, various moguls, Maria's brothers and miscellaneous cousins, including Caroline and John.

I hadn't seen or spoken with John in months. John was impetuous and had too quick a temper. He wouldn't return my calls. His cousin Anthony, who had asked me what I "really" thought about *George*, had repeated it to John, who felt I was bad-mouthing him around town. I shouldn't have been so direct with Anthony, but I thought it was all in the family; on reflection, that had made it worse.

John was across the living room with Carolyn Bessette, Matt's office mate at Calvin Klein and now Mrs. JFK Jr. Then Maria came over and said, "What is the problem with you two?" She wanted me to go over and break the ice, but I was stubborn, not one to bend the knee. She pulled me up and sat me down with John. We traded some barbed small talk and made a date to ski together the next day.

We had a great day skiing, catching up on our lives, and competing. I could still beat him down the hill, and he could still crush me in the bumps. He skied down early to get his plane back to New York. It was the last time I saw him.

CHAPTER 55

ONLY THE GOOD DIE YOUNG

IFTEEN STUDENTS AT Columbine High School were butch-ered in a bloodbath by fellow classmates with assault weapons in the privileged white suburb of Littleton, Colorado, the very heart of the American Dream. It was still the early days for this new signature rite of American education. Our "violent culture" was being blamed, anything to avoid pointing the finger at the gun industry. Clinton was calling for a White House summit. A witch hunt into the video game business was ramping up — more people were obviously being killed by people with their thumb on a game console button than their fore-finger on a hair trigger. The willful blindness was stupefying.

I composed a new Letter from the Editor: "We have got to accept the reality that violence is part of the human condition and sometimes snaps in inexplicable and chaotic ways, and despite this, the United States — alone among Western industrial societies — lets its population have access to guns. Something went terribly wrong with two children, and the parents were powerless in the face of it. It was evil, and like all evil — great and small — it is a mystery.

"Students, when they arrive in their classrooms, don't want to know whether schoolmates have been playing video games but whether they are carrying guns. Clinton offers to 'bury the hatchet' with the NRA and asks its leaders to sit with media executives in search for solutions. This is ridiculous.

"Are we a better society if we demand that musicians and filmmakers and game designers not portray violence? Are we safer if children can't play *Dungeons and Dragons*? It's not culture that created the killing fields in Springfield, in Jonesboro, in West Paducah, in Pearl, in Littleton, or the place where this happens next. It's the guns."

I wish I had added, "Melt every damn one of them into the ground."

THE PHONE RANG on a mid-July morning, 5:30 a.m., as it sometimes will. One of the Shriver kids was trying to find Caroline Kennedy, who was on a raft trip in the Idaho wilderness that I had arranged. He told me that John was missing on a forty-five-minute flight he was piloting from New Jersey to Martha's Vineyard the night before. His wife and her sister were flying with him. Wreckage was found floating in the Atlantic and it looked like the worst.

I was in disbelief: to accept the worst, while there was still slim hope, would be a kind of betrayal. I turned on the news, diluting my private grief with public curiosity. The last time I had spoken with John was on a catch-up phone call two weeks earlier. His marriage was on the rocks. He had flown after sunset, two hours late, chose a route over open water despite low visibility, instead of along the well-lit shoreline.

John was cremated and his ashes scattered from a Navy destroyer off the coast of Massachusetts. The memorial service was at the small church where Jackie had taken the kids when she moved to Manhattan. The first person I saw there was Maria Shriver; we collapsed into each other's arms, crying. I loved John. He was my good buddy, a little brother, and now a mythological fallen prince.

There was a luncheon afterward at Sacred Heart, Caroline's childhood school. Uncle Teddy, jacket off and sweating, led Irish drinking songs. I sat with Anthony Radziwill, just John's age, who had become weak and frail, the punishment from three years of chemotherapy. We had become very good friends. I never saw him again; three weeks later he too was dead.

BOZ ASKED ME to take on his son, Austin, as an intern or anything I could provide. He was nineteen. I hadn't seen him since he was in sixth grade and couldn't believe how much he looked like his dad back in the day, a physical embodiment of youthful times and enchanted places. He had his father's Southern voice, and it was Luke and Elrod time again. We called each other "boy." Austin suggested we ought to form an office band to play our Christmas party, and I could be the rhythm guitarist. Thus was born the Rack of Lambs, and its backup girl group, the Mint Jelly. We rehearsed on the weekends; I sweated it out to match the fluidity of the considerable number of wannabe musicians who worked at the office. At the Christmas party, I sang "Don't Let Me Be Misunderstood," "Sweet Little Sixteen," and "Love Me Tender." We played about an hour and a half. Lenny Kravitz jumped up and played drums on our encore, "Like a Rolling Stone." We had nailed it. We killed it. Our own music critics were in awe, or so they told me.

BRITNEY SPEARS WAS a new pivot point for her generation, the Mouseketeer from Kentwood, Louisiana (population 2,400; motto "Drive Carefully, Live Prayerfully"). The David LaChapelle portfolio of her in a bra and super-short shorts, in her bedroom and on her pink bicycle, would have been out of the question for teenage girls when I grew up. On our cover, she was lying on pink satin sheets wearing a black brassiere and polka-dot underwear. She was snuggled up to the purple Teletubby doll with a triangle on its head that was rumored to be a gay symbol. A gay doll! I was accused of pandering to a teenage audience, but this was social history, a report on young America and current sexual attitudes and culture that I knew to be absolutely true. LaChapelle went right from Britney to Eminem, totally naked and holding a fake stick of lit dynamite as if it were his penis. Eminem was the giant crossover of rap into the white world, a sweet-looking boy with ghetto cred who appealed to white kids yearning to act and think black. Dr. Dre himself had produced Eminem's first record; he was a major talent, and rap had a mainstream star.

CHAPTER 56

ALL OUT FOR AL

I WANTED TO DO whatever I could for Al Gore. Clinton was in my age cohort, but Al was my generation. Bill was an Elvis fan. Al was a student of Bob Dylan. I met with him in a Detroit school classroom between campaign events to do his first formal *Rolling Stone* interview. I brought senior editor Will Dana along as my road manager and tape jockey. We waited in the kindergarten room for Al to finish a teachers' union event. By the time he appeared, forty-five minutes late, I was seriously pissed off. Will told me later, "Wow. You just yelled at the fucking vice president." Al apologized and instantly pulled me in. Will said, "He seems like a man who enjoys a hard-won sense of casualness."

I wanted our readers to get a feel for the guy I knew, not the cartoon blowhard the press was pushing, repeating the fake accusation that he had claimed to have "invented the internet." After a tough summer and fall, he was now the Democratic front-runner. We started talking about music, not foreign policy, establishing his passion for it, singing a verse from "Just Like a Woman." We discussed guns and drugs, which he danced around with words like "education," "prevention," and "rigorous scientific study." He was punting; we both knew it. That's politics, and I felt sure that when the time came, he would do the right thing. We hitched back to the airport in his motorcade, a bulletproof, zero-traffic ride on deserted streets and empty freeways, ramps blocked until we passed. It was as if civilization had been frozen.

Bill Greider, who had been our deeply moral conscience for seventeen years, was no longer at *Rolling Stone*. I thought his essays had gotten repetitious, so I had asked him to go out on the road again and report on the political campaigns. He thought that would be repetitious, too. It had been a long, important run. He had been the voice and the intellectual engine of our politics for nearly two decades. Nonetheless it was time for a change, sadly an unhappy one for all of us. Bill moved over to the *Nation*, wrote *Frontline* documentaries and more books.

NOT HAVING A full-time political reporter, we thought we might get great nonpolitical fiction writers on the road to cover the campaign. The first and only one who said yes was David Foster Wallace, and only if he could follow John McCain. David spent a week on the Straight Talk Express, snubbed by the candidate and his high command, either owing to his motorcycle jacket or the fact that he was from *Rolling Stone*. Because of sudden changes in political fortune, we needed the piece on a four-day deadline. David turned in 28,000 words, which was cut in half by our editor, whom he would address only by his last name, Mr. Tonelli. David was a perfectionist, but also the politest and nicest person to work with, which is hard to believe as a piece gets cut in half. "The Weasel, the Twelve Monkeys, and the Shrub" ended up winning the National Magazine Award.

I told Al I would put together a fund-raising concert in the fall. Which is how I became introduced to the bully Harvey Weinstein. Luckily, he was gone for most of the summer to Italy, but he would call in to my planning meetings with self-serving ideas that would waste everyone's diminishing time. He was never in the room where it happened. Karenna Gore Schiff, Al and Tipper's oldest daughter, married with two kids, hosted a small event for them at her apartment. Of all places, it turned out to be the duplex Jane and I had lived in for ten years. I gave the Gores a tour and filled them in on where all the bodies were buried and what the walls might say.

FOR THE FUND-RAISER, we went to Radio City Music Hall with Al and Tipper in their motorcade. Our route was again completely blocked off by the Secret Service, streets empty as if during a plague, and Al said he intended to stop this practice when elected. With a little gentle hair-pulling, I got Bette to do the show. Her set included one of the best versions of "The Rose" I ever heard. She also brought on Darlene Love to do "He's a Rebel" and "River Deep, Mountain High." Crosby, Stills & Nash, the Eagles, and Paul Simon each did half-hour sets, and the entire cast closed with "Teach Your Children Well," at the start of which Jimmy Buffett grabbed Al and Tipper and brought them onstage to sing. We had movie stars and comedians introducing the acts, and they took moving political stands. Much like the Hall of Fame dinners, it was a night of music, stirring emotion, and common purpose.

In the month before the general election I flew to Silicon Valley to meet Al and fly back to Washington with him on Air Force Two, where we could sit quietly for however long we needed and do the interview for his cover. Air Force Two was a first-class Boeing 757, with a six-person private cabin in front, comfortable but strictly utilitarian. He was flying with Secret Service, a small press corps, staffers, his best friend and brother-in-law, Frank Hunger, a silver-haired Southern gent ("Everything is just more relaxed when Frank's here"), and an Air Force major carrying "the football," an attaché case containing the nuclear launch codes. Just in case.

When we landed at Andrews Air Force Base, Al invited me to come along on Marine Two. He put me in his seat, the one with the big window and the view, while he changed into a tuxedo for his next event. It was a spectacular ride through the nightscape of floodlit and illuminated monuments and government buildings, a shining vision that Al narrated for me. We landed at the Reflecting Pool, just south of the White House.

In every issue we had pounded on Bush. We zeroed in on his environmental record as governor of Texas — Bush and his oil-well buddies were guilty of gang-raping the planet is the plainest way of saying it. We published "All Hat, No Cattle," about his feckless business career and indolent term as a governor. Al Franken did a piece about Bush's public comments, titled "Is Bush Dumb?" With it we ran a cartoon by Bob Grossman that showed Bush with his arm around Dick Cheney, who wore a T-shirt that read, "I'm with Stupid." Bush's lead in the polls had evaporated, Al had inched ahead, and we were smelling victory.

Us WEEKLY HAD BECOME stuck, despite a circulation of over a million, and it had started losing money. I had pride and an investment on the line, and a sense that something was there, but I couldn't figure out how to put it across. The man who had sold it to me had an idea: go weekly, head-to-head against *People*. The staff would triple, printing costs quadruple. We would have to reckon with the power of Time Inc. and the *National Enquirer,* which together controlled weekly distribution in supermarkets. Those guys were not going to let us be next to the cash register in checkout lines; we would be forced to start out at "mop level," the magazine rack closest to the floor. We had to find four printing plants across the country that didn't have most of their time already blocked out by the four Time Inc. weeklies. We also needed a fleet of trucks going to every sizable city in the country. The logistical challenges extended everywhere: post offices, paper mills, production houses, computer terminals, pads and pencils. It was high-risk, but we convinced ourselves. Millions of dollars were on the table and the adrenaline was pumping.

Then, within ten issues, *US Weekly* hit the rocks. We had been selling barely half of what we had budgeted for on the newsstands, a million-dollar shortfall each month and probably another million-dollar reduction in advertising. This would soon eat up every bit of money *Rolling Stone* was making. To conserve our cash, we had to cut the press run and publicly lower our rate base below the magic million. We were tagged "Wenner's Folly." It began to crack my confidence. I was facing failure. I didn't know what to do, how to fix it, or if it was even fixable. I was depressed, which I was having a hard time concealing.

Tina Brown asked me out for lunch. I told her my tale of woe, and she told me hers. As if her triumph at *Vanity Fair* hadn't been enough, she moved to the sleepy *New Yorker* and set it on fire with her brand of hot editing. (It was the same shuffle that brought Graydon Carter in to take over *Vanity Fair*, a brilliant choice. I knew Graydon from his pre-*Spy* days, when he wrote a long profile of me for *Gentleman's Quarterly* on his way to legend status.) Tina had been seduced and suckered by Harvey Weinstein to leave *The New Yorker* and start a new magazine. They called it *Talk*, and it was a turkey with all the trimmings, such as a multimillion-dollar launch party on Liberty Island. Her tale of woe had to do with the horrors of Harvey's interference in everything and trying to sell it to Hearst behind her back. Harvey was a nightmare of lies, broken promises, and self-dealing, quite the monster, as it turned out. The idea of two renowned editors sitting together, crying in their soup, two well-known killers confessing their secrets and setbacks to each other, made me laugh. Tina saw no humor in it at all. She had life-and-death problems. I did not.

KATE HUDSON, WHO played the groupie Penny Lane in *Almost Famous*, was a must for the cover. The movie was a love letter by Cameron Crowe, to his time at *Rolling Stone*. It caught all the fun and seriousness that we brought to our jobs, the whole experience of spending days — often moving in — with a rock and roll band, that fantasy in which we all wanted to play a part. I used to see Cameron more in the rock and roll world we lived in than in the office, not just as my cub reporter but as an insider. He had asked me to play a small part in the movie, but the schedule conflicted with a trip. When I got back, he was filming in New York and asked if I could do a cameo, five seconds of screen time, because I was his good luck charm. I am, per the official on-screen credits, "The Legend in the Cab."

I WAS GIVEN THE "exit interview" with President Clinton, a considerable journalistic prize. I got to the White House two weeks after interviewing Al on the campaign trail, on a stunning fall day. I was scheduled from two to six in the afternoon, and Bill was late, as usual, this time because he was signing a bill to normalize trade relations with China, passing out pens to dignitaries gathered around his desk. The morning had also included the first-ever presidential meeting with the commanding general of the North Korean army. Bill was feeling his oats. We took the private elevator to the family floor. First, he wanted me to see his music room with his saxophones, then an Elvis guitar and a McCartney bass. We settled into the solarium to talk. It was decorated in yellows, very informal, nothing like the rest of the White House. It was their private family room. On the coffee table was a set of Russian nesting dolls, painted as Bill and Hillary. We looked out over the South Lawn to the Washington Monument. He put an unlit cigar in his mouth, and we sat. No company.

Bill was both easy and difficult to interview, since he was a nonstop talker, probably the reason he was always behind schedule. It was hard to get him off a particular subject or to interrupt an answer you had already heard a dozen times. He agreed to a second session. We would do it on November 2, five days before the election, aboard Air Force One, flying to California for his only campaign appearance of the election. Al's people had kept Bill off the trail because their polling said that the stain of Monica Lewinsky would cost them undecided voters in swing states.

I showed up at Andrews Air Force Base. You walk to the custom-built Boeing 747-200SP not through a terminal but right to its steps, and you are startled that the plane is so massive, almost ten stories high and 70 feet shy of the length of a football field. It is a vast machine sparkling in the sun, the most unearthly vision of American technology and power I have ever seen.

Bill gave me a tour of the plane: his private office and bedroom in the front, the series of club chairs and tables for his traveling staff and guests, his personal conference room, and a main conference room with a table for twenty-four people, projection screens, phones, and computers. Aboard was a squad of armed Marines, a dozen armed Secret Service, and, in the last cabin, the traveling press corps, six reporters. The big names were on the trail with Al. Before taking a seat, I told Bill we had to start on time, and he snapped at me about how I was "getting more god-damned time" than he was giving anyone. I went to my seat and waited.

THE COVER OF Al came out, timed to be on newsstands for the two weeks leading to Election Day. Seliger had shot him in a desert background, thumbs hooked in his pockets, khakis, a black tee under his denim work shirt. Out of nowhere, the radio talk shows and even the political press were abuzz with a rumor that we had airbrushed his pants in order to make him look big where it counts. Al called me to laugh about it: "Jann, let me just ask you: Is this a bad thing or good thing?"

Al invited me to a campaign rally in Pittsburgh where organized labor showed up by the tens of thousands. It was three nights before the election. James Taylor was scheduled to play, so we all flew in together. The *Rolling Stone* cover was everywhere, and I was getting the golden-boy treatment from the campaign, quickly swept into a holding room with Al, John Kerry, and Bob Kerrey, three men my age, of my generation, who each wanted to lead the country.

Al wanted me to walk the rope line with him and show me what a big deal the *Rolling Stone* cover was. The rally had been rousing, with a quick sprinkle during James' "Fire and Rain," of course. Al came off the stage drenched in sweat and gave me a bear hug. The Secret Service grabbed onto the back of his belt and held him as he walked the rope with me in tow right next to him. I was surprised by the diversity of age, color, and sex, by the expressions of joy and yearning. Quite a few were holding up the new issue of *Rolling Stone* for an autograph, or had a button, or a post-card of the cover, waving it for a signature or a blessing.

We put together a last-minute election watch party at our house, the usual mix of celebrities and civilians. I would get an hourly telephone update from the campaign with results that started upbeat and soon turned tentative. The votes were coming in and it was too close to call.

The back-and-forth in Florida was a nail-biter, but it was over before that. The deck had already been stacked.

MICHAEL DOUGLAS AND Catherine Zeta-Jones got hitched at a semi-royal wedding in the ballroom of the Plaza hotel, just before Thanksgiving. Matt and I were discreet as a gay couple, no PDAs (public displays of affection) out of concern for others', especially Jane's, sensitivities. I was still not comfortable with what people thought about me being gay. But there comes a time when it all feels right, and you've had the right amount of vodka, so Matt and I went out on the floor and let it rip. Matt was a natural, supple, and sexy dancer. Finally, we cut in on Michael and Catherine. I danced my heart out with Catherine, who was a professional dancer, but all eyes were on Matt and Michael.

THE WHITE HOUSE Christmas Party, a dinner and dance under a tent on the South Lawn for a few hundred people, was also a thank-you and goodbye from the Clintons. Matt and I were staying across Pennsylvania Avenue at the Hay-Adams. Before retiring for the night, we walked to the Washington Monument and then the Lincoln Memorial. It was our farewell to the White House for years.

A few days later we were back in Washington. Al and Tipper were having a Christmas party at the vice president's residence, a rambling nineteenth-century Victorian on the grounds of the U.S. Naval Observatory. Karenna came down with us. It was a small gathering of the Gores' old pals, a few of the campaign staff whom I had gotten to know, neighbors, and relatives from out of town, a time for a little holiday cheer and sympathy. Al pointed out to me which of the guests were gay. We sat upstairs with Karenna and her folks in their bedroom, a whirlwind of books, papers, files; they were either packing up or hadn't had a chance to put anything away in the eight years they lived there. I tried to be cheery; Al was giving it his best, and he was a pro, but too many of the conversations were memories from the campaign trail, which ended first in laughter and then in the sound of silence. We were all drinking, but as cheerful as we tried to be, it was bittersweet, it was sad, it was goodbye. The dream was over; what can I say?

Karenna's parting words were "I'm going to join the resistance."

IN THE BACK-TO-BACK interviews I had done with Bill and Al, my purpose was to take the measure of both men. The day-to-day battles were already old, although the behind-the-scenes maneuvering on something like being cornered on Don't Ask, Don't Tell ("that dumbass policy," Bill called it) was revealing inside baseball. I wanted our readers to see how deeply the men I had gotten to know thought about stuff, how much they believed in what they were doing, how tough and how hard it was to get it done. I also felt an obligation to the history books to catch a man with the presidency in his hands or in his sight, fighting to hold on to his idealism and humanity. These were men of enormous intellectual capacity and compassion.

Bill was the third-youngest person ever to be president, after Teddy Roosevelt and JFK. As he sat back, reminiscing on his triumphs and his trials, he said, "It's the job I'll miss the most. I love the work. Every day, even on the worst day. Even in the worst times of that whole impeachment thing. I just thank God every day I can go to work. I love the job and I always loved it."

Bill and Al were smart guys, the best and brightest. I chided them both about being show-offs about their knowledge, which got a good laugh. The two of them returned again and again to three themes: the expansion of human rights — gay, black, and female; income inequality — the threatening consequences of tax cuts for the rich and turning over Social Security to Wall Street; and the environment — the projected melting of the ice caps, global warming, and certain devastation within fewer than fifty years. Both interviews are documents of the American Dream.

CHAPTER 57

MY CITY OF RUINS

WE JOINED JOHNNY PIGOZZI for my fifty-fifth birthday on the *Amazon Express*, a sixty-seven-meter tuna trawler he had converted into an expedition boat, anchored on the west coast of Panama, where Johnny owned miles of oceanfront and thousands of acres of rain forest, surrounding a bay lined with white sand beaches and featuring an island on which he was building a modern castle. We landed by helicopter on the upper deck, where Johnny and his girlfriend waited with umbrella drinks for us. The helicopter came again the next day, landing Mick and his new girlfriend, L'Wren Scott. Bags, hats, scarves, and skirts flew in the wash of the rotors. It looked like a *Vogue* shoot.

The week began with my birthday dinner. Mick brought me a set of caviar spoons and Johnny gave me a Panama hat. Each day we visited different beaches to picnic on. We took jet skis into the mangrove swamps and sailed to small islands in the national park preserve. Matt and Mick went fishing together in the afternoons, like two beer-drinking buddies from the Ozarks, only they wore sarongs.

Johnny had installed a small-gauge railway to bring construction supplies to his mountaintop building site. The train was going to make its first ascent while we were there, so we decided to have a ceremony, followed by a picnic dinner on shore. Princess Olga (of Greece, Johnny's girlfriend) did the ribbon cutting and L'Wren was her lady-in-waiting;

Mick was the BBC reporter, and I was his cameraman. The dinner was in a palm grove lit by candles in the branches. A four-foot snapper was cooking in the pit. Mick had brought his guitar. He sang "Don't Be Cruel" and "Queen Jane Approximately." I asked him to sing "No Expectations." He had his groove going; it was ballad time. He sang "Angie" and "Wild Horses," and then something I would have never imagined, "You Can't Always Get What You Want," slowly, sadly, gorgeously.

WHEN I GOT back from Panama, Michael Eisner, Disney's CEO, called to ask if I was still looking for an investor in *US Weekly*. Why he called, I didn't know, although the speed bumps I had hit were widely known, while the magazine itself was getting pretty good. We were still in the red, and as a practical matter, it was worthless. I proposed that Disney put in $35 million for 49 percent of the equity, and Michael agreed. I was a rare fan of Eisner's; he was unabashedly blunt but didn't interfere once. Michael and I had a press conference the next week in the studios of *Good Morning America* in New York. Scrappy and shaky *US Weekly* was now backed by the Walt Disney Company, the family entertainment colossus. Wenner's folly was suddenly worth $70 million.

I WATCHED THE TWIN TOWERS fall while I was having breakfast. I wasn't thinking of people jumping out of windows on the eightieth floor, firemen and office workers suffocating, or passengers burning in exploding jet fuel. The spectacle overtook all that, and heroes and villains hadn't yet come into focus. It was beyond "What the fuck?" Michael and I met at an outdoor café on Columbus Avenue around the corner from our homes. It was a beautiful day and almost totally quiet. There were few cars, no rumbling subways, no planes or helicopters in the skies. Fighter jets occasionally circled in the distance. We walked south down Central Park West, flooded by the exodus of the Manhattan workforce going home.

It wasn't computing with me at first as a human tragedy but as a calculable, predictable cost of the geopolitical war for oil, and the billions and billions of dollars in soldiers and weaponry we spent every year to guard the oil, that the U.S. government was always fighting in the Middle East. The next day, my top editors were waiting at the door to my office. It was the unspoken assumption that *Rolling Stone* had a responsibility to respond with a special issue; it would also be a way for each of us to deal with the tragedy.

For us — I suppose for all magazines — it was a hometown story, so we assembled an opener based on reactions in the musical community, people who lived in New York, like Lou Reed and Yoko. Kurt Loder, our longtime writer and MTV personality, lived three blocks away from the towers and wrote "My Neighborhood Vanished." Jimmy Breslin, New York's singular newspaper columnist, wrote about watching the tragedy unfold from the street. Mark Seliger made a portfolio of grim-faced first responders at work. Two of our best reporters, Jeff Goodell and Pete Wilkinson, went back to the homes of the firefighters and the steelwork-ers who were excavating the center of mass death. David Foster Wallace, who lived in Bloomington, Illinois, wrote a wonderful account of trivial-ity and community, an inspirational story about watching the coverage on television with his neighbors, "The View from Mrs. Thompson's."

It seemed that amid the flag-waving we needed some sanity. We gave a page to a photo of Yasir Arafat, chairman of the PLO, donating blood to the Red Cross for the victims. I did not trust the mood that was descending upon America.

I wrote a Letter from the Editor: "A Pivot Upon Which We Will View Our Future." I said, "Discussing our enemies as men who live in caves — who should be 'hunted down and smoked out like animals' — underesti-mates the true nature of those who conspired to attack the World Trade Center. Vice President Cheney talks of Osama bin Laden's 'head on a plat-ter.' This kind of offhand imagery does not prepare us for the complexities and subtleties of what's ahead. Our allies want to see America act with cali-bration and certainty, not with frontier justice and swaggering crudeness.

"These are not cave-dwelling animals. These are people who sacrifice their lives for what they feel is right (which is generally how we might define courage). They are on a long-term mission and have grievances that we ignore at our own risk. Is it plausible that the United States — as Britain once — is perceived as an imperial, colonial power occupying impoverished Muslim lands and appropriating their oil riches in collusion with corrupt monarchies and dictatorships? We have to ask ourselves which side of history are we on and make sure we are on the right side, so that we survive with our own freedoms intact, not in the grip of a national-security state under siege from constantly renewing terrorism."

Matt and I went to Ground Zero with Bette and her husband, Martin von Haselberg, on a police boat. Street access was closed. The daily imagery of the twisted steel, of broken skyscrapers and lines of dump trucks, workers with blackened faces, all of this was not enough warning for what we saw. Four square blocks were demolished, the ruins of the buildings still smoldering and smoking, with the stench of chemicals. Not just twisted steel, but the frames, the structures, the sides of giant buildings emerged from the black pits, burned skeletons reaching out from the burial ground. The devastation of Ground Zero was so wide that the trucks and fire engines seemed like toys. It was just too much; all you could do was cry.

JOHN LENNON HAD released "Imagine" on September 9, 1971, almost thirty years earlier to the day. What gave "Imagine" such power? Twenty-two lines of lullaby rhyme. It was a Buddhist idea, that imagination precedes action, that visualization anticipates a new reality. No religion, no heaven or hell, no countries, no possessions, no need for greed. "You may say I'm a dreamer, / but I'm not the only one. / I hope someday you'll join us, / And the world will be as one." It was from the sixties, a radical manifesto. It was now a global anthem, the common prayer for peace.

MICK SETTLED INTO an impressive duplex suite at the Carlyle. I went to a session he was doing with Wyclef Jean for Mick's new solo record.

Watching Mick and Wyclef weave together a rhythm was bewitching, especially after a little pot. They were recording straight into a laptop sitting on the unused 48-track recording console. Before Mick put out *Goddess in the Doorway*, I listened to it for days, headphones at dangerous volume during workouts. I hadn't written a record review since *Slow Train Coming*, and once again I had listened so carefully and continuously that I felt called to spread the joyful news. It was a rave, "better than any Stones since 'Miss You.'" Mick's singing was rich, the writing was strong, humorous, and introspective. It was a great collection, and I still think so.

When I submitted it, the record review editor put four stars on it. There was no problem with my adding an additional half a star. Bob Dylan had once patted me down backstage, looking for where I kept that extra star. No guts, no glory, and I kicked it up to five stars. There was some snickering about being on Mick's leash, but so what, and what if I were?

Mick's solo albums never sold well. My review didn't change that. Keith called the album *Dogshit in the Doorway*. A sweetheart. That's what friends are for. Dylan also got five stars for *Love and Theft*, his forty-first album, which our reviewer Rob Sheffield called a "stone-cold Dylan classic. Relaxed, magisterial, utterly confident." It had an energy and lyrical explosion that reminded me of *Highway 61*. The release date was September 11.

AFTER FIFTEEN YEARS and four hundred issues, Fred Woodward retired from *Rolling Stone*. No other art director had stayed as long. He won *Rolling Stone* more international design medals than any other U.S. magazine, plus enough gold and silver medals from the Art Director's Club in New York to set the record for the most awards in its history. Only at a distance, looking back at those covers, those pages, those spreads, where the typography merged with the image and the story, did I fully realize that Fred Woodward, that quiet but stubborn guy from Noxapater, Mississippi, was a genius in our midst.

WE LOST KEN KESEY. As much as anyone, he was a Founding Father of the sixties, and had a vision of the American Dream. His family buried him on a spot he had chosen on his Oregon farm, next to his son, who had died at seventeen. Ken's wife, Faye, his high school sweetheart, said that he always had loved the John Wayne movies where the cowboys gather in a little cemetery to lay one of their own to rest. That very scene was also one of the most resonant memory fragments from my childhood. It was in a black-and-white movie I have never seen again, where the cowboys stand around Boot Hill, their hats over their hearts, and sing "Home on the Range." I was a little boy, and I cried.

Kesey started writing for *Rolling Stone* in 1969, and did seventeen pieces for us, the last one in the year he died. He was raised on a dairy farm as a kind of all-American boy, a star football player, actor, and wrestler in high school, voted most likely to succeed. He wanted to be a writer, and became a great American novelist. When we went together to interview the governor of Oregon years earlier, Kesey had worn Stars-and-Stripes clothes, like Uncle Sam. He wanted to absorb and refract the power of that symbol of America. He was a prankster, and he was a patriot.

THE LAST THING we did in 2001 was "Broken Lives, Broken Dreams," twenty profiles of *Rolling Stone* readers who had lost their lives at the World Trade Center. It was directly inspired, a copy, really, of the *New York Times* series "Portraits of Grief." The editorial staff tracked down the relatives and friends of the firemen, the stockbrokers, the secretaries, and the bond traders who had *Rolling Stone* subscriptions and had died in the smoke and flames. They were passionate about their careers, their families, and their love of music. They were cut down as their lives were coming into flower. It was heartbreaking, every bit of it. Once again, our wars were killing the innocent. But you never ask questions when God's on your side.

CHAPTER 58

MY PRIVATE IDAHO

A T BROADFORD FARM the orchards and pastures were covered in deep new snow, Christmas-card perfect. Matt set the fires in the morning and would return in the afternoon with reports on how what I called the Matt Pack had skied so brilliantly that day. Everyone was "stoked" or "*en fuego*" and had their "fun meter set at ten." I had broken my ankle over Thanksgiving playing tag with Gus and was getting around on crutches.

Arnold was out of commission, too, having broken several ribs in a motorcycle accident. We had lunches in town and showed up together at the base lodge to take a bow and show our purple hearts. He was toying with running for governor of California as a Republican, although he was socially very liberal. I liked him a lot, as confident as they come. He used to laugh about showing those legislators how he would "crush their bones."

I knew Rita Wilson only a little, but she and her husband, Tom Hanks, invited Matt and me for dinner, squeezed around a table with Arnold and Maria, Martin and Nancy Short, and Bruce and Patti Springsteen. At dessert, Bruce told a long and winding personal parable, as he generally does. The moral at the end, based on his experience with Patti, was that once you get married, there's another person you have to be considerate of and share your life with, your equal. It was a sermon. Silence. Arnold stood up, turned to Maria, and in a loud voice said, "Time to go. Maria! Heel!"

I invited Bruce and Patti to the house for lunch to open the new year. I didn't know Bruce that well, although we had had some good laughs and a healthy respect for each other. We spent hours at the table, talking about our parents, our childhoods, our children, our partners, our jobs, and our dreams. There was this need to catch up on our lives, to create a history together. It was intense and there was an urgency in it. It felt like something deep had happened.

OUR NEWEST EDITORIAL commitment was a series on immigration. We sent a team to profile eight Mexican men at a border crossing in search of work. They had a brutal escape across the hot desert by night with no water, dangers all around in that wilderness, poisonous snakes, border patrols, and vigilantes. They saw the bleached bones of human beings lying in the sand. In part two, we caught up with the men living together in a motel room on the outskirts of Greenville, a Baptist city in South Carolina where they spent twelve-hour days hanging sheetrock. For part three, we went back to Mexico and wrote about the wives and children they had left behind.

We sent a distinguished foreign-affairs correspondent, T. D. All-man, to dig into what had happened to "Plan Colombia," the hundreds of millions of dollars Clinton had spent to get America off drugs and save that country. It was now four years later and there was more cocaine in the U.S. than ever, and Colombia had fallen into full-scale civil war. The only winners were the defense contractors in Connecticut who built Black Hawk helicopters. Our government had spent $354 million on helicopters and $68 million for alternative crop development.

WE ALSO SPENT summers in Idaho at our farm. We had settled in, digging a new pond with a swing rope tied to a nearby tree, and put in cherries and pears. It was a battle with the local deer, which we called "rats on hooves." We set up beehives. We had beekeeper suits and bottled sage-flavored honey. We owned about thirty chickens and guinea hens, who lived in a Matt-designed, two-level coop. Robin Williams visited and asked why it was necessary for the chickens to have a penthouse. We had great friends and neighbors we really liked, who had kids in our cohort. The kids had their friends come out for long stays. Theo's best friend was Vito Schnabel, oozing charm and trouble. Alex had his boarding school roommate, a super-polite football star. They graduated together. He died a freshman in college, falling down a fraternity staircase one night at a drinking party. I started Alex and Theo on motorcycles, Theo on a Honda CBR600 and Alex on a Harley-Davidson. They each made it about a hundred feet the first time.

WHEN MATT AND I headed back to New York, we detoured for a visit with Gil and Janet Friesen in Santa Barbara, a Labor Day tradition. We had become a tight foursome. Gil had scheduled four days of activities. We spent a day on a picnic and surfing at Hollister Ranch with Jackson Browne. We stopped on the way back in Indianapolis to visit Jason Priestley, who had introduced me to the Yamaha FZR1000 crotch rocket when we first met during his *Beverly Hills 90210* stardom. He had crashed his racing car into a wall at 180 miles an hour coming out of the second turn in the final practice for the Kentucky 100. He broke his back and both feet, but had no brain damage. He looked like a car wreck — bruises, lacerations, trussed up and suspended in his hospital bed by various cables.

BETTE AND MARTIN had won a week at Versace's mansion on Lake Como in a charity auction; Matt and I, along with Ned and Cathy, joined them at the oversized, overstuffed, and over-the-top faux-Roman villa. There were reproductions of statuary everywhere, including ten-foot-high naked wrestlers in our bedroom. Bette is wonderful to travel with. She overflows with wit and inspires it in everybody. We had a particularly funny time at that joint. From there we went to Croatia and sailed for a week, stopping at deserted coves and eating in small towns until we got to Dubrovnik. The six of us would travel the world together in the years to come. We called ourselves the Twelve-Legged Monster, and ended up in Cuba and Mexico, Syria and Israel, India and Bhutan. Not to mention Paris, Venice, and Vienna.

Us WEEKLY WAS gaining traction, chasing the Whitney Houston drug-abuse story and buying the rights to Catherine Zeta-Jones' baby pictures. In fact, our newsstand sales had been rising slowly but unmistakably since launch. It turned out we didn't need the infusion of cash from Disney; however, the infusion of confidence was incalculable. I hadn't fully realized yet that it was very much a magazine for women.

I hired a new editor who had a sixth sense for women who lived their lives through the stars, the glamorous, and the good-looking. She was unafraid to bring the stars down to earth. She created wonderful departments like "Stars, They're Just Like Us," which would have a paparazzo shot of a star putting out their garbage or picking up after their dog. I added "Fashion Police," in which we got various wits and snarky people to give us one-liners about what stars were wearing. My son Theo came up with "What's in My Bag?," an annotated archeological dig into a star's handbags.

For *Rolling Stone* I brought in a Brit, who was then the editor of *FHM*, number two to *Maxim* in the new laddie-magazine race, magazines that were loud, overdesigned, in-your-face fare for rebellious college boys. "Random Notes" suddenly exploded with photos, shapes, and colors; the covers were so busy you needed to catch your breath to look at them. I started hearing about "points of entry," the notion that any given editorial page ought to have a set number of items for the reader to look at: boxes, lists, cut-out photos, and, on top of that, small photos bleeding off the pages, plus digital-looking typefaces and the pointing-mouse arrows. The thought was that we needed to compete with the internet by imitation. All of a sudden, we were giving away prizes for "our favorite letter." We ran a feature titled "Rock's 50 Greatest Meltdowns," a compendium of stale drug stories and egos. Then we had these three cover headlines in a row: "Asia Argento, She Puts the Sex in XXX"; "Bound, Gagged and Loving It, Meet the People Who Pay to Get Kidnapped"; and last, "The New Girl Next Door and Her Astonishing Sexual Requirements." The Brit's last issue was a cover of Christina Aguilera, naked, of course, except for buckles, leather straps, and black boots. She lay on red sheets, red fingernails resting on her left breast and a well-placed guitar between her legs. The headline read "Inside the Dirty Mind of a Pop Princess." Even I was appalled. That editor was a one-trick pony, and I sent him out to pasture.

BRUCE RELEASED THE RISING, his first album in seven years and his first record with the E Street Band in nearly two decades. It was his eleventh *Rolling Stone* cover. We gave it five stars. It was a reckoning with 9/11. Bruce said that a few days after the attack, he was leaving the beach and a man drove up, rolled down his window, and yelled, "'We need you!' I thought I'd probably been a part of this guy's life for a while. People want to be around things they are familiar with. So, he might need to see me right about now. That made sense. Like 'I've got a job to do.'"

Bruce addressed a nation that had lost its certainties and its way. We had lost our sense of safety, our immunity from the problems of others in the world, our sense of righteousness, and the American Dream that had sanctified us. Bruce was not asking for vengeance, but for us to rise above it, accept the losses, transcend the ancient hatreds, and celebrate the yearning for human connection.

This confirmed and expanded my faith in rock and roll. It was a new benchmark against which the work of other artists would be measured by the commitment to human justice. A new rock era was in the making, a new North Star was shining. The title song, "The Rising," was about a fireman going into the tower fires and perishing. "Sky of love, sky of tears, /…Sky of mercy, sky of fear, /…Come on up for the rising, /… lay your hands in mine." What follows that song is "Paradise," about a suicide bomber who puts explosives in his backpack, kisses his family goodbye, blows himself up, and waits for paradise. It is a profoundly sad song. The last song is "My City of Ruins," with a gospel choir and the mighty, heavenly majesty of a Hammond B3 organ. "My city's in ruins / Now with these hands /…I pray, Lord, for the strength, Lord /…for the faith, Lord / for your love, Lord, with these hands…/ Come on rise up!"

I was filled with hope and purpose. Make no mistake about the greatness of this album. It is a masterpiece.

AL GORE CALLED to have lunch just after Thanksgiving, wanting to talk about his future. I was moved that he wanted my thoughts. Karenna urged him to run again; so did most of his close advisors. They had the hunger for another fight. Al had a list of pros and cons that we ran through; one struck me the most: "I want to stop having to lie, I want to tell the truth again." That thought, more than any other, came from his innermost self. Al was drained, still not fully back to a future. The defeat had been profound. I told him I would be thrilled if he would run again, happy to double my efforts, but I also told him that I didn't hear him say that he really wanted to. The lunch left me depressed.

He was in town to host *Saturday Night Live*, thin ice for an aspiring president, but he was excited about it, proud of his humor. "Hi, I'm Al Gore. I am a recovering politician." We went to watch him perform on *SNL*, and he was a natural. The next week he announced he wouldn't run.

MY MOTHER TURNED eighty. The three of us kids and our husbands took her to the Hana Ranch in the noncommercial wilds of Maui. There was hiking and visits to waterfalls, and one day we headed for one of those paradise-like beaches on the other side of a small mountain. The path was narrow, steep, and slippery, since Hawaii is so often wet. She was grabbing my arm to steady her footing and I instinctively pulled it away from her. There was nothing this eighty-year-old lady on a slippery path wanted from me other than a helping hand. It was tricky terrain, and she was scared. I couldn't believe that I was pushing her away from me, trying to get away from her.

Somewhere along the line I realized that I didn't like being around her. I hated feeling that way; I felt like a bad person. She had moved to Hawaii after we got out of college. We were all okay with that. She seemed happy, enjoying her exotic and somewhat glamorous life. I don't recall feeling deserted, but I'm not so sure that growing up independently of the family was necessary and that we didn't miss a lot. When she got involved with the sex-and-scam cult in 1971, I began to keep her at arm's length. How could she fall for that, be so duped? She used to talk about it all the time. She was disrespectful to Jane, always making some cutting remark. No love was lost. Even our little dog growled and snapped when she showed up.

I could never get comfortable with her declaration that she had become a lesbian. I don't know if my reaction was my refusal to face my own facts by avoiding hers, or whether her self-aggrandizing declarations were too uncomfortable and off-putting. I wasn't disapproving or negative; I just didn't want to hear any more intimate information. What son wants to hear about his mom's sex life?

We rented a house back on the Big Island. She had moved to the Hilo side, not only the rainiest place in Hawaii, overgrown like a jungle, but one with a simmering volcano, flowing lava slowly eating up the area a few miles from where she had bought a new home. We flew in her friends and had a birthday luau. The lesbian striptease was embarrassing but funny. How many women get a striptease on their eightieth birthday? It was the toasts that told the tale. Sim took them over and became the master of ceremonies, managing, correcting, adding to all the wonderful things people said about her. That was my mom.

CHAPTER 59

WATCHING
THE RIVER FLOW

MY OLDEST SON, Alex, turned eighteen and graduated from high school in 2003. We went full family, sat on folding chairs in the sun and watched him in a parade of green caps and gowns. We met his new girlfriend, Emily Eisen-Berkeley, and her family. He married her a few years later, his high school sweetheart. Alex was a little over six feet, in varsity football shape, with sparkling blue eyes, but also a loner and difficult to read. I doted on him. He liked heavy metal, and I put my foot down about tattoos and piercings but promised that I'd go with him on his eighteenth birthday and we would both get a tat. Paul Booth, the King of Ink in the world of heavy metal, gave Alex and me the black-carpet treatment. He lived above his shop in the Village and brought us sodas while we waited upstairs, where he had a collection of dead animals, body parts, and human fetuses in glass jugs. When we went down for our tattoos, everyone was in costume and makeup for the monthly zombie day. I had a simple line drawing of the eye of the Egyptian goddess Isis inked on my ankle, about two inches in size. Alex had the eye of Isis, too, but two of them, from one edge of his back to the other, fully two feet wide and fully inked, like a painting. We had come of age.

Us WEEKLY HAD found the very ganglion of American culture. A gentler celebrity coverage — witty, ironic, and youthful — was born. This was a new generation of stars. One of the early scoops was a picture of an actress kissing Justin Timberlake on a surfboard. She was unpleasant to deal with; she told one of our researchers, "I hope you get cancer." We had a new supercouple — not Liz and Dick or Sonny and Cher — to whom we gave a new style of merged name: Brangelina, for Brad Pitt and Angelina Jolie. The *New York Times* wrote, "*Us Weekly* is one of the most intoxicating cultural artifacts of our age." And *Advertising Age* named *US Weekly* Magazine of the Year, saying we had become a "cultural reference point, if not an entire worldview."

Rolling Stone, which was dedicated to covering American culture, also got the celebrity itch. Jessica Simpson was a staple of *US Weekly*, and we put her on the cover of *Rolling Stone* in a tight T-shirt and underpants, pushing a Swiffer WetJet mop. Jessica and her dad, Joe, came up for lunch with the *Rolling Stone* and *US Weekly* editors. Like Britney, she had been a Mouseketeer. Her breasts nearly fell out of her dress.

Angelina was a stunning *Rolling Stone* cover. She mentioned that after divorcing Billy Bob Thornton, she hadn't had sex for a year and wasn't meant for marriage. Then back to Justin Timberlake, paired with Christina Aguilera, *American Idol* stars, and the inevitable, the Olsen twins. *Rolling Stone* was almost a combination of two different magazines, one silly and one serious.

I COMMISSIONED BOBBY KENNEDY JR. to write a manifesto on Bush's war on the environment, the rewriting of energy laws in secret meetings with Cheney and the oil companies, and the ferocious three-year rollback under way on environmental laws. It was an indictment. We titled it "Crimes Against Nature."

In nearly every issue we published a serious piece about the environment and the climate crisis. The science left no doubt about what lay ahead. The laws of physics were clear. It would be a five-alarm global holocaust. I asked Al Gore why the national media weren't meaningfully covering global warming, and he wrote "Climate of Denial," about the media and the merchants of carbon death. What, he asked, was so badly dysfunctional with the free press in our democratic society? "The conversion of all truths into questions of power has attacked the very heart of the distinction between true and false. The wealthiest individuals and corporations have overwhelmed the nation's ability to make intelligent collective decisions." I asked Al to address his piece directly to our influential readership in the establishment press. It was time to send a message that they were failing their country.

The biggest threat to democracy was Rupert Murdoch. We ran a 20,000-word report on Murdoch, Roger Ailes, and Fox News titled "The Fear Factory." They ran an around-the-clock propaganda mill that manufactured misinformation, paranoia, the Tea Party (which they birthed), white supremacy, warmongering, conspiracy, and climate denial. They had emasculated the other networks into a cowed neutrality. Murdoch rivaled Goebbels, and then he gave us Trump.

WE EMBEDDED A writer — whose previous jobs had been at *Hustler* and a pornographic website — for two months with a squad of Marines on forward reconnaissance patrols in Iraq. The men were considered the toughest of the Marines and trained with Navy SEALs, thus the title of the piece, "The Killer Elite." They were in all kinds of hairy combat situations, and our writer was riding in the front seat. "They return fire and redecorate an apartment building with about a dozen grenades fired from a Mark 19. Dead bodies are scattered along the edge of the road. Most are men, enemy fighters some with weapons in their hands. The Marines nickname one Tomato Man because from a distance he looks like a smashed crate of tomatoes. There are shot-up cars and trucks with bodies hanging over the edges. We pass a truck smashed and burned with charred human remains sitting up in the window. There is a man lying in the road with no head and a dead girl, too, about three or four years old, lying on her back. She is wearing a dress and has no legs."

This was the first report of war crimes in Iraq, well before Abu Ghraib. Commanding Marine General James Mattis defended the piece, calling it honest and accurate. HBO turned it into a series. And the beat went on.

Bob dylan's tour bus was parked outside the Sun Valley Lodge, where I found him leaning against a tree with a cowboy hat slid down over his face. We were going to spend the day hanging out at Broadford Farm. We went for a walk of the property, ending up at the Big Wood River, where I had an old safari tent with a table and chairs. We sat there all morning shooting the shit and watching the river flow. He was writing Chronicles, and told me how he was researching it. We gossiped about Bruce and Mick, and he told me his stories of John Lennon. We traded notes on investments, real estate, trust funds for kids. Bob was a family man with five kids and fourteen grandchildren. He was incredibly open. He was in his late fifties.

Matt and Gus made lunch and we ate in the apple orchard. Bob carried the conversation through the meal, stories that cracked us up, charming and witty chitchat, the ideal guest. He fully engaged thirteen-year-old Gus, who was learning guitar, just getting comfortable with it. Bob picked up Gus' guitar and played "Johnny B. Goode." Gus asked if he would show him how to play "Hurricane." Bob told him to listen to Charlie Christian and he would be all right. I could resist no longer and picked up my camera. It was a little intrusive, but I had to save the moment — my little boy with his head of unkempt curly hair, axe in hand, at the foot of the master. Bob sent Gus a Charlie Christian box set, and a few months later, for his birthday, signed a guitar inscribed "Don't forget to tune it."

John Kerry was in Sun Valley shortly after, and we took our Harleys out for a ride to the top of Galena Pass, and then to Cristina's, the Elaine's of Ketchum, but with good food. We talked about his run for president.

He had had the fever for years. I gave him one piece of advice, which I thought was live or die: throughout a campaign, I told him, all kinds of people would be telling him different things about what he should do, and the problem would be that they were all highly experienced, highly paid people, and probably all of them would sound right. The ability to win would be based on him trusting his own judgment and instinct, by finding his own true north. Otherwise, I said, he would get lost, would never figure out whose advice to follow. I specifically named one person to watch out for and not listen to. He hired that person at the top of his campaign.

YOKO TOOK MATT and me to Japan. We checked into the Hotel Okura, staying in the suite where she and John had once lived. She showed us the sights, her childhood and the mansion in Tokyo she had grown up in, now an embassy. She came from one of Japan's richest families and had been a playmate of the current emperor. Her family fled to the countryside during the war and sold their furniture and dishes.

Yoko wanted us to see ground zero at Hiroshima. It was roughly a square mile of cleaned-up rubble, with hollowed-out buildings on the fringes and a plain museum with sobering artifacts and documents on display. It was far from an American-style interactive experience, no reenactments like a Civil War battle at Gettysburg. We took in Kyoto and its gardens and stayed in *ryokan*, the old-style hotels. Back in Tokyo, we went to a concert honoring John, featuring Japanese artists ranging from the latest teen sensations, pretty pop boys and teenage girls dressed like dolls, to a very fish-out-of-water hippie in his sixties, the Bob Dylan of Japan, all singing Lennon songs.

I was struck by how precisely ordered the society was, whether waiting in line for trains or in shops. Why was everything you bought so beautifully wrapped, so perfectly presented, the rules of society so scrupulously obeyed? My flash of insight about the mentality of following orders was that the need for strict discipline, and discouraging original behavior, was ultimately about pure survival. That many people living in that tiny country who thought only as individuals, like Americans do, would sooner or later kill each other.

JOHNNY CASH WAS dead at seventy-one, the victim of hard living and grief at the death of June Carter, the woman at the center of his life. I had seen him play at San Quentin. We covered him regularly, with nearly rock star treatment. John, as his friends called him, was Old Testament in presence and voice. Bob Dylan wrote a piece for our tribute issue about hearing "I Walk the Line" in 1956: "The record sounded like a voice coming from the middle of the earth. It was profound, every line deep and rich, awesome and mysterious all at once." Mark Seliger had done the black-and-white cover portrait of Cash eleven years earlier, with wisdom written in every wrinkle and in the ease of his smile and countenance.

CHAPTER 60

KERRY LOSES

I STARTED OUT FEELING blasé about my own induction into the Hall of Fame in 2004 but ended up with my head in the clouds. Prince, Traffic, George Harrison, ZZ Top, Bob Seger, and Jackson Browne were in my class, all of whom were close to *Rolling Stone*, in our world. Sharing the night with Jackson, whose songs and comradeship were such treasures for me, made it even richer. A week before the show, Ahmet told me that he had gotten Mick to come in from London to induct me.

We sat in a cluster of tables with Keith Richards and his daughters, and Mick's kids; Olivia Harrison was at the next table with her son, Dhani, his father's doppelgänger, and Yoko and Sean. It was a mess of Beatles and Rolling Stones and my kids, who all knew each other. I had Jane, Matt, the three boys, Don Henley, Tom and Sheila Wolfe, and Mick. It was a black-tie family picnic.

Prince opened the show with three blazing songs. Stevie Winwood, who I never realized was such a serious guitar player, did a ferocious solo on "Dear Mr. Fantasy" that was a full knockout. Seger had been off the road for many years, but the Waldorf ballroom felt like a juke joint when he ripped "Old Time Rock and Roll." Bruce spoke proudly about Jackson, his "meticulousness of craft, matched by deepness of soul." He also called him a "bona fide, rock and roll sex star," and admitted being jealous of his hair and the number of hot girls that came to see him play: "Jackson was drawing more women than an Indigo Girls concert."

Ahmet walked onstage with his cane, introducing my induction and giving a shout-out to Jane and Ralph Gleason. He spoke with gravitas. I tried to stay in the moment and take in the historical weight of Ahmet's speech. Then he said, "To further my remarks, Sir Mick Jagger." There he was, smiling wide with his tooth diamond sparkling, dressed in a black suit. I was able to relax into a groove of the pleasure, the treasure, the measure of this extraordinary moment. I wanted it to take me over. Mick made a gracious bow to Jane — "She was there at the beginning and she's here tonight" — who was beaming and blushing.

Mick looked down at Keith: "We remember the early days of the Stones in America, when the teen magazines asked really deep questions about what kind of girls you liked, blondes or brunettes, or Chinese food versus Italian food, what kind of socks.

"But this innocent triviality was swept away when in 1967 *Rolling Stone* changed all that by inventing the very *long* interview. Now you had to spend hours describing your views on everything from Vietnam to the Beatles, as well as, of course, your sexual preferences. Now intrepid *Rolling Stone* reporters hang out on tour with you and you must provide the drink, drugs, and even food to produce the interviews Jann demands . . .

"I must tell you that not so long ago, Jann decided he was going to do a very long interview with me and visit us on tour in small places where there wouldn't be interference. After a couple of interviews, he said, 'You know, I'm really getting into this. It's like I feel like I'm a cub reporter again.' I said, 'Yeah, Jann, you're a cub reporter with the Gulfstream G4 waiting at the airport.'

"Jann was one of the first music critics and editors that really understood how we as artists felt and could sympathize with our yearnings. Jann almost single-handedly pioneered the idea of popular music and of rock and roll in particular as a vibrant art form. It was Jann who elevated our music to a place where it enjoys the status of other musical forms.

"This is a wonderful, heartfelt occasion, and I will treasure the memory of it all the way to the airport."

I had prepared a speech, given it a lot of thought, and had much to say and many to thank. "To the two most elegant men in the room, Ahmet Ertegun and Mick Jagger, I am honored by you. Ahmet, you are a national treasure. You have done so much for me.

"Sir Mick Jagger [I made a bow], how cool it is to be inducted by you. You still have the world's greatest rock and roll band. I always set my compass to you, Mick, and guided *Rolling Stone* by how you conducted yourself as an artist and as a driving force, how you held it all together with such intelligence and integrity. It's been a pleasure to be your friend for all these years, and you coming here tonight means the world to me."

At the end of the proceedings Prince stepped out of the shadows into the all-star ensemble performance of "While My Guitar Gently Weeps." His playing was transcendent. I remember standing there, my mouth open, tearing up, in dumbstruck awe. It can be seen today on an Imax screen at the Rock and Roll Hall of Fame in Cleveland. The greatest performance in the history of the Hall of Fame was that night.

THE LAST GREAT revival of *Rolling Stone* began. Our new art director, Amid Capeci, came over from *Newsweek*, where he must have picked up his love of ripping up layouts on deadline and the energy of a big story. The editors liked hanging around in his office, cracking jokes and writing headlines. Amid always kept an open can of cashew nuts for me on his desk and called it "Jann's salt lick." He had a running war with our production department, saying that the man in charge was running a prostitution ring. Amid was always trying to find some new color variation for the logo in each issue. I had to give him a memo with a list of colors that were banned without formal written permission: pink, purple, yellow, and green. Amid took the best of the formal traditions that Roger Black had so impeccably crafted and Fred's whirlwind of unrestricted creativity, and tamed the sea of sidebars into something practical and fun, combining them all into what was ultimately the fully elaborated and quintessential version of *Rolling Stone*.

ONE ISSUE THEN was a particular favorite: "Doonesbury at War," a Garry Trudeau drawing of a soldier on a stretcher with one leg blown off, waiting for a medevac helicopter. We ran the first interview with Garry in twenty years, in which he talked about his childhood buddy Howard Dean and his Yale classmate, the frat boy George Bush. We excerpted Tom Wolfe's upcoming novel, *I Am Charlotte Simmons*, a wildly intimate look at college life in the 2000s (Tom was now seventy-four), which we titled "Knight of the Love Skull." We also had a Sebastião Salgado portfolio, masterpieces of black-and-white photography, this time from the Galápagos.

I WAS ON FRIENDLY terms with Tom Cruise. It was hard not to like the guy; his smile was so unnaturally dazzling it was like his superpower. I used to think of him as a comic book hero, Tom Terrific. He managed his press carefully. I knew I was being managed. He put 1,000 percent focus into everything. He met our latest writer, Neil Strauss, on his movie set for a trailer visit and motorcycle stunt training. Our last Cruise profiler had ridden in a stunt plane with him and now we were going to be allowed to meet his mom and sister, briefly, during a guided tour of the Scientology center. It seemed he was opening up, but in the end he said nothing; he thoroughly deflects. You walk away thinking you know the guy, but all you know is that here is a confident and extremely polite man. He wouldn't even reveal whether he was for or against Bush. What the fuck is he guarding? Why is he in a super-secretive cult? He is a great talent. He is Super Tom. All his secrecy gave rise to the suspicion that he was gay. I never got a ping on my gaydar, but gay people persisted in what Bette one night called "swishful thinking."

THE YEAR 2004 was another high-stakes election year. Bruce saw that he could no longer stand on the side and just be hopeful. The Iraq War had to be stopped. Jobs were being shipped overseas and justice every-where denied and sidelined. I had put the matter to Bruce at the begin-ning of the year, as he was trying to reconcile his artistic and political consciences into a single, actionable statement. I was certain where he would come out. It was time for action. He decided to headline the Swing State Tour, a fifteen-day, old-fashioned cavalcade of the stars that raised $15 million. I was considered an official of the Kerry cam-paign by virtue of the two fund-raising concerts I produced for them, and was legally forbidden from "coordinating" with the Swing State Tour. We put the tour on the cover. I had never actually interviewed Bruce before; I enjoyed just being friends. Anything about work went through Jon Landau, per Bruce's mandate. Jon said Bruce wanted to talk to me about his decision to be openly political, to "come out."

Matt and I drove down to Jersey on a sunny afternoon, our first visit to the new farm. Bruce and Patti piled us all into his Mustang, top down, and gave us a tour of Asbury Park, where he played, where he lived, where he met Patti. He loved to revisit his childhood, the fount of his mythology and wisdom. They had just bought their new farm in horse country and were spending the night in a guest cottage on the property. They served us a fancy dinner, then Bruce and I walked up to the stables, where he had his writing office on the second floor of the barn. We got out our notes, pencils, and a tape recorder. He was consulting a spiral notebook in which he had written down questions he wanted to answer, the insights he wanted to share.

Bruce is one of the most thoughtful, measured people I have ever met. He studies, reads, thinks about stuff. I've never seen anybody have so much fun onstage before, yet he is a deeply inward and serious man. His audience had an uncommon faith in Bruce, a relationship based on his integrity and humanity. The greater part of that audience was work-ing and middle class, his people, where he came from. Taking a stand against the president of the United States, and in the middle of a war, was a considerable decision. He did not hold back: "You serve at the behest of your audience's imagination. You are asking people to welcome the complexity in the interest of fuller and more honest communication. The artist and audience are valuable to one another as long as you can look out there and see yourself and they can look back and see themselves.

"Sitting on the sidelines would be a betrayal of the ideas I had written about for a long time. I don't want to see the country devolve into an oligarchy, watch the division of wealth increase, see another million people below the poverty line this year. To see the country move so far to the right has removed whatever doubt I had."

Three weeks after interviewing Bruce I flew out to interview Kerry in Denver, where he was preparing for his second debate. I watched him do a spur-of-the-moment press conference set up outdoors with the snowcapped Rockies as his backdrop. It had just been announced that there were no weapons of mass destruction in Iraq, and Donald Rumsfeld admitted there was no connection between Saddam Hussein and Al-Qaeda. John should have then and there demanded Bush's head on a platter, or perhaps immediate impeachment, but he didn't. Back in his hotel suite, he got out of his blue suit into chinos and running shoes and leaned back in his chair. His battered guitar case was in the doorway. John was long-winded and took his time making an effective point. He had won the first debate. Hopes were high, but he seemed to float over the real world.

I DECIDED TO PAY a visit to our licensees throughout the world. Moscow is heavy-duty and oppressive. It has the grandiosity of a great world capital but is decrepit once you get away from Red Square. It was way cool to see *Rolling Stone* in Russia. I would never have imagined such a thing. It seemed to indicate a new level of meaningfulness. Three guys in their late twenties owned the license, the sons of a KGB officer, a nuclear submarine commander, and a general who had been awarded a Hero of the Soviet Union medal. Their office was in a renovated warehouse looking out on a river, a sanctuary in Greater Moscow, with posters of *Rolling Stone* with its clarion logo. I spent the day in meetings, talking story ideas with the editors, debating whether putting a pop star on the cover would compromise "our" integrity. It was a nostalgic moment, the same conversation I'd had years ago. I smiled. The prophecy had been heard, even in Mother Russia: "Calling out around the world, / Are you ready for a brand-new beat?" It's apparently obligatory in Moscow that you drink lots and lots of vodka. I did my best.

Our first overseas editions began in Australia and Germany in 1981. Now editions were established in Russia, India, Japan, South Africa, the Middle East, Germany, Mexico, Brazil, Argentina, Indonesia, Italy, and Spain. We began an annual conference for the licensees in New York to bring them into design and editorial harmony with the mother ship. They had become an important part of *Rolling Stone* and its potency, with serious political coverage of their own countries. The Chinese government shut down our edition there after six issues. Hearing artists tell me that they had been on the cover in Russia gave me goose bumps.

HUNTER WAS IN no shape to cover the campaign, but John Kerry was so clearly the fruit of our efforts together in the seventies that he wanted some kind of role and asked to write about it. Hunter had not done any original writing for five years. I had given up. He couldn't even do short stuff that was crisp or funny. His weekly column for ESPN was a throwaway, bringing in some money on top of his book royalties. He didn't do lectures anymore because travel was too difficult. But our friendship and loyalty to each other were permanent.

I arranged for him to meet John at the Aspen airport and spend a few hours with him at a local fund-raiser. It was wonderful to get on the phone and work again, but it was painful to edit it. There was little there — scraps, old memories, no scenes, no reporting. He was going in circles. I did like his description of Houston as "a shabby, sprawling metropolis ruled by brazen women, crooked cops and super rich pansexual cowboys." I was happy to indulge him once again, even though he had, as he and I both knew, lost his edge and his relevance. It would be his last piece.

I wrote my own Letter from the Editor about John, rich in rhetoric and flourishes. "Our current leadership seems to have lost its moral compass. Dishonesty has become a national policy. We have abandoned scientific and medical research, bowing to narrow religious beliefs. We have handed over even more of our national wealth to the rich and taken it from the working man. We have made war on nations because we think we hear God telling us who is evil..."

At the final rally of the campaign, 10,000 union members and their families were waiting in downtown Cleveland, in sight of the glass pyramid of the Rock and Roll Hall of Fame. The last few days of polls showed Kerry up two or three points. People were high-fiving. Bruce was asked to sing, so he, Patti, Jon Landau and his wife, Barbara (our long-ago copy editor), Matt and I, plus Gus and Sam Springsteen, flew out. John dropped by our trailer for a visit and let ten-year-old Sam talk his head off. John's wife, Teresa Heinz, took the stage first and with her thick, European-esque accent talked about herself for ten minutes. Bruce got up, spoke for two minutes — he was following Ohio senator John Glenn — and sang "No Surrender." John got under way, and we slipped out and headed back to New York.

In the plane's guest book, Bruce drew a picture of the plane he called "Jann Air." In it, the passengers were waving from the windows as the plane crossed over an ocean from a continent labeled "Bushland" to another continent, shaped like North America, captioned "The Promised Land."

BUSH BEAT KERRY. For our last issue of the year, we interviewed the young Barack Obama as one of our People of the Year:

> *What advice do you have for people who feel hopeless after the Kerry loss?*
>
> Get over it. Go to the movies, go to the park, go on a date — get some perspective. Losing an election is not a tragedy. Tragedies are losing my mom, getting cancer at fifty-three and dying in three months.

Are you thinking about Obama '08?

Not going to happen. I do not intend to run for president in the next election.

What transformative changes are required right now?

How do we integrate a world economically, culturally, politically, while still valuing life on a human scale? How do you have global free trade that doesn't lead to wages settling at the lowest common denominator, in which you have a few gazillionaires and everyone else on the wage scale of China?

What would most surprise people to learn about you?

Probably that I'm a failed jock. I love basketball, but my love for the game always exceeded my talent. Also, I'm a reformed smoker, but when you are on the campaign in a car driving through cornfields, occasionally I bum a cigarette or two. But I did all my drinking in high school and college. I was a wild man. I did drugs and drank at parties. But I got all my ya-yas out.

CHAPTER 61

HUNTER THOMPSON, R.I.P.

HUNTER SHOT HIMSELF in the head at Owl Farm. I don't remember what time of day it was or who told me, just the old leather chair I was sitting in when I heard the news. I sat in that chair for hours — I called Jane right away — alone in the house as night came. I was back at Broadford Farm for the month of February, day after day of exhilarating skiing. Matt was on his way to Kenya to see the gorillas.

I let the memories and crazy days drift through my mind. I sat back in the chair, my feet on the desk, and vividly remembered our conversations, our great partnership, our great friendship. I wasn't surprised that he had committed suicide. It was no mistake, no crazy impulse. Hunter was calculating and careful. If he did it, I knew it was the right thing for him to do. I wasn't angry at him or anyone. I was just sad, terribly, awfully, lonely sad. I loved him.

I flew down to Aspen later in the week to see Anita, whom he had married only a year earlier, and his only son, Juan, and his wife. They hadn't left Owl Farm since the day of the suicide. The iron buzzards were still mounted on the gate, a red Cadillac was in the driveway, and the peacocks in their outdoor cage on the porch. After the hugs and tears, Anita and Juan left me alone in the living room with my thoughts and memories. How many times, for how many years, had I sat with

Hunter in that room with the fire roaring, sometimes at 3:00 a.m. in the dead of winter, while his two stacks of speakers pumped out "Gimme Shelter" or "One Toke Over the Line"?

This house had been an office and a retreat for me. Headquarters was the kitchen; Hunter would stand on one side of the counter, on which sat the red IBM Selectric typewriter he had appropriated from *Rolling Stone*. The wall phone was within his reach, with a Polaroid of Jane pinned next to it, the television always on news or sports, drinks within easy refilling reach, memos, notes, clippings, photos, menus, letters pinned or Scotch-taped to everything, half of them intersecting with our mutual adventures. This was where Hunter ran things from. It was odd to see so many familiar, almost intimate bits and pieces, but they were no longer mine, not just because I was older, but because it was now a museum, everything now more memorabilia than memories.

I gathered up the survivors and we drove into Aspen for their first time out of the house since Hunter's death. We went to Poppies, which had been his favorite restaurant. We stayed until after it closed, laughing, crying, telling stories, our private family wake for the man we shared, who lived in each of us. It was helpful for me, to share the loss. We talked through ideas for his memorial service as I tried to mediate and keep a delicate family peace. Here I was again in Aspen, another weekend working for Hunter, doing Hunter duty, but no Hunter. I used to sit with him in Poppies late at night, reading aloud something he had just written, and he would slowly wave his hand back and forth, like a conductor, hearing the music and the rhythm of his words.

Hunter had left me a message on my machine, which I had picked up after New Year's. He was calling, he said, just to say he was thinking about our old times together, how much fun we had, something about those times being over, the good old days, the laughs, hitting the highwater mark. I had paid too little attention to the message; I didn't listen carefully enough. I didn't know it was goodbye. I had called him back, erased the message, and never heard from him again.

EVERYONE WAS IN love with Hunter, and everyone had something going on with him that felt individual and special to them, but everyone also knew that they shared Hunter with many others, and with multitudes. Each of us had held on to something precious, a time or moment when Hunter had been the catalyst for our journey. All wanted to be part of our tribute issue. I pulled in two former junior editors, Corey Seymour and Tobias Perse, who had helped me work with Hunter in the past (a job they described as "one part editorial assistant, one part cabana boy"), to help me assemble an oral history.

Johnny Depp was a teenager when he first read *Fear and Loathing in Las Vegas*. Like Hunter, he was raised in Louisville, Kentucky, another adolescent with lots of issues. The affinity was natural. Depp had lived with Hunter while getting ready for the *Vegas* film. He had picked up Hunter's nervous tics, sudden gestures, and whooping and screaming sounds. He even dressed in Hunter's clothes: "We would wade out of the house like freakish twins, a pair of deviant bookends on the prowl. He was the most present and loyal friend I ever had."

Sandy, his wife of eighteen years, wanted to "acknowledge and honor all the women who loved him…and there were many…we all felt his love…his tenderness…his pain." She knew him the longest and the best, that he was tortured, that he could become a "monster." Who knows what goes on in a marriage? His father died when Hunter was three, his mother was an alcoholic, his brother died of AIDS. Jack Nicholson was Hunter's peer in the fun, fame, and pussy game, barely hinting at it and instead talking about the presents Hunter had given his kids. The same presents he had given mine: the black plastic rat, the Bedazzler, and the hammer that made a frightening sound of shattering glass when you hit it.

Doug Brinkley, the historian,* met Hunter in 1993, and Hunter

---

* Brinkley's books include *The Wilderness Warrior: Theodore Roosevelt and the Crusade for America; The Unfinished Presidency: Jimmy Carter's Journey Beyond the White House;* and *Cronkite*.

designated him his official biographer. Through the years Hunter opened up his life to him; they were in constant touch, and slowly he let Doug into his heart of hearts. Doug wrote about Hunter's final months. The years had slammed him hard. He had broken his leg and had to spend three days detoxing before he could have surgery. He was in a wheelchair and could barely travel or make it up the stairs. He wore a diaper. He must have understood that he could almost certainly end up living in institutionalized care and would never be able to escape. Instead, he chose to die by his own hand, on his own terms, and at his own time.

Juan, his son, wrote, "He was a wild man, a brilliant writer, a warrior king."

TWO WEEKS LATER I was back in Aspen with Jane for a memorial at the Hotel Jerome, where Hunter had presided at the bar and had his campaign headquarters. It was a sunny mountain afternoon and a hundred of us were there: bartenders, dope dealers, the sheriff and some of his deputies, neighbors, locals who watched out for him, the football gamblers who gathered every Sunday at his house, a few fellow journalists, his several editors, movie stars, girlfriends, and family.

I brought the cover of the tribute issue with me, mounted on a four-by-five-foot board, which we set on an easel at the memorial. I had chosen the photo, a familiar one, his eyes looking down in mid thought, a thread of smoke curling up from the cigarette holder in his mouth. He was a handsome man. "Dr. Hunter S. Thompson 1937–2005. Tales from a Weird and Righteous American Saga." In the bottom right corner was a double-thumbed fist that held a peyote button shaped as a dagger, with one word across it: "Gonzo."

I had written a farewell to Hunter and read most of it as my eulogy. It was titled "My Brother in Arms." Every time I practiced reading it, editing it for speaking, I cried. Some phrase or scene or event put me in touch with how sad I really was. I missed him, and as I pronounced him gone, began to absorb that finality, I had found the words I wanted.

"These are sad days at *Rolling Stone*. I struck the National Affairs Desk from the masthead after thirty-five years. Hunter's name is now listed at the bottom, along with Ralph Gleason, on what Hunter would have called 'the honor roll.' It's very hard to give him up and say goodbye."

I began to describe our first meeting, how he poured out his satchel of paraphernalia on my desk; our first pieces, the Battle of Aspen, the Chicano rebellion in Los Angeles. Suddenly somebody was shouting, and I saw Warren Hinckle in the audience, my boss at the first job I ever had, and who had been Hunter's editor just before me. He was heckling me. The audience remained quiet; Hinckle's weird outburst added more electricity and drama to the moment.

I described a typical HST deadline, the logistics, personnel, tactics, writing strategies, food and fuel it would take, comparing it to a military siege. I talked about our life off duty, stories of "bad craziness" and gonzo behavior that everyone there shared: "It was part of what was so addictive about Hunter. It was an adrenaline rush to be with him. Walking with him, you knew you were likely going to come to the edge of the cliff, to sense danger, to get as close to the edge as most of us get in our lives."

The silence was total. I was the only one there. I was in the zone; I was speaking slowly, with dignity.

"We were both into politics and shared the same ambition, to have a voice in where this country was going, and we created the National Affairs Desk. We deliberately set out to do this and we became partners in this, as mad as it may have seemed at the time, a rock and roll magazine and a man known for writing about motorcycle gangs, joining forces to change the country.

"It was powerful stuff and it put both of us on the map in a big way. We could have probably done most of it each on our own, but together we let it roll and we hit the high note. It was scorching, it was original, and it was fun. He was my brother in arms.

"Now those days are gone. Once I had Hunter all to myself and now, I don't have him at all.

"His suicide was not careless, not an accident, and not selfish. He already lived longer than he, or any of us, had expected. He had lived a great life, filled with friends, his genius talent, and righteousness."

And then I read a letter from Hunter which I found while we were going through my files for the issue.

Dear Jann,

Just seeing you and me and Joe [Eszterhas] mentioned in the same paragraph still gives me an atavistic rush. My memory of those days is mainly of tremendous energy and talent and rare commitment running almost amok, but not quite. It was like being invited into a bonfire and finding out the fire is actually your friend. Ho ho . . .

But just how hot can you stand it brother, before your love will crack?

That was the real question in those days. I think. Or maybe it was just about how much money you were being paid. Or how much fun you were having. Who knows? Some people were fried to cinders, as I recall, and some people used the heat to transmogrify themselves into heroes. (Which reminds me that you still owe me a vast amount of money — and you still refuse to even discuss payment for my recent politics memo.)

Anyway, my central memory of the time was that everything we were doing seemed to work. Or almost everything. What the hell? Buy the ticket, take the ride, eh? Like an amusement park, or the Circus Circus Casino. It depended on your personal definition of "acceptable loss."

I know Joe considers his days at *Rolling Stone* to be an utter waste of time and talent, or maybe he just says that for his own vengeful reasons. Some people are too weird for their own good.

But me, Jann, I just say thanx for the rush.

Yr. Buddy, Hunter

426 • SETTLING DOWN

I don't remember whether there was applause or silence. Depp took me upstairs to his suite to show me a little surprise. He had on his table a scale model of a fifty-foot cannon he was going to have made, from which we would shoot Hunter's ashes.

For the record, Hunter and I never had a fight with each other, not once. I'm sure he called me a "cheap and greedy waterhead," and I called him "washed up and brain-dead," but he was always carrying on about people. I never canceled his health insurance when he was in Vietnam, nor did I secretly bury 7,000 first editions of *Vegas* to sell after his death. We were having fun, lots of it. I love him still and hope when I die I end up in the same place he is.

CHAPTER 62

HUNTER REDUX WITH JOHNNY DEPP

I HAD FIRST MET Johnny Depp when he was a wannabe rock star and charismatic teen actor. He was a student of the Beat era, a rock fanatic, a charmer, and created a secret world that you, as an honored person, entered into. He was not unlike Hunter. We bonded in the brotherhood of the wrong stuff. Johnny had three days off during filming of the second *Pirates of the Caribbean* movie and invited us to come down and hang. Matt and I chartered a sailboat named, oddly, *Darling*. We followed the winds for a few days to Dominica, a non-tourist island with black sand beaches and a rain forest. The *Black Pearl* had just arrived in the harbor, a barge done up like a pirate ship and rigged for filming. We all swam over because Johnny was anxious to have a reunion with it and see the crew. We took Johnny out scuba diving.

Dinners were aboard a motor yacht that he rented from Nicolas Cage. The interior had lots of Elvis photos and Elvis paraphernalia. Johnny had brought aboard all his stuff — scarves, candles, beads — and draped them over lights, walls, and couches, like Keith Richards' back-stage dressing room. We got good and drunk; he was well provisioned with high-end reds. On the second night we had the big Hunter talk. We were having one more night with the Good Doctor.

Johnny was troubled and finally explained that he hadn't returned calls from Hunter in the last year or so. It was a tough confession to make, that he had turned his back on Hunter when he was reaching out for help or perhaps just a hand to hold. Hunter had made Johnny a totem for his life, and Johnny had created an enchanted version of Hunter, a living, breathing sculpture. Johnny had become central to his life. He loved the charming and magical Mr. Depp — Johnny was a touchstone for him. My instinct was that Hunter saw Johnny as the curator and custodian of his ethereal estate.

But when the movie's over, it's over. Everyone goes home. I had also been out of touch with Hunter, other than through sporadic phone calls. Talking with Hunter was frustrating; he wanted to discuss stories I knew he wouldn't be able to write. Being with him in person meant drugs, and the more coke he took, the more ineffective and unfunny he became. I didn't like being around it. I told all this to Johnny. Telling him my story made us both feel better. Hunter wasn't having fun anymore; he had become a burden. Johnny was young, a druggie, a movie star, and maybe that's why he wouldn't pick up the phone. I gave him forgiveness. He loved Hunter, and I knew it.

The visit had been great for the both of us, in a way I had never expected. I needed someone to console me and help me, who could understand and share the tragedy and the guilt that comes with it. He needed it, too, which I hadn't realized, and we went deep. The person I needed to answer my questions turned out to be Johnny. Or Hunter in the person of Johnny? I could have both my confession and one more rambling night? "When the going gets weird," Hunter used to say, "the weird turn pro." Selah.

JOHNNY MOVED AHEAD with his salute to Hunter, a cannon the height of the Statue of Liberty. It cost him a million bucks. Hunter would have been thrilled to see such a spectacle as a way to say goodbye to him. In fact, it had been his idea in the first place. He dreamed it up in 1977 and asked Ralph Steadman to make a drawing of a Gonzo Fist Memorial.

Johnny brought in movie-production people and erected the cannon in the field behind Hunter's house. In front of it was a tented pavilion for a party, hung with memorabilia, stuffed peacocks, blow-up sex dolls, and photos of Hunter's literary heroes. Ten mortar shells packed with gunpowder launched Hunter's ashes from the cannon while Norman Greenbaum's voice rang out "Spirit in the Sky."

I had driven out with George McGovern and John Kerry. John said he offered Hunter the vice presidency the last time he saw him. George, the gentlest person I'd ever met to run for public office, found in Hunter a man of "deep goodness and justice and compassion and idealism." They had come to pay a grateful nation's final respects, and I was proud to walk with them.

It was a king hell spectacle, and people came from far and wide. I spoke again, but I had already said goodbye. The one last thing I wanted to do was a proper biography of Hunter, so I used our tribute issue as the basis for an oral history, which I edited into a remarkably revealing biography, far and away the best book about Hunter until Brinkley does his. I read in the obituaries that *Fear and Loathing in Las Vegas* was a "landmark, defining work" like *Moby-Dick*, *The Adventures of Huckleberry Finn*, and *The Great Gatsby*, "peering into the best and worst mysteries of the American heart."

CHAPTER 63

MAGAZINE WARS

I HADN'T FULLY RECKONED with *US Weekly*, which was now overshadowing *Rolling Stone*. The competition with *People* was intense, and choosing our cover each week was a several-hundred-thousand-dollar decision that took steady nerves. I met with the top editors on Thursdays to review preliminary choices, to craft the two-to-ten words that would become the cover headline, and make some informed guesses about what *People* and the other celebrity magazines might do for the next week, how to program and counterpunch. *People* threw its weight around, writing big checks for interviews and exclusive photos. They always got the biggest weddings and the biggest babies. Our secondary competitors had the advantage of being willing to make stuff up. We had one hand tied behind our back thanks to my insistence on accuracy, fairness, and reasonably good taste. So we had to be plucky and fast on our feet.

Plucky, lucky. A photographer we worked with received a tip that Angelina Jolie was at a resort on the coast of Africa on a secret trip with then-married Brad Pitt. The tipster further specified a time and place where they walked every day and suggested we could "secretly" do a photo ambush. We got the photo, we got the proof, we had the worldwide scoop, the debut of Brangelina. The tipster was Angelina.

I MADE WILL DANA the managing editor of *Rolling Stone*. Will was from a divorced Connecticut family — country clubs, Taft boarding school to Middlebury College. When he first interviewed for a job in 1997, he critiqued, correctly, my pole positions in a show-off photo on the wall of me skiing off a cliff. In eighth grade he saw *Rolling Stone* in a record store and had read every issue since. His ninth grade "What I want to be" essay was about living in San Francisco and working at *Rolling Stone*.

There was the tingling sense of *Rolling Stone* coming alive again. Putting out the Hunter tribute issue reminded us of our roots, the richness of our history and our traditions, the promises we had made to ourselves.

Will had already brought in Matt Taibbi, who would turn out to be the closest we ever got again to Hunter. Matt was a Boston kid pushing the edge, coediting an English-language newspaper for the expat community in Moscow. He had already been kicked out of Uzbekistan, moved to Mongolia (where he was on the state basketball team), and was back in Moscow writing, drinking, and playing around with drugs. His dad was an on-air NBC correspondent. He had been expatriated back to the U.S., and Will found him looking for work.

For his first piece Matt joined the Kerry press caravan, dressed up in a Viking costume. It brought some nice color and wit to a well-worn story line and had this little nugget of wisdom at the end: "Rather than focus on the whole country, the press corps focuses exclusively on a rigorously stage-managed soap opera of the democratic process, where all of America looks clean and hopeful. It's a never-ending advertisement for the health and functionality of the system, even though half the country considers the system neither healthy nor functional. The campaign represents a bunch of rich people talking to each other in front of the help."

Taibbi stood out from the get-go. He covered such things as Burning Man and the Michael Jackson trial, which were no-brainers if you wanted something to mock. When he spent a month on Capitol Hill with Bernie Sanders' staff working on legislation, or when he went undercover as a GOP campaign volunteer in Florida, it got special. He was a political animal, a beast and an angry one.

OUR CLIMATE COVERAGE was outpacing everyone other than the science journals. Our principal environment writer, Jeff Goodell, was in his eighteenth year at *Rolling Stone*. Bill McKibben had been a regular contributor since 1989. He — like Jeff — was born in Silicon Valley. Bill had been editor of the *Harvard Crimson*. Tim Dickinson covered the look of it from the West Coast or traveled to Washington, D.C., for reports on the crime scene. Al Gore regularly contributed essays and manifestos. They were a formidable team. Environmental reporting and writing would be one of the great parts of our legacy. We published yet another special section trying to raise the alarm, titled "The Planetary Emergency." McKibben pulled the science together, writing, "We are entering the 'Oh Shit!' era of global warming." Al Gore helped edit the issue and wrote in the opening manifesto, "Stronger hurricanes and typhoons represent only one of many new dangers as we begin what someone has called a nature hike through the Book of Revelation." He quoted Churchill speaking about the rise of the Third Reich: "The era of procrastination, of half-measures, of soothing and baffling expedients, of delays, is coming to a close. In its place, we are entering a period of consequences."

THEO GRADUATED FROM boarding school; he had been on the bicycle team, raced kayaks, milked cows, and chose to study photography. His girlfriend was a concert violinist and his two best friends were the grandson of Pierre Matisse and the godson of Wavy Gravy. I asked Sebastião Salgado to give Theo a summer internship at his studio in Paris, where he would get his very own master class working on projects under Sebastião's tutelage. Matt and I were on our way to a summer visit to Patmos in Greece and stopped in to see my beautiful teenage son, eating baguettes and cheese on benches in the dappled light of Paris in June. He was staying at Annie Leibovitz's apartment on the Left Bank. Some kids have no luck.

On our way home from Patmos we stopped in Dublin to see U2 play at a new soccer stadium that had been built on the site of the original Bloody Sunday massacre. Onstage, Bono wore a headband decorated with the Islamic crescent, the Star of David, and the cross. It was revelatory for me, as Bono showed himself to be a preacher, a religious and political figure channeling Martin Luther King Jr. His vision of brotherhood in a time of hostile seas frightened me. His wife, Ali, was standing with me, and I asked her if she was worried about someone taking a shot at him, as had happened to the Reverend King. I didn't want to cause her anxiety, but she said sometimes she was terrified.

We hung out with the band after the show at the hotel they owned in Dublin. We lunched the next day at the home of their manager, Paul McGuinness. I told him I wanted to do a big interview with Bono, like the ones I had done with Mick and John Lennon.

HURRICANE KATRINA WHOMPED and nearly destroyed New Orleans. The levees burst and left bloated bodies floating in the streets and tens of thousands of people stranded in football stadiums. It had struck at the birthplace of jazz, the cradle of R&B, a genetic link to rock and roll. Millions of dollars were raised from concerts and telethons by the music world. It was a disaster that exposed truths about racial injustice almost as ugly as a forest of trees with black bodies hanging from the branches. We quoted Jesse Jackson saying that the shelters reminded him of "the hull of a slave ship." Bush floundered and fumbled. Katrina killed Bush, whom I had come to despise, and I was happy to help put another nail in his political coffin whenever possible.

Matt Taibbi hooked up with Doug Brinkley and Sean Penn to chronicle their volunteer rescue efforts, working in the oozing beast with fouled black water in its bleeding veins. I followed the story on CNN, watching as Anderson Cooper betrayed his own grief and horror. Sometimes he openly wept. It was the most honest reporting I'd seen. We interviewed him for the issue: "I think it's a copout to get caught up in this 'I've seen it all' crap. Your job is to come here and be moved. Open your eyes, and open your ears, and heart, and relay that. It's very simple. It's not brain surgery; it's not really a very impressive thing to do, but you have to do it consistently and fairly; and if you can't do that, if you can't keep your mind and your eyes open, then you ought to leave the business."

Words to live by.

I TRIED TO BACK out of interviewing Bono because of all the work involved and the fear of not doing a good job. I loved listening to their old records but hadn't mastered them, didn't know the lyrics, didn't recognize songs by the first chords or their titles. I called up McGuinness to back out, but he wouldn't let go. Bono was prepared, they had allocated his time. It was too late to change. In fact, in two weeks they would be in Cancún, Mexico, between stops on the *Vertigo* tour, saving them tax-free days in the States, and I was expected.

Bono had rented a house on the ocean, at the edge of the jungle. The night before, they chased off two jaguars, and a humongous boa constrictor was in the driveway when I got there. Matt and the McGuinnesses had flown off earlier in the day to climb a Mayan temple. Bono's kids were terrorizing the house. A tropical storm was gathering; we talked until dinner and resumed the next day, ten hours in all. He is Irish. He loves to tell a story, setting a scene, then backing up with the relevant history and character biographies, and then, with his full imitative powers of dialogue, moves into his narrative. The characters are as often a pub owner as a prime minister.

Because his songs were so plainly autobiographical and anchored to specific locations, talking to him about songwriting was going to be talking about his life. To get to the man, I began with the boy. Bono had grown up in a lower-class neighborhood with a "constant sense that violence was around the corner." His mother and grandfather died within days of each other, and he and his brother were raised by his father, "a house of men, and all that goes with that. Quite macho men, and the aggression thing is something I'm still working on. That level of aggression is neither normal nor appropriate. We were not really encouraged to have big ideas, musically or otherwise. To dream was to be disappointed. The blandness — its very grayness — is the thing you have to overcome." The father-son relationship was a key to Bono; I told him I thought he owed his father an apology, not the other way around. He started to figure that out for himself as we talked.

By the end of the next day we had gotten to know each other well. Another brother. McGuinness had been telling him how much alike the two of us were. The last question was whether he had found what he was looking for: "I wasn't looking for grace, but luckily grace was looking for me."

IN EARLY NOVEMBER I made a few whirlwind trips to Las Vegas to check out the idea of building a *Rolling Stone* hotel. We had been approached by a real estate developer who had a huge nonrefundable deposit for us. I never liked Las Vegas. But it was fun to imagine a guitar-shaped swimming pool, a nightlife complex of blues clubs, folk music coffee shops, rock joints, and, my favorite, the Chapel of Love, where you could tie the knot. In the end I was spared a life of twisting arms, restless nights, and sunning by day at the Fender pool. I floated the idea that if the Stones guaranteed to play there once a year, they would get a piece of the action, the way Frank Sinatra had done at the Sands. It was all scheme and dream. One upshot, though, was that Mick and I finally came to an agreement on the joint ownership of the *Rolling Stone* name. We signed the agreement, nothing changed, we went our merry ways and never had a problem. It always gave Mick and me a bit of shtick at dinner parties, with a mock showdown over whose name it was. Did he own the magazine, or did I start the group? We also had laughs when I would take guests with me for a visit to his backstage dressing room. To amuse my friends, we would sort through his wardrobe trunks and pick out his outfits for me to try on. Mick sent me a note: "In return for my consent to allow you to register the name 'Rolling Stone,' what do you offer so far as cover stories, special small ad rates, and summer clothes coverage?"

FROM VEGAS I went to Los Angeles to meet Matt and see the Stones at the Hollywood Bowl. We took Tom Hanks and his vivacious and hilarious wife, Rita Wilson, and after the usual backstage backslaps and comedy from Keith, we went to find our seats. The Hollywood Bowl has boxes in front of the low stage, and we were in the center box, less than ten feet from the stage. I was in eye contact with Mick the whole evening. I wish I could say it had been the concert experience of my life; it certainly was the greatest seat of my life. But I was trying not to distract him — which I'm now sure was unnecessary — so I kept my own singing and waving arms in check. Furthermore, it was almost clinical, watching Mick and everyone onstage in the closest-up view, examining and dissecting the performance. It was less than ecstatic — more like fascinating. Mick asked me about it afterward. He said I barely moved, no matter how hard he had tried. Sometimes you are just too cool for your own good: "I worked my butt off, and you didn't even tap your toes."

ON THE WAY back to New York we stopped in Idaho to see our new home. We had been trying to expand our privacy at Broadford Farm, but we were trapped by a light industrial district to the north and a suburban sinkhole to the south. Then we came across an enormous all-glass house set in a private mountain valley, a river running through it, surrounded by some of the highest peaks in Idaho. It was tucked in at the base of the Pioneer Mountain range. It was 200 acres and surrounded by U.S. Forest Service land. Our nearest neighbors were a mile away,

Chuck Christopher and Cally Galpin, who had a shooting range that SEAL Team Six used for practice. The first time I saw the property with Matt, I was coming off a day of skiing and pot cookies, and couldn't keep my cool, even with the real estate agents following us. This was a dream, and I just had to have it. It was going to be my own private Idaho.

CHAPTER 64

THEY SAY IT'S YER BIRTHDAY

J ANE, MATT, BETTE, and Martin hosted my sixtieth-birthday party. I suspect that's the best of all birthdays: at last you've become smart, you still have your health and your looks. Getting older had so far turned out to be a good thing. You have achievements and satisfactions and you ain't done. No fat ladies lurk on the near horizon, whispering to themselves, measuring your box. Furthermore, you can afford to throw a party. And this might be the last chance.

Three banquet tables for fifty people each ran the length of Le Bernardin, one of my go-to restaurants and pretty fancy. There was a bottle of vodka in a block of ice at every other seat. The room was full of penguins and glittering dresses. My family was all there: my mother and sister came in from Hawaii, and I sat my mom next to John Kerry. Ned and Cathy came from San Francisco, and I sat them with David and Iman. Jane sat next to Michael; Matt sat next to Laurie David. I put myself with Patti Scialfa. That morning I got a telegram from Bob Dylan — "Happy Birthday, Jann. How does it feel? Now you know. Bob."

The evening began with a New Orleans brass band marching among the tables. Matt lined up people to deliver toasts throughout the dinner. Michael went first: "I'm getting tired of all this wunderkind bullshit. The reality is that Jann hasn't changed much in the thirty-five years I've known him, only he's richer and gayer...For years I thought Jann was just a wonderful and compassionate guy rather than a star fucker." He turned to Jane and Matt: "I might only add how complemented you are by a couple of people in your life. Jane, you've been an integral part of all of our lives for so long; and Matt, well, we saw you coming. You have conducted yourself like a true gentleman."

Ahmet got up. "Hello. I am a distant friend of Mr. Wenner's." He talked about our history together from the first issue to building the Hall of Fame. "And he is, with all his toughness, obtuseness, his difficult ways, one of the best friends I have ever had."

Sister Kate shared childhood stories about my earliest empire-building efforts. Caroline Kennedy recalled my picking her up at Harvard in a long white limousine: "I was captivated by his understated style...There aren't many people who are equally good friends with my mother, my brother, and myself. When John was looking for what to do, he looked around at the people he knew and asked himself, 'Who has the best life, the coolest friends, and the most fun?' And he decided to start a magazine. I am happy to be a part of your life."

"Hello, I'm Al Gore. I am a contributing writer to *Rolling Stone*. I used to be the next president of the United States...I am one of many who have stood in the arena and have looked around and asked, 'Who is going to help me?' John Kerry is here tonight — he was on the cover, too. He was one of the many over the years who have benefited from the passion, commitment, and intelligence of a man who was saying to all his readers, 'Here is what I believe is best for the United States of America and the world.'" Al was pouring sweat and he, like quite a few people by this point, had been hitting that vodka bottle. He was whipped up, and shouted, "In closing, the main point is, Jann Wenner is hot!"

It was around eleven when Bruce rose. He can quiet a crowd just by standing up. After a poke at my movie career, he told a story about his teenage years when he saw the first issue of *Rolling Stone*, with John Lennon on the cover, at a record store near his house. "I can't begin to tell you how shocking it was to find something that seemed to be speaking directly to me. For us young musicians in the outlands, it was the only thing we had that gave us information and inspiration about what we aspired to and what we hoped to be. And the community we wanted to be a part of. So, in honor of Jann, I have written a song, it's kind of a little bluesy thing. It goes:

> I got to know the man a little bit, by and by
> I've never seen so much innocence and cynicism walk side by side.
> I never guessed a man whose magazine once changed my life
> Would one day want to have a threesome with my wife.
>
> Champagne, pot cookies, and a Percocet
> Keep him humming like a Sabre jet
> Champagne, pot cookies, and a Percocet
> Keep him rolling stoned...
>
> I've been on the cover quite a few times, mon frère
> But these days I'm going to need tits, a bikini, and a belly wax to get me there
> The last time I figured was the very last, I supposed
> But now I'm up here kissing ass, so who knows?
>
> I told him I never did any drugs one night
> He said, 'Son, it's not too late to throw away your life.'
> Champagne, pot cookies, and a Percocet
> And you'll be playing that guitar mellow
> I called him a few days after the election was done
> And all he said was, 'Fuck, there goes our ride on Air Force One.'
> Big finish:
> I'd like to say happy birthday old man, and thanks for the good years

And for the message you sent back in the day that said, 'You ain't alone out there.'

So, if this song tonight don't have my debt covered

I know just what I am gonna send one old crazy motherfucker

Champagne, pot cookies, and a Percocet. A lot of years gone, a lot better coming yet."

I should have died and gone to heaven right there. But Robin Williams got up to close the evening, drunk, literally one night away from rehab. Matt had told him to "go as low as you want to go." He came up with a revival-tent gloss on *Brokeback Mountain* that began, "Long before there was a Cocksucker Ranch, there was two men being rump wranglers, way before everybody else. Yes, indeed! He has lived beyond us all, now that is true, and we're here right now to say, 'God bless you, Hebrew.' Matt said to go way low, oh, dear sweet Jesus, you know what we know."

I heard shouts of "Hallelujah." I was laughing my head off but saw Jane frowning. I could see her friends sending her protective grimaces. I had the three kids there, but it was for them to deal with what was, in the end, love and acceptance. Robin was having a good roll, quite in control even if unhinged. He kept going lower, taking the "jism trail" up *Brokeback Mountain*. "Happy birthday, Brother Jann," he said, and presented us with a pair of handcuffs, so even though we couldn't get married "at least you are fucking joined forever. I say dear Jann, dear Matt, enjoy yourself in wedded bliss. Until that day you can be one together. Let us enjoy ourselves no matter. Sweet Jesus, amen."

Round midnight, Paul Shaffer and the Hall of Fame Orchestra, as we called it, plugged in. John Mayer opened and brought Gus up to play with him; Robbie played a New Orleans ballad that Dylan had taught him; John Mellencamp did "Wild Night." Peter Wolf was the emcee, dressed in black, black hair flying, juking and jiving like it was talent night at the Apollo. He did a Sam Cooke song and "Looking for a Love."

Paul brought up Darlene Love, who performed "River Deep, Mountain High." Then she sang "He's a Rebel."

Bette took the stage: "There's so much love in this room. So much money, too. I don't want to follow Darlene, so come back up, honey, and sing this old chestnut with me." They sang "Da Doo Ron Ron," but this version was "Da Doo Jann Jann." She did some banter about my asking her not to sing "Wind Beneath My Wings," and then sang a gorgeous weeper, "The Glory of Love," also from *Beaches*. What I wanted to hear was "The Rose," a song of fear and the redemption of love: "It's the heart, afraid of breaking / That never learns to dance / ... It's the one who won't be taken / Who cannot seem to give." She could make me laugh; she could sing and make me cry. One of the people in the world I felt closest to.

Standing by the cake, I thanked those who raised toasts. "You have been my friends for many, many years. The things you said tonight are hard to take in and not say, 'Wow. Is that me?' If I were to look out tonight and say that at sixty it's over, I would just have to say, 'Gosh, it's enough. I was lucky. What a chance to have good times, to laugh, to take great risks, and to do great things. To work with John and Al, and all of you, to try to change the country and make lives better. That was my great honor.'"

Matt and I stayed there with Bruce and Patti till three thirty, replaying the night. We were the last to head home.

THE YEAR HAD the best snowfall and ski conditions in two decades. I was sixty and still getting better and faster. Gus was getting better, too. He was sixteen, a strong, athletic kid with glutes. "Making the call," i.e., choosing the runs, requires a knowledge not only of the hill but also how the conditions change based on the weather, crowd patterns, and time of day. It's sensing the vibe for the day, tailored to the group, and finally making a story, a plot that has narrative and maybe a little character development.

I'm serious. If you're with a good skier, let them make the dance card and find yourself on the tail of amazing tracks, maybe a few secret stashes. You want to be on that train when it comes by. Most of the time I made the calls. One day I noticed Gus making a call, and then another, more of a challenging run than I would likely have picked. Then another, another, and I realized I was following him. He was now the lead dog. He made a few cracks: "Torches were passed, egos were shattered." I was so proud.

I WENT AFTER SEAN WILENTZ, a Princeton professor whom Arthur Schlesinger Jr. called "one of the best historians of his generation," and asked him to take a dispassionate look at Bush in a historical comparison to all other American presidents. There were a handful of fairly bad presidents, but when Wilentz laid out the historical record, it was unmistakable: Bush was the worst in 230 years, "The Worst President in American History." I gave the story to Bob Grossman, who gave me back a cartoon of Bush sitting on a stool in the corner of a classroom with a dunce cap on his head. It was simple and damning, an image worth a million words.

After we came out with the dunce cover, the establishment press began to shift. Whereas they had been perplexed by how to present Bush as president, now there was an acknowledgment that we were being misled by a terribly, woefully bad president. Al had won the popular vote but lost the election in the Supreme Court. As a result we went to war, and had the worst economic collapse since the Depression and an incalculable setback on climate. Al could have been one of the best presidents ever — he had aptitude, energy, experience, and a moral compass.

WE DID TWO more preelection issues, and I couldn't restrain myself. Bob Grossman did a cover of the dome of the Capitol tipped open and figures popping out dressed as pigs drooling for cash, oil wells holding money, fundamentalists, torturers holding battery cables, Lady Justice peeking through a blindfold, and a congressman chasing a male page around the roof. Matt Taibbi wrote, "Very little sums up the record of the U.S. Congress in the Bush years better than a half-mad, boy addict put in charge of a federal commission on child exploitation."

WHEN THE ELECTION was over, we published a meticulous investigation and presented extraordinary evidence, never challenged or discredited, that stated that Bush had stolen the 2004 election. Exit polls — not preelection surveys — that were highly accurate and considered almost a science had Kerry ahead and winning beyond the margin of error in Ohio. Kerry led in the exit polls by 8.8 percent but lost by 2.1 percent in the final count. The secretary of state in Ohio was Bush's campaign chairman; the irregularities at Ohio polling places were specific and widespread. The reporting team was led by Bobby Kennedy, Tim Dickinson, our top political reporter, and a special research unit. It was heartbreaking.

CHAPTER 65

THE WHEEL OF LIFE

MATT AND I were keeping a secret: we were having a baby. With only Gus in the house, Matt had discovered how devoted he had become to the boys, taking them to the park, buying skateboards, helping to make a papier-mâché Eiffel Tower for French class. It had come so naturally and been so rich with purpose that he wanted another child, one of our own. I had heard Jane call Matt "their stepmother." That was snarky, and funny, but it was a reminder that it's a tough slot. It was the best kind of secret to share. And a secret it would remain.

When it came time to tell the kids, in my enthusiasm I thought it would go down pretty hunky-dory. I gave Jane a heads-up but she took it hard, which she didn't conceal, and so the kids figured that something ominous was afoot. I scheduled a family dinner to share the good news, and they were by then expecting something bad. I was oblivious to the dynamic, and startled when Theo and Gus stood up and stared hard at me. One of them said, "I don't even know you anymore," and walked out of the restaurant. It broke my heart.

In the first few years of the separation, holding on to the boys and their love was a key to my happiness and sense of self. At no price would I lose these kids. Now I was hearing old echoes and ricochets, faint but fearful. Back at the house I talked with Gus, who was crying. He wasn't against a sibling, but he did not want to accept Matt. He had held the anger for years and now he burst out that he "hated" him. I looked my little, curly-haired man in the eye and asked, "Do you want me to be alone?" He was quiet and then whispered, "No." A few days later Theo gave me his wisdom: "Dad, this is not a science experiment."

When August came I waited outside the swinging doors until Matt walked out, wet with tears, in a hospital gown, holding a newborn baby boy. Two days later we were in our new home in Sun Valley with Noah Jaspar Nye Wenner. His first visitor was Rita Wilson. Gil and Janet Friesen, with their new baby boy, came for a cozy new-parents weekend. They had held our hands the whole way. Matt and I cocooned with the swaddled infant. As a parent you are doing God's work, and every aspect of it, however trivial or ordinary, is joy and humility. Changing dirty diapers is an act of love. We stayed put in the mountains for a month.

THE TIME HAD come to put out our thousandth issue. A three-dimensional cover had been on my idea list for a few years. I wanted to re-create the *Sgt. Pepper's* concept, so we made a collage of a hundred or so people in our world, plus the Gonzo fist and a flaming Stratocaster. I figured we could sell a 3D back cover to an advertiser to help pay for it and offered it to Steve Jobs. I wanted the Apple logo, not a beer can. Steve got back to me with a yes, but he called a week late. Target already had taken it, so the back cover was their pretty cool bull's-eye. No magazine I could remember had been so self-referential and had put out more special issues about itself than we had. We threw a party to celebrate the event. Solomon Burke played a set and so did the Strokes, with Eddie Vedder and Lou Reed joining them.

US WEEKLY HAD its all-time biggest issue with "Janet Jackson: How I Got Thin: Sixty Pounds in Four Months." Britney and Brangelina were still big-time breadwinners. There was a confluence of pop-culture rivers with *Rolling Stone* — e.g., John Mayer said Jessica Simpson was "sexual napalm." We started an *US Weekly* website, and it went through the roof.

Bob Iger, who had succeeded Michael Eisner as CEO of Disney, took me out to lunch at the Four Seasons and told me he wanted to sell their half ownership in *US*. I had wanted us to merge *ESPN* magazine, which Disney owned, with *Rolling Stone* and *US* and have the fourth-biggest magazine company in the country. A year earlier, Eisner's top financial guy offered to sell me the Disney share at a price we could privately negotiate. I was happy to have Disney as a passive partner, and I had passed on that without thinking it all the way through. It would have been the shrewd move. *US Weekly* was making $50 million a year, after *People* possibly the most profitable magazine in America, and I had even made the *Vanity Fair* "New Establishment" list for a few years.

I was not going to let go of control, and I was assured we could easily borrow from a bank. No one was sounding any alarms or giving me the slightest counsel on the consequences of taking on that kind of debt, i.e., I would owe a bank $300 million to buy Disney out. I put up the whole company, including *Rolling Stone*, as collateral. No warning bell sounded. I didn't ask anyone about it, and puffed myself up with the idea of owning something valued at $600 million, on top of what *Men's Journal* and *Rolling Stone* were worth on their own. At the high end, the market was near its top, and this was plausibly the billion-dollar enchilada.

At the same time we were in discussions with Hearst, which had made an offer for the whole company. They promised me independence. We started to negotiate a deal in which they would buy 25 percent of everything and would have a path to buy the rest of it within a few years. In other words, the strength and stability of a huge company as well as independence, at least on paper. The deal was fully negotiated. I asked for a weekend to consider it.

What did I really want? I hadn't had that discussion with myself, even though I had pushed the negotiations forward. The business guys, especially Kent Brownridge, who had come to work for me in 1972 and had become my all-purpose general manager and right-hand man in business, put no pressure on me despite the potential payday for himself; neither did my longtime counselor, Ben Needell. Of course, lawyers are always making money either way — up, down, and especially around. Jane would walk away a wealthy, beautiful divorcée. Matt would have to live with the impact on me. It was a decision I would have to make on my own. The two big what-ifs were, what would I do with myself and what would I do with all that money?

Picassos? Gauguins? Légers? A yacht? I already had a plane that could take me anywhere on the planet with a few hours' notice. I thought the odds were fifty-fifty at the very best that I would last as someone else's employee for more than a year. Teach? Travel? What would I do with all my energy? I loved public policy and had an eye for politics, a pretty shrewd sense for the long game, but neither the patience nor nuance to practice it. It was too much work in any case.

As talented and as passionate as I was, I didn't think I would ever be able to repeat the success of *Rolling Stone*. I could start another magazine, for sure, and a good one, but it would never have that magic, that mojo.

My social life and my friends? So much of that was based on *Rolling Stone* and the opportunity it afforded me to be places, share experiences, and have a meaningful role in music and with the artists I loved. As editor of *Rolling Stone* I had access to a rarefied world of musicians who prized substance and currency. It was my world.

What I had been given, the responsibilities and the purpose, could not be traded for money that I had no need for. Having so much money didn't mean that much to me. The risk was enormous, the reward meant little, and I said no. I never regretted it.

IN LIEU OF a baptism or circumcision for Noah, we had a blessing ceremony at Bette's triplex on upper Fifth Avenue overlooking the reservoir. Zac Posen made Noah a gown. The Buddhist scholar Robert Thurman said the prayers, in both English and Tibetan, and passed along some of his Buddhist wisdom. Janet Friesen, Gil's wife, came; she was one of

Noah's godmothers; Bette was the other. His godfathers were there, too: Ned Topham and Sean Lennon. Bette serenaded her godson, playing a ukulele and singing "Take Me Out to the Ball Game." Bruce and Patti came, Ahmet and Mica. Jane came with our three boys. David Bowie and Iman held the baby for the blessing. We drank champagne and Ahmet made a toast. It was the last time I saw him alive.

THE STONES WERE filming with Martin Scorsese at the Beacon Theatre in front of sixteen movie cameras and a private audience. Ahmet went backstage to visit Keith and fell backward on the stairs. He was taken to the hospital and the next day went into a coma. A watch began in the cold, featureless corridors with silent doors that guard the rooms of the sick and dying. I went over twice a week. Mica had uncommon strength and composure, but she was scared. Her life was Ahmet. The idea that a man of such power and love of life could so suddenly disappear was unsettling to our certitudes about great men.

Mica and I would sit on either side of him as he lay motionless in bed. One evening I said to her how amazing Ahmet looked. They had been shaving him and keeping him groomed. In fact, he looked healthier than I had seen him in years. "Well, of course he looks good," Mica said. "He hasn't been drinking."

AHMET WAS EIGHTY-THREE when he died. We flew with his body to Istanbul. It was an overnight flight, an eerie passage, with a coffin in the forward cargo hold and a dozen of us huddled in the nearly empty cabin of a chartered commercial jet. We planned a quick stop in London for Mick and Jimmy Page, but they couldn't make it; both paid very substantial homage soon enough. Linda Wachner, Johnny Pigozzi, Lyor Cohen, and Kid Rock were with us. Lyor was new to Ahmet's life, but as the current president of Atlantic Records had an important symbolic role, which he handled with dignity. Bobby Ritchie, a.k.a. Kid Rock, had been an addition to Ahmet's life in recent years, and the two of them adored each other. Forever young.

The next day Ahmet's body lay in a grand mosque, open to any Muslim but not to nonbelievers. We stood outside as he was taken back by his faith and his homeland. His body was carried out by hundreds of mourners, and we could not get close. The coffin was escorted by a government motorcade sent by the president of Turkey up the hills to a Sufi house of worship, a tekke, with a grand view of Istanbul. The body was wrapped and lowered into a dirt grave in the garden. Ahmet was buried next to his brother, his father, his grandfather, and his great-grandfather, the sheik who had founded the tekke, the first one in Turkey. I stood there for a while with Mica, who was unmoving. They had been together fifty years, and now Ahmet was unalterably gone, and what seemed to lie ahead was empty. She was as strong as anyone I knew, but now she was so utterly alone.

I looked into his grave, at his shrouded body, and in my mind said what I wanted to say to him. He had reached out, guided me, and had loved me. With Ahmet's death, as had happened before when I said a final farewell to someone important in my life, I breathed in and breathed out and breathed in and tried to feel his wisdom enter me.

CHAPTER 66

≤🖎

IS IT ROLLING, BOB?

OUR FIRST PROFILE of Barack Obama, titled "Destiny's Child," had a painting of him, arms carefully folded, a stately red curtain behind him, looking presciently presidential. A detail that might seem trivial, but which I found fundamental, was that he acknowledged using marijuana and cocaine in school. It was time to stand up and unequivocally call bullshit on this culture-war crap. If you didn't have the balls, the honesty, and the smarts, after all this time, then I wasn't all in. Obama said something else I thought very intriguing for a forty-year-old: "Just being president is not a good way of thinking about it. You want to be a great president."

Our writer Ben Wallace-Wells visited Trinity United Church of Christ in Chicago, to which Obama belonged. It was led by Reverend Jeremiah Wright. It wasn't Martin Luther King Jr. preaching; it was Malcolm X. We wrote about the Reverend Wright's history, reporting that lay dormant until the press made it a hot potato. We created the first crisis of his candidacy. It forced Obama to directly address race in an eloquent speech that was a high-water mark of his campaign.

I WAS OVERSEEING ROLLING STONE'S fortieth anniversary. Much like we had done two decades earlier, the three special issues would be interviews with major players of our past — the baby boom, more or less —

about what they had learned since their idealistic twenties. These were not personality profiles. We asked each for their thinking on the state of our times.

I did Bob Dylan, but it had to wait until three days before deadline. He was on tour; his only free day was in Amsterdam. Matt and I went to the Van Gogh Museum and the Rembrandt House Museum and bicycled around the canals. A beautiful city.

Bob has a grin that says mischief is in the air, and I know I'll soon be laughing about something. Hunter was that way. I was now on a bro-hug basis with Bob, but after the hugs, I become a reporter, with a legal pad and digital recorder. I am there on business and I am right on deadline. The sound file will be sent via the internet to New York ten minutes after it's done, and I'll have the transcript in the morning. No shooting the shit; I need every minute to get this right. Bob, of course, is in no hurry and not going to give up his fun. He has a new record, the first in a long while, a dark, resigned statement. I want to discuss why he's feeling that way. Bob doesn't want to.

YOU'VE BEEN ON *the road pretty steadily for forty years. What is it that is so enjoyable?*

The groupies and the drinking and the parties backstage. Why would anybody? Performers are still performers. Why do you edit your magazine?

You just released this amazing new record, Modern Times. *Is there a general theme?*

You would probably have to ask every individual person who hears it. It probably means many different things on many different levels to many different kinds of people.

Do you think it looks gloomy on the horizon?

In what sense do you mean?

Bob, come on.

No, *you* come on. In what sense do you mean that? If you're talking about a political sense…

In a general political/spiritual/historical sense. You are talking about the end of times on this record, you've got a very gloomy vision, you're saying, "I'm facing the end of my life and looking at all this…"

Aren't we all always doing that?

No, some people are trying to avoid it. But I am trying to interview you, and you're not being very helpful with it.

Jann, have I ever been helpful?

You have been in the past.

Yeah, but I wasn't on tour when I was doing them. Now I'm thinking about amps going out and…

You don't have people taking care of these for you?

You would hope.

You can't find a good road manager? Is that the problem here?

Yeah.

What can I do to get you to take this seriously?

I am taking it seriously.

No, you're not.

Of course I am. You're the one who's here to be celebrated. Forty years now with a magazine that obviously has intellectual recognition. Did you ever think that would happen when you started?

Look how far you've come. You're the one to be interviewed. I want to know just as much from you as you want to know from me. I would love to have you on our radio show and interview you for an hour. You've seen more music changes than me.

Oh, please.

No, no please. You please, you've seen it all from the top…I've seen it maybe from…also near the top.

AT THIS POINT we just looked at each other and began to laugh. I had gotten worried. I didn't really think Bob was going to leave me empty-handed, but the presses were ready, and I was in the hands of fate. Bob went on and talked about the "old America" he grew up in, and the metaphysical weight of the atom bomb on modern civilization and faith. It turned out to be personal stuff, which he usually preferred to leave obscure. I thought the opening was funny and to print it would be a treat for Dylan lovers. Everyone loved it, especially Bob.

I HAD ONE MORE thing to do for Ahmet, his memorial. We began with a band led by Wynton Marsalis, winding through a packed theater at Lincoln Center. Solomon Burke spoke, sitting in a red-velvet chair built for his XXXL frame, and introduced Eric Clapton, in a proper suit and tie, who played some of Ahmet's favorites. Ahmet loved his friendship with Henry Kissinger, and I knew that it would please him to no end to have Henry honor him. Henry told funny stories from their travels together; he caught the boyish essence of his irascible friend. It was a tender eulogy. Bette sang "Princess Poo-Poo-Ly Has Plenty Papaya," accompanied by a ukulele. Crosby, Stills, Nash & Young reunited; Neil and Stephen as a duet did "Mr. Soul." Many of the early Atlantic greats were long gone, but the second wave of Ahmet's historic signings all came to pay homage, like Jimmy Page and Robert Plant.

When I spoke, I looked down at Mica, at whom I'd been glancing throughout. She seemed to me in great pain from the memories that deepened the intensity of her loss. I told a few Ahmet stories, including the one about sitting at his bedside with Mica. I said, "To have lived a life so filled with music, to have been so deeply a part of it, and to have contributed so greatly to it. To have always been insistent on doing the right thing, to have lived so fully, and to have had so much fun. How lucky the world has been to have such a man. How lucky for me to have had such a friend."

Mick was the last speaker. He said he had heard Ahmet referred to as a father figure, but to him Ahmet was the "wicked uncle with the wicked chuckle." The stories he told, "My Adventures with Uncle Ahmet," were hilarious but never too risqué. Everyone fell under the charm of Mick's twinkling toothy smile and laughter. Mick had meant the world to Ahmet; he indeed had been his wicked uncle, and Mick brought Ahmet onstage one last time.

GUS STARTED A summer internship at *Rolling Stone*. He was one of those appealing, enthusiastic, and clever kids to whom everyone gravitates. He could write, too, so he was doing news items and tiny profiles of new artists. I was flying out to Chicago to meet Robbie, who was playing with Eric at the Crossroads Guitar Festival, and asked Gus to come with me on a father-and-son trip. We had done a lot of ski trips but this was a business trip with Dad, if you want to call a blues festival a business trip. No goofing around. You are with the old man, in his workplace.

David Fricke had an interview scheduled with Eric. Gus and I were seeing a different side of things from backstage, so I told Gus he ought to write a piece, too. John Mayer sat down with him for an interview. I watched Gus write the first draft of his story in a reporter's notebook on the plane back. I checked over his shoulder and was shocked to see how he put it together. He deftly broke up and moved quotes and scenes for better effect, wove the incidental color and data into casual phrases and subordinate asides. He picked up something Robbie said to me and led with it: "All that was left was a pile of burning guitars." Gus brought the reader backstage, and wrote it with economy and flair. We printed what was essentially his first draft, with his byline at the top of the piece. He was sixteen and could have joined *Rolling Stone* then and there.

THE CLINTON GLOBAL INITIATIVE had its annual conference at a hotel two blocks from our office. The night before, Matt and I had dinner with Al and Tipper, and then went with them to catch a Melissa Etheridge show. Bill had invited Al to speak at the conference at the last minute, when he heard Al was in town. Seeing them on the panel together was funny, as each of them, by second nature, tried to top the other with tales of the great humanitarian efforts for which each was responsible.

Steve Bing, a wealthy real estate heir with a love of politics and rock and roll, took me to the green room; Mick came, too, and the three of us sat and listened to Bill handicap the elections. Brad Pitt was also speaking at the conference there. I had never met him. He was so exquisitely tailored that his silk suit made his face look ordinary. He had come to give a presentation about the affordable houses he was building in New Orleans, and we talked a bit about architecture. He seemed like a genuine guy.

Obama came up to my office for a private dinner, tall, thin, and all business. I didn't get any of that charismatic rhetoric or the hip wit. We talked politics, not policy. Two things stuck out: how much younger than me he was, and that he took notes. He seemed a very serious man, and I had the feeling a real person was there, not some rehearsed act. He was quite direct, unusually so for a politician, and wasn't carefully turning his conversation to conceal a lack of knowledge or duck anything controversial. I couldn't make a judgment on his viability as a candidate nor did I sense any magic powers, but he was no bullshit. It was my first step on the road to Damascus.

I JUMPED IN TO work on the last of the three fortieth-anniversary special issues, the one in which we would look ahead to what was coming down the line. We had assigned interviews with Tim Berners-Lee, Craig Venter, Jane Goodall, and Bill Gates. Bill Clinton would be the closing interview, and Al would be the opener, which I would do myself.

We were going to have lunch at his home in Nashville. I was listening to *Slow Train Coming*, Bob's album about the reckoning, on the plane down, flying over the mountains and river valleys of Kentucky and Tennessee, images of the Civil War floating through my mind, in a fugue state about home, country, and roots. Al and Tipper were at their front door waiting for me with a bottle of Cristal; the very day before, he had won the Nobel Peace Prize. They had been up late celebrating with Sheryl Crow and the gang. There were hugs, kisses, and high fives.

Al threw steaks on the barbecue and set a bottle of Jamaican pepper sauce and a bottle of Château Latour on the picnic table and we settled in. When we got to dessert, Al brought out orange brandy and a box of chocolates. We talked about nature and the needs for the future and what would be his own best role. "What politics has become requires a tolerance for triviality, artifice, and nonsense that I personally find I have in short supply," he said. "We are the only nation capable of leading the world and establishing a set of conditions that can promote the general advance of justice and prosperity everywhere on the planet. Those challenges are currently seen as political problems, but they're actually moral imperatives in disguise, and we have to enhance our capacity for dealing with them. The survival of democracy depends on it."

WE SPENT A good amount of time with Bruce and Patti that fall. They did two shows at Madison Square Garden. One night backstage they had a present, and out comes this fancy bag tied with ribbons and wrapped in cellophane, and inside, a bottle of champagne, a plate of pot cookies, and a baggie with Percocets. Matt and I went down to the farm in New Jersey on weekends. They had horse pastures and riding trails in the woods. The main house had a long front porch with wicker chairs, a campfire going in front, and someone bringing out drinks on a tray. After years on the road and the intense inward focus that Bruce needed for his artistic process, as well as an emotional isolation he needed to manage his sanity, it was a delight to see him at ease.

Even with a bunch of people around he was still a loner, sitting quietly on the other side of the room. Patti, bless her soul, was a social, red-headed woman with the right mix of wonder and wisdom. She had an ethereal singing voice. We would laugh and laugh, and then analyze our friends, records, and America. They played Washington, D.C., and we went down to see the show. John Kerry was waiting backstage. Their older son, Evan, who was then doing an internship at *Rolling Stone*, came. Bruce dedicated "Thunder Road" to Matt and me. The police who escorted our car back to the airport had cleared the streets. Fans were lined up for a few blocks behind barricades. Bruce said, "Watch, I'm going to Pope it." He rolled down the window, stuck his head and arm out, and waved his hand to the crowd from the wrist down, like he was John XXIII. It was done with the utmost sincerity.

Bruce was a motorcycle guy. He had a few Harleys; he rode a custom one that took your full body weight on the brake to stop it. New Jersey has some beautiful roads. I got a guided tour of his childhood, the home where he was raised, and met the guy who lived there now. We went to his high school, his lower school, to the corner radio repair and record shop he patronized as a teen, and where he bought his first issue of *Rolling Stone*.

Seeing Bruce perform is a joy. I have never seen anyone take more pleasure from being onstage. His is total, radiant happiness. In a small out-of-town arena the vibe is easier, more relaxed — driving through quiet streets, parking backstage, walking in through the kitchen door. When you leave New York, journalists and industry folk no longer linger in hospitality suites or outside dressing rooms. You are not at a carnival. I generally don't visit just before a show because I don't want to disturb the equilibrium of the pre-performance process. Patti has a spacious setup. We smoke a few cigarettes, pour the red, shoot the shit until Bruce pops in and says it's time to go onstage.

In Hartford, Connecticut, on the *Working on a Dream* tour, Max Weinberg's son was sitting in on drums. There's a lot of buzz about this, and Bruce thinks it would make a perfect *Rolling Stone* story, which it will. Clarence Clemons, Bruce's iconic sax player, is taken from his dressing room to the stage on a golf cart. It's trimmed in purple. He has a cape on and he sits majestically. I notice a forklift, which places him onstage. This will be Clarence's last tour.

Watching Bruce work up close in a concert with the fans mobbed in front of the stage, you can see his ecstasy as they reach out to him while he's singing, bathing him with adoration and showering him with energy. It is a transfiguration, and unbelievable to witness. After the show Bruce throws his arms around me, wrestles me onto the couch, and lies on top of me. "Did you hear your name? I dedicated 'Outlaw Pete' to you." He knows my son Jude, his godson, loves that track. I get a tape of the show a few days later. I can see myself in the crowd, but it is him, leaning into worshippers, at the moment he splits the atom.

We went down to the farm for his sixtieth-birthday dinner on a perfect fall day, fifty or so people eating on the back lawn. Bruce had decided on relatives only, his and Patti's, so it felt like a Fourth of July picnic. Nobody from the band, just the household, Jon and Barbara Landau, Matt and me. I was grousing to myself, since U2 were opening that same night at Giants Stadium, just up the New Jersey Turnpike.

THE NEXT NIGHT we went to see U2. They were on a worldwide stadium tour, and the set was massive. They were playing a style of music made for huge venues, a modern electronic sound full of effects, echo, and synthesizers, and simulcasting the show on the multistory overhead screens built into the top of the stage that provided an up-close look for every seat in Giants Stadium, 75,000 blissed-out customers.

Bono gave me a ride over. On arrival, he decides to get out of the car and walk along the chain-link fence lined with fans. There's a solemnity, a formality to the gesture, almost like a religious leader and his faithful. The parking lot has what looks like a hundred semis, trailers, and buses that take the tour from city to city. There are actually two stages, which leapfrog each other on the tour, since it takes three days to set one up. When you drive down under the stadium you enter a nighttime world of people scuttling around on golf carts and forklifts, shuttling the paraphernalia and tools of this artificially lit, subterranean civilization.

The show pulls out all the stops, every one of them. We assemble near the exit, before the last song, to be a part of the "runner," the police-escorted caravan that leaves the stadium the minute the show finishes, to beat the traffic. The last song tonight is "Moment of Surrender," a hymn of suffering and redemption, a confession and plea, a very Bono mash-up of religion and mysticism, delivered as a hypnotic chant. I am mesmerized. The band leaves the stage, but Bono decides to run back up, one last message to the audience: "I want everyone to know we sold more tickets tonight than when the Pope was here last month."

BONO AND HIS family had moved around the corner from us on Central Park West. We could wave at each other from our terraces. He was usually out on some nighttime mission, but he was early to rise, and we would breakfast at each other's place or have afternoon tea with Ali and Matt. Ali was the least likely rock star wife I ever met. She was running a home with four kids and prepared to handle Bono and his parade on sudden notice. I don't believe that Bono, unlike Bruce, had been shy for even a minute of his life. I can talk a blue streak, but Bono can talk a category four storm. I don't know if we ever completely finished a topic. One night I went for dinner at the Spotted Pig, a semi-chic downtown watering hole. Rupert and Wendi Murdoch, Bill and Melinda Gates, and Sean Penn were waiting for us. This, I was learning, was a typical Bono collection. He was on a first-name basis with every important international leader except Putin...which would surely come later. Sean refused to sit at the same table with Murdoch and set up a chair nearby. I held Murdoch personally accountable for mainlining poison into American democracy, but nonetheless my instincts were to be cordial; there was nothing to be gained otherwise. Nothing I could say or do would cause him a millisecond of regret, nor would it make me feel any more righteous. What do you learn or accomplish by not talking with your adversaries? He said to me, "The trouble with you is you believe what you read in the New York Times." I said, "The trouble with you is that you believe what you read in the New York Post."

THE FORTIETH-ANNIVERSARY issue was anything but a celebration. We were conducting a colloquy about the future of America and humanity. The country was coming off an unleashed right-wing President that had started two wars and disfigured democratic safeguards. We walked away from global climate rescue. On the near horizon was the potential to elect a black or female president. What that would say about us. The special issue was heavy reading: two men who ran for president, plus scientists, political activists, economists, historians, and futurists. I believed we also must always listen to the poets — actors, comedians, musical artists, and writers — for they are scholars of human nature and often have the gift of prophecy.

"We cry out for good leadership," I wrote in my Letter from the Editor. "For the past seven years, we have been fed fear and deceit. We have been led into a war with neither purpose nor success, taking the lives of tens of thousands and turning millions into refugees. Our president has stood numb and mute as evidence of catastrophic climate change has become terrifying. Private interests have looted the treasury and the administration has sanctioned fraud and corruption. We have watched Congress and the press become weak, willing handmaidens to those who would rip apart the fabric of our democratic society.

"Our elected leaders hired private armies and ran secret programs of wiretapping and kidnapping and torture. They abandoned poor people desperate for health care and left an entire city devastated by natural disaster. We don't need leaders who wear flag pins in their lapel, but rather men and women who have the guts to tell us the truth. Like those who speak out in this anniversary issue, we hunger for the restoration of hope and common sense and purpose."

I was imbued with the call of the Declaration of Independence. The people who spoke in this issue were my cosigners, my fellow patriots.

IN OUR FINAL issue of the year, Jeff Goodell visited Dr. James Lovelock, one of our eminent men of science, who had postulated the Gaia theory, which states that Earth is a self-sustaining, integrated organism capable of self-destruction but also has the mechanisms for cycles of self-renewal. He said global warming was irreversible and believed that, as a result, Earth's population would be culled from 6.6 billion people to as few as

500 million, with most people living in the far latitudes — Canada, Iceland, Scandinavia, and the Arctic Basin.

When the annual National Magazine Awards came around, we were given the top honor, the General Excellence Award, once again the best magazine in America. We had been nominated for it five times, and this was our second win. "*Rolling Stone* remains as forward-looking as ever," the judges said. "The magazine is uniformly smart, deeply reported, and beautifully written."

CHAPTER 67

BURNING MAN

H AVING A CHILD was having its traditional effect. My life was settling down. Matt and I now had twins cooking. They arrived in January, born in San Bernardino, in the desert east of Los Angeles. I watched the delivery — my third C-section — organs being lifted out of the stomach and laid onto cheesecloth. It didn't bother me. The nurse handed me the first baby, and I almost shouted at her, "It's a girl, I've never had a girl before!" I now had six children to love and protect.

India Rose Moon got her name when we were driving down a 15,000-foot mountain pass in Bhutan. I was good with Matt's choice of India but also liked Rose, a gorgeous and rarely used name. Caroline's oldest child was named Rose, and was a beautiful Jackie look-alike. Moon was Matt's grandmother's maiden name. Altogether a magical incantation. We called the second baby, a boy, Jude Simmons Nye Wenner. We knew we wanted a name starting with J, a nod to the hero of *The Red and the Black*, the Stendhal novel we had both just read, featuring the beautiful young man who had charmed all of France. Simmons is my mother's family name.

We took the babies to Sun Valley and stayed put. Our nurse's specialty was twins, and she could prop them on her knees and feed them simultaneously. There were guests, family, and children galore, but mainly it was a time for nesting, snuggling, and sharing the wonder of three new lives. We headed back to New York with our new family in tow in April.

FACEBOOK WAS TURNING four years old and had seventy million users, so we decided to profile Mark Zuckerberg, who refused to cooperate. But we did dig up the Winklevoss twins, and a few other Harvard students, who said Zuckerberg had stolen the idea of Facebook from them. We didn't try to prove anything one way or the other, though huge financial settlements were made later. The article compared Zuckerberg to Donald Trump. "How many people has he burned and he's only 24?" asked one friend. "The fact that he's a grade-A asshole doesn't mean he did anything illegal." Words to ponder...

At the same time, eerily enough, we sent Naomi Klein to China to report on "The Golden Shield," a massive undertaking based in the city of Shenzhen, where the Huawei tech empire was being built with the help of U.S. defense contractors. We specifically warned that they were building prototypes for a high-tech police state. Words to ponder...

I MET UP AGAIN with Obama in Chicago and jumped on his chartered 757 for an interview and complimentary airplane breakfast. The primaries were essentially over, so it was a low-key day traveling to a town hall in Appleton, Wisconsin. I brought Theo along with me, and we were having a father-and-son road trip. He started to shoot pictures of Obama and me sitting next to each other, but once breakfast came, Obama shooed Theo away; he said he didn't want any photos out there with a fork in his mouth.

Presidential candidates, more than presidents in office, are indoctrinated to stay on their predetermined, group-vetted message. Spontaneity and truth telling are not your friends. Anything on a controversial issue has been memorized and said about a thousand times. The wrong word can be used by the opposition to rattle, even ruin, your campaign.

I wanted to introduce Obama to the *Rolling Stone* readers, about seven million of them by this time. I always asked a subject about music to get a sense of the private citizen. Bob Dylan had just endorsed him, as Bruce had already, and I asked about his favorite Dylan song. "I've got probably thirty Dylan songs on my iPod, and the entire *Blood on the Tracks*," he replied. "One of my favorites during the political season is 'Maggie's Farm.' It speaks to me as I listen to some of the political rhetoric." Any other politician would have chosen "Blowin' in the Wind," or something like that. But "Maggie's Farm" is about the Man, ain't going to work for him anymore, ain't going to slave, ain't going to do what anybody tells me to do. "Well, he puts his cigar out in your face, just for kicks / His bedroom window, it is made out of bricks."

They were playing "The Rising" at Obama's rallies, along with Aretha and Stevie Wonder. "Not only do I love Bruce's music, but I love him as a person," Obama said. "He is a guy who has never lost track of his roots, who knows who he is. When you think about authenticity, you think about Bruce Springsteen, and that's how he comes across personally. We actually haven't met in person. We had a phone conversation, and he was exactly how you hoped he'd be. He's passionate and humble." And you call him the Boss? "You've got to."

We were using a photographer then, Peter Yang, who brought back one of the most endearing portraits of Obama ever taken — looking down, eyes nearly closed, and grinning in some kind of wonderfully happy state. It was an obvious beauty. Once again, this was one that needed no words or headlines. It won all the Cover of the Year awards.

BURNING MAN WAS not on my radar. Taking drugs twenty-four hours a day with thousands of people in the windblown desert a hundred miles outside of Reno, Nevada, was not on my bucket list, more like my fuck-it list. Nonetheless, when Tom Freston invited me, I didn't think twice. He had gotten two RVs in the "camp," organized by Bob Pittman and his new wife, Vera, and a group of his friends and fellow partyers including his son Bo. Tom, Gil Friesen, and I would be in one trailer and Jane Buffett, Jimmy's wife, and Alice Michaels, Lorne's wife, in the other.

Pittman had been a Burner for years. He filled the camp with fellow ecstasy fanatics, free spirits, and babes. There was more than enough sensuality to be had, but three guys in their sixties traveling with the wives of their close friends was like traveling with private detectives.

The place felt incredibly sexy, good-looking people in their twenties and thirties in terrific shape, walking around half naked most of the day. About thirty thousand of them. Silicon Valley fortunes had been spent on space-age discos, giant abstract statues and installations, and a universe of custom vehicles, such as buses turned into giant roving ducks. There were uniformed sheriff's deputies regularly patrolling the encampment, who seemed out of place until you realized they were making it one of the safest places on earth to take drugs. We walked around in the afternoons visiting art installations and camps that offered all kinds of entertainments. The pop-up city was a psychedelic carnival. The costumes were a sideshow in themselves. You do it again at night when everything is lit up, including the thousands of Burners, who themselves are adorned with twinkling fluorescent lights. The drugs are even more plentiful, and open-air discos are pumping the cosmic pulse at either end of the mile-wide encampment. And the next night.

The highlight is on Saturday, when the thousands gather to watch a bonfire consume the Burning Man, a ten-story-high wooden effigy packed with gasoline. Tom's son, Andrew, was in a camp called Robo Heart, which had a customized triple-decker bus mounted end to end with about 100,000 decibels of speakers. I watched the Man dematerialize in the inferno from the roof of the bus, vibrating and pounding with music. I expected to be thrown from the top into the dancing and writhing Burners at any second and was nervously looking forward to it.

Burning Man was a mash-up of *Star Wars* and *Apocalypse Now* and Disneyland and the Las Vegas Strip. I had barely scratched the surface. The next year I would return and bring Matt and Theo. On the flight back to New York after that second visit, Theo wrote in the plane's log, "Burning Man…hmm…where to begin without getting anyone in trouble? 1) Helicopter ride from Reno to the Black Rock Desert.

2) Arrive at 'Burning Man Customs' and are forced to roll in the dirt while shouting 'I'm home.' 3) Unpack at our camp, named 'Squid Row,' and meet up with the Pittmans, who had 'accidentally' just taken MDMA by drinking the wrong bottle of water on their nightstand. 4) Eat lunch, pasta and truffles, and start exploring around Burning Man. 5) Night falls and we all travel to the 'Opulent Temple.' 6) Bedtime around sunrise and wake up at 3 p.m., standard and acceptable Burning Man hours. 7) Meet tons of weird and creepy people, but Lobster Man and Butterfly Boy definitely take the cake. 8) Explore by day, dance and party by night — ride bikes and Segways, check out all the art installations. 9) Our turn to cook dinner for the Squid Row camp. Dad claims to have made the pasta sauce for the entire camp (which had been prepared days earlier by his private chef). 10) Befriend the surrounding camps like Robo Heart (home to all the Euros) and Pink Pussycat, home to Dr. Reed and a dude who claims that Vito is moving into a building he owns, not realizing that he was lying to the person who actually is Vito. 11) Dad almost got taken down by the cops on a bike ride with Vito...apparently, you're not supposed to ride through the middle of a group of cops arresting somebody. 12) Each moment that passed, our costumes got more decked out and lit up. Matt debuted his disco pants at dinner. 13) Around 9 p.m. on the final night, midst a dust storm, our RV turns into a makeshift Ibiza, working disco. 14) We all almost get our balls chopped off by a feisty Russian girl for smoking in her trailer — seriously the scariest part of Burning Man. 15) Ride the Giant Squid into the desert to watch the burning of the Man. 16) Vito and Theo, and Matt and Jann, go their separate ways. Matt and Jann return to the RV around 4:30 a.m., only to find Vito and Theo cozy in bed with a lot of fish-stick wrappers everywhere. 17) Leave the next morning; on the helicopter ride back, we begin planning next year's trip."

THEO GRADUATED FROM Bard. He had studied photography and during the summers had interned with Mark Seliger and Annie, as well as Salgado. We started Theo on small assignments, something he felt comfortable with, and he did an exceptionally good shot of Sean Lennon. I sent him out to do Jackson Browne, who gave Theo the longest hug ever and said, "You look just like your old man." Theo hit a triple with Robert Pattinson, the heartthrob vampire of *Twilight*. Pattinson was looking hot, beyond what the publicists wanted, far beyond virginal. We resold that photograph around the world. Theo's métier was not guitar players; it was pretty women. Gus started his first year at Brown, the hip Ivy League school. It was clearly right for Gus, who had been turned on by the academic, competitive ethos of Collegiate School in New York. College meant the end of his teenage rock group. Alex and Emily, now married, had moved to San Francisco, where he was working at Electronic Arts, writing analyses of new video games. Bing Gordon, one of the EA founders, and his wife, Debra, took Alex under their wing, but he and Emily missed the family and moved back east after two years.

The older boys invited Jane to a long weekend in Sun Valley. Matt was fine with it. I prepared myself for tension at every meal — a round of table tension, anyone? It was late fall, parka weather and leaves turning gold. We got an amazing family picture, with the three older kids each holding their baby siblings, and Matt, Jane, and me in the middle. The only tense person there was me. Jane wrote a few words in the plane log: "WTF! It was really great."

AFTER FORTY YEARS, we shrank *Rolling Stone*'s size and turned it into a standard-size magazine. The 2008 recession and the power of the internet suddenly became a double whammy hit to our once lucrative ad sales, which were now on a clear and irreversible slide. By downsizing we saved millions of dollars buying paper, fit into more newsstand racks at more places, and made it easier for advertisers, who were no longer doing lavish campaigns designed for our luxurious space. The oversized format seemed integral to our history, part of the soul of *Rolling Stone*. The loyalists thought that size was sacred; I was convinced that in fact it would improve the magazine. Once we did change, we lost nothing except nostalgia.

With the smaller size we did a redesign that embraced my own classical leanings and penchant for formality. The newsy feel had to change; our music news coverage was already headed straight to the internet. The times were more serious, and I wanted that reflected. Writing and photography were *Rolling Stone*'s strengths, the magazine business's only collective advantage over the internet; we needed to emphasize both elements. The result was, thankfully, another great design iteration of the magazine. And new mojo. Will recruited the art director of the *Los Angeles Times*, Joe Hutchinson, to join us. I asked him for something that looked more like a monthly. He was the calmest art director I had ever met.

Those of us who ran magazine companies could read our own numbers and knew what the competition was doing. The internet was no longer a looming threat: it was at the goddamned front door, a vampire with several hundred million untethered tentacles, the ubiquitous iPhone. It was also causing our circulation, as well as our advertising, to drop. This was serious trouble.

I thought magazines could fight back if we played to our strengths: photography, design, and writing. But most magazines were trying to look like websites, imitating what the internet could do better, quicker, and give away free. Not a good strategy at any level. Magazine publishers had been discounting and sweepstaking subscriptions for so long that they had created the aura of low value and the expectation of low prices.

We had been making respectable money licensing our online rights to midlevel companies, lucrative deals put together by a good friend of mine, Tommy Cohen, a freelance financier who worked out of our offices. We were the only magazine company making money on the web then; big companies like Time Inc., Hearst, and Condé Nast were losing hundreds of millions trying to transplant traditional print orthodoxies onto new age digital "platforms." I wanted to wait until it was figured out.

When we added online advertising it seemed we had found our little piece of the digital pie and our business would survive, as lost advertising spending started coming back. We had five years of growth and profits. But the three dragons of Silicon Valley — Facebook, Apple, and Google — as if they didn't have enough billions of dollars, came to steal what was left. They appropriated for themselves the intellectual property created by magazines and newspapers, repackaged it, gave it away free to our customers, and sold ads to our advertisers. They tricked publishers into thinking they were building traffic for their own websites. That was a lie, and one day the dragons walked away, leaving their victims in the news and journalism business to bleed out.

DAVID FOSTER WALLACE hanged himself at age forty-six. I had sent one of our best new feature writers, David Lipsky, out to profile Wallace when *Infinite Jest* was first published in 1996. I liked the long-haired, headband-wearing photo of him in the book review section. He looked totally *Rolling Stone*. I had to put Lipsky on something else midway through, and we lost the piece but had gained Wallace as a contributor. The two Davids had vibed well; Lipsky lived with him in his house for a week. Wallace, it turned out, was a big fan of *Rolling Stone* and me. When he died we had hours of tape of him trying to explain his life. Lipsky had the brilliant piece in hand. We won the National Magazine Award again; it became a bestselling book and a terrific movie.

Obama laid a smackdown on John McCain. Other than substantial editorial support in nearly every issue, I had no role in the campaign. They didn't need money and rock and roll fund-raisers. I didn't need to recruit artists, as everyone was already on board. Bruce had performed at the big campaign rallies. Youthful voters — coast to coast, border to border — turned to Obama. Al had carried young voters by two points; John carried them by about nine points. Barack Obama carried them by thirty-four points. At long last, it was time for me to find a comfortable rocking chair and a nice place with a view from the sidelines.

We packed up the three babies, two nannies, three grown sons, and new daughter-in-law, and headed for Kauai. We rented a ridiculous eight-bedroom house that more properly belonged in a gated community in Florida. My mother was a crazy old lady now, a silver fox. The general riot of children, nannies who were sleeping on cots in the hall, surf instructors, my sister Merlyn, her husband, who is a shaman and aya-huasca farmer, plus Merlyn's three kids, threw my mother into a pretty full spin occasioned by not getting the kind of attention she needed to breathe.

I had a baggie of peyote chocolates. After a few nights of woulda, coulda, shoulda, we — Matt, Gus, Theo, Alex, and I — bit the brown bullet. That evening we sat and giggled in the outdoor Jacuzzi. Alex's wife made garlands for all to wear, and the boys' bodies glistening in the night made them look like the gods at play. A wind-whipped storm came up, palm trees bent, and the rain was blown in sideways. Matt and the boys decided to hike down the cliff to the beach and challenge the roar-ing waves. It was a beach with the highest fatality rate in the Hawaiian Islands. I stayed behind, waiting. And waiting. Trying not to worry. Did the gods want a sacrifice? Speculating on this was not useful, so I began the hike down to see. Out of the dark curtains of rain they came, laugh-ing, having braved the waves, more godlike than ever.

CHAPTER 68

'HIGHER AND HIGHER'

LADY LUCK STILL wasn't completely done with me. The year I bought Disney out of *US Weekly* we were splitting $27 million a year in profits. The next year, when I became the sole owner, the earnings jumped to $50 million a year for the next ten years, once topping $64 million. Of course, I still had to pay down the bank loan, which I began to do, but I was in no hurry. *US* was an outlier in the magazine business, and despite the dramatic drop of *Rolling Stone* profitability, so much money was coming in, I didn't want to ask questions or rock the boat. One golden goose was just fine.

IT WAS NOVEMBER 2009 and the time for the Hall of Fame's twenty-fifth-anniversary concert was at hand. I wanted to take it to the limit, to use the knowledge and experience I had absorbed in over forty years of friendships and the trust of so many artists. I wanted to do the best rock and roll show of all time. I quickly understood that this would take two nights and two different shows.

A year earlier I had asked Bruce to headline one night and asked Bono to do the other. I had told Mick that I wasn't sure what he would do, we would figure it out, but he had to commit to being available that particular week. The Stones would not be touring, and reassembling that vastly complicated machinery was not going to be possible. With their promises in hand, I booked Madison Square Garden for a two-night stand on October 29 and 30.

I wanted McCartney and Dylan, not for ticket sales but to complete and close the historic circle. Paul said yes, then no, then yes, and then no again. Dylan was another matter; I thought for sure I could get him. My relationship with Bob was solid; I would talk him into it. I made him every offer under the sun: walk-on solo, duet with Bruce, solo with the E Street Band, ride in on a chariot. I would even turn off the TV cameras. But it was always no. I decided not to announce Mick at all and save him as the penultimate "surprise special guest." He would appear on the last night and sing "Gimme Shelter" with U2.

THE MAGIC, THE big heavenly magic, came quick. We opened with Crosby, Stills & Nash, with their guests, Jackson Browne, Bonnie Raitt, and James Taylor. If there was going to be a Simon and Garfunkel reunion, Paul insisted on having his own solo set as well. For his section, Paul brought on Dion, with Little Anthony and the Imperials as special guests. Artie asked me to get Paul to give him more verses in "Bridge Over Troubled Water." Taking these calls is what a "producer" does. When I mentioned this to Paul, he said that giving that song to Artie was the biggest mistake of his life. I guess some people are just meant for each other.

Artie came on: "The Sound of Silence," "Mrs. Robinson," "The Boxer." These were songs bound into our lives, that resonated with everyone's personal history. When it got to "Bridge," Artie followed the piano opening: "When you're weary, feeling small / When tears are in your eyes / I will dry them all..." As they sang together, and as the chorus expanded in its great buildup, the roof was lifting off the building, and by the time the audience stopped cheering, the roof had disappeared altogether. I was certain that this was the greatest performance of that song they had ever done.

Stevie Wonder set up a three-ring musical circus onstage, a festival of musicians and polyrhythms. Stevie killed it. He brought out Smokey

Robinson for a duet on "The Tracks of My Tears" and John Legend for a Michael Jackson tribute, "The Way You Make Me Feel." Not enough? B. B. King ("The Thrill Is Gone"), Sting ("Roxanne"), and Jeff Beck ("Superstition"). It was nuts. Stevie could have and would have played all night.

By this time it was nearly midnight, and we still had Bruce. I wasn't that familiar with "The Ghost of Tom Joad," Bruce's tale of Depression-era poverty and homelessness, a solemn melody with fierce lyrics. Tom Morello joined him onstage; his guitar playing was like fireworks exploding one after the other, trails of sound streaming and screaming through the sky. My self-awareness left me behind where I was sitting, an out-of-body experience, into what felt like a heaven never ending.

My heart swelled when Aretha walked on, resplendent, as it is said, in a red gown. This wasn't just a concert; this was Mount Rushmore. Aretha had been nothing but trouble for two days. She even asked us to shut down the air-conditioning in the Garden while she performed. I watched her arrive in the afternoon: a double-stretch white limousine drove up the backstage ramp, and she came out with two double-stretch bodyguards. She was wrapped in white fur, turban to toe.

One week before showtime, Eric Clapton said he was having emergency gallstone surgery. Jeff Beck, already booked as Eric's guest, put his band together and stepped in. Sting sang "People Get Ready." Buddy Guy, the last of the blues greats still standing and burning, ripped it; Billy Gibbons joined him on "Foxy Lady." The closer was Jeff's trademark operatic version of "A Day in the Life," with John Lennon looking down from the giant screen above, a part of the visual script that we had built for the show.

U2 had finished their world tour in Vancouver the night before and flew into New York overnight. (They had to pay additional taxes for prolonging their days in the States.) They opened with "Vertigo" and "Magnificent." When Mick suddenly appeared from side stage, impeccably tailored, the Garden erupted. We had pulled the lion out of the hat. "Beautiful Day," one of their greatest pieces, which they have performed at every concert since they wrote it in 2000, was the grand finale. It builds and builds to a chorus and chiming guitars, the sound of a mighty cathedral, set in a mountain valley. As Bono reached the middle of the song, he sang, "It's a beautiful day / Don't let it get away / Touch me, take me to that other place / See the world in green and blue / Jann Wenner right beside you."

The Hall of Fame concert was shown on HBO over Thanksgiving, and the next day Dylan called. "How come I wasn't there? Those were my people. I should have been there." He brushed past my reminder to him that I had asked him five ways to Sunday and gave me a review of every performance. That was a cool call to get.

Bob was playing New York and asked me to drop by. As we were sitting around, he asked me how "your friend Bruce" was doing. I told him Bruce was just fine, and on his new tour each night he was performing an entire album, like *Darkness on the Edge of Town*. Bob grinned and said, "Maybe I should do that. I could do, maybe, *Dark Side of the Moon*."

Jodi Peckman, our creative director, had carried a large leather-bound book backstage at the Hall of Fame concert and asked the artists to each sign a page. She was always looking after me as well as the magazine. She gave the book to me for Christmas; on one page the inscription read, "Jann, Only you! Love, Bruce."

CHAPTER 69

THE RUNAWAY GENERAL

THE STONES WERE putting out a new edition of *Exile on Main Street*, which was another excuse for a party at our house. It's always fun to watch Keith arrive anywhere, never a quiet entrance. He's just got so much in motion on him: earrings, bracelets, rings; things twisted into his hair, headband, and hat; shirt unbuttoned; scarves, beads, and necklaces, plus a belt with a skull or something similar. In addition to the usual suspects, I invited Chris Martin, whom I had just met that day at the office, a giant rock star at thirty-three but still a wide-eyed newbie. After dessert I was squeezed in between Mick, Sting, and Bruce on a couch in the living room, and Chris sat at our feet, asking the sweetest, sincerest questions of the senior citizens. When he left, Jimmy Fallon joined Mick on our stoop to do their Mick dance for the benefit of our curious neighbors.

IN AUGUST 2010 we had the latest beefcake teen vampire on the cover in a wet white T-shirt, arms over his head, biceps bulging, armpit hair peeking from his short sleeves, titled "Teen Wolf." The letter from a reader in Mesquite, Texas, was a classic. In full it read, "Gayest. Cover. Ever." Vampires were good for business. *True Blood* was an HBO soap opera set in Swamp County, Louisiana, about the struggle between greedy locals, civic-minded vampires, and a smallish colony of intermarrying, shape-shifting werewolves in a fight for the lucrative artificial-human blood franchise. Wow! What a concept! The three stars posed naked with blood splattered over their intertwined bodies. The cover headline read "They're Hot. They're Sexy. They're Undead."

WILL DANA AND senior editor Eric Bates walked into my office with a reporter they wanted to hire, a baby-faced guy, thirty-year-old Michael Hastings, a Canadian and a graduate of New York University's journalism school who had been covering Iraq for *Newsweek*. He wanted to go to Afghanistan to profile General Stanley McChrystal, who once ran special ops for the Department of Defense and was now in command of the war. This was a fresh angle, and I loved the idea of a major profile of a wartime general. Michael was the kind of dogged reporter you love.

Michael was worried about access to McChrystal, but Eric reassured him: "You'd be surprised how much access the military gives *Rolling Stone*. After all, their goal is to recruit our readers and send them to their death." Eric was no-nonsense. His parents, from West Virginia, had raised him on a farm with no electricity, and were targets during the McCarthy years. His childhood heroes were Woodward and Bernstein.

In a simple twist of fate, while Michael was on the assignment, a sudden volcanic eruption shut down air traffic, so he stayed over with the general and his staff in Paris. In the course of that, McChrystal's closest aides dissed Obama's team, and in particular shit on Vice President Joe Biden, who thought we should get out of Afghanistan as soon as possible. When he got to Afghanistan, Hastings found dissatisfied troops and allies angry about McChrystal's failing new strategy. The piece was titled "The Runaway General."

An embargoed copy we had given to the Associated Press made its way to Biden, who immediately put it into Obama's hands, who read it and ordered McChrystal to return to Washington the next day. It was an awesome thing to sit in our offices, watching television as the president of the United States relieved the general of battlefield command. Obama mentioned a "magazine article," but didn't give us credit or a name-check, which I thought was clearly deliberate. He wanted to protect himself from the backlash. Of course, our name was everywhere, and on this for all time.

We had never tried to pretend that *Rolling Stone* was neutral. We were going to be scrupulously accurate and tell the truth. The word "objective" was a red herring, a claim that stating an opposing point of view was necessary even though that view might be a blatant falsehood. "Objectivity" didn't mean fairness or honesty; it was just covering your ass. I thought that prejudicial adjectives and liberal clichés in the reportorial copy undercut the power of the facts. And I didn't want to repeat what I could read everywhere. We had to find something new and meaningful to add, not be the third or fourth article about the latest cause *du jour*. Nothing was going to be gained by blowing up. It was time to buckle up.

Michael Hastings, unscathed by the Pentagon, would continue on a roll. He obtained an interview with Julian Assange, who was in hiding in the English countryside, and spent hours interviewing him, learning very little other than that Assange was an asshole. A few months earlier, Michael had done a blow-by-blow, gotten the deep inside dope, on the fight between Obama and the Pentagon over troop levels in Afghanistan. Michael's newest was "Drone Wars," about our ability to go to war by remote control. The White House had a secret list of assassination targets they were always updating and had just wiped out the family of two U.S. citizens, albeit members of Al-Qaeda, in their home in Yemen. It wasn't called an assassination or a hit but a "targeted killing." The drone operators with joysticks, which guided the weapons from a secret base near Las Vegas, called it "bug splat."

A WEEK AFTER GETTING back from Burning Man for the third time, I was in the Oval Office with Obama. He complimented me on my multicolored striped socks, saying if he weren't president, he could wear socks like mine. It was the eve of the midterm elections, with Democratic control of the Congress in play. Obama faced criticism from his left, grievances both real and sometimes inflated. He thought of *Rolling Stone* as one of his "progressive" critics. We sat next to each other in the twin high-back chairs underneath the gold-framed portrait of George Washington. I glanced at him palming a nicotine gum from his pocket. The interview was a report card of what he had and hadn't done, the bitterness of a brazenly hostile Republican Party. Obama spoke in his very measured way, holding his anger, hopeful that steadiness and reason could still work. He looked strong and stern on the cover shot we chose, hands in pockets. The headline was "Obama Fights Back." I was all in on Barack.

MATT HAD FOUND a new home for our family near the village of Tivoli, in upstate New York. It was a small house set on the bluffs above the Hudson River, with a majestic view that had been captured by the moody luminescence of the Hudson River School of painting. The land had belonged to Chancellor Robert Livingston, who with Jefferson, Ben Franklin, Roger Sherman, and John Adams drafted the Declaration of Independence. He had administered the oath of office to George Washington. The property had been named Teviot, and belonged to one of Livingston's direct descendants.

The house was hidden among overgrown willow trees. We plunged in, reclaiming the views, unveiling the giant oaks, protecting the eagle's nest where two were born every year and grew up flying around the property. We restored the house and added rabbits, chickens, and peacocks. Wild turkeys were already there.

Our new family life was taking shape at Teviot. I was commuting by train along the Hudson, a stunning ride, and Annie Leibovitz lived twenty minutes downriver. Our daughters were becoming fast friends. In the spring, Annie staged an Alice in Wonderland Easter egg hunt, and in the fall the kids picked apples from her orchards, put them in an old-fashioned apple press, and bottled the juice. We also started to spend a lot of time with other parents, inevitably younger than us, with kids the same age as our wildcats, who upped the trouble factor.

We settled in for the summer, basing out of Tivoli, hot, occasionally thick humid days and lightning storms. We spent the afternoons at the pool house or beside the pond, playing with the children and watching families of deer meander along the river at sunset. We got out to Sun Valley to stage another motorcycle trip to the northern tip of Idaho, up in white-supremacist territory, along rivers, through forests, up mountains, past vast fields of potatoes to the lake town of Coeur d'Alene. It was Gus's first rodeo, but by the last day he was doing twisties with ease and on one straightaway passed me doing 110 mph.

KEITH HAD FINISHED his autobiography with the help of James Fox, a writer Jackie Onassis had once sent to me and who had then written for us. Keith was a great talker, always a good story, with a witty aphorism at the end plus a barb about somebody. But who would have expected this louche and seemingly loosely-held-together person to come up with such a brilliant memoir? We serialized it and put Keith on the cover. There was wonderful stuff in it, his eccentric, Dickensian English childhood, how the Stones began, and a great section on playing and tuning the guitar. The tours and the extent of the drug abuse were beyond hairy. It was the *Beowulf* of drugs, perhaps the *War and Peace*. No redemptive rehab, no regrets, no apologies. He held nothing back, including his mixed emotions about Mick. He gave Mick credit — a lot less than was due — but otherwise took a knife to him, reopening old wounds, rivalries, near deaths, deaths, and the death throes of their friendship, even to the point of discussing Mick's penis size. Keith said he hadn't visited Mick in his dressing room in twenty years.

Mick was infuriated. He could get pissed off at people who did stupid things, but this was betrayal. He loved Keith, and he had been hurt. Mick and I had often commiserated about working with Keith and Hunter, brilliant people whom we cherished and depended on but who were both addicts. A junkie is a junkie, and you can never truly depend on a junkie. We talked through how he should respond; it was obvious the less said — in fact, nothing said — the better. It would have its life and then go away. They restored their working relationship and went back on the road. The pot of gold at the end of the road was enormous. They never successfully wrote songs together again.

I SAW A STORY about an explosion in the Upper Big Branch Mine in West Virginia. Twenty-nine miners dead. The mine was run by the most powerful coal baron in Appalachia, Don Blankenship, a hometown boy, born in Stopover, Kentucky, and raised in a trailer with his mother and three siblings. Now he lived in a mansion on a hill, with a Bentley in his garage. His cruelty and greed had killed his men, his neighbors, the people he had come from. It reminded me of a poem I read in high school by Edwin Arlington Robinson titled "Richard Cory":

> *So on we worked, and waited for the light,*
> *And went without the meat, and cursed the bread;*
> *And Richard Cory, one calm summer night,*
> *Went home and put a bullet through his head.*

Blankenship had a black heart, as black as coal. I asked Jeff Goodell to find the man. Because of our story he was indicted by the government and sent to jail. The last of the Coal Barons.

THE WALL STREET banks had been up to their eyeballs in crime, and I thought the government should put those bankers on trial. Matt Taibbi agreed, but I think he wanted firing squads. The gravity of the injustice was extraordinary. Matt wrote a two-year series that laid out the complexities of investment swindles with fierce hilarity, *tours de force* of analysis, and Swiftian humor. The first one, "The Great American

Bubble Machine," was about Goldman Sachs, the world's most powerful bank. He reviewed Goldman's history of creating artificial stock bubbles, bundling underwater mortgages and credit default swaps, selling them to "suckers" or to fellow co-conspirators to sell to other "suckers," draining their profitability, and leaving the losses for everyone else. Matt described Goldman as "a great vampire squid wrapped around the face of humanity, relentlessly jamming its blood funnel into anything that smells like money."

Goldman, just by itself, stripped nearly $5 trillion from the economy in just a few years. In 2008, the year of the crash, they paid $14 *million* in taxes on $12 *billion* in total profits, an effective tax rate of 1%. "The bank is a huge, highly sophisticated engine for converting the useful, deployed wealth of society into the least useful, most wasteful and insoluble substance on earth—pure profit for rich people." Goldman was never properly investigated for its crimes, but the phrase "vampire squid" will stick to it until the last Goldman banker's dying day.

THE ELECTION RESULTS were depressing. The Republicans picked up more than sixty seats in Congress. We had scheduled our annual morning-after assessment at the office, a colloquy to be published in the next issue. As usual, the session was with Peter Hart, establishment Democrat, and David Gergen, establishment Republican, and this time, Matt Taibbi, who had spent a week on assignment with Tea Party people the month before.

Taibbi: "What we saw last night was the Tea Party taking over the Republican Party. That more radicalized, extreme wing of the party is going to play a kingmaking role in the presidential election of 2012, and that's going to make it impossible for the Republicans to take the White House. To me, the main thing about the Tea Party is that they're just crazy. If someone is able to bridge the gap with these voters, it seems that they will have to be a little bit crazy, too."

For David, God bless his old-fashioned belief in civility in politics — whenever that had been — Taibbi, who also had blasted Wall Street, was just too much. "That sentiment is what the business community objects to."

Taibbi: "Fuck the business community."

Gergen: "Fuck the business community? Is that what you just said?"

We were all sitting in the boardroom. Eric Bates was with me, and I was trying to attempt an erudite analysis. Gergen and Taibbi were standing their ground, their red faces fixed on each other across the generation and ideological gap, widening as we sat there.

Gergen: "I'm putting my money on Jeb Bush as a potential star who might emerge and unite the party."

Taibbi: "Whew. I was already depressed this morning, but thinking about another Bush as the better-case scenario in an either-or political future makes me want to douse myself with kerosene and jump into a blast furnace."

Gergen: "The looming, transcendent question is whether we can govern ourselves as a people or whether we are going to drift into a serious decline."

Hart: "In the late nineties, under Clinton, there wasn't Fox News. Fox not only demonizes everything Obama says and does, it is the major vetting group for Republicans and will not allow any kind of compromise to exist. I don't think we're going to get there."

CHAPTER 70

THE WRECKING BALL

JANE AND I finally got divorced. Not doing so had been an emotional crutch we both needed; she still wanted to be married and, whatever the circumstance, might have taken me back. At least that's what she told herself, without really thinking it through or talking to me about it. I was afraid of anything that would break the threads that bound me to the kids, to the idea of family. I wanted to keep her, too. Matt was amazingly accepting of this. He understood that it was necessary for everyone's happiness.

Once, a few years earlier, we had appeared in front of a judge. We rode downtown together and met our lawyers in the judge's courthouse chambers. After some chitchat and procedural stuff, the judge asked why we were there. She told us to leave and come back when there was something to discuss. When the time finally came, we wrapped it up, out of court, property and all, in a few days. In the end nothing changed, except the lifting of some hanging sword and a new deepening of the family relationships, including Matt, based on truth.

The best line in the saga came from Fran Lebowitz. She said, "When they separated, I took Jane's side. Jane, however, took Jann's side."

OUR FAMILY MET up with Michael Douglas and his family to sail the Pacific coast of Panama for New Year's Eve of 2012. As soon as we boarded, he broke down crying in my arms. My dear buddy, Mikey, the tough guy with the big heart. He had suffered through a battle with stage-four cancer and survived. But now he had just lost the battle for his oldest son, Cameron, my godson, who was in federal prison for using and dealing heroin. Cameron had been trouble for Michael since he was a teenager, and now in his early thirties faced another stretch, this time in maximum security with long periods in solitary. Michael had pulled every lever he had, spent every dollar he could, yet he was helpless to save his son. Michael had endured a tough few years, a struggle to save his marriage and then a hard-fought battle with throat cancer. But this long-running crucible was as close to breaking him as anything I had seen.

But they weren't going to get Mikey. Not on my watch. We talked it out, man to man and margarita to margarita, for a few days at sea. We were two couples, Catherine's brother, five little kids, and our nanny. The coast of Panama and the coastal islands were untouched national park land, empty beaches with long surf breaks and outdoor cafés with fresh fish and cold Pepsis. It was a good old family mash-up for a week.

Pigozzi was throwing himself a sixtieth-birthday party. When we sailed into Baie Longue, we could see Johnny's 20,000-square-foot, post-modern, multistory mountaintop castle in the distance. Isla Simca was Pigozzi's pastel redoubt on the summit of a jungle island, a place I hadn't seen since our visit with Mick. The other boat at anchor in the bay was the 400-foot *Luna*, property of Roman Abramovich, the multibillionaire oligarch who was one of the closest to Vladimir Putin. His wife, Dasha Zhukova, was also there for the party. Our expedition boat, *Latitude*, looked sad bobbing quietly next door to the *Luna*, which had nine decks.

We jumped into a waiting jeep for the ride on a narrow road that wound up the mountain. It felt as if we were visiting one of the James Bond villains, like Dr. No. There were bedrooms on the first two floors, above which were swimming pools, terraces, and great rooms with sprawling collections of contemporary African art and kitsch — wooden alligator side tables, life-size portraits of jazz quartets from Zambia, and paintings of juked-out Disney characters. The staff was still uncrating beds and mattresses for the guests. Mick canceled at the last minute. It was a weekend of jet-skiing in the mangroves, ATVs in the jungle, and big dinners. Dasha hosted a party on the rear deck of the *Luna*, which had its own stunning swimming pool. It was a cross-dressing party. Jane Buffett had flown in from St. Barts and stayed on our boat. She loaned me her clothes and Catherine did my makeup. Matt and I won the dance-off.

I WENT BACK TO the White House to interview Obama again. His reelection campaign was shaping up to be a showdown with the new Republican Tea Party. He was still talking reason and hope. Before the interview I gave him a few pairs of socks, since he had commented on mine last time we met. One pair was salmon colored with pink squares and the other had black and pink stripes. He handed them to an aide and said, "These may have to be second-term socks." Mick had just performed at the White House, and Obama had been in New York singing impromptu with Al Green at the Apollo, so he enjoyed telling those stories. We got sidetracked into gossiping about Bono, whom, he said, he had drunk under the table one late night at the White House. When I left, Hillary Clinton was sitting in a chair outside the Oval Office waiting for us to finish. It was kind of pinch-me time.

BRUCE RELEASED WRECKING BALL, his testimony on greed and destruction during the Bush presidency. The tour opened with a performance at the Apollo in New York, and in the middle of the show, he went into the audience and walked across the rows of seats to where I was, then stood on my armrests playing a solo above me. Twenty minutes later he was in the balcony, hanging off the edge, looking right down at me and shouting, "You again!"

My connection to and love of Bruce's music deepened further with *Wrecking Ball*, his most radically political effort, and in a way his most spiritual. It was based in working-class New Jersey, no longer about lost and found teenage dreams. It was about the life of people and their — I use this phrase advisedly — capitalist oppressors. "Jack of All Trades" is about a man who loses his job but can still hammer nails and take a car engine apart; he tells his wife that he will still provide for her. It breaks your heart to hear the pain, the bravery, and the acceptance: "If I had me a gun, I'd find the bastards and shoot 'em on sight / I'm a jack of all trades, we'll be alright."

"Death to My Hometown" is about the businessmen who shut the factories and took the workers' homes: "Send the robber barons straight to hell / The greedy thieves who came around / And ate the flesh of everything they found / Whose crimes have gone unpunished now / Who walk the streets as free men now." I was ready to pick up a torch. He closed the record with "Land of Hope and Dreams," a call to rise up, put your hands in the air, and get on the glory train.

It was gospel, rock and roll gospel, a preacher and a choir, lifting us up, higher and higher. It was the church of rock and roll.

GIL FRIESEN CALLED to tell me he had leukemia. Matt and I had been at his seventy-fifth birthday party just a few months before. We left for Los Angeles by the end of the week and moved into his house in Brentwood with his wife, Janet. I would show up at the hospital each morning, and Matt and Janet would head for Malibu with all the kids, surf, relax, get Janet away from the grim situation and her difficult patient. I would settle in for the day with Gil, who was getting chemo. Gil was taking phone calls, a visitor now and then, and working on his documentary, *Twenty Feet from Stardom*. I didn't think I would have the patience, but it turned out to be a wonderful way of hanging out; unhurried and intimate. The whole situation was suspended in time. I spent the day helping him out, reading the *New York Times*, enjoying his company, and his friendship. I wanted to devote my time to him, to act with love.

MY MOTHER WAS now living in Palo Alto, the tree-lined city that borders the Stanford campus. We had found a small apartment building for older people. I rented her a small grand piano, which she could still play though she was in a wheelchair when I visited. I would go over, roll her to a nearby restaurant, and then spend the afternoon with her in her garden or as she lay in bed. She was fully there, and when visiting her alone I was relaxed. I was not the dutiful Jewish son who worshipped his mother who was still living upstairs, but I asked her to move back east and offered to get her a place close to my house on the Hudson. She declined. Mother knows best. Three weeks later Sim turned ninety, so I returned for a family reunion, a birthday breakfast, and an afternoon picnic at the Gordons'. She was in her glory. My sister Katie — who had taken charge of Sim's medical issues and money, with all the sensitivities to be reckoned with — handled her like a child. It made me uncomfortable, the feebleness, the face of a frightening future.

After a few months back at his modern home set among trees and lush gardens, Gil returned to the hospital for a bone marrow transplant. Based on my experience with Dad, I was wary. The cancer specialists told Gil they could transplant his bone marrow and he'd have a shot at a cure, or he could enjoy a fairly normal life without one that would fade out in two years. However, because of the type of leukemia he had and his age, his chances of surviving the transplant were not great. I was against it but didn't say so. Was it my place to throw a shadow over his decision, either way, or stand by him and his terrifying choice? He had two little children who had lit up his life, and he wanted to grow old with them.

GUS AND I had our first proper discussion about a future for him at *Rolling Stone*. His mom had always called him "little Billy Gates." I told him it was a tough job to learn and was not sure he would enjoy the daily realities of being a businessman. The gap between our ages — I was sixty-six and he was twenty-one — made it unlikely that he would have gotten enough years of experience to take it over by the time I was ready to retire. He didn't want to be a writer, though he had that talent in spades. So, I made him the assistant to our new chief digital officer, from which spot he would be able to learn every area of the operations.

GIL DIED. I had visited him once more while he was getting the bone marrow transplant, an awful process. He had patches of black skin and bruises all over his body. There were nurses, lab technicians, and doctors in and out of his room, a swarm of people sucking his vitality and killing him. I wanted to get Gil out of there, let him spend his last days at home. That was the last time I saw him.

He stayed alive another week. His bed was moved into his living room, looking out on his beautiful trees and gardens. Bob Thurman came and sat with him a long time and reported that Gil's energy was still strong. His wife, Janet, put him in his favorite pajamas and played Miles Davis' *Sketches of Spain*, which he had long ago asked for in his final hours. The sun was setting, his children and friends were by the bedside. Janet called me and said Gil was still conscious. She gave him the phone so I could say goodbye. Gil's last spoken words were to Janet: "I love you."

One of his Ed Ruscha paintings, *Exit*, was on the wall behind him. Janet sent me a photo of the farewell. It was everything Gil would have wanted, and it made me feel happy.

CHAPTER 71

THE ROAD TO RIO

I STAYED IN LOS ANGELES after the memorial service for Gil and had breakfast with David Geffen at his Beverly Hills estate. David had a way of making you feel bad because you weren't as rich as he was, that you were the chump who didn't know better than to sell your business at the peak. I was looking for advice on handling our bank debt. His advice was to sell the company.

I never liked bankers, even the ones who loaned me the money to buy out Disney, and I had already paid half of it back. We had been a reliable, honest company for forty years and always paid our debts. But now that print magazines had been put on the endangered species list, the bankers increased our interest rates, tightened our collar, and shortened the leash. They wanted to scoop up nearly all our excess cash after operational costs. It meant I would not have the chance to make the changes in our business model necessary for any magazine to survive the digital transformation. They killed our chances for building a digital publishing business.

The new reality, the race to pay back the bank before they forced us to sell, meant fewer pages, cheaper paper, and cutting back editorial — no more Sebastião Salgado portfolios, no more full staffing. We narrowed our range, pulled back on the bravado. The mission was to save money, which became a filter for everything. The fun started going out of it. Instead, it became a question of running out the clock. I would miss my plane, my home away from home, but those times of go-anywhere adventure were already gone.

I was certain Wenner Media wouldn't survive as an independent company. It was the twilight of stand-alone magazines. The time was on the near horizon when we could survive only under the umbrella of a big company. Within the next three years, I expected to sell, take a short-term employment contract, and at the fiftieth anniversary, in 2017, take my bow. The outsize profitability of *US* was also shrinking—internet, advertising decline, and look-alike copycats—and soon I would have to sell it to pay off the remaining bank debt with its new harsh terms. I would hold on until then. The money play would have been to sell quickly, but I loved it and was not yet ready to let go.

I RAN INTO PAUL MCCARTNEY here and there over the years. He'd been to my house a few times, but we never had a serious talk or a big hangout. He was incredibly polite, and his Beatle magic was powerful stuff, with an accent that could melt you at fifty feet. *Lennon Remembers* had hurt Paul, but his relationship with *Rolling Stone* was always good, producing many interviews and covers. Still, we remained the keepers of the flame for John. I thought Paul was angry about that, but perhaps I was imagining it, steeped as I was in Yoko's partisan anti-McCartney stance and my loyalty to her.

Paul was putting out his first new album in seven years and wanted to line up support from *Rolling Stone*. When he came to pick me up for lunch at the office, staff were standing by their doors. The only more remarkable reception was when Jerry Lee Lewis walked down the hallway amid a standing ovation. Paul, for his part, was delighted to shake every hand and answer every question. He was enjoying himself. The fairy dust was everywhere. Our lunch was gossipy and relaxed. Paul was anxious to talk about John, and kept coming back to him. He wanted to make sure I understood the depth of his love. John was a complex, difficult character, and Paul's feelings, however competitive and conflicted about credit, were nonetheless pretty simple. Paul didn't want to be in a fight with the John cult; he wanted to be a part of it.

We went over to the studio and he played me his next record, *New*. The music struck me as more in tune with the times, while Paul's song-writing seemed more in touch with his own history, including his early days with John. Paul was looking inward, trying to reach the level of honesty and depth that John had. His melodies and his voice were soft and pretty, lovely. I could hear him making a reach with this album, historic in his own arc.

When I told Yoko about my visit with Paul, she said something to the effect that I had fallen under his spell. She was a hard-ass about it and had her reasons, but I didn't want to be a party to it anymore. I thought that Sean should have a solid relationship with his deceased father's oldest friend. Paul had finally reconciled with his own feelings about John. We were all growing up.

The show Paul did that week in Brooklyn was joyous, a lot of stage business and fireworks at the end. He embraced his heritage and the achievements of the Beatles. He was celebrating the Fab Four and dedicating songs to John. All you need is love!

Two LOVELY OLDER ladies ran the justice of the peace office in a tiny hamlet across the Hudson River in the Catskills. Matt and I kissed in front of the justices as they looked on with moist eyes. I got very sentimental. Matt was smiling ear to ear. We were married. Things became more real, more intensely felt. I wanted a big celebration, but the far-flung nature and numbers of our friends and families were logistically daunting.

We kept it secret. I didn't want to be tabloid entertainment again. The three older boys had figured it out already. It took me a long time to call Matt "my husband." Being a married man is a whole lot different than being someone's "partner." The law, or religion, gives it sanctity; you are now part of one of the official and sacred rituals of mankind. There are rules and laws, moral and civic, you have to follow. Now when you argue, walking out is no longer a response. You give your husband greater respect, greater love. The family was official, and our relationship was fundamentally altered by that vow, "till death do you part."

AT ROLLING STONE we had to make global warming feel viscerally and personally threatening. I wanted a piece that would fit the headline "Goodbye Miami," a city built on porous limestone, where water was already running through the streets. Jeff Goodell spent a month there and talked to academics, engineers, developers, and government officials. He wrote, "When the water receded after Hurricane Milo in 2030, there was a foot of sand covering the famous lobby of the Fontainebleau in Miami Beach. A dead manatee floated in the pool where Elvis once swam. The 24-foot storm surge overwhelmed the low-lying city. The old art deco buildings were swept off their foundations. The storm knocked out the wastewater treatment plant on Virginia Key, forcing the city to dump hundreds of millions of gallons of raw sewage into Biscayne Bay. Tampons and condoms littered the beaches and the stench of human excrement stoked fears of cholera. Salt water corroded underground wiring and the city was dark for months. Miami became a popular snorkeling spot to swim with sharks and turtles and check out the submerged ruins." No one, neither the banks nor the government, would be able to save Miami. Jeff reported this in 2012, and nothing has changed since. It's just one randomly aimed monster hurricane away.

SOME DAYS IT'S just better to stay home. Like when I expressed my displeasure with an upcoming cover. Didn't we have any other choices? One of the junior editors piped up that the best story we had in-house was on the Boston Marathon bomber. I had been intrigued with a photo of the nineteen-year-old on the front page of the *New York Times*, dark moody eyes and a mass of curly hair like Jim Morrison, an early Bob Dylan, or thousands of other college students. That would make a powerful and on-the-news cover.

The decision was made, and the next day my two top business guys, who ran ad sales, were in my office to sound an alarm, warning me that we would lose a lot of advertising and alienate big clients if we put the bomber on the cover. That kind of discussion got me angry every time. Who the fuck were the advertisers to tell me what I couldn't do? I dug my heels in, even as ads started to drop out over the next few days.

The first signs of trouble were phone calls from each of the three network news anchors and two morning show hosts asking me to be their special guest on their shows as soon as possible. I wasn't winning a Nobel Prize, so this could only mean trouble. Apparently, Boston was in a citywide uproar. The mayor had called us out and a boycott was afoot. I was hardly going to go on a talk show to explain that the need to learn that terrorism can wear a friendly mask and live next door is somehow more consequential than the suffering of the maimed and the innocent.

I was taken by surprise, entirely. Advertisers based in Boston wouldn't pay for their advertising and banned us for a long time. We lost schedules from State Farm insurance and Mercedes-Benz. It was a two-million-dollar hit, a whole roaring river of spilled milk.

Nobody was interested in our expressions of sympathy nor "*Rolling Stone*'s long-standing commitment to serious and thoughtful coverage of the most important issues," blah blah blah. The *New York Times* and *The New Yorker* published eloquent editorials in our defense. The story itself, "Jahar's World," by Janet Reitman, was a terrific piece of reporting on how this once popular, promising student was failed by his family, fell into radical Islam, and became a monster. It was a finalist for the National Magazine Award.

ERIK HEDEGAARD, ANOTHER *Rolling Stone* stalwart, was a wonderfully eccentric individual, a surfer with a master's in creative writing from Columbia who loved to ask questions about sex just to see what people would volunteer. Depp once called me after his interview with Erik and asked why I had sent him a proctologist. Erik's mother raised him as a single parent; she was an alcoholic and burned him with cigarettes. His dad was a Pentagon bigwig. So, he had a leaning toward the tragic side of life. Like Charles Manson.

Manson had spent the past forty-four years in prison and was still Crazy Charlie, with those black-hole eyeballs that stared out from his *Rolling Stone* cover decades ago. After three months of letters and phone conversations, he agreed to meet with Erik. This was a full catch-up on Manson, his life in a prison housing unit with other serial killers. He still got hundreds of fan letters a month. After their day together, Manson began calling Erik at home, at any hour, to talk about the environment, his prophecies, Jesus Christ, his sex life with his pillow and his "Roscoe." He was half mad, a devil posing as an elf. The letter he wrote us once asking for a free subscription in prison was the most popular curiosity in our archive. He was still a stigma on a generation, a symbol of something dark in our era.

CHET FLIPPO, ONE of our very first readers and, by 1970, a full-time editor, died at sixty-nine. He had the writing gene and went on the road with the Stones and on holiday with Dolly Parton. His wife, Martha Hume, another one of our top writers, had died just six months earlier. Chet carried our ethos deep and was our ambassador to Nashville. His death was sad for those of us in that original gang, the "lifers." The day before Chet's death, Michael Hastings, our new rising star, thirty-three years old, had plowed into a tree in a high-speed crash at 4:30 in the morning in Los Angeles. Hastings was an incredibly likable guy and had the ability to get in anywhere. He was a bug-eyed kid, mischievous, the kid who always had the firecrackers. A nearby camera showed his car bursting into flames. The engine flew fifty feet in the air. Michael's body was burned beyond recognition. Because he had been working on a CIA piece, rumors about an assassination via a remote-control car device followed immediately. His brother and wife, who had been preparing for an intervention with Michael, thought he had been drunk. A CIA hit job on a journalist seemed far-fetched; they only kill elected officials.

Rachel Maddow eulogized Michael on her show: "Michael was angry about things that weren't right in the world...and it made him fearless when he realized he had found something important to report."

DOWN IN JERSEY one late afternoon, we were having drinks around the outdoor fire with Patti and Bruce, listening to stories of Parents' Weekend at Duke, where their daughter, Jessie, and my young cousin Cliff were good friends. Bruce was throwing me some shade about not having gone on his European tour that summer, and how extravagant the crowds had been, nearly a hundred thousand fans singing along in English in Nuremberg, where Hitler once played. Why didn't Matt and I come see him in Brazil in a few weeks?

When we got to the hotel in São Paulo there was Jon Landau, waiting to take us to breakfast. I ducked out for lunch later that afternoon with the publisher of the Brazilian edition of *Rolling Stone*. The show that night was an hour by caravan across São Paulo to a campus gymnasium, a *Back to the Future* throwback. Bruce was a giant international star, but not in Latin America. The first and last time I had seen a rock show in a college gym was the Jefferson Airplane in Berkeley, 1965.

The next day we went to Rio and checked into the Copacabana Hotel. It was a day off, so Bruce took us, along with his magisterial piano player Roy Bittan and his wife, Susie, to a prettier, less crowded beach. We bought a lot of drinks in freshly opened coconuts and emptied a few bottles of tanning oil. The waves were pretty serious, and Matt and Bruce barely let me wade in, while they went in headfirst. Bruce was in great shape. He said one night onstage a few months earlier he had looked up at his screen projection and saw "the fat Elvis." Now he was buffed, wearing tight T-shirts.

I didn't know that we had been followed across town by some paparazzi, who shot Bruce and me walking on the beach. By the time we picked up our towels and went for nearby langoustines and cerveza there was a message from the office. They emailed pictures of us on the beach, which had just been sent from a photo agency. Obviously, I hadn't had any warning to suck up the gut. I showed Bruce, who said, "You can't go anywhere these days. The minute you go anywhere, you are everywhere."

After dinner, Bruce, Matt, and I hit the locals' nightlife district, a maze of cobblestone streets, small plazas, public gardens, family restaurants, open-air clubs on every block, music and singing in the air. No tourists, no Americans. No one recognized Bruce. What a pleasure. We wandered the streets, drinking. Matt and I were pointing out girls for Bruce, he was picking out guys for us. We would poke into the clubs, listen to some amazing drummer — a fourteen-year-old girl at one place — and then move on to another, loud with the music of Brazil, into the early hours of the morning.

We decided to rejoin the tour in South Africa. Patti had heard all about our Rio adventures and said she was coming, too. This would be a couples trip, not boys on the town. I was enchanted with Patti. I got wrapped up in her kids, her horses, and her life on the farm. Her tremolo singing voice was haunting. She poured out the love and the pain. Bruce was closemouthed about his work and comings and goings, but Patti loved to talk about their adventures. Patti swept you up in her laughter, her sophistication, and her sense of wonder. Without seeing it, I had developed a real crush. When we met up at the airport for the fourteen-hour flight to Cape Town, no Patti. She had been packing for two days and changed her mind when she woke up that morning. I gave Bruce the WTF look, and he just smiled and shrugged: "That's the missus."

The shows were at an indoor bicycle racing track, the audience was 95 percent white, but it was still about sending a message, performing "Sun City." I watched the solo encores from the side of the stage, and when Bruce walked off, still spiking adrenaline and with sweat coming off him like a squeezed sponge, he would spot me and go for the ten-second, drenching bear hug. Tom Morello, on his first tour with Bruce, told *Rolling Stone*, "The first show felt like the Normandy Invasion. The E Street Band cut a destructive path through South Africa and planted the flag of victory."

CHAPTER 72

THE MILLION-POUND SHIT HAMMER

OUR BESTSELLING COVER of 2014 was Pope Francis. This was probably as far away from the predictable as we ever got, but in my mind central to how I defined the magazine. The headline under his name read "The Times They Are a-Changing." The new pope condemned greed and despoilers of the environment, and pursued a profoundly humanistic moral agenda. When asked about homosexuals, he famously replied, "Who am I to judge?"

The statement "I'm from *Rolling Stone*" usually opened every door, and this time it got our reporter, Mark Binelli — a lapsed Catholic, son of Italian immigrants, his father a knife sharpener — an interview with an ultraconservative Opus Dei official inside the group's Rome headquarters. After lunch he asked Mark if he had read the new memoir by Steely Dan's Donald Fagen.

We had another find on our hands in Matthieu Aikins, a very young, competitive guy who liked to get his drink on, dedicated to journalism and danger. After college he went backpacking through Europe, across India, and into northern Afghanistan. Matt was half Japanese, and because of his Asian looks could go places others couldn't. He befriended Pakistani drug smugglers and moved to Kabul. His first story for us, "The A-Team Killings," was about Special Forces soldiers who kidnapped and killed Afghans. It won us our third George Polk Award, an honor equivalent to the Pulitzer inside our profession. He did two more Afghan pieces for us: "Last Tango in Kabul," an evocative piece about the coming endgame, and one about what we would leave behind after a decade of war, the crumbling foundations of a country.

I WAS LOOKING FOR more cuts, and the axe fell on two of our longest-serving and best-known senior editors, Peter Travers and David Fricke. Travers had been at *Rolling Stone* reviewing movies for twenty-five years. When he came to us, he asked how he should treat my friends in show biz. I told him, "Don't do me any favors." It wouldn't have mattered; he was Mr. Integrity. He became one of the important American film critics. I introduced him once to a singer who said, "Oh, you're the guy with four names: 'Peter Travers, *Rolling Stone*.'"

David was a tall, slender guy with a Prince Valiant haircut and thick glasses. He looked like he actually worked at *Rolling Stone*. He wore a motorcycle jacket and often was mistaken for one of the Ramones. He had written a freelance piece for us in 1977 and went full-time in 1985. He went on more than a hundred tours. David had been with us forty years. He's now a well-known voice on the radio. He and Peter had both landed on their feet, but I never felt good about saving that money.

A few years earlier we were churning out a thick, large-format magazine, now we were publishing an eighty-page, standard-size magazine. About half the content was music, the other half of the magazine was politics and general-assignment reporting. I loved music as much as ever, but it's a general truth that nothing is as special as what you grew up with. I would rather listen to Van Morrison or Ray Charles than whatever. There was new stuff I liked—Green Day, Weezer, or the

Nightsweats—right in my sweet spot but not deep in my heart. Rap fit every criteria in the rock and roll playbook, the best of it undeniably brilliant and powerful. It deserved to be in *Rolling Stone* and the Hall of Fame, no matter that it was not to my musical taste nor from my cultural maelstrom. I left our coverage in the hands of our much younger music staff. Whatever the new forms and rhythms, the music was still a passionate voice to and for its audience. Like classic rock, the force of Afro American music and culture was at its center, and as Plato said, the walls of the city were still shaking and falling. My focus was politics and reporting, and I had two excellent editors who put together an all-purpose team of contract writers who knew how to doggedly report and write clean, descriptive narrative.

THE SINKING AD sales signaled ever more dangerous waters. I started weekly meetings to brainstorm ideas to sell to big-ticket advertisers. These began as gung ho group therapy and then faded into sessions of frustration and futility. *US* was carrying the company. Celebrities were still cheating, breaking up, marrying, having babies, dropping dead, and now transitioning, too. The profits were still handsome, but declining.

The *US* and *Rolling Stone* websites had a nicely profitable business going on. Gus had revamped the operation — in fact, when he took over, he quickly and quietly replaced everyone on the staff. We watched a half-dozen similar website launches with eye-popping valuations. Despite our credentials and potential, big money wanted "pure play" digital deals. Owning magazines was owning "legacy" media. I hated that word. We had missed that bandwagon.

When I put Gus in charge of *rollingstone.com,* the first move he made was to start *rollingstone/country.com.* I flew down to Nashville with Bruce to see his show and meet up with Gus, who was so proud to take me to the new bungalow office with the *Rolling Stone* sign outside and a kitchenette. I took him to the show that night — yet another sweat-dripping, postshow embrace—and he flew back with us. I was trying to nap, but Gus stayed wide awake, pitching advertising to Landau.

Gus asked to sit in on my meetings. Occasionally we would sneak a glance at each other with the "Are you thinking what I'm thinking?" look. He was getting it. He was a smooth operator. He was starting to shed the college costume and the unshaven look. I put him in charge of a team that landed a $5 million advertising deal—our largest ever—to launch Google Play in *Rolling Stone*. My cold appraisal was that it wouldn't have gotten done but for Gus.

PUTTING ROBIN WILLIAMS on the cover of his memorial issue was like burying a family member. He had killed himself by his own hand. We had had dinner with him and his new wife just a few months earlier. Robin had been funny that night but not in his usual manic, center-of-attention way, just warm and intimate. Now I was choosing a cover, editing a piece, making sure the details were all correct, attending to the requirements when death comes to such a life, the clothes of a public burial. These deaths were now becoming too familiar to me, an endless sad parade of losses.

L'Wren Scott, Mick's girlfriend for what seemed like forever, hanged herself in their apartment in New York while Mick was on tour in Australia. The photo of him leaving a restaurant after getting the news, with a look of terror and fear, was a Mick I had never seen. We didn't speak about it, nor did he talk about it with any of our friends. You didn't want to ask "Why?" It was something Mick never saw coming, and I'm not sure he knew "why." Who really knows what's in the human heart? I couldn't go to the memorial service and sent Gus and Theo to represent me. Mick sang "Just Like a Woman."

BONO WAS ALWAYS in and out of New York, speaking at the United Nations, on his way to Washington, D.C., having dinner with the Clintons, meeting with moguls to raise money, and occasionally recording a new album. Bono is a great storyteller and an excellent mimic. He is a late nighter and an early riser. Ali is an angel who found him early on, willing to support his dreams and absorb his energy. Their four kids were in local schools, so the family were bona fide New Yorkers for a year.

If Bono was coming over for a family meal he arrived with an armload of presents, a rapscallion uncle. His inborn charm and Irish showmanship dazzled. We would settle in for a few hours to catch up on our crusades, the coming agendas, the families. B, which is what I called him, was also a world-class first-name dropper...Bill, Barack, Angela (Merkel). I always felt as much respect and curiosity from him as I felt for him. We were becoming good friends and were both out to change the world. He had his band, and I had my magazine. We saw it as all one.

Songs of Innocence was in the works. Bono would play me the latest mix, rearrangement, or new song, and update me by email. The album was about his childhood as well as other states of innocence. He was a whirlwind of thinking about it, explaining each new track, where it came from, what it meant. I thought it was one of their best. Soaring and majestic. *Rolling Stone* gave it five stars, without me having to weigh in.

Bono flew into New York to launch the album in November, landing at about 4:00 a.m. Without much rest he went for a morning bicycle ride in Central Park, crashed, and woke up in an emergency room. When I visited him after surgery, his arm was trussed up like a lamb on a spit. His face and body were terribly bruised. The X-rays of the rods and screws they put in his shoulder and arm looked like the structural plans for the Eiffel Tower. I left for Thanksgiving and he stayed put. He sent me an email: "Who knew drugs could be this good? I wake up every morning like I have been in a car accident and by mid-day I am in Disneyland talking to Snow White...and feeling like Mickey Mouse. It's evening here now. Sun and pain killers fading...a sense of uselessness has come over me. It's so hard to have your hands tied behind your back and not be singing these songs from the rooftops now...I've never been more excited about going on tour. The band are very emotional about being chosen *Rolling Stone*'s album of the year. I don't know if she mentioned, but Ali and I are going to be looking for a house for the month of July if you know of anyone near you...it would be nice to be close...Up the Jewish Irish...or as they're known around here...the cashews. LOVE and gratitude for so many things. B."

In november 2014, Will Dana and features editor Sean Woods sat across from me at my round table, the command center of the empire. Will looked scared. We had just published "A Rape on Campus," about a brutal gang assault in a fraternity house at the University of Virginia. It was getting a huge readership on the internet and national pickup in the press. However, the writer had just called Will and told him that "our worst nightmare has come true." The *Washington Post* was re-reporting our reporting and finding it wasn't holding up. The "victim" wasn't returning calls and had disappeared. This didn't seem possible; it was too screwy to happen. But it was very possible. The *Post* began going after us every day. They were on a crusade, and they made it a circus.

Our intention had been to closely examine one case of sexual assault on campus, through which we could show all the complexity of the problem: the ostracism of the victim, the *a priori* masculine prejudice, the college's self-protective instincts, the judicial roadblocks. Sabrina Rubin Erdely, through her earlier stories on rape, had been able to tap into the victims' activist network, which led us to the case of a coed at the University of Virginia, a hometown school for the Washington, D.C., elite, and named by *Playboy* as party campus number one.

I had read the story in draft when it came in. It had a powerful opening scene of a naive freshman at her first-ever fraternity party lured into an upstairs bedroom, thrown onto a low glass table, shattering it, and raped. Seven different men for three hours. The rest of the piece explored her journey into a labyrinth of emotional destruction and legalized discrimination against women.

I thought it was terrific and authorized publishing it. It didn't occur to me to remind anyone about fact-checking and secondary sources. We trusted the writer. We had a widely regarded fact-checking department, a legal review process, experienced editors, and a near-flawless track record. Our budget cuts had left us understaffed; still, pseudonyms, lack of corroborating sources, and our sympathy for the victim, which made us reluctant to challenge her, were all warning signs. The victim, pseudonym "Jackie," had been vouched for by the UVA dean's office. The problem was that she had made the whole thing up.

Donny Graham called. He had just sold the *Washington Post*, his family's newspaper, and wanted to give me advice based on a similar hoax perpetrated by a *Post* staff reporter. He suggested we hire an outside ombudsman to investigate and print the results. It was sober advice, and we commissioned a report by the dean of the Columbia Journalism School, himself a noted journalistic heavy, Steve Coll. It was a high-minded idea, but ended up backfiring.

We had been humiliated, humbled, and shamed. The holier-than-thou magazine had finally flown too close to the sun. Our fuckup was a good, old-fashioned, red meat story in its own right, but I felt many of our peers were reporting it with relish. It would be years before we could shake this one. It was no consolation that the *Times* and the *Post* had each survived the same flogging for a piece of fraudulent origin that got past a systemic organizational flaw. But they were institutions with big money. I was on my own. I wouldn't take calls from "crisis management consultants." I expected that the review would somewhat exonerate us, if not for our practices, at least for our integrity and intentions. Hunter had a phrase: "The Million-Pound Shit Hammer." It was coming down.

CHAPTER 73

BAD MOON RISING

I GOT OUT OF New York before Christmas, took the family to Idaho, and didn't return for three months. We enrolled the children at a local school. It was a relief to be gone. The beat of the bad news arrived every day as the *Washington Post* came out with one story after another about how badly we had gotten it wrong. The phrase "crucified in the press" described the experience fairly. When I got back, going into the office each morning was painful, a lot of shuffling and soft talk, like at a funeral. At this point the concern was reputation and pride. I hadn't considered lawsuits, staff morale, and the damage to our sterling trademark. The editors involved offered their resignations, which I turned down. We all make mistakes, we all deserve forgiveness, and as I have said before, I'm not one for selling postcards of the hanging. All we could do was lower our heads and wait.

As pledged, we published the investigation from the Columbia Journalism School, itself a fascinating piece of journalism about journalism. We had been the victim of some kind of psychotic fantasy. In looking back, after the fact, the unverifiable statements in the coed's story about her gang rape should have sent up a red flag. But both our sympathy for her and the premeditated stonewalling by the fraternity and the UVA administration (who refused to provide us with crucial information) clouded our decisions and judgment. The university added credibility to her accusation. They had taken her seriously. For our part, total discipline and unerring oversight would have prevented all this.

If I thought we were off the hook, I abruptly discovered how naive I was. Publishing the report wasn't seen as contrition or journalistic responsibility in the face of adversity. It became an excuse for a new, even more detailed rehash of the whole affair, another round of national shaming that would blacken our name. The effort to do the right thing hadn't helped. I would have been better off without the report, just letting it all fade away. I thought we should take the high road, be recognized for openness and honesty, our willingness to take the consequences. The world I had chosen to live in didn't quite work that way.

And then came the lawsuits. The ombudsman report was like a free private investigator's report for lawyers. The fraternity and the dean in charge of rape victims wanted their measure of flesh. These were the very people who blocked important reporting avenues and had steered us, wittingly or not — which remains unknown — on the wrong course. The frat knew there was no party and could have proved that to the reporter rather than give her a nondenial denial. And the dean, who had agreed to talk to our reporter, suddenly canceled on her, stonewalling her close look at UVA, a school already put on notice by the Justice Department for suspected violation of the Title IX laws. She could have likely undercut the "victim." The federal government would later call UVA "a hostile environment" for victims of sexual assault. They could have and should have been open and forthcoming. Instead, they made it seem as if they had a lot to hide. It didn't matter if we had been suckered. The wheels of the legal system were grinding their way to our door.

THE TWELVE-LEGGED MONSTER, our peripatetic group of six travelers, made what turned out to be its last trip, returning to Venice. Microsoft's Paul Allen had offered us the neglected palazzo he had just bought on the Grand Canal. We felt like the down-on-their-luck heirs of a once wealthy family, living a threadbare life together in the childhood home. We came to see the Biennale, the art fair, which was just an enjoyable excuse to spend time together. Every meal and expedition was a set piece, whether it was a hilarious loud lunch at a café on the canal, generally with Bette and me carrying on, breaking plates and throwing silverware; a dramatic shopping disaster, which would involve Bette and Cathy carrying on; or the complicated translations and choices on the menu, the province of Ned, Matt, and Martin, each proudly steeped in culinary issues. We could be childish, eccentric, or sophisticated. It didn't matter. Bette and Martin, Ned and Cathy, were people I loved and with whom I felt at ease and valued. These were people lodged deep in my life and who would be forever. I suppose that's one of the definitions of family. With that comes unspoken, unconditional love, and the safety to be totally yourself.

THE GRATEFUL DEAD were back, this time as the Dead, with John Mayer standing in for Jerry. It had been years for me, at least forty, and never out of the ballrooms of San Francisco. I smoked a little pot and got glued to the patterns and interlaced movements of the light show, wonderful memories from long ago. Theo and Gus came with me. I casually knew Bobby Weir and we lived worlds apart, but there was a big bear hug, an affirmation of fellowship, travelers on the long, strange road, a brotherhood that yet survived. Theo and Gus watched all this. I could see their loving smiles.

Don Henley and I, for all the years and all of our prickliness — or being pricks — were friends, comrades in the conspiracy and mutual admirers. He was playing the Beacon in New York. Theo, as big a fan as I was of Don's brilliant solo albums, came with me. We went to his dressing room. He had his twentysomething daughter with him, working on the tour. She was doing his makeup, his shirt open to a chest of curly gray hair. The years, the years... Theo drank it in with such affection.

The highlight of summer at the beach was the Hewson family: Bono, Ali, and their kids, who were staying at the house Jane and I had once owned in Amagansett. The topper had to be dinner at our new home in

Montauk with them and Paul and Nancy McCartney — moonlit, looking out on the silvery ocean, past midnight. We served drinks on an old Beatlemania souvenir tea tray that Peter Wolf had given me. Paul lit up: "Oh, it's me and me mates," and the twinkling Beatle magic dust filled the air. No one is immune.

I WAS ASKED TO introduce Michael Douglas at a luncheon sponsored by AARP. Bob Love, one of my former managing editors, was featuring him on the cover of the association's magazine where Bob was now the top editor. I was happy to go anywhere on Mikey's behalf. We had stood side by side for years and come into our careers, our families, and our adulthood as if hand in hand. He was doing work for the United Nations, spending serious time at it. I was always so damn proud of my old buddy. There we were, both of us in our seventies. We both still got such a kick out of seeing each other. On the road we traveled together…drugs, divorce, tough times, good times, wonderful times…he was always there for me and I for him. We had both had big success. Our dreams were the same. We celebrated each other. The friendship itself became a special thing, with its own life. We were made in the same batch.

I PUT TRUMP ON the cover in September 2015. This was before the primaries, but he was out there chewing the scenery, mesmerizing crowds with his angry bullshit and nearly illiterate mumbo jumbo, turning his rivals impotent with mockery. I didn't know if he was unstoppable, but the tea leaves were in plain sight. I did feel certain that this was not a lark for Trump, not just a marketing stunt, although he was an absolute whore for publicity. He would fuck over anybody for a few lines of ink. Trump was drooling for the cover and attention from us.

None of our political writers were interested. Taibbi ducked; Trump was too low-life and a clown. Will recruited Paul Solotaroff, one of our steady contributors, a veteran of twenty-five years at *Rolling Stone*, whose specialty was tough guys, crime, and tragedy. He was a former steroid-using bodybuilder. On their flight to a rally in New Hampshire, the only other reporter aboard Trump's custom 757 was from Breitbart News. It was on that flight that Trump remarked to Solotaroff about Carly Fiorina, "Look at that face! Would anyone vote for that? C'mon, folks, are we serious?" When the quote was picked up and became an early controversy, Trump stated that he had never said it and that "Wenner personally made that up and forced the writer to put it in." From the moment Paul boarded the plane, Trump began lying, starting with the size of the plane ("bigger than Air Force One"). Paul could smell the breath of the dragon, calling Trump "a top-of-the-food-chain killer...gaining strength and traction by the hour." I wrote the cover headline, "Taking Trump Seriously," because people didn't believe it was possible. I did.

WILL DANA HAD recruited a major-league team of writers, a dozen men and women constantly on active assignment. This team rivaled the gang I had put together in San Francisco, the so-called golden era of *Rolling Stone*. But the UVA debacle had drained Will. He lost his confidence and his spirit. There was no way I was going to throw him to the wolves...for what purpose? But he was going to have to heal by himself, and I needed to get *Rolling Stone* back on the right footing. It had been a year since the Erdely piece. He knew it was coming, was probably past due, a sad day played out under a gloomy cloud. No farewell luncheon, no golden watch. We tried for some valedictory words between us but they felt hollow; it was more like walking away from a house that had burned to the ground. There was nothing left to say.

SEAN PENN CALLED to say he had a story, but couldn't tell me what it was because his phone was tapped. He started dropping hints and clues; he was bursting with excitement and the code words of conspiracy. He couldn't hold it in: he had been in contact with the Mexican drug cartel overlord Joaquín Guzmán — El Chapo — and he had agreed to an interview. That was an old-fashioned "Holy shit!" moment. El Chapo was, plain and simple, the most wanted man in the world. He was guarded by a private army of remorseless killers. Finding El Chapo would be insane.

The advice I offered Sean was useless. I had no experience in evading international law enforcement, and Sean wouldn't have listened anyway. He had to get to El Chapo's high-security hideout, which so far had apparently eluded armies and spy satellites. My chief concern was being trapped in some hoax by a genius prankster or perhaps a random fabulist. We needed some proof — a fingerprint, a photograph, a voice recording — to analyze. Meanwhile, Sean was off to Mexico.

Some weeks later he came to see me. It was now time to "read in" — a CIA phrase I always loved — a "special operations group" to work with Sean and run the cover-up necessary to keep this a secret. We had assembled for lunch at my house when Sean pulled a manuscript out of his backpack, stood up, and for half an hour read it aloud. We sat astonished by the gauntlet of heavily armed men, roadblocks, and checkpoints he had passed through to get to El Chapo's hideout in the mountain jungles of Mexico. With his metaphor and simile-filled story, he was a simulacrum of Hunter, whom he idolized. Sean and El Chapo had spent a long night over tacos and tequilas until they were suddenly awakened before sunlight and forced by approaching military to depart through the jungle. In the end, Sean hadn't gotten the interview, just the promise of one. But even without it, this was an amazing piece. We would wait while the return trip was arranged. Weeks of negotiating over encrypted phones began.

EL CHAPO AGREED to answer written questions via videotape from his hideout. We asked how he felt about the death and destruction he had caused and to describe his business, his day-to-day life, his ethics. What we got back was a video of him wearing a baseball cap, a simple farmer on his farm, ignoring the questions. I decided we would go with just that; the visit itself was itself fascinating, more than enough.

Sean was a florid writer. He wanted to make some points about the drug trade, morality, and journalism, which was fine. However, dialing him back for his own best interests was a tug-of-war, a battle over every fucking word, a war of attrition that he won.

We set up a locked room called the Red Dragon Lounge for essential staffers we needed to process the piece. There would be a last-minute secret switch with the cover-up cover. We had a photo of Sean grinning and shaking hands with El Chapo. On deadline day, two hours before we went to press, El Chapo was captured.

We put the story online before we got printed copies out. Gus came in to hit the "publish" button when the time came. We were in another newsbreak tsunami, adrenalized, riding the big one again. It was a repeat of Patty Hearst and General McChrystal, including the usual jealous journalists who had their bitchy issues. Sean refused to respond, which added more oxygen to the media fire. In the end he went on *60 Minutes* — a nothingburger, but great publicity. It was soon revealed that the federal police had followed Sean and the woman he was with — a Mexican soap opera star whom El Chapo had set his eye on. They unknowingly led the *federales* to El Chapo. The Mexican government had postponed the initial raid on his compound because they knew Sean and the actress were still there.

EVERY YEAR I got a Christmas card from a longtime *Rolling Stone* reader from Massachusetts, Dean Conway; it would contain a neatly handwritten letter thanking me for particular stories we had done that year, sharing his own thoughts on the spiritual and political state of the nation, and bringing me up to date on what his children were doing. Dean was a teacher and soccer coach. He impressed me because he got all the nuances of what I was doing, so I always wrote him back, and finally, after ten years of correspondence, I invited him down for a Christmas lunch. He was a delightful guy, a family man trying to make a better world.

CHAPTER 74

THE GATHERING STORM

FOR MY SEVENTIETH birthday, Gus had a surprise waiting at the top of Sun Valley's Mt. Baldy. The guys I had spent the past twenty years skiing with had assembled to make a celebratory run down Warm Springs, the high-speed barrel of the highway to the bottom: the twins, local racers Kitt and Cody Doucette, Curt "Hollywood" Hansen, the poster artist Jack Weekes, X Games gold medalists Reggie and Zach Crist, and Olympian Terry Palmer. Scott "Stork" Hanson was MIA in the state penitentiary. I didn't know what was up when I saw the first familiar faces. I would have cried, except for how macho the scene was.

By the end of the season, my back went down again. The spinal fusion I had in 1990 had transferred the nerve pain to another vertebra. I counted my steps and looked for the nearest place to sit on the way back to New York. Matt arranged for a wheelchair to meet me at the airport check-in. There was no choice; I prepared for the stares. When I was put in the wheelchair Noah looked at me and said, "Don't worry, Papa, you've still got your looks." And this time I did tear up. He was ten. I went to Düsseldorf, Germany, for a series of shots that held off the pain for two more years.

DAVID BOWIE, MY fellow Capricorn, died two days after his birthday in January 2016. No one knew he had cancer. The record he had just made, *Blackstar,* was his farewell, a testament at the time of his dying, a beautiful, eerie album that starts with a musical evocation of his last minutes, rising into the ether, an aural vision of the transubstantiation, the turbulence, the joy, and the disappearance into space. Major Tom, he's dead: "Look up here, I'm in heaven / I've got scars that can't be seen…Everybody knows me now." David talking from the beyond, from the other side. "Where the fuck did Monday go?"

David and I had a book club, and we would send each other reports on our latest reading. He turned me on to contemporary fiction. We debated Churchill. He liked to exercise his intellect and humor, and delighted in crossing swords with elegant repartee. If whatever at hand was something new, avant-garde, or forward-looking, David liked it. He turned me on to bands like Arcade Fire and TV on the Radio. He dismissed the Stones as retro. He turned me down when I begged him to come in person to accept his Hall of Fame induction. It meant nothing to him. The nicest guy, a gentleman from an earlier century. It just didn't seem right to lose him.

I SLOWLY FELL OUT of regular touch with Mick. After L'Wren's death, he moved back to Europe and I remained stateside. He sent Matt and me terrific Christmas gifts every year. I stopped going to the new Stones tours when they came through. My love of their music never wavered, but to go through the hassle of a stadium to watch an oldies review, distanced no matter how good the tickets, just didn't feel worth the stamina. It was tough on me to turn away from all that atavistic energy. It had been a long run. Mick and the Stones had been on the cover twenty-five times.

I WENT TO THE next Hall of Fame induction with little heart. The artists I loved had by now mostly been honored; there were a few more to go, but my work was done. Jon Landau was still running the nominating committee; a redesign of the museum was completed and money was being quickly raised for an additional building. We had a solid partnership with the city of Cleveland. What I had set out to do was complete. I was editing a multiscreen, supersonic-sound film of the great highlights of music from the ceremonies. I chose Jonathan Demme as the director. He was a major music fan, and it was like being back in Hollywood again. The film runs every day in Cleveland. It's a powerhouse. The workload was minimal, the decisions were second nature, and the heavy lifting had been done. Great years had passed. I was a caretaker without any emotional attachment to its current business. I announced my intention to retire as chairman of the Hall of Fame.

My only worry was the pressure to compromise the integrity of the nominating and voting. I should have known better; I should have played the game better, seen people a little more cynically than my nature allowed. After I resigned, I was told that music business power-brokers on the board were going to be inducted. These individuals had made not one iota of difference to the history, present, or future of the creation of music, which was the explicit criterion. But they had accumulated influence and wealth. It was an inside job.

That was fast.

My mother died in March. She was ninety-three, bedridden, and in the hands of caregivers who loved her. The whole family had been with her the year before, when her doctor said she might not make it through the night. We had a late-night family meeting at the time to make a pull-the-plug decision, a roundtable in the lounge of her residence for the elderly in Palo Alto. We voted her off the island. I say this sarcastically, but it's true. Over the years she had just squashed the sentimentality out of our relationships with her. I spent a good amount of time visiting her, bringing her both sets of my children, taking her on vacations. I sent her a monthly allowance, though she hardly needed it. But I minimized time alone with her. I didn't like being with her, feeling the guilt and sadness of that knowledge, aware that it hurt her. I couldn't change what had become so ingrained, so deeply rubbed in by her hand.

The last words she spoke to me when I was kissing her goodbye after a quick visit were these: "Get your filthy hands off of me." Matt and I looked at each other in amazement. What a classic. She was on a drug that provoked anger and hostility, and she must have been unimaginably frustrated that she had become an immobile old woman in a wheelchair with a television screen that she could barely see. The grand piano, the two-bedroom garden apartment, the night-and-day care, and her cat no longer had a palliative effect. When I heard the news, I was happy to have done with it. It was sad, but not a tear.

My sisters put together a memorial service in Marin County. My mom had been in the Navy, and a small squad of uniformed sailors showed up with a folded flag to present and a bugler who played taps. Kate, who had been a documentary filmmaker, put together a story of our family — kids on bicycles, washing cars, Sim in shorts gardening, and studio portraits of her and her parents from the twenties. Our childhood was a vision of the suburban fifties.

We all spoke of our relationships with her. She had been a dominant parent, and we had trimmed our little lives to her wishes. The older grandkids in the three families spoke, something she surely would have been proud to behold...and then criticize. Noah, age ten, the shyest of all my kids, stood up on the spur of the moment, saying there were a few things he thought of and wanted to say. He had the tenderness of a young boy and the elocution of a mature man. I wish my mom could have seen that.

My eulogy opened, "My mother was a great beauty as a young woman. She was my defender and the sun shined. My childhood memories are at Rainbow Road, and I think of it now as a place of enchantment. I try to learn from that time in raising my own kids — about love, the feeling of safety, guidance, and letting go. It took me many years to get over being sent away at twelve. 'But what the hell,' as she might say, 'you turned out pretty okay.' In her phrase, 'You're on your own, Buster Brown.'"

And ended: "My mom was a mixed blessing. A beauty, even at ninety-three. She was smart as a whip, sharp, witty, curious, and fearless. She came from her own tough emotional crucible, did her best with it, and was fiercely her own person, and in her life did everything she felt like doing, on her terms and to the fullest."

We held the service at the foot of the Golden Gate Bridge, with all the blue magic of the Pacific Ocean, the skyscrapers and hills of the city, and the engineering wonder of the bridge span to behold. Jane came with her share of the children. Our San Francisco family, Ned and Cathy, Bing and Deb Gordon, were there. Afterward we went back to Rainbow Road, the one place we called home, to scatter our mother's ashes. I knew I wanted to say a few last words to her, inwardly. It was not emotional, not driven by tragedy or loss, just a simple thank-you for everything she had done for me. I had learned politics, how people think, found my love of music, and learned how to write. I wanted to reassure her that I would be okay, and so would all of us. One adult to another. Then I threw her ashes into the air and said goodbye.

I WAS EXCHANGING LETTERS with Robin Gracey. I had a sudden desire to reconnect with the boy I met splashing in the river that summer fifty years ago. I wanted to revisit that fantasy, to daydream, to imagine the road not taken, fall back into that long-ago children's story. Robin caught me up on his life, poetry, his gardening, his marriage, his children. We still saw the world in the same words, but our lives had turned out to be so different. The letters back and forth became a wonderfully intimate attempt at understanding our lives. At twenty-one you run into a stranger and find a saint. What would happen if we had met now, as old men? I don't know.

WE GOT DOWN to work on the *Rolling Stone* fiftieth anniversary. The one thing off the table was the intoxicated, starlit evening, the million-dollar bash. The Hall of Fame was putting together a yearlong exhibition about *Rolling Stone*, re-creating my original office. We were doing a supersize coffee-table book. The most ambitious and consequential piece was a documentary by Alex Gibney that would run as a four-hour special on HBO. Gibney was a master documentarian. He had done a film about Hunter, which was how I met him. His questions had brought me to tears. The film he made about our history was a mix of *Almost Famous* and *60 Minutes*.

MY 2016 SUMMER highlight was the political season, watching the Republican and Democratic conventions on television. Trump's celebrants were foaming at the mouth. Taibbi wrote that he had never seen anything like Trump, "impulsive, lewd, grandiose, disgusting, horrible, narcissistic and dangerous." Now, that's entertainment. Nancy Pelosi and her husband, Paul, came to Montauk for lunch on Labor Day weekend. Nancy does most of the talking, pausing only to expand and articulate further on an idea she's in the middle of, and does so with a startling certainty and authority. She was pretty sure we would take back the House, and I was sure Hillary would win, too. We had a long afternoon in high spirits.

I SAW TOM WOLFE for the last time. We talked on the phone every few months, keeping alive the notion that he was doing another piece. Neither of us expected that, but it was just fun to talk about. He was slow, but funny and graceful as ever. I hadn't seen him in nearly two years, so we went for a chic East Side lunch. He walked in with a trekking pole in each hand. He was severely hunched over. Tom wouldn't use canes — "too old-man-looking" for him. Trekking poles, he thought, were sporty. They went well with a white suit. He still had a child's ability to light up with amazement, but his voice was soft and you had to lean in close to hear him. I adored Tom. I drove him home — his building was between

Art Garfunkel's triplex and Mayor Bloomberg's mansion — and said goodbye. He had told me that as he got older, the worst thing was hearing someone call him "spry." I had been blessed by this graceful man who, just as his career had gotten incandescent, chose to throw in with me. He was probably the greatest writer I ever worked with. He had been generous with himself in every way; sharing his talent was part of that, and being a part of his life was an enormous pride and joy, from that nervous moment I first shook his hand after I tracked him down in San Francisco so long ago.

THAT SAME NIGHT we celebrated Mica Ertegun's eighty-ninth birthday at La Grenouille, the last of New York's café society French restaurants. Tom had used it as the location for one of his greatest set pieces in *The Bonfire of the Vanities*. I was at the head table with Bette and Martin; we were the young ones, in our early seventies. I was seated with Annette de la Renta, a dinner party friend of mine for years, now eighty and the court-appointed guardian of Brooke Astor. Rounding out the group was Sir John Richardson, Picasso's biographer and bon vivant, ninety-two; Alexandra Schlesinger, widow of Arthur Schlesinger Jr., the great Harvard historian, also in her eighties; and Henry Kissinger, the oldest at ninety-three. The host was Linda Wachner, once the only female CEO on the Fortune 500. This was the end of the dinners and the weekends; this was all that was left of the world that Ahmet and Mica had introduced me to. It was now history, theirs and mine as well.

THE NOBEL PRIZE for Literature was given to Bob Dylan. The affirmation of Bob's talent was obvious and overdue. He was one of the twentieth century's literary masters, and this was the world's highest honor. No artist meant more to me. The Nobel committee had specifically cited the form of the work, a validation of the art itself, what we all had lived by, rock and roll. I was over the moon.

We went to trial with the dean of the University of Virginia. The prosecution team blindsided us and leaked the confidential deposition videos to ABC News, which ran salacious promotional spots all week hyping their "exposé." That's another thing that is so nice to wake up to. We had big-city lawyers; they had their Virginia-based home team, who saw this as their shot at becoming a big law firm with this famous case as their calling card. They were aiming for a settlement or jury award of $50 million or more. That would certainly be curtains for us.

A secretive Silicon Valley billionaire had just financed a libel lawsuit against *Gawker*, an outspoken website, bankrupting it and driving it out of business. I was scared. Who was paying this law firm?

The jury delivered their verdict in November, the day before the election, which unequivocally declared that *Rolling Stone* was not guilty of libel, but faulted the reporter. They said we had behaved properly and in good faith. Nonetheless, because we did not immediately remove the piece from our website when we knew there might be a problem, and even though we added a disclaimer alerting readers to the story's flaws, we were "republishing" a piece we thought might be false. This was a new interpretation of the law, and a large group of news organizations was ready to join us to overturn the ruling. But the distinction was barely made in the news coverage; we were tarnished and not given the benefit of "rehabilitation" from the underlying decision of not guilty.

The dean got a small jury award for damages and her lawyers were devastated. The insurance company paid for 90 percent of our costs and settlement, and the verdict had, in fact if not appearance, vindicated us. I was told I should be happy. I was pissed off, dissatisfied by having to pay a penalty, and felt that the cloud would linger. I wanted exoneration. I couldn't finance an appeal, so it would take years for this cloud to lift. The dean got her reputation back, with a promotion; we got cleared too late to make a difference; and the lawyers, as usual, got the money, far, far more than anyone else did.

THE NEXT NIGHT we watched the election results come in. It was like a bomb, leaving devastation everywhere. I went to sleep drunk; I just couldn't face thinking about it. What is there to say? What can be done? How do you rebuild? What will you do with survivors?

Months earlier, Obama had agreed to an exit interview, and it was to take place in the Oval Office the morning after the election. I had spent the week reviewing questions about his achievements, how they would be building blocks for the future, his triumph over racism and Republicanism, his advice for President-elect Clinton.

I got up early and called the White House to see if the president wanted to put our interview off a few days. He called back and wanted to get it done. This had to be one of the worst days of his political life. It would be our fourth interview together and his tenth *Rolling Stone* cover. He had agreed that Gus could come and sit in. I had been planning to bring Matt, but he said that turning over the keys to your son included the privileged ritual of meeting with the president in the Oval Office.

It was a dull, cloudy day. The streets and broad avenues were quiet. It had been a long and unhappy night at the White House, and only a skeleton crew remained. The West Wing was lifeless, but the boss himself was in. The last time I had been there, Hillary was chilling outside the Oval Office; now it was her ghost. The president walked in, sat right down, and said, "Let's do this."

It was a sober conversation, and a tricky one. Despite his contempt for Trump, he had to hold his tongue out of respect for the office, the tradition of an outgoing president's deference to his successor. Obama also had to give comfort to his supporters, his party, indeed to the entire world. He had to give us a reason for hope. We discussed the future of marijuana, the climate, Obamacare, the party, the press, and on each he gave the long view, assessing the durability of his legacy. I thought some of it was wishful thinking, but I was reluctant to challenge him, since I didn't want to bum him out. We had not only been beaten, we were now in peril. At one point he said, "Listen, if you want to persuade me that everything is going to be terrible, then we can talk ourselves into that. Or we can act. It is what it is.

There's been an election. There's no benefit that's derived from pulling into a fetal position. We go out there and we work. We slog through challenges and over time things get better."

I asked if he thought the weight of history would to some extent restrain Trump. He said, "I think sitting behind that desk is sobering and that it will have an impact on him as it has on every president. The most important constraint on any president is the American people themselves, an informed citizenry that is active and participating and engaged. And that is something that in my own modest ways I will continue to try to encourage for the rest of my life."

Obama had enraptured us. Whether it was his sophistication and humanity, his looks and color, or that he embodied our dream of America. But with charisma came hubris. He made the mistake of misreading the Republicans, their cynicism and ferocious cruelty, and thinking that his own personal strengths would substitute for the cold reality of wielding political power. He wouldn't play politics. It was a big mistake.

PART FIVE

GOODBYE TO ALL THAT

CHAPTER 75

SELLING
ROLLING STONE

I HAD BEEN SURE Hillary would be president and that after fifty years I could lay down my sword, knowing the country was in good hands, that I had helped bend the arc of the moral universe toward justice. But history doesn't proceed in a straight line. Instead of our supremely qualified and humanitarian first woman president, we had been saddled with a moron.

Every day brought some new lunacy and lie. Would we survive this onslaught on the truth, was this the end of the informed consent of the governed? What could we do, what could anyone do? For the first few months, until the Women's March, I was in a funk of helplessness. But that national, nearly spontaneous protest was the signal of sanity and resistance. Matt and Jane joined the Fifth Avenue march, taking Noah, who carried a hand-painted sign: "Obama cared, do you?"

WE PUBLISHED INVESTIGATIVE profiles of people who were appointed to positions that were once unthinkable: they weren't there to build; they had been picked by Trump to destroy. They were saboteurs. His interior secretary blamed climate change on "rising ocean temperatures." Bill McKibben wanted to know why he thought the oceans would suddenly be getting hotter all by themselves. Walruses peeing? Washington was in the grip of the fossil-fuel gangsters. Activism had become our marching orders.

We interviewed Professor James Hansen, whom I thought was the man above all others to listen to on climate science. He said, "We have not hit the disastrous level, which would knock down global economies and leave us with an ungovernable planet. But we are close. The energy system and the tax system have got to be simplified in a way that everybody understands and doesn't allow the wealthy few to completely rig the system. Young people will have to figure out how to get carbon dioxide out of the atmosphere. Or figure out how to live on a radically different planet."

WE PUT US WEEKLY on the market. In addition to paying off the loan balance to the bank, we learned that we owed taxes that had been deferred over the years, due to a break granted to magazine publishers. I put Gus in charge of finding a buyer. I was still sneaking cigarettes, and Gus and I had a father-son ritual: we would meet at the elevator, go across the street, and sit on a park bench (Gus called it the "pigeon drop"). There we would smoke a "grit," share the day's news, and brainstorm. "Grit time" became our decision forum and brought us even closer.

The obvious players for US were our competitors. They could benefit from the elimination of millions of dollars in duplicated costs that would drive up their profits. Time Inc. was looking to sell itself, which left American Media as the only viable customer; its CEO, David Pecker, offered Gus $80 million. As usual, at the last minute an offer came in from another company, one that had a reputation for some erratic high flying. They offered more than $100 million. We all advised Gus to take the bird in the hand, but he took the big offer. Five days later, as the papers were being prepared, they pulled out. Gus moved fast and got Pecker to raise his offer to more than $100 million to match the deal that had evaporated. Gus had balls.

THE FATHER OF rock and roll, Chuck Berry, died in March 2017. He was ninety. We honored him with a beautiful farewell cover doing his signature duckwalk. Another of my favorite covers. We ran a biography wrapped inside a tribute by Mikal Gilmore, who explained Chuck's yet-to-be-fully-understood place in the larger American story. When we ran a photo from his funeral, the open casket revealed that he would be buried with his red Gibson guitar.

Chuck had been the first person inducted into the Hall of Fame. I dedicated our next ceremony to him: "No one in this room tonight would be here but for this man. He's called the Father, the inventor of rock and roll. He put the poetry of the common man to the beat, and then he added the revved-up, motorvatin', double-string guitar that laid down the laws for every rock and roll musician that came after. Tonight we say farewell to the founding father." That was my last speech at the Rock and Roll Hall of Fame.

OUR FIRST COVER of Trump as president, by Victor Juhasz — who had succeeded Ralph Steadman and Bob Grossman as our political cartoonist — was a drawing of an orange whirlwind, a cyclone, forming the shape of Trump in profile. I was reaching for the imagery and language of the Old Testament. The headline: "Trump, the Destroyer." These were heartless people bent on extirpating government protections of our liberties, our health, and our happiness.

Trump was a crook, but something else was wrong with him beyond sadism and dishonesty. My sister Kate hit it. She said Trump had clinical narcissistic personality disorder, something that affects 6 percent of the U.S. population, including our late mother, who had struggled with it her entire life. Of all the recognized personality disorders, this mental disorder was nearly impossible to treat. I commissioned a piece by one of our newest contributors, Alex Morris, titled "Trump and the Pathology of Narcissism." It made it clear that the sickness had overwhelmed

Trump, the pathological man to whom the country had entrusted its safety and future.

IN APRIL, I. M. PEI turned one hundred. His adult children had a party for him on the roof of the St. Regis Hotel. Talk about "It was an older crowd." When I went to I. M.'s table after the cake, he looked up at me, puzzled, drawing a blank, and then his happy smile opened up with the memory. He pointed at me and said, "Rock and roll!"

SHORTLY AFTERWARD, I solemnly packed a bag and flew to San Francisco to sit with Cathy Topham on her deathbed and spend time with Ned, my dearest old friend, as he managed the death of his wife. They had fit into every stage of my life, from college to becoming irreplaceable members of the Twelve-Legged Monster. Ned was stoic, his always reserved self; his grown son Ned Jr. — who came to work at *Rolling Stone* for a few years in his twenties — was in tears. Cathy was set up on a bed moved into the family room. I held her hand, but she was unmoving, a victim of a rare brain disease that froze her functions. She stared at the ceiling, her mouth locked in a grimace. I talked to her, because you think that somehow there must be some level of communication, something spiritual, beyond consciousness. But it was upsetting. Her mouth clenched, as if she was angry. John Warnecke, the third member of the LSD Musketeers with Ned and me, had died fifteen years earlier. He had been fifty-four, and left two daughters whom Ned and Cathy looked after. The years were closing in, and I was back in my hometown, watching a long stretch of my life fade away — not just the growing up part, but that richer, powerful bond of a lifetime friend of fifty years.

US WEEKLY MOVED out and with it, two-thirds of Wenner Media. I also sold *Men's Journal* to David Pecker, who owned a similar men's magazine he would merge into it. The moment the US Weekly sale closed, a switch was thrown and, other than fraternal, poignant small talk, I could no longer command or even advise the hundred-plus members of the team I had led to publishing, cultural, and financial glory. A hundred people who spend five days and nights every week closing on a deadline make a lot of soothing, comforting noise. When they moved out, it was hard to look down the end of the long hallway from my office and see the US offices, built in the open style of a daily newsroom, empty and dark, lifeless. I had to reckon with that sight every day. Coming to work was never really a happy thing ever again.

Gus — whom I had promoted to chief operating officer — and Tim Walsh, our chief financial officer, who had worked for me for twenty years, scheduled a meeting. Gus gave me a heads-up: Tim was coming to tell me I would also have to sell Rolling Stone. I go calm and analytical when dealing with something tough, and save the fears and tears for down the road. I was worried about Tim. He had seemed depressed, almost angry, at every meeting over the past year during the weeks and months of relentless bad news. At first I thought he was panicking, but he lined up the facts carefully, and he was right. There was no choice. I instructed them to start looking for investment bankers again. We were on a sinking ship. Gus wasn't just learning the ropes — these were the ropes.

A MONTH LATER I was in the back of an ambulance, unconscious, on the way from Tivoli to Weill Cornell Medical Center in the city. I had been watching Noah play tennis and decided to show him how to improve his toss. This was not requested, not wanted, and utterly unhelpful. I fell forward and broke the biggest bone in the body, my femur, in half just below the hip. When the shock wore off, pain ripped through me each time I even slightly moved the leg until the ambulance and the morphine arrived. By the time we got to the hospital, I had also had a severe heart attack. It was Sunday morning.

The doctors told my family that they should take the opportunity to spend time with me. Theo described hearing that and no other sound, nothing but the echo of those words. When he came into my room, he found me unconscious and intubated. There were tubes down my throat. My skin was pallid, bloodless, and translucent; I was in a coma.

The very explicit message was that I was dying. The surgeons didn't want to operate because my vital functions were so poor that they felt the valvuloplasty (a balloon inserted to open the artery) that could save me would most likely kill me. They refused to do anything. They asked who would make the decision. My family all turned to Matt and said, "His husband." The use of that word was a turning point for all of them. Matt told Jane, Kate, and my kids that they were all equal in making the decisions.

David Blumenthal, my personal doctor and a cardiologist, arrived for his daily rounds. By the hand of fate, he saw me being moved on a gurney, and realized that I had had a heart attack. The metabolic functions of my body were failing fast. He demanded that the on-duty surgeons immediately catheterize the arteries and reopen the valve. I was moved to the Intensive Coronary Care Unit and lay there for two days while my family waited to make their decisions, if necessary. When I finally awoke from the coma someone was looking down at me, and what I remember was a hallucinatory backdrop that combined elements of Disneyland and a Tahitian landscape by Gauguin. No LSD required.

Before they would open and operate on my heart, I had to stabilize. For a week I lay in bed with my leg suspended in traction, weights strapped around my feet. In addition to all the drips and monitors stuck in me, there was a separate tube through a needle into my upper leg, barely relieving the pain at the break. When the nurses came to move me or adjust the wires holding my leg up, I would scream. The pain was horrific. They weren't going to look at the leg until I recovered from open-heart surgery, which was still days away. I had become delusional, hearing things, seeing things. I was in for a battle.

At night I would panic when Rachel Maddow signed off and my mind wandered. I was short of breath. I needed oxygen. Would I die tonight? I felt that it was time for some quasi-deathbed wisdom. As corny as it was, I could not dismiss the time I had. I told Alex how sorry I was for the mistakes I had made with him as a first child. I admonished Theo to stop smoking—look what it had done to me. Gus was wrestling with choosing bankers to sell *Rolling Stone*. Apparently my wisdom to him was about bankers. A control freak to the very end.

I had by this time met my surgeon, a six-foot-three-inch ex–high school football player who had just finished a tour in Iraq and Afghanistan as a combat doctor, not the kind who operates at an air base hospital but in a tent on the front lines, where the casualties come straight from the battlefield. For no particular reason, this was reassuring. He mentioned how good it was to have music during surgery and that research had suggested that music in the OR was associated with better outcomes. My surgery would take eight hours.

I mentioned this on the phone to Bruce, and when he and Patti showed up the next afternoon, they brought along a six-hour mixtape. The surgeon couldn't believe it. We would be rolling in the OR to a soundtrack handpicked by the Boss. I was never nervous, even in the gown, being prepped for surgery. I don't know why I was so calm about it. The anesthetics were working, that's all I needed to know. I had a triple coronary bypass and a valve transplant. A week later I had the hip and femur operation.

I settled into hospital life: the nurses attentive, the painkillers liberally available, and a great mixtape. The food was tasteless and texture-free, boiled chicken and Jell-O. Matt was organizing the visitor schedule and take-out meals, with someone coming to dine every other day. The kids would come and we would have a Chinese meal family style in the visitors' lounge.

My visitors meant a lot. They had to get to and through a complex hospital maze at the end of which lay a disheveled old man, bedridden and possibly smelly. These are people who came to show their love. Love heals. On the day of the surgery, Bono wrote, "Please know that the Hewson clan are holding you in a tight grip of prayer and deep affection. We love you. B." They came for visits during days off on the *Joshua Tree* tour. Tom Freston, Tommy Cohen, Steve Simmons, Helen Marden, and Caroline Kennedy were also flower bearers.

During an operation you accumulate a lot of fluid, and in the male of the species these excess fluids accumulate in the scrotum. Mine was now the size of a head of cauliflower — not a grapefruit, not two papayas. A fucking cauliflower! It was a scary thing to see attached to your body. The nurses made a little platform for it so I could lie down comfortably. Most people would not enjoy my sharing that, but Bette and Martin were steady visitors, and I knew Bette would get it. I dramatically undraped it. And after some minutes of gasping and mock shock, lewd jokes, and peals of laughter, Martin took photos for the scrapbooks. I wanted Bette to be my nurse.

Jon Landau came by. He had helped me put together *Rolling Stone* when he was a college kid and had been my longtime éminence grise and counselor on the Hall of Fame as well. His gravitas made a huge difference in what we did and how it was accepted. Now Jon was on a bench in a garden outside the hospital, beside me in a wheelchair. What had rock become? Did we have a place in it now? When do we turn the Hall of Fame and *Rolling Stone* over to younger people? We had achieved what we set out to do, written a full and true history of rock and roll and honored the people who created it. We had realized goals beyond our dreams.

Sister Kate would stay with me on the nights Matt was worn out. They were the team taking care of me. My life had gone to the edge. I don't know which of the drugs was affecting my mind, but at one point I told Kate I urgently needed to write a book about my experience. I had nearly lost my life. I was having an epiphany. I asked her to write down what I was thinking about.

"*The Impatient Patient. Why did this happen to me? What did I learn about life when I was dying? Treating yourself badly... Thinking I was so*

smart that I could get away with anything…Disguise makes you a liar…
Take five slow deep breaths and turn it positive…De-involve…Stop managing other people's business…Fire yourself…Pay attention and you will learn
something…The long, sustained work of understanding yourself…Why not
shut up and trust somebody?…Why am I trying to run the show?…How
important is it to be right?…It's annoying, but what are you going to do about
it anyway? Be polite and get on with it…The freedom to act from your true
self—why I came out…People repeat themselves…So do you…Sister
Kate…How Matt became my husband (getting over shame)…Your gut—
you were right from the beginning…That fucking iPhone…Talking shit
about some of my closest friends—the karma must build up…These are my
families…The End…I hope I've given you a good cry."

After a month and a half in bed, my muscles were atrophied to such
an extent that I could not lift my legs while lying down. I could not walk.
When I was wheeled up to the rehab floor—two sessions a day and a
group of patients in a world of hurt far worse than mine—I struggled
with a walker and had to be talked through how to make each step. I had
lost both strength and muscle memory. They would not release me until
I learned how to put on my socks, push a walker down a hallway, and
turn around. I graduated to how to get in and out of a car, and finally to
managing stairs. I was in pain, but I did what I had to do.

It was summer; the days had become long and the visitors few. I
wanted to see my kids again, I wanted to sit in the sun, feel the breeze on
my skin, and look out at the ocean with a glass of wine in my hand.

HOME WAS HEAVEN…on wheels. I did rehab every morning, and
Matt had rearranged the house and gotten the latest old people's toilet
seats and shower chairs. I had a shopping bag of pills. Finally, after six
weeks at home, we got out and went to Jimmy and Janie Buffett's fortieth
wedding anniversary. I walked into this baby boomer bash with a cane in
one hand and holding on to Matt with the other. The tables were can-
dlelit, lanterns hanging in the trees. I felt like Grandpa, finding the

nearest seat and receiving well-wishers. We had been able to keep it out of the media, but my brush with the fates was common knowledge here, and it seemed that everyone came by to welcome me home.

WE ANNOUNCED THAT *Rolling Stone* was for sale in a large front-page story in the business section of the *Times*. There was no moment of emotion for me, just pride in the place of honor which carried the news. It had a very handsome photo of young Gus at his desk, the image that we wanted to project to potential buyers. I said I hoped to find someone who "understood our mission and had lots of money. It's time for young people to run it."

I owed David Pecker a lunch. He was an outspoken, Mar-a-Lago–style Trump supporter and thought of the president as a personal friend. *Star* and the *National Enquirer*, his tabloids, had run outrageous attacks on Trump's opponents. That's not all, David told me. He had been buying and then spiking stories from women who had been sleeping with Trump. He was very explicit about Trump's knowledge, approval, and encouragement. I just thought of this as David bragging about being buddy-buddy with the president. I mentioned it to Gus and forgot about it.

ONE YEAR AFTER my open-heart surgery and having my femur reconstructed, I was back in an operating room, this time for a spinal fusion. I could barely walk due to a near-total compression of the nerves inside the spinal column. It took four doctors to discover that I needed a new back operation, my third. I was in danger of paralysis. The "best back surgeon in New York" happened to be a serious Rolling Stones fanatic. I was on the operating table by Memorial Day. It had been less than a year since my triple bypass, my valve replacement, four eye operations, my broken femur, a second heart procedure, and five days in the hospital on an IV for an infection. There was no certainty that this operation would work, but we had no choice.

I was back home after two days, but five days later I became delusional and was readmitted to the hospital to have my spine opened up again to clean out a staph infection and to undergo yet another fusion because of the infection. I was in the hospital for another month and this time went over the edge. Every night was some kind of nightmare hallucination of being in a new city: trapped and strapped in a bedroom in Berlin while Bette and Martin partied on in a house we had rented; left by Matt in a medical clinic fronting as a whorehouse in Paris while he went to a Stones concert. Another night I was staying at a hippie hotel in Toronto and then moved to a boutique hotel in Montreal and was later abandoned to a panicked mob backstage at a U2 show. The worst was ending up at a gang headquarters in Spanish Harlem, or it might have been in Miami, handcuffed on the floor, my wound open to a new infection from all the junkies slumped next to me.

It sucked, but you have to suck it up and get on with it. Getting old was becoming a daily battle, all the wounds and injuries. I was still up for the fight. The retreats were tactical, but no surrender. When I checked out again for home, drainage tubes were still inserted in my back. But I could walk. Very slowly. My progress was in inches, but it was progress, and progress was hope, and hope was life. I went back to the city to speak at the memorial for Tom Wolfe at the New York Public Library. I sat with Tom's family, which I had been a part of for many years, but still it had a quasi-official feeling — an assembly of the remaining chroniclers of a great era that was passing.

I MADE IT TO our fiftieth-anniversary party via a service elevator, walking on Matt's arm through the kitchen and the waiters' entrance into the Pool Room of the Four Seasons. It was the same place where we had so grandly celebrated our twenty-fifth anniversary, but the twinkling stars were long gone. HBO was putting on a modest premiere to promote the Gibney documentary, *Rolling Stone: Stories from the Edge*. It was the de facto fiftieth celebration, encompassing nearly all staff, old and new, and a treat for the current, younger *Rolling Stone* family, getting a taste of high living from what they called, so heedless of the sting of the words, "back in the day."

Gibney hit it right on the head, totally getting the politics and rock mix, putting the UVA story up for scrutiny, and catching the joy and sense of purpose at the center of *Rolling Stone*. It was also a love letter to the magazine. They had found some video from 1968, when a local TV station had come to our first loft office to film a "what the kids are doing" piece. I had completely forgotten about it, but the clip was a revelation about my very much younger self, a twenty-two-year-old in a T-shirt. He was a kid on a mission, self-confident, exuberant, sparking with energy. You just wanted to go with that kid. He could talk you into anything.

I KNEW THAT IF I didn't start going to the office, I would end up staying at home in slippers and sweatpants. I had stopped wearing suits, and my new look was black jeans and sweaters, dark blue with the occasional green or camel. If you care. Bruce and Patti had rented an apartment a few blocks away from where we lived during the long Broadway run of his hit show. It was a nice change to have the Springsteens in the city, in the hood, for breakfasts and lunches. Bono was also in town, healthy again, and a steady visitor as he bounced between the studio and statesmanship.

I DIDN'T HAVE MUCH to do at *Rolling Stone*. I had already been backing away from editing and story ideas; it was repetitive and restrictive. The business side was on hold, in a defensive posture, treading water while Gus tried to sell the company. I had privately checked out. I wanted to get it over with. Gus presented two buyers who had agreed to a price. They were media companies, but neither was in the magazine business and they didn't have the infrastructure or knowledge that would be needed.

I thought the buyer ought to be Jay Penske, a good-looking young man with a terrible haircut. His dad was the former race-car driver Roger Penske, now a billionaire businessman. Jay was already in the magazine and online businesses, having aggregated a small group of once formidable trade magazines such as *Variety* and *Women's Wear Daily*. I was impressed by his energy, ambition, and smarts. He didn't have experience or an intuitive feel for general-interest, large-circulation magazines, but he had the money and motive. Jay also had the strategy for survival, put the pedal on online instead of print and become a player in music events and promotions. He and Gus would pull it off smartly. It would be a big one for him. We had to close the deal in two weeks, by Christmas Eve. It was a day-and-night marathon for the two teams of lawyers. But at the end of the day, there was a pot of gold. We were home free.

CHAPTER 76

THE ROAD
TO RECOVERY

T HE LAST THING I did in the final days when I was still in charge was an interview with Bono. It was antithetical to what the new regime had in mind, the new millennial, or perhaps post–new millennial, *Rolling Stone*. No more baby boomer covers. It had been thirty years since U2's first cover — "Band of the Eighties" — and this would be Bono's sixteenth, either alone or with the band. Their new album, *Songs of Experience*, was at number one.

We met up in the kitchen of my house and got down to business. He was just coming off the road and needed a major rest. We talked about the biblical David and Paul of Tarsus. At the end, I asked Bono what his thoughts were after such a difficult year. What were his "last words of wisdom"? "I want to be useful," he said. "That is our family prayer, as you know. It is not the most grandiose prayer. It is just, we're available for work. That is U2's prayer. We want to be useful, but we want to change the world. And we want to have fun at the same time. What is wrong with that?"

BY CHRISTMAS I was no longer in a position to change the world: I was stuck at home with the walker, an awkward exoskeleton on wheels with two tennis balls on the front legs. We were in Sun Valley, but my skiing days were over for good. I had been jumping out of helicopters for years, but no longer. At that point, I didn't care; I just wanted to walk. I couldn't get to sleep, lying awake making an inventory of every nerve pain and muscle flutter. What about my renovated heart? Would it hold? At high altitude, breathing is harder and shallower. I took sleeping pills, one after the other. I stumbled around or lay in bed expecting to die. Even to get into bed, I had to use my hands to lift my legs up; I had no feeling in my feet, they didn't move. I was helpless and afraid.

It was my fault, and my fault alone. Put aside fifty years of Marlboros. Blame that on peer pressure and the tobacco companies. But I also had diabetes. I had been injecting insulin at mealtimes for thirty years, which is actually easy and painless. High blood sugar corrodes your vessels and builds up plaque, restricting blood flow to your nerves, feet, and heart. Especially to the micro blood vessels in your eyes and penis; thankfully the boomers got Viagra. At first I had been strict about not eating sugar and carbs — the stuff you love, like pasta, fresh fruit, and cinnamon rolls — but I slowly let it slide. It was the same old risk-taking indulgence, exceptionalism, and faith in karma that characterized so much about my life.

That had eventually resulted in the loss of muscular control in my feet, on top of a quickly detaching retina, all of which led to the fall on the tennis court when my back foot didn't move as my body accelerated forward tossing a serve, which led to the systemic shock, which triggered the heart attack. It was my stupid fault. I brought it on myself. Now I was in deep shit. I wasn't suicidal, but some careless accident, another fall, seemed more and more likely.

As someone who felt the loneliness of death with so much unconcealed grief, I was so deep in my own trauma drama I couldn't offer any comfort to my own family when it looked like I might die and abandon them to a world turned upside down, hollowed out, and adrift, especially Matt, Jane, and the little kids. As I slowly recovered, I wouldn't accept my responsibility, my helplessness, and my escape from death. I would not accept my truth and would not face the fear with them.

As it turned out, God wasn't taking me, and Matt took away the pills. Sister Kate told me about Lexapro, an antidepressant. I was going to need something to get through all this. Two months later I was back in the hospital. I had arrhythmia, some irregular electrical pulse in the ticker, which meant snaking a tube through the groin into the heart. Two weeks later, my other retina tore and I had to have another eye surgery. I increased my Lexapro; it was working. I was telling people that I was suffering from "TMB." I had heard that one from my old friend and cousin-in-law, Alan Hirschfield, who told me his doctor diagnosed his problems as "Too Many Birthdays."

WHEN I SOLD *Rolling Stone*, I didn't negotiate for a place on the masthead or a continuing role in the magazine. I clearly understood that if I ever sold it, whoever got it would do whatever they wanted. It was always that way. Jay's intentions were honorable, and he often told me of his reverence for our history. One thing was clear, though; he was in charge. The first thing he did was fire our star photographer, Mark Seliger. Mark was born in Amarillo, Texas, and fell in love with photography as a kid while looking at *Playboy*. He left home for the Big Apple to find his future and dropped his portfolio off at our front desk. Mark ended up shooting 188 covers of *Rolling Stone*, 588 assignments altogether. He was at the heart of our creative excellence, the visual expression of the soul of the magazine. Jay took direct control of the editorial budget and enjoyed cutting costs. He felt we were throwing away money as if we were *Vanity Fair*, which was demonstrably not the case. But many of our good writers were forced out. The new mantra was clear: What counted was not the power of the printed word but the number of "hits" on the website. I thought this was a false dichotomy and did not believe quality was inconsistent with quantity. I thought quality was the road to get there.

I wanted to remain with *Rolling Stone*, to have some relationship with my baby. Could I be the uncle? The grandpa? The brother-in-law? Nope, I would be the ex-wife. Gus wanted to take over. He listened to me with respect but impatience. He had been seduced by the critique that was by now a cliché: *Rolling Stone* was only about the sixties and only wrote about old stars and classic rock. In fact we had covered pop, punk, and especially hip hop — first, best, and definitively, as always. Our readership was getting older because we were still holding on to the baby boomers as we also pulled in the succeeding generations. The average age of the reader had gone from twenty-one to thirty-five, a fourteen-year increase over fifty years. We had stayed in the sweet spot, the folks born between 1946 and 1996. Maybe it wasn't as sweet anymore.

The mix of politics, journalism, and music was crucial. No other music publication ever came close to our circulation. I believed that we should follow the news and cover what was timely, including in music. If a genre or artist was hot, we would get on it, no matter what or who it was. There was no purity test. If we were genre-deep, it would be in the main river of rock, but we wouldn't be genre-exclusive. And neither were we generation-specific. We wrote about astrophysicists, animal rights activists, politicians, and dope dealers. This "newer and younger" audience didn't particularly read print; this was an iPhone-based generation. You were never going to persuade them that *Rolling Stone* had now become a rap magazine.

I tried to tell them, but of course I was now in my seventies, standing in the way of progress, stubbornly locked in my office listening, it was assumed, to Bob Dylan and Neil Young. I was not invited to meetings. What should have been an exciting redesign and translation of *Rolling Stone* from a newsmagazine to a feature magazine ended up garbled and lackluster.

To the outside world, to my friends, colleagues, and peers, I had lost no prestige, no status. As for the benefits of fame, meh. The issue was how to navigate vis-à-vis the young Turk, my usurping doppelgänger. I was proud, even giddy, about turning it over to him. How he ran the business, God bless him, was no concern to me. But editorial, what was on the pages, was something I should be able to influence, even decide. For fifty years and a few generations I had rolled with the changing times. I mean, wasn't I the world's unquestioned expert on what was right for *Rolling Stone*?

Apparently not. Gus had his instincts for it, and he was slowly developing confidence in those instincts. I was just going to have to learn to live and to let this go; he would figure it out at some point. Gus had to face the current reality, not get into some pointless fight about our legacy. He clearly intended to keep his relationship with me. Sometimes our meetings were contentious, quarreling over small things that were symbolic of bigger, tougher-to-confront disagreements. It was the pathetic cliché of the old bull storming and snorting around, ready to knock down the whole barn. Gus would call or come back and make peace, and I would be so happy that he did. I told Gus I wanted some clear answers about where I stood. It took my assurance that he should tell me the truth without fear of my flipping out or being angry with him to get him to man up and tell me. In so many words, I was out. I had been joking about it for a few years — I loved to rib him about *Tommy Boy*, the Chris Farley movie — but now it was true. "I'd like you to meet my boss, Gus Wenner."

After Bono read the interview, he sent me a letter that I prize. "Above and below the usual concerns I have about my volubility and vulnerability, I have two thoughts... One, how come there is no other place for an interview like this? And two, your own role as inquisitor and interlocutor is again a kind of phenomenon, a rare point of view. Thanks for all the hard work. Thanks for the sheer joy of discovery that you bring. Your fan, B."

JACKSON BROWNE WAS playing at the Beacon, around the corner. It was time to get out of the house, back to my life. I had my cane, but needed a strong arm, too. Jackson had earlier in the day walked every step I would have to make when I arrived that night, and now he met me at the stage door and led me by the arm. We hadn't seen each other for a while, and we went big into Bro Land. The fact that we were both in our seventies, one helping the other on a cane, was feeling deep. Jackson had set up a chair for me onstage. I asked him to do "Linda Paloma" mid-show, and afterward he said I now owed it to him to put Warren Zevon into the Hall of Fame. I was so happy to see him, to have the lifetime of friendship, to be in the music, to drift and dream. His delightful eccentricity, his spirit, and his song were in my heart.

We went to Paul Simon's farewell concert at Madison Square Garden. He was seventy-seven; I never thought someone could retire from rock and roll. Paul's music triumphed over his stiff personality, and the show went right onto my all-time-best list. With a twenty-piece ensemble backing him, he conducted a tour of his solo years, which had been so sophisticated, with changes in arrangements that revealed ever more depth of melody and harmonics. He then went on to the Simon and Garfunkel years. I was in awe.

As Paul came to the end of the show, the end of his brilliant career, what had started out as so joyful took on a sadness. He was singing these songs in public for the last time. He closed with "The Sound of Silence," his first hit, written in his bathroom in Queens fifty-five years earlier. His career had come full circle. His last words from the stage were "It means more than you can know."

The next day I sent Paul a letter praising the genius of his catalogue, his writing and singing, and what his work had meant to me personally and to a generation. I was not going to let this unpleasant and ungenerous person spoil his music for me. He sent me back an email: "Thanks. Paul." A cold man to the very end.

Bruce's broadway run was sold out, award-winning, and a triumph. Each show was different and as powerful as the one the night before, about Bruce growing up, what he learned, and who he became. It was a journey that lifted you up, brought you into his small town and his Jersey childhood; and to the working class and his troubled father. You laughed, you cried, and in the end felt the redemption. It was as if Bruce had written the movements, the interludes and the refrains, the reprises of a singular lifelong work. It had the emotional range of life itself, of having lived a meaningful life, one that worked toward the good. He was a phenomenon onstage, a place far different than any I had shared with him. He seemed so intimate with us in a theater, yet was typically so reserved in his own living room. For all the years we had known each other, the truest Bruce I saw was onstage, singing.

BOB DYLAN WAS in town for a run at the Beacon, a few blocks from my house, which was becoming a regular stop for performers in my age group. It had been built in 1929, a vaudeville and movie palace. Bob called and asked if I would visit. I invited sister Kate to come. She had often seen but never met the great one, and I wanted to give her that moment and see her reaction.

When we got to the dressing room, me with cane in hand, the first thing Bob did was quote something my mother had told me as a kid: "You're on your own, Buster Brown." He was smiling, having fun, gently teasing me. It took me a beat to figure out that he had been reading about me. I noticed that the line he chose to repeat echoed so clearly — "How does it feel to be on your own, like a rolling stone?"

After we caught up on families, friends, and real estate, we began to talk about writing, how he had written *Chronicles*, what hard work it had been for him, and how much time it took. I told him I was starting to write mine, that I even had done a trial chapter about him. I told him one of the scenes. He told me he always read my pieces, that they were "clean, direct, and funny. Make your book like that."

My sister asked about the audiobook of *Chronicles* — she thought the passages about New Orleans were the most evocative descriptions of that city she had ever read. This led to talk about Hunter. He had willed

Bob his red IBM Selectric typewriter. I said it was stolen from me, and I wanted it back. Bob said his own first drug experience was getting bennies at a truck stop in Idaho. We reminisced about Jerry Garcia and playing with him in the early days. After the third warning for curtain time, we left with big, warm, family-style hugs. He used to shun shaking hands, so many years ago.

Bob played the best show I had heard him do in recent times, a selection from across the years, the old ones in new arrangements, not thrown away or ticked off a list, but suited to his mature voice, with melodies and vocal emphasis shifted. In addition to singing his newly written songs, he was discovering new meanings in what was still such familiar work. It was a display of his musical brilliance and incredibly beautiful poetry. He turned "Don't Think Twice" into a hymn. His encore was the Hendrix version of "All Along the Watchtower," and he closed with "Blowin' in the Wind."

Still lucky to be alive.

CHAPTER 77

MY LAST LETTER
FROM THE EDITOR

WRITING A BOOK about your life is slow work. You have to concentrate, wait for the memories to surface, stir them up, let them cook, and then serve. I was surprised at how it worked, how one piece interlocked with another like a jigsaw puzzle, the clouds and the trees down to the prowling tigers at the bottom.

I decided to do my own reporting and research. One ex-girlfriend hung up on me. I got in touch with Charlie Perry, our first paid employee. He had retired as the food critic of the *Los Angeles Times* but was still the head of the Lovers of the Stinking Rose, an international group of garlic fans. Ben Fong-Torres, his credentials burnished into the *Rolling Stone* Hall of Fame by the portrayal of him in *Almost Famous*, was still, at seventy-six, the dean of San Francisco music journalism.

Laurel Gonsalves had been my confidante in building the business in the early days, a soul mate. She was funny, smart, preternaturally sophisticated. She got it. She got me. We had a falling-out soon after moving to New York and hadn't seen each other for thirty years. When she came for lunch, a rush of happiness, almost giddy and girlish, came over me. It reopened the past for me, the spirit of those times, the dreams and the friends who shared them with me.

MONTAUK WAS A special place for writing. We built a modern house, and every room opened over the beach and onto the ocean. Matt and I took a break and went to Greece without the kids. Helen and Brice Marden had lent us their home in Hydra, a small port on a small island with cobblestone streets, whitewashed houses, and outdoor restaurants that served grilled squid. Leonard Cohen lived there in the sixties. I sat in a sunny room opening onto a walled garden. I wrote fluidly and easily. The vibe of writers, including Joni Mitchell, from the past was in the air, and the breeze moved me forward.

I WATCHED GRETA THUNBERG'S speech to the General Assembly of the United Nations: "I shouldn't be up here. I should be back in school on the other side of the ocean. Yet you all come to us young people for hope. How dare you! You have stolen my dreams and my childhood with your empty words. People are dying. Entire ecosystems are collapsing. We are in the beginning of a mass extinction, and all you can talk about is money and fairy tales of eternal economic growth. How dare you!" Hers was as simple an analysis of the problem as was ever spoken: "fairy tales of eternal economic growth." It was a clarion call: "How dare you!" As with the recordings of Martin Luther King Jr., I heard a voice of prophecy.

I wanted to do one last thing at *Rolling Stone*, one more special issue on global warming, a last warning about humankind's looming self-destruction, a last call for sanity and salvation. Gus agreed and gave me his full backing. I started on it immediately, to finish it in time for Earth Day 2020. Greta Thunberg would be the cover, maybe as Joan of Arc.

BRUCE WAS TURNING seventy and had a party at his house in Los Angeles. It was a balmy September night, with about fifty people at tables set up under the oak trees in a hacienda-style courtyard. Patti and daughter Jess were wandering about barefoot. Bruce was trying to be a dutiful host but looked as if he'd be more comfortable in a corner. I dragged him into his office to open my present and to give him one I had brought from Bono.

I sat down next to Bob Dylan and his wife and spent the evening with them. David Geffen was a chair away, talking about record business stuff, drawing a blank from the rest of us. Mostly it was Bob and me teasing each other. I would say how bad his current records were, he would trash the gossip rags I had put out, as each of us tried to top the other with one-liners.

Bob's office called a few months later; he was going to be playing the Beacon again, and would I come again and visit? This time I took Jane with me. He had an eye for pretty girls and always remembered her. Years ago he had put his arm around her and told her, "Stand by your man." He was looking good in a black dress shirt with sparkles and white patent-leather shoes with pointed toes. He was feeling good, poking fun at my cane.

He asked about something we had published on Jack Kerouac. He recalled seeing T. S. Eliot read in St. Paul, Minnesota, and on another occasion watching Billy Graham preach. Bob talked about his childhood in Hibbing. What haunted him, what he always remembered, was the wind. The houses in Hibbing are made of brick and have small windows. The iron pits are as big as the Grand Canyon. The wind is brutal. The winds never stop, the winds of Hibbing.

It was another magic show, words and a voice that you fell into, spellbound in the dark, adrift in the music, guided by melody into reveries of the past, the here and now of the moment, and the hopes and fears for the future. At the end of the show, he said, "Jann Wenner is here tonight, the father and the publisher of *Rolling Stone*. That's the magazine of sex, drugs, and…politics." Then he sang "Gotta Serve Somebody":

You might be a rock 'n' roll addict prancing on the stage
You might have drugs at your command, women in a cage
You may be a businessman or some high-degree thief
They may call you Doctor or they may call you Chief
... But you're gonna have to serve somebody, yes indeed

JACKSON BROWNE CAME to have lunch and see my new office. When I was with old friends, we would review our signs of aging. Everyone seemed to talk about their health now. We were grandparents. Matt and I went to visit Yoko, now in a wheelchair, at the Dakota. We had so much history; the apartment was thick with memory. We brought over the kids for another visit. It made her happy. She had once written, "A dream you dream alone is only a dream. A dream you dream together is reality."

BONO STARTED WRITING his autobiography. As Lin-Manuel Miranda said of Alexander Hamilton, "The man was nonstop." He would come over to read me what he was writing. He was learning a more relaxed, simpler prose style, forgoing his image-packed wordsmithery. He wanted to hear me read what I was writing, but I wasn't ready, as he said, to show him mine if he showed me his. We agreed to call them "buuks," and he presented me with a red Montblanc pen.

I got this email from him: "Thinking of you and yours today apropos of nothing. Are you getting back to fitness? Is it harder or easier? I've been writing me buuk and I must admit enjoying every moment of it, even the queasiness and nausea of stormy passages and the squirminess of discovering the creepy-crawlies of one's youth under various stones. How's your buuk? Can we agree on a common strategy for both buuks and that we describe ourselves as tall? You don't tell on me and I won't tell on you sort of thing?"

The man is a giant of his times.

I SPENT ABOUT SIX MONTHS in the new offices. Gus came up for a daily drop-in. Working on the special issue on the climate crisis put me back in touch with *Rolling Stone*. On one level it was fun, conjuring a compelling issue, creating something of consequence. I had to be polite while rejecting weak story ideas and explain myself patiently, a long-overdue breakthrough for me. After this, I wanted to be done.

Editorial idea meetings had once been the magic factory, where the best and the brightest would pull up chairs to the round table or sit on the windowsills, sparking off each other, until we had an idea and chose from the best writers. A year or two before selling the company, I realized those days were over for me when in the middle of one meeting, as I recalled some editorial crisis or drama of yore, I noticed the young faces around the table hanging on the tale, eager for more. The glory days were coming to life for them, hearing history from the old man. I was loving it, like I was in a rocking chair with a pipe in my hand.

FIVE YEARS EARLIER we had anticipated the coming presidential election: "A Republican victory will signal a comprehensive, regressive offensive unlike any yet seen in modern American politics, a full-scale assault on basic democratic principles, the living egalitarian idea from which American progress has flowed."

The prophecy had come to pass. Few expected it to overflow with such hatred and grievance, led by a man of such naked dishonesty, amorality, and greed. Trump and Republican rule had become the dominant fact of life, a daily drill of hate and destruction. It sank in deep. It was like being trapped in a house with an abusive parent, a drunk with a belt strap. We were the guilty victims.

The special issue of *Rolling Stone* devoted to the climate emergency was published, and Greta was on the cover. I wrote my rhetorical analysis that wove together information and ideas I had been accumulating as

I watched and brooded. I wanted to fully understand and let my readers be aroused and armed. It was my last Letter from the Editor.

"Greed is a disease. The unending craving for more money, the addictions to luxury and power, may destroy our civilization. Is World War III an economic clash over our endless consumption of resources — food, forests, and the oceans — stolen and then resold to us by the merchants of death? The carbon industries — the drug companies, gun manufacturers, sugar and the fast-food giants — knowingly spread disease and death. And in those big shiny skyscrapers where they keep all their money, they are heard saying to one another, 'What does it matter? I'll be gone, you'll be gone.' Are we too spoiled to make the necessary sacrifices? We will answer for what we did to protect our children and the miracle of nature and her diversity of species on this planet, when we still had the time. How much fight do we have left?"

THEN ONE DAY the plague came. We were in Idaho when the outside world stopped. Our area was too remote for good phone service. Matt watched over me and the kids. We took three meals a day together and learned how to thrive on each other. We turned inward, finding new friendship inside the family. No one was knocking at the door. I was home and happy.

When we made our way back to Montauk to spend the summer at the beach, I wrote while looking at an ocean sometimes whipped into vast fields of white-capped waves. The kids — Noah, Jude, and India — were boisterous. They surfed in the right weather and were a daily variety show of mischief, which I watched with endless love. They were now beginning teenagers, adolescents driven by what Fitzgerald called "a form of chemical madness," the hormonal rituals and the yearning for self-determination. I could sit back and watch it with perspective; Matt, however, was fully, frontally engaged. The great pleasure was watching them come into their different selves, become so interesting, funny, and enchanting. These kids seemed to be on the same path to confidence and inner light, a joie de vivre, just like the first batch of my kids. The pride and joy of watching your child grow, to be in the presence of the great miracle, is the greatest joy of all.

Jane was just a few minutes away, on Further Lane, where Gus, my dynamic and beguiling successor, and Theo, a superb photographer and my doppelgänger, stayed throughout the summer and fall. My oldest son, Alex, was thirty-six, with a look-alike ten-year-old son plus three little girls. He and his wife, Emily, had followed us to the Hudson River Valley, where they built a home and opened a craft brewery. In Montauk we lucked into great neighbors, the Bieler family, with kids the same ages as ours.

The divorce with Jane never fully worked out. We were parts of a finely woven cloth — it was easier to keep it all in one piece. Not easy to do, but I felt it was my responsibility, perhaps even something redemptive and rewarding, to make sure she landed on her feet. She expected me to do it. She made it her business for me to succeed at my new life with another partner, at *Rolling Stone*, and as a father to our children. There was a lot that only the two of us could fully share, enjoy the same way and to the same measure: time the irreplaceable, the work that became historic, and children who were each such deep reflections of ourselves.

Everybody saw it, and no one took sides. Matt, foremost above others, took Jane into the heart of our new life. And vice versa; they had a lot in common. I was blessed with family. Matt had wanted to think of the six kids as one family. Jane let her hair go gray but was still a striking beauty. She was, in a family phrase, a "happy camper."

DURING LOCKDOWN I read *The Price of Peace*, a biography of economist John Maynard Keynes, one of the principal architects of the twentieth century, the world we still live in. It was a dive into monetary policy and the nature of the social fabric. As it came to an end, I was stunned by this paragraph:

"Optimism is a vital and necessary element of everyday life. It is the spirit that propels us to go on living in the face of unavoidable suffering, that compels us to fall in love when our hearts have been broken and gives us the courage to bring children into the world, believing that even in times such as these we are surrounded by enough beauty to fill lifetime after lifetime."

I wrote a fan note to the author, Zachary D. Carter, and got a long letter back. He had been reading *Rolling Stone* since he was nine years old. He wrote, "You have been a companion along all the important creative currents in my life. In no small way, *The Price of Peace* reflects your influence, built issue by issue, and idea by idea, over decades. Thank you for that."

I NEVER THOUGHT I was a "spokesman" for a generation. Even to the extent that there was some truth to that, I recoiled from the idea. It was a trap. Mine was a generation that was looking for leadership, especially moral leadership, but those who thought they were that leader usually weren't. Bob Dylan was allergic to the idea. Now I accept the fact that I had helped shape the way my generation viewed itself, its responsibilities, its way of laughing, its achievements. But I didn't speak for it; I spoke to it.

The run-up to the election finally ended. Joe Biden won by the biggest margin since FDR in 1932. Bruce and I spoke every day as it came closer, virtually holding hands, trying to convince each other that we were going to win this time. We had shared some painful commiseration before. We were on the sidelines this year but invested more fearfully than ever. My hopes for Joe Biden and Kamala Harris give me courage as I set down my sword and shield. Contrary to a widespread delusion particular to young people, politics matter, politicians count, and some of them are heroes.

My generation wanted to serve the country, sacrifice ourselves if necessary, but instead we paid the price for the stupidity of our elders. The wholly unnecessary invasion of Vietnam — a lost war against the right of self-determination — had stolen so much of our precious time. I found a truth about myself in a Jackson Browne song: "I have prayed for America, I was made for America, I can't let go till she comes around." The struggle has not stopped.

My generation is passing. The world has doubled in size and doubled in danger. But there are still places to go where you can see the stars at night and understand your place in the universe.

"FOREVER YOUNG" WAS a generation's mantra, an unforgettable Bob Dylan song. We all knew what it meant, that we stay young in our outlook, our actions, and our hopes.

> *May you always be courageous*
> *Stand upright and be strong…*
> *May your heart always be joyful*
> *May your song always be sung*
> *May you stay forever young*

I have always tried to keep that in mind. It's a new feeling to have to adjust to the realities of my seventy-five years, to walk with a cane. I am an old man and yet still feel so young in my heart. Kids, all six of them, all good. Spouses, all two, all good. Weather fine, the ocean rolls in, and the sun makes the ocean sparkle. The dog sleeps at my feet.

ACKNOWLEDGMENTS

I had a great time writing this book. I looked forward to the daily hours at the keyboard, waiting for the right word and figuring out how to move along a complex narrative. I wasn't expecting this to turn into a voyage of discovery and self-examination, but a well-told, well-written memoir demands this. In returning to my history, I ended up reconnecting with many of the people in my life, "lovers and friends I still can recall…some have gone and some remain." What a pleasure that turned out to be.

The nature of my work and passions opened many worlds and walks of life, and my walk and way gathered many colleagues and companions. I called upon them again to help with this book.

Bob Wallace, one of the most skillful and delightful top editors I ever had at *Rolling Stone*, was my principal editor in the three-year process. Paul Scanlon, my managing editor in the San Francisco era, got me started. In the final stages, two of my oldest colleagues and dearest friends, Jonathan Cott and Jon Landau, tuned the manuscript, with a deep understanding of my voice. Jon and Jon were on the masthead of issue one. Tom Freston, Michael Douglas, Wade Davis, Doug Brinkley, Kate Wenner, and Matt Nye all read the manuscript and gave me notes and put the wind to my back.

I asked Roger Black, a pivotal *Rolling Stone* art director to design the book. Jodi Peckman brought her *RS*-trained eye to the photo edit. My assistant, Susan Ward, carefully managed the logistics and the drafts. Annie Leibovitz took the cover. What could be more perfect?

Bruce Nichols, the editor in chief at Little, Brown, was my backer from his first read and also an expert editor when he made his cut. Thanks also to production editor Michael Noon. As always, thanks to Lynn Nesbitt, my crack agent and confidante, who worked together with me handling Hunter Thompson and keeping an eye on Tom Wolfe.

I had a wonderful, soulful time having lunch, talking on the phone, and reading the memories of the writers and editors with whom I had spent so many hours and days and years in the trenches. I was your beneficiary working on this book as well. We fought the war and had fun. We kicked ass, and I'll never forget any of you.

In approximately chronological order: Charles "Smokestack El Ropo" Perry, Ben Fong-Torres, Paul Scanlan, Greil Marcus, Sarah Lazin, Barbara Downey, Christine Doudna, Marianne Partridge, David Dalton, Joe Eszterhas, Cameron Crowe, Michael Rogers, Howard Kohn, Laurel Gonsalves, David Felton, Robin Greene, Annie Leibovitz, Terry McDonnell, P. J. O'Rourke, Nancy Collins, Bob Love, Chris Mundy, David Fricke, Peter Travers, Will Dana, Eric Bates, Sean Woods, Toure, Marc Binelli, John Colapinto, David Lipsky, Janet Reitman, Matthieu Aikins, Eric Hedegaard, John Rasmus. Mike Steele, and Jason Fine.

I thank all of you and the many people I name check in the book for their ideas, the use of some wonderful phrases, and for always reminding me of the spirit of *Rolling Stone*.

PERMISSIONS AND CREDITS

The author is grateful for permission to quote lyrics from the following songs: "The Rose" words and music by Amanda McBroom © 1977 (Renewed) Warner-Tamerlane Publishing Corp. and Third Story Music, Inc. All rights administered by Warner-Tamerlane Publishing Corp. "Lazarus." Words and music by David Bowie © 2016 Nipple Music. All rights administered by Warner-Tamerlane Publishing Corp. All rights reserved. Used by permission of Alfred Music. "Girl Loves Me." Words and music by David Bowie © 2016 Nipple Music. All rights administered by Warner-Tamerlane Publishing Corp. All rights reserved. Used by permission of Alfred Music. "That Lonesome Road." Written by James Taylor and Don Grolnick © 1981 Country Road Music, Inc. (ASCAP) Used by permission. All rights reserved. "God." Written by John Lennon © 1970 Lenono Music. "Imagine." Written by John Lennon and Yoko Ono © 1971 Lenono Music. "California." Words and music by Joni Mitchell © Crazy Crow Music (SOCAN) / Reservoir Media Music (ASCAP). All rights administered by Reservoir Media Management, Inc. All rights reserved. Used by permission. "Do You Believe in Magic." Alley Music Corp. (BMI) / Trio Music Co. BMG Bumblebee (BMI). "For America" lyrics used courtesy of Jackson Browne © 1986 Swallow Turn Music. All rights reserved. "Beautiful Day" MUSIC: U2 LYRICS: BONO Courtesy of Universal PolyGram Int. Publishing, Inc. on behalf of Universal Music Publishing Int. B.V. (ASCAP) "Jack of All Trades" "Death To My Hometown" "Land of Hope and Dreams" © 2012 Sony Music Publishing (US) LLC and Eldridge Publishing Co. All rights are administered by Sony

Photographs in the inserts are provided courtesy of:

Insert A, page 2, top, courtesy of Kate Wenner; page 2, bottom, courtesy of Kalei Wenner; page 3, courtesy of Kalei Wenner; page 6, © The Baron Alan Wolman Collection, Rock & Roll Hall of Fame; page 7, top, © The Baron Alan Wolman Collection, Rock & Roll Hall of Fame; page 8, top, © The Baron Alan Wolman Collection, Rock & Roll Hall of Fame; page 8, bottom, Annie Leibovitz; page 9, top, © Jim Marshall Photography LLC; page 9, bottom, Annie Leibovitz; page 10, top, Stephen Paley / Getty Images; page 11, top, © Jim Marshall Photography LLC; page 11, bottom, © Camilla and Earl McGrath Foundation and *Face to Face: The Photographs of Camilla McGrath*, Alfred A. Knopf, New York 2020; page 12, Annie Leibovitz; page 14, top, Annie Leibovitz; page 14, bottom left, Annie Leibovitz; page 14, bottom right, Annie Leibovitz; page 15, top left, courtesy of Jon Landau; page 15, top right, courtesy of Jonathan Cott; page 15, center left, Annie Leibovitz; page 15, center right, Annie Leibovitz; page 15, bottom, Annie Leibovitz; page 16, Annie Leibovitz.

Insert B, page 1, Annie Leibovitz; page 2, top, Bettmann / Getty Images; page 3, top, © Jean Pigozzi; page 3, bottom, © Jean Pigozzi; page 4, top, © Camilla and Earl McGrath Foundation and *Face to Face: The Photographs of Camilla McGrath*, Alfred A. Knopf, New York 2020; page 4, center left, © Jean Pigozzi; page 4, center right, © Jean Pigozzi; page 4,

INDEX